The Defortification of the

In the early modern period, all Ge
contemporary jurists defined "city" as a coherent social body in a protected place, the urban environment had to be physically separate from the surrounding countryside. This separation was crucial to guaranteeing the city's commercial, political, and legal privileges. Fortifications were therefore essential for any settlement to be termed a city. This book tells the story of German cities' metamorphoses from walled to defortified places between 1689 and 1866. Using a wealth of original sources, *The Defortification of the German City, 1689–1866*, discusses one of the most significant moments in the emergence of the modern city: the dramatic and often traumatic demolition of the city's centuries-old fortifications and the creation of the open city.

Yair Mintzker is Assistant Professor of European History at Princeton University. His PhD dissertation won the Elizabeth Spilman Rosenfield Prize of Stanford's Department of History in 2009 and the Friends of the German Historical Institute's Fritz Stern Dissertation Prize in 2010. His articles have been published in *History of European Ideas* and *Réflexions Historiques*.

PUBLICATIONS OF THE GERMAN HISTORICAL INSTITUTE

Edited by Hartmut Berghoff
with the assistance of David Lazar

The German Historical Institute is a center for advanced study and research whose purpose is to provide a permanent basis for scholarly cooperation among historians from the Federal Republic of Germany and the United States. The Institute conducts, promotes, and supports research into both American and German political, social, economic, and cultural history; into transatlantic migration, especially in the nineteenth and twentieth centuries; and into the history of international relations, with special emphasis on the roles played by the United States and Germany.

Recent Books in the Series

Winson Chu, *The German Minority in Interwar Poland*

Christof Mauch and Kiran Klaus Patel, editors, *The United States and Germany during the Twentieth Century*

Monica Black, *Death in Berlin: From Weimar to Divided Germany*

J. R. McNeill and Corinna R. Unger, editors, *Environmental Histories of the Cold War*

Michaela Hoenicke Moore, *Know Your Enemy: The American Debate on Nazism, 1933–1945*

Cathryn Carson, *Heisenberg in the Atomic Age: Science and the Public Sphere*

Matthias Schulz and Thomas A. Schwartz, editors, *The Strained Alliance: U.S.-European Relations from Nixon to Carter*

Suzanne L. Marchand, *German Orientalism in the Age of Empire: Religion, Race, and Scholarship*

Manfred Berg and Bernd Schaefer, editors, *Historical Justice in International Perspective: How Societies Are Trying to Right the Wrongs of the Past*

Carole Fink and Bernd Schaefer, editors, *Ostpolitik, 1969–1974: European and Global Responses*

The Defortification of the German City, 1689–1866

YAIR MINTZKER

Princeton University

GERMAN HISTORICAL INSTITUTE

Washington, D.C.

and

 CAMBRIDGE
UNIVERSITY PRESS

CAMBRIDGE
UNIVERSITY PRESS

32 Avenue of the Americas, New York NY 10013-2473, USA

Cambridge University Press is part of the University of Cambridge.

It furthers the University's mission by disseminating knowledge in the pursuit of
education, learning and research at the highest international levels of excellence.

www.cambridge.org
Information on this title: www.cambridge.org/9781107644236

GERMAN HISTORICAL INSTITUTE
1607 New Hampshire Avenue, N.W., Washington, DC 20009, USA

First published 2012
First paperback edition 2013

A catalogue record for this publication is available from the British Library

Library of Congress Cataloguing in Publication data

Mintzker, Yair.
The defortification of the German city, 1689–1866 / Yair Mintzker, Princeton University.
pages cm. – (Publications of the German Historical Institute)
Includes bibliographical references and index.
ISBN 978-1-107-02403-8 (hardback)
1. City walls – Germany – History – 18th century.   2. City walls – Germany – History – 19th century.
3. Fortification – Germany – History – 18th century.   4. Fortification – Germany – History –
19th century.   I. Title.
UG430.G47M56   2012
623′.194309034–dc23   2012000071

ISBN 978-1-107-02403-8 Hardback
ISBN 978-1-107-64423-6 Paperback

To my parents

פְּתַח לָנוּ שַׁעַר.
בְּעֵת נְעִילַת שַׁעַר.

Open us a gate
Even as a gate is closing

Neilah le-Yom Kippur

Contents

Illustrations

Acknowledgments

It takes a village to raise a child, goes the old saying, and the same is surely also true for writing one's first book. It gives me great pleasure to thank those individuals and institutions that helped me in writing mine.

My greatest thanks go to James J. Sheehan, my PhD advisor at Stanford, who followed this project from beginning to end, and whose advice, encouragement, and critique shaped this book and the kind of historian I am in innumerable ways. Many thanks also to other members of the history faculty at Stanford who have contributed so much to my intellectual development over the years: Paul Robinson, Carolyn Lougee-Chapell, Paula Findlen, and especially Keith Baker. Jelena Batinic, Daniela Blei, Andrew Gradman, Kevin Hilke, Roz Route, Julia Sarreal, and Kari Zimmerman read previous drafts of this book. I am most grateful for their comments. As I was writing this book, I also benefited from the advice of David Bell, Peter Brown, Dan Diner, Michael Gordin, Tony Grafton, Carla Hesse, William Chester Jordan, Tom Laqueur, Ted Rabb, Barbara Stollberg-Rilinger, Wendy Warren, Eric Weitz, and the two anonymous readers of the manuscript for Cambridge University Press. Much of what is good about the following pages I owe directly to all these individuals; the book's shortcomings, needless to say, are my own.

The research and writing of this book were funded by Stanford's history department, the German Academic Exchange Service (DAAD), the Ms. Giles Whiting Foundation, the Stanford Humanities Center, the American Council on Germany, Princeton's history department, and the Institute for Advanced Study in Princeton. I am deeply grateful for this remarkably generous support. Visiting close to two dozen archives, I also benefited from the knowledge and advice of many archivists, curators, and librarians. Special thanks go to Rainer Braun (Munich), Kurt Westtengl (Frankfurt am Main), Helga Mögge (Hamburg), and Stephen Ferguson and John Delaney

(Princeton), who went out of their way to help me locate the documents and images I needed. I am especially grateful to the German Historical Institute in Washington, D.C., for awarding me the Fritz Stern Dissertation Prize in 2010 and for its assistance in the publication of this book. David Lazar at the GHI and Eric Crahan and his crew at Cambridge University Press have been the best editors I could wish for.

Finally, I would like to express my gratitude to friends and family who have followed and encouraged me over the years I spent working on this project. Katie Route, whose love and companionship I cherish more every day, Itai Ryb (get better soon!), Junko Takeda, Veronika Nickel, Per Urlaub, and Marwan Hanania – thank you all. It pains me greatly that Gadi Brinker did not live to see this book in its final form. His friendship meant the world to me. Last, but by no means least, I would like to express my deep love to Yishai, Lihi, Yaara, Uri, Karen, Mia, and my parents Hannah Mintzker and Yohanan Mintzker. It is to my parents that I dedicate this book.

Princeton, New Jersey
February 2012

Abbreviations

Bayer. HStA	Bayerisches Hauptstaatsarchiv
Bayer. HStA KA	Bayerisches Hauptstaatsarchiv, Abteilung Kriegsarchiv
Br. LHA	Brandenburgisches Landeshauptarchiv
BSB	Bayerische Staatsbibliothek
DSB	*Deutsches Städtebuch*
GLA	Generallandesarchiv
GStA PK	Geheimes Staatsarchiv Preußischer Kulturbesitz
HGM Wien	Heergeschichtliches Museum, Wien
Hist. M.	Historisches Museum
ISG	Institut für Stadtgeschichte
LA	Landesarchiv
LHA	Landeshauptarchiv
ÖNB	Österreichische Nationalbibliothek
ÖSB	*Österreichisches Städtebuch*
ÖStA KA	Österreichisches Staatsarchiv, Abteilung Kriegsarchiv
S.H.A.T.	Service historique de l'armée de terre
StA	Staatsarchiv
StdA	Stadtarchiv

Figure 1. Central Europe with major German regions and cities, ca. 1700

Introduction

"I can imagine a time," wrote the novelist Hans Wachenhusen in 1867, "perhaps a hundred or two hundred years from now, when a historian will sit down and write a simple sentence: 'Once upon a time, the city of Berlin was surrounded by walls.' Oh! If only that future historian could know the history of these city walls and, what is more, the tragic end they met!"[1]

Almost 150 years later, I sit in my study, writing the lines that you are now reading. And I cannot help beginning my story with the same sentence that Wachenhusen suggested, so long ago, that I would use. Once upon a time, the city of Berlin was surrounded by walls. So too were Vienna, Munich, Nuremberg, Augsburg, and more than 1,000 other German cities, let alone other European ones. This book is about those walls, and about the tragic end they often met. It is about the reasons for – and the experience, consequences, and significance of – their demolition, a process known as "defortification."

I assume that when traveling to a European city today, you, just like me, do not expect to see physical barriers separating that city from the countryside. Unless you intentionally seek out one of the few European cities that still retain their medieval fortifications, you do not expect to see walls, palisades, gates, or moats around the city, nor do you anticipate being stopped at the city gate, asked to show your passport to a local guard, and having a special fee demanded of you in order to pass through the gates. On approaching a European city today, you have no reason to worry about arriving too late, after the gates' lock-out hour in the evening, a mishap that in premodern times often forced even the city's own burghers to spend the night outside the walls, waiting for the gates to reopen in the morning.

---

1 Hans Wachenhusen, *Berliner Photographien* (Berlin: Hausfreund Expedition, 1867), 2:232.

1

We "moderns" tend to take both the reality and the idea of the open city for granted.

The situation could not have been more different before the modern period. Up until the mid-eighteenth century, the fortifications of many European cities were enormous monuments. Standing twenty or even thirty feet high, these massive constructions dominated the surrounding country-side and could be seen from a great distance. They contained moats, bastions, towers, elaborate gates, and several layers of walls, sometimes stretching for many miles. As late as 1750, more than 2,000 city walls still stood in central and Western Europe, with a total length that likely rivaled that of the Great Wall of China. So important were walls for premodern European cities that they commonly formed part of the city's very definition. No settlement – no matter how big, populous, or rich – deserved the title "city" unless it was surrounded by strong fortifications.

This book represents the first comprehensive treatment of defortification in a single European country. As is often the case with projects such as this, my goals in writing this book have changed over time. I began researching it with rather limited aims in mind and with a small group of professional historians as my intended audience. Yet over time, it developed into a work that may, I hope, be of interest to anyone who is interested in the history of the Western city and the history of early modern and modern Europe in general.

My original aim was to furnish professional historians with enough evidence to demonstrate how insufficient are common explanations for the emergence of open cities in Europe. Historians have written a great deal, of course, about urban demography, social structure, and politics in eighteenth- and nineteenth-century cities, but very little indeed on defor-tification and its significance. With only a few exceptions, historians of the general development of the modern city have written very little or nothing at all about defortification. This includes Max Weber, Lewis Mumford, and Mack Walker, among many others. The few historians who have written about defortification tended either to focus on very particular cases or to use one of three meta-narratives that, instead of explaining defortification, only managed to trivialize it.[2]

2 Some notable exceptions are: Peter Grobe, *Die Entfestigung Münchens* (München: Stadtarchiv, 1970); and Hans Lehmbruch, *Ein neues München: Stadtplanung und Stadtentwicklung um 1800* (Buchendorf: Buchendorfer Verlag, 1987). A very extensive documentation of Vienna's case is Renate Wagner-Rieger, *Die Wiener Ringstrasse, Bild einer Epoche: Die Erweiterung der inneren Stadt Wien unter Kaiser Franz Joseph*, 8 vols. (Wien: Böhlaus, 1969). For Vienna, see also Carl Schorske, *Fin-de-siècle Vienna: Politics and Culture* (New York: Vintage Books, 1981), 24–115. A few regional historians elsewhere have begun to pay attention to the defortification of particular cities. Two representative works for

I call the first of these three narratives the "expansion thesis." This is the idea that as more and more people migrated to European cities in the eighteenth and nineteenth centuries, urban centers began to expand rapidly into their adjacent countryside and in the process "swallowed" their walls. Such descriptions appear in many different places: in general works on urban history such as Paul M. Hohenberg and Lynn Hollen Lees's *The Making of Urban Europe, 1000–1950*; in works on German urban history such as Peter Johanek's edited volume; and in lexical works such as the historical handbook edited by Karl Bosl and others. It is not surprising that the most succinct (and telling) example for this thesis comes from such a lexical entry. "The city expanded," one author characteristically wrote about Munich's case, "and the walls disappeared."[3]

The second narrative tries to establish a connection between the demolition of city walls and industrialization. Here, the idea is that with the changing nature of society following industrialization and the increased need for easy transportation between city and countryside, the walls simply had to go. Although less common than the expansion thesis, one can still encounter such arguments in professional literature: in Wolfgang R. Krabbe's description of the nineteenth- and twentieth-century German city, for instance, or in the concluding remarks in Michael Wolfe's new book on French walled towns.[4]

Finally, the third narrative is of a military nature. It is the claim that sometime in the early modern period, when the firepower of the artillery reached a certain level, the military defenses of towns and cities lost their usefulness and were consequently razed. This argument is typically applied either to the cases of specific cities or, in the work of Martin Van Creveld, to the Napoleonic Wars in general.[5]

Of these three narratives, by far the most problematic is that of industrialization. As this book shows, industrialization occurred after most of the

---

the cases of Basel and Saarlouis are: Georg Kreis, "Der Abbruch der Basler Stadtmauern," in *Stadt- und Landmauern*, ed. Brigitte Sigel (Zürich: Institut für Denkmalpflege an der ETH Zürich, 1993), 135–43; and Anne Hahn, *Die Entfestigung der Stadt Saarlouis* (St. Ingbert: Röhrig, 2000).

3 Paul M. Hohenberg and Lynn Hollen Lees, *The Making of Urban Europe, 1000–1950* (Cambridge, MA: Harvard University Press, 1985), 301–03; Thomas Tippach, "Die Rayongesetzgebung in der öffentlichen Kritik," in *Die Stadt und ihr Rand*, ed. Peter Johanek (Köln: Böhlau, 2008), 213–34, esp. 213; and "München," in *Handbuch der historischen Stätten Deutschlands*, ed. K. Bosl (Stuttgart: A. Kröner, 1981), 7:81.

4 Wolfgang R. Krabbe, *Die deutsche Stadt im 19. und 20. Jahrhundert* (Göttingen: Vandenhoeck & Ruprecht, 1989), 78–79; Michael Wolfe, *Walled Towns and the Shaping of France: From the Medieval to the Early Modern Period* (New York: Palgrave MacMillan, 2009), 170.

5 See, for instance, Ortwin Pelc, *Im Schutz von Mauern und Toren* (Heide: Boyens, 2003), 70ff.; and most importantly Martin Van Creveld, *Supplying War: Logistics from Wallenstein to Patton* (New York: Cambridge University Press, 1977), 40–42.

cities in Western and central Europe had been defortified and therefore could not have been its cause. The same is true for expansion – contrary to the common assumption, there is only a weak correlation between expansion and the demolition of city walls in the eighteenth century, and the nineteenth century witnessed an inverted correlation: the biggest, most rapidly expanding cities, at least in central Europe, demolished their walls later than other cities, not sooner.

The military argument is by no means as problematic as expansion or industrialization, but it too needs to be considered with caution, because the argument, as it is usually formulated, lacks sufficient nuance. To speak about the demolition of city walls in terms of their decreasing usefulness without asking usefulness for whom and for what purpose is to lose sight of one of the most important arguments in favor of defortification in the eighteenth and nineteenth centuries. Paradoxically, this argument held that the continuing usefulness of urban fortifications should be the main reason to dismantle them.

The most serious criticism of the three traditional narratives to explain defortification, however, should concentrate on the common thread connecting them: the assumption that the demolition of city walls was a self-evident, natural development, whether demographic (expansion), socioeconomic (industrialization), or technological (military firepower). All too often, historians tend to use the term "disappearance" in describing what happened to European city walls.[6] Even Ilja Mieck, who concedes that it is the lack of fortifications that most distinguishes the modern city from its predecessors, uses the word disappearance to describe what happened to the old walls.[7] This term, probably unintentionally, might lead one to conclude that at one point in time the walls were simply gone, without anyone really doing anything to make this happen; without the authorities making a decision to tear down the walls; without anyone writing about defortification, reacting to it, arguing about it, fighting over it; without, in short, any substantial political dimension. As will become evident on almost every page of this book, nothing could be further from the truth.

In the course of the research and the writing of this book, it became increasingly clear to me that my main preoccupation was in fact much broader than just a refutation or a fine-tuning of three old narratives about

---

6 Two examples for the use of the term "disappearance" in conjunction with the demolition of city walls are Bosl, "Munich," 7:81; and Jürgen Osterhammel, *Die Verwandlung der Welt: Eine Geschichte des 19. Jahrhunderts* (München: Beck, 2009), 432–33.

7 Ilja Mieck, "Von der Reformzeit zur Revolution (1806–1847)," in *Geschichte Berlins von der Frühgeschichte bis zur Industrialisierung*, ed. Wolfgang Ribbe (München: Beck, 1987), 1:407.

defortification and its causes. I felt that I had something to say not only to urban historians, but also to anyone who is interested in early modern and modern European history. Immanuel Kant, who as a young man held lectures in Königsberg about the science of fortification, once commented that "human reason so delights in constructions that it has several times built up a tower and then razed it [just] to examine the nature of the foundation."[8] Part of what Kant meant, I think, is that we often understand something – be it an idea, a piece of machinery, or even (as archeologists know) a whole culture – only after dissecting, dismantling, or even destroying it completely. By examining its broken pieces, we get to see, perhaps for the first time, an object's hidden parts and understand its operating principles.

When burghers demolished their city's walls with pickaxes, hammers, and shovels, or when they blew them up with gunpowder kegs, they stood in front of a hole in the ground. Looking with them into the void and at the surrounding fragments of the old walls, I felt a chance to follow Kant's suggestion: to understand, exactly at the moment of their destruction, the kind of communities the fortifications helped sustain, the basis of these communities' ways of life, the "true foundations," as one Frankfurter put it in 1801, of their communal spirit.[9] This is why this book is not only about defortification. It is also about the old world to which the walls once belonged and the modern world that replaced it.

It is the general significance of defortification as a metaphor for, or a parable about, the replacement of a whole older world by a new one that explains why, as it unfolded, defortification was everybody's business. It was the business of monarchs, state officials, generals, architects, travelers, the local peasants from the city's surrounding countryside, and, of course, the burghers themselves. The following pages will excavate these actors' long-forgotten voices. Through them, we will look at defortification not only from the historian's bird's-eye view (although we will do that, too), but also from the perspective of the people who supported, opposed, or merely witnessed defortification. Without these voices, the story will always be partial, always incomplete.

Defortification was, of course, not unique to German cities; all but a very few European cities experienced it at one point or another. Why devote a book to the German case, then, and not to Europe as a whole or to any

---

8 Immanuel Kant, *Prolegomena to Any Future Metaphysics*, trans. James W. Ellington (Indianapolis: Hackett, 2001), 2.
9 "Der alte Frankfurter Brückenthurn wurde abgerissen im August 1801, der jüngere, der Sachsenhäusser war geboren 1345 und starb 1765," His. M. Frankfurt am Main, Grafische Sammlung, C 3129g.

other European country? Beyond the fact that a comparison with France will play an important role in this book, I have two broad answers here: one intended for a general public, the other for specialists in the field.

"If a scholar from another planet were to come to earth in order to investigate different forms of government," wrote the journalist Rudolf Zacharias Becker in 1796, he would find Germany "to be the best school for his purposes. Here one can investigate from up close the advantages and disadvantages of any conceivable form of government."[10] Indeed, no other European country (except, perhaps, Italy) displayed such a diversity of institutions, traditions, and urban centers as early modern Germany. Lacking a centralized bureaucracy or a nation-state framework, Germany's many states and cities moved along several distinct trajectories from the mid-seventeenth century onward. The result was an unparalleled diversity of defortification projects in the German lands that represents a broad illustration of the general forces behind the modernization of European cities in general. Unlike in France or England, for instance, in Germany one cannot reduce defortification to a single factor. My decision to concentrate on German cities is therefore motivated not only by my professional background as a historian of early modern and modern Germany, but by an analytic claim as well: early modern Germany was a microcosm of Europe as a whole.

Christopher Friedrichs recently criticized another book about German cities, Mack Walker's *German Home Towns*, by arguing that the communities Walker described in it were not all that unique compared to Europe's other urban centers.[11] I personally find this to be an advantage rather than a flaw. Because seventeenth- and eighteenth-century Germany was Europe writ small, the story of its transformation from a country full of walled cities to one containing almost exclusively open cities is Europe's story, too.

A narrower answer to the question "Why Germany?" relates to more specific aspects of Walker's book. In *German Home Towns*, Walker set out to explore the history of those countless middle- and small-size communities that were so characteristic of premodern Germany. For many good and important reasons, his book is still considered the classic in the field,

---

10 Quoted in Holger Böning, "Gotha als Hauptort volksaufklärischer Literatur und Publizistik," in *Ernst II. von Sachsen-Gotha-Altenburg*, eds. Werner Greiling, Andreas Klinger, and Christoph Köhler (Köln: Böhlau, 2005), 326.

11 Mack Walker, *German Home Towns: Community, State, and General Estate, 1648–1871*, 2nd ed. (Ithaca: Cornell University Press, 1998). Christopher Friedrichs, "How German Was the German Home Town?" (Paper presented to the annual meeting of the German Studies Association, Louisville, Kentucky, 2011).

at least in the English-speaking world. It demolished superficial historiographic boundaries between the early modern and the modern, and it told the history of the German lands from the bottom up and not, as had been so common beforehand, from the top down.[12] At the same time, certain assertions in Walker's work have always seemed problematic to me. By concentrating on "home towns" – urban communities with less than 10,000 inhabitants – Walker drew a line dividing them from larger cities. Seventeenth- and eighteenth-century Germans did not make these distinctions: they described what in English one would call "boroughs," "towns," and "cities" with a single term – *eine Stadt*. When they did make distinctions between different cities, early modern Germans did so according to political rather than social criteria: Imperial cities, residence cities, provincial cities, and so on. They probably did so for a reason. Thrusting a social definition of the city on early modern Germans rather than using their own native concepts could be misleading.

Walker furthermore paid no attention at all to the physical footprint of German towns, to their internal layout, the location of their communal institutions, or the towns' different parts. He even termed the typical early modern tendency to define all cities by the existence of fortifications as intellectually lazy.[13] Whether in the clear line he drew between home towns and large cities or in his disregard for towns' and cities' external appearances, Walker's methodology served a purpose: to show, despite their slow decline, the continuity and extraordinary stability of urban communities in Germany from the Peace of Westphalia in 1648 to German unification in 1871 and even beyond.[14] It is a central argument of this book that overemphasizing stability can be misleading and that the material environment of cities and towns is not a superficial aspect of their history but part of their very fabric.

It is clear to me – and should be clear to the reader from the outset – that there is more than one way of telling the dramatic, and often traumatic, story of the defortification of German cities. In the book's seven chapters, ordered chronologically, I concentrate mainly on politics and what has been called "political culture" – the set of discourses and symbolic practices that shape political claims.[15] Other historians could have chosen a different way

---

12 For an evaluation of Walker's achievement, see Christopher Friedrichs, "But Are We Any Closer to Home? Early Modern German Urban History Since 'German Home Towns,'" *Central European History* 30, no. 2 (1997): 163–185; and James J. Sheehan, "Foreword to the Cornell Paperback Edition," *German Home Towns*, by Walker, xiii–xvii.
13 Walker, *German Home Towns*, 30.   14 Ibid., 5.
15 Keith Michael Baker, *Inventing the French Revolution: Essays on French Political Culture in the Eighteenth Century* (Cambridge: Cambridge University Press, 1990), 4.

of describing and analyzing my sources. A social historian would probably have devoted more space to the question of migration in and out of cities, to the social groups that inhabited the city's margins, and to questions of health and sanitation; an economic historian could have analyzed in depth the fluctuation of real estate prices within and outside the walls and their effects on defortification decisions; and an art historian would have surely devoted much, much more time to discussing the re-planning of defortified cities than I have done here. The story of the demolition of city walls and of the collapse of the world to which they had once belonged is a complicated one; other historians might certainly use different analytical methods to shed more light on it. Be that as it may, my intention while writing the following pages has never been to present a "total history" of the transformation of German cities from fortified to defortified ones, nor has it been to claim that my interpretation is the only valid one. My aim, above all else, was to draw the attention of historians and laypersons alike to one of the most important, but also most neglected, chapters in the history of the European city; an important chapter, indeed, in the history of the transition between premodern and modern Europe.

Last but by no means least: this book describes a historic demolition of fortifications, but it also seeks to demolish certain walls itself. Historians of the transition between premodern and modern Europe are often trapped in boundaries of their own making: the distinction between large cities and home towns, between industrialized and nonindustrialized towns, between German and other European cities, and – most generally – between the premodern and the modern. I am not certain that these distinctions are always useful and I am absolutely sure that, in the story of the emergence of the open city, they need to be treated with great caution. Wachenhusen was right: in many cases, the demolition of city walls was a tragic event. Tearing down historiographic boundaries, on the other hand, should cause no anxiety. We should follow Kant's lead here: razing historiographic boundaries could help us realize the nature of their true foundations. Whether we then choose to rebuild them or not is a different question.

PART I

Beginnings, 1689–1789

1

The City and Its Walls

Throughout its long history, the German city was always a dynamic organism. It continuously changed in size and appearance, and its economic and political relationships with the outer world were often in flux. The defortification of the German city in the eighteenth and nineteenth centuries was a significant moment in the city's history. It signaled a fundamental transformation of the urban environment on three interrelated levels: the city's defense against military intervention from the outside; public security and police within the city; and the symbolic way both locals and foreigners imagined the urban community.

Contemporaries wrote a great deal about the transformation of cities from closed to open places. Whether supporting or opposing this transformation, they wrote with much passion; all felt that something very important was at stake. Some burghers (citizens of towns) argued that even the smallest change in the old walls was absolutely unacceptable. The burghers in Jena, for instance, sent a delegation to their duke one day around 1800 with the urgent request that His Highness put an immediate stop to the demolition of a small part of Jena's walls. The burghers evoked "their old, honorable city walls" and claimed not to understand how anyone would think about demolishing even a small section of them (the adjective "honorable" was very frequently associated with the walls before, during, and after their destruction).[1] Others would hail the prospects of similar action in other cities as "the liberation of the city from its old 'pressing belts'"[2] or write poems and even compose music for the occasion.

1 Johann Wolfgang von Goethe, *Gespräche*, ed. Woldemar Freiherr von Biedermann (Leipzig: Biedermann, 1890), 260–61. There are a great many other examples of the use of the term "honorable" in relation to city walls in the eighteenth and nineteenth centuries. Two such examples are Amalie Muenster-Meinhövel, *Amaliens poetische Versuche* (Leipzig: Voss, 1796), 128; and Hans Wachenhusen, *Berliner Photographien* (Berlin: Hausfreund Expedition, 1867), 2:33.
2 Napoleon Weinhagen, *Studien zur Entfestigung Kölns* (Köln: Selbstverlag des Verfassers, 1869), 3.

In many cases, contemporaries viewed the defortification of a city as nothing short of magic. "Many years had passed since I last saw this friendly city with its high standing castle," wrote, for instance, one traveler to Gotha in 1810, "and how speechless I was, when – coming from Erfurt and traveling along the street before the Siebleber Gate – I saw the great and pleasant transformation that had taken place in that area." In the past, "a traveler had seen here the city's walls and deep moats and had been forced to go through the dark, long passage of the gate into the city. But now everything had changed as if by a magic spell into a wonderful park with large grass lawns, little grottos, groves, and small waterfalls."[3]

A few years earlier, Katharina Elisabeth Goethe echoed a similar sentiment in a letter to her illustrious son. For many of her fellow burghers in Frankfurt am Main, the demolition of the old walls was a moment of great melancholy. For Katharina Elisabeth, however, it was a joyful occasion. "It is all really like magic," she wrote about the defortification of the city in which her husband had once served on the city council. "Our 'old wigs' would surely have waited until the Second Coming before daring to do such a thing of their own volition."[4]

The reactions in Frankfurt to the demolition of the city walls contain three of the most important leitmotifs of defortification stories in general: contests over the fundamental transformation of the city (the "old wigs," who would never have dared to defortify the city of their own volition, were nonetheless forced to do so); a sense of wonder when it finally arrived ("it is all really like magic"); and accompanying nostalgia for the world just lost (sadness about the demolition of some beautiful gates and towers). Such sentiments, although conflicting, were almost always related. Together, they signaled that the destruction of the old barriers between city and countryside meant much more to contemporaries than the demolition of a physical object. Contemporaries had strongly contradictory views about defortification because they viewed it as a metamorphosis of the urban environment as such: a fundamental transformation of what the city actually was. This transformation was the source of burghers' nostalgia and the reason for their sense of wonder after the walls fell; the sense that through defortification the old city had suddenly turned into a totally different place, as if by a magic spell.

---

3 "Bemerkungen über die neuen Anlagen und Kunst-Sammlungen in Gotha," *Journal des Luxus und der Moden* 25 (1810): 756.
4 Letter from July, 1, 1808. Katharina Elisabeth Goethe, *Briefe an ihren Sohn Johann Wolfgang, an Christiane und August von Goethe* (Stuttgart: Reclam, 1999), 287.

Indeed, many contemporaries had a hard time calling an open city a city at all. Some felt the expression was inadequate; others viewed it as an actual contradiction in terms. French military theoreticians around the turn of the eighteenth century, for instance, used the expression "to raze a city to the ground" (*raser*) as a synonym for the destruction of the city's fortifications and not the destruction of the city's footprint. To raze a city was equal to demolishing its defenses because by doing so one turned it "back" into a village.[5] In German, on the other hand, the verb "to raze" (*schleifen*) was reserved in the early modern period for what one did to the walls, not the city. Thus, the walls were razed to the ground, while the city was either physically destroyed or merely defortified (*entfestigt*).[6] But on the whole, men of letters in eighteenth-century Germany held a similar view to that of their French counterparts. An unfortified place is simply not a city, argued the important eighteenth-century German jurist Johann Gottlob von Justi. Echoing the old German proverb that what distinguishes the burgher from the peasant are the city walls (*Bürger und Bauer scheidet nichts als die Mauer*), Justi claimed that a place could be big, beautiful, or densely populated, but if it was not physically surrounded by a wall it lacked the most important sign of a city and should therefore not be called by that name.[7] Even in the early nineteenth century, one sometimes encounters a similar sentiment. Goethe himself shared it when writing about newly defortified cities. They were nothing more than big villages, he argued.[8] The fact that the market, streets, churches, and all other buildings were left intact did not matter. With the destruction of their walls, these places ceased to be towns and turned back into rural communities.

What was behind such arguments? In what sense were the walls "honorable?" Why did one refrain from calling a large though wall-less settlement

---

5 Camille Rousset, *Histoire de Louvois et de son administration politique et militaire*, 3rd ed. (Paris: Didier, 1863), 4:160.

6 The etymology of one of the names for a city in Latin, *oppidum*, signifies a similar idea. It comes from *ob-pedum*, that is, "an enclosed area." The English term "town" comes from the German *Zaun* (a fence) for the same reason, as does an old Hebrew word for a city, *kirya*, which comes from *kir* ("wall").

7 Johann Heinrich Gottlob von Justi, *Staatswirtschaft* (Leipzig: B.C. Breitkopf, 1758), 1:491. A similar idea can be found in Diderot's *Encyclopédie*: "[une Ville est un] assemblage de plusieurs maisons disposées par rues, & fermées d'une clôture commune, qui est ordinairement de murs & de fossés. Mais pour définir une *ville* plus exactement, c'est une enceinte fermée de murailles, qui renferme plusieurs quartiers, des rues, des places publiques, & d'autres édifices." Louis de Jaucourt, "Ville," in *Encyclopédie, ou dictionnaire raisonné des sciences, des arts et des métiers*, eds. Denis Diderot and Jean le Rond D'Alembert. (University of Chicago: ARTFL Encyclopédie Projet [Winter 2008 Edition], ed. Robert Morrissey, http://encyclopedie.uchicago.edu/, 17:277).

8 Johann Wolfgang von Goethe, *Sämtliche Werke nach Epochen seines Schaffens, Münchner Ausgabe*, ed. Karl Richter (München: C. Hanser, 1985), 9:459.

a city? What, in other words, was at stake in the contests over the defortification of German cities, and why, when it finally happened, did it make one feel that something magical and transformational had just taken place? These questions take us back to the late seventeenth century: first, to the issue of the overall spread and geopolitical characteristics of urban fortification in Germany; and second, to the daily routines of the city and the symbolic meaning of its walls.

THE FORTIFICATIONS OF CITIES IN GERMANY BY
THE LATE SEVENTEENTH CENTURY

Down to the late seventeenth century, German cities had a long tradition of political independence that was manifested by strong fortifications. Comparing his days with those of the ancients, Sir Roger Williams wrote in 1590 that "Alexander, Caesar, Scipio, and Hannibal... would never have conquered countries so easily had they been fortified as [present-day] Germany, France, and the Low Countries."[9] "The cities of Germany," wrote Niccolò Machiavelli a few decades earlier (not without a slight exaggeration), "are completely free, they have little surrounding territory, they obey the emperor when they wish, and they fear neither him nor any other nearby power." They can do all of this, Machiavelli claimed, because "they are fortified in such a manner that everyone thinks their capture would be a tedious and difficult affair. For they all have sufficient moats and walls; they have adequate artillery; they always store in their public warehouses enough to drink and to eat and to burn for a whole year." Finally, Machiavelli added, German cities "hold the military arts in high regard, and they have many regulations for maintaining them."[10]

Much would change in central Europe from Machiavelli's time until the late seventeenth century, when German cities began to be permanently defortified. The sixteenth and seventeenth centuries were a time of great upheaval in the Holy Roman Empire, the ancient political framework in which almost all German cities existed. The Reformation and the religious strife during the sixteenth century and the Thirty Years' War in the seventeenth century brought the Holy Roman Empire to the brink of collapse without, however, revealing an undisputed winner in the conflict. The military impasse after three decades of war and the peace treaties of Westphalia

---

9 Quoted in Geoffrey Parker, *The Military Revolution: Military Innovation and the Rise of the West, 1500–1800* (New York: Cambridge University Press, 1996), 6.
10 Niccolò Machiavelli, *The Prince*, trans. Peter Bondanella and Mark Musa (New York: Oxford University Press, 1984), 37–38.

in 1648 established a delicate political equilibrium in the Empire that would last – at least in some parts of Germany – until the Napoleonic Wars and the Empire's final demise in 1806. This delicate balance was one of the two factors that shaped the physical appearance of Germany's numerous fortified cities in the century and a half after 1648.

Based on the status quo painfully achieved by the end of the Thirty Years' War, the Peace of Westphalia strove to prevent conflicts within the Empire from turning into another general war of all against all. It created a political mechanism that historian Mack Walker called "perpetual frustration of disruptive energy and aggressive power."[11] The treaty did not abolish the Empire, and the Imperial Diet (the Empire's highest representative assembly) could still declare a general war against the Empire's external foes and raise an Imperial army for that purpose. But the treaties also gave the German states – the building blocks of the Empire – the right to form and break alliances independently in defense of their liberties, and they designated the Great Powers of Europe as guarantors of the peace. The result of these arrangements was that no one, not even the emperor himself, could garner enough power to dramatically change the status quo of 1648. In theory, at least, the Empire was meant to be sufficiently strong to protect itself as a whole, but never strong enough to deprive its members of their liberties.

The impact of the political arrangements of Westphalia on the physical form of German cities was unmistakable. Unlike the situation in other European countries such as France, England, or parts of Eastern Europe, the idea of a wall-less, defenseless city remained for a long time a contradiction in terms in the German lands. In France, as a later chapter will show, the king demolished many an urban wall in the seventeenth century, and in England (in the words of an Italian traveler), "the sea served as the wall and moat" of a united, even if not completely pacified, country.[12] Because every member of the German Empire had the constitutional right to defend itself and external threats did not disappear but had to be dealt with on a case-by-case basis, it was almost unthinkable for a German city to demolish its defense systems.[13] The Peace of Westphalia was not only, as Catherine the Great once put it, "the very basis and bulwark of the constitution of the

---

11 Mack Walker, *German Home Towns: Community, State, and General Estate, 1648–1871*, 2nd ed. (Ithaca: Cornell University Press, 1998), 11.

12 This is Girolamo Lando, as quoted in Colin Platt, *The English Medieval Town* (London: Secker & Warburg, 1976), 43.

13 See, for instance, article VIII (2) in the Instrumentum Pacis Osnaburgensis. *Die Westfälischen Friedensverträge vom 24. Oktober 1648. Texte und Übersetzungen* (Acta Pacis Westphalicae. Supplementa electronica, 1). http://pax-westphalica.de/ (accessed May 2010).

Empire."[14] It was also the reason why so many physical bulwarks existed in the Empire at all.

The second factor determining the outer appearance of contemporary German cities was continuous innovation in military technology. By the late seventeenth century, German cities – which Machiavelli had hailed as "fortified in such a manner that everyone thinks their capture would be a tedious and difficult affair"[15] – were no longer well defended by contemporary standards. The introduction of gunpowder to European warfare in the late Middle Ages contributed to a slow "military revolution," which by the mid-sixteenth century had fundamentally changed the nature of the defense of cities.[16] It was the result of a vicious cycle in military technology. In order to counter the rise in the besieger's firepower, the city's fortifications became stronger; the stronger the city walls, however, the greater the need for further development in firepower, and so on.

In the sixteenth and seventeenth centuries, it became clear that the simple stone walls of preceding centuries were no longer sufficient. But strengthening the old walls was not enough. One also had to reevaluate the layout and functions of fortified places more generally. Some of early modern Europe's greatest minds contributed to this reevaluation: not only famous military engineers such as the Marquis de Vauban and Menno van Cohoorn, but also such figures as Albrecht Dürer, Leonardo da Vinci, Galileo Galilei, and even Immanuel Kant.[17] The size and complex structure of the new fortification systems made war on the continent much more sophisticated and especially more expensive for the defender. For the besieger, too, war had become more costly. One had to keep a much larger field army and supply it with ever more expensive equipment in order to have a chance of taking a city fortified according to the new style. Not every member of the German Empire was strong enough or wealthy enough to do so.

Together, the political compromise of Westphalia and the change in the nature of the science of fortification and the art of siege explain the particular character of seventeenth- and eighteenth-century fortifications of German cities: practically all German cities were fortified, but only a few

14 As quoted in Johann Stephan Pütter, *An Historical Development of the Present Political Constitution of the German Empire*, trans. Josiah Dornford (London: T. Payne, 1790), 3:203.
15 Machiavelli, *The Prince*, 37.
16 See Michael Roberts, "The Military Revolution, 1560–1660," in *The Military Revolution Debate: Readings on the Military Transformation of Early Modern Europe*, ed. Clifford J. Rogers (Boulder: Westview Press, 1995), 13–36.
17 Albrecht Dürer, *Etliche underricht/zu befestigung der Stett/Schloßz/und flecken* (Nürnberg: 1527); Galileo Galilei, *Breve Istruzione all'Architettura Militare* (1592). About Leonardo, see Pietro C. Marani, *L'architettura fortificata negli studi di Leonardo da Vinci* (Firenze: Leo S. Olschki, 1984). About Kant, see Allen W. Wood, *Kant* (Walden, Massachusetts: Blackwell, 2005), 6.

were fortified well. The Empire, it was agreed, should not have a standing army or any fortress towns directly under its control.[18] In case the Imperial Diet declared a general war, the emperor was allowed to raise an Imperial army and use existing fortified cities to support his campaigns. But it had been the general consensus at least since the Peace of Prague in 1635 that the emperor and the Diet should have no say in the construction of new fortifications in the cities and no right to interfere with the decisions of particular territorial states to fortify or defortify cities and towns.[19] Such provisions were recognized as part of the constitutional liberties of the Empire's members, which were now even entitled to raise money for the overall defense of their territories without the need of their estates' consent.[20] Because the essence of the treaties of Westphalia was defensive in nature, offensive operations were made deliberately difficult, while defensive measures on the part of the Empire's members were unrestricted. The construction of modern fortifications in post-Westphalia Germany was never, and could never have become, a general matter for the Empire as a whole.

With the Empire playing little or no part in the financing of city defenses, the construction of new fortifications could be funded only by a territorial state or a wealthy city. Several cities belonging to territorial states such as Prussia, Bavaria, or the Habsburg lands were indeed fortified by the state in the new, modern style. Such cities were nevertheless relatively few in number, as states fortified in the modern style only the cities they deemed strategically important – princely residence towns (e.g., Berlin, Vienna, or Munich) or cities along their borders. Several wealthy, independent cities such as Hamburg, Bremen, or Nuremberg were also able to finance – single-handedly – the construction of modern fortifications. But the vast majority of German cities lacked the independent financial means to strengthen their fortifications and could not rely on the support of any territorial state to do so. They therefore refrained from strengthening the fortifications altogether, had to compromise the quality of the fortifications because of the

---

18 For the question of the military constitution of the Holy Roman Empire, see Helmut Neuhaus, "Das Problem der militärischen Exekutive in der Spätphase des Alten Reiches," in *Staatsverfassung und Heeresverfassung in der europäischen Geschichte der frühen Neuzeit*, ed. Johann Kunisch (Berlin: Duncker & Humboldt, 1986), 297–346.

19 The history of these agreements was often discussed in the 1790s. See, most importantly, Dietrich, *Gedanken über die Frage: Wann und wie sind die Reichsstände verpflichtet, in die in ihren Landen befindlichen Festungen . . . Reichstruppen zur Besatzung einzunehmen?* (Frankfurt am Main: 1794).

20 As, most importantly, in the *Jüngster Reichsabschied* of 1654, §180. Karl Zeumer, ed., *Quellensammlung zur Geschichte der Deutschen Reichsverfassung in Mittelalter und Neuzeit* (Tübingen: J.C.B. Mohr, 1913), 2:460.

huge sums of money involved (so in Frankfurt am Main, for instance[21]) or, after spending a fortune on their construction, neglected the maintenance of their walls. One traveler to Cologne in the 1790s had this to say about its fortifications: "[T]his pompous enclosure . . . with its hundred turrets and twenty-four principal gates, is in such a state of dilapidation that I am apprehensive it would tremble and fall at the very report of the besieging cannon as effectually as the walls of Jericho yielded to the sounds of ram horns."[22]

A general map of fortified cities in Germany during the first half of the eighteenth century demonstrates the resulting spread of urban fortifications (figure 2).

The map shows the differences between three areas in central Europe: the north, the center, and the southeast. The north and the southeast were what the nineteenth-century historical geographer Wilhelm Heinrich Riehl called Germany's "centralized country": the two areas traditionally under the control of the strong territorial states of Prussia (north) and Bavaria and Austria (southeast).[23] The centralized country contained many fortified cities, although it had significantly fewer cities than in Germany's midlands. It was in the north and southeast, too, that one could find the greatest number of well-fortified cities because the strong, centralized states had the means to finance the buildings of modern fortifications.

The majority of German cities lay outside the centralized country, in a belt running through the middle of the country – roughly from Saxony, through Thuringia, Franconia, and Swabia, to the southwest. Here, in the lands Riehl termed "the individualized country" because of the variety of small and medium states they contained, lay most of Germany's middle-sized cities and home towns. As opposed to the north and southeast, the individualized country contained very few modern fortifications. There was simply no one who could finance the strengthening of the old city walls in these areas. Middle Germany's cities and towns lay outside the sphere of influence of the great territorial states, they could not apply for money for new defenses from the Imperial Diet, and they lacked the financial means to embark on such an expensive project independently.

Even in small German cities and towns, where by the second half of the eighteenth century the city walls possessed little or no military significance,

21 Johann Georg Battonn, *Oertliche Beschreibung der Stadt Frankfurt am Main* (Frankfurt am Main: Verein für Alterthumskunde, 1861), 144–46.
22 Thomas Cogan, *The Rhine: Or a Journey from Utrecht to Francfort* (London: G. Woodfall, 1794), 1:244.
23 Wilhelm Heinrich Riehl, *Land und Leute*, 2nd ed. (Stuttgart: Cotta, 1855), 132–35, 139–41, 159–217; Walker, *German Home Towns*, 1ff.

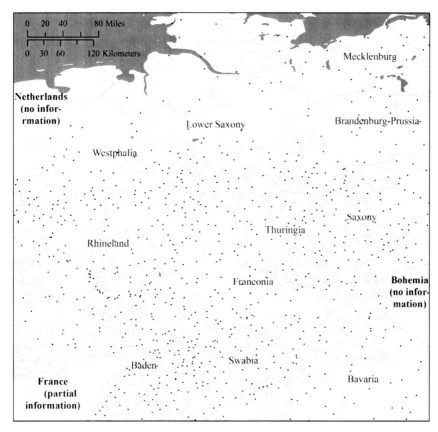

Figure 2. Distribution of fortified cities with a population of more than 1,000 inhabitants in early eighteenth-century central Europe.

there were heated debates over whether to defortify the city or keep its walls intact. Such debates were caused by the fact that city walls were important not only militarily; they were also crucial to internal security and to the community's symbolic self-definition. To understand the contests over defortifications, it is therefore not enough to describe the walls' military functions. One also needs to picture a typical early modern German city in its daily routines and its physical as well as symbolic form.

THE CITY AT NIGHT

The police role of the walls was especially evident after dark. Indeed, approaching a city like Gotha, Jena, Frankfurt, or Munich in the early modern period was something a traveler would dare to do only during the day.[24] At night, the city gates were bolted, the drawbridges raised, and the city's surroundings engulfed in pitch black. By the late seventeenth century, German cities no longer hung heavy chains across their streets after dark.[25] Even so, nocturnal city streets were quiet and human movement rare. Only a couple of German cities had public streetlights before 1750, and even then more to prevent garrison troops from deserting than anything else. In some towns, a gibbet just outside one of the city gates would provide a solemn warning to soldiers who might entertain the idea of fleeing their posts. Still, many managed to escape into the night, never to return.[26]

In one or more of the city's towers a night watchman kept an eye on the city, calling the hours throughout the night. His main role, as the motto on the Holsten city gate in Lübeck solemnly proclaimed, was to ensure that both *concordia domi* and *pax foris* would be guaranteed. The night watchman's highest task in assuring "domestic harmony" was to ring the alarm bells in case a fire broke out somewhere in the city. Fire was by far the gravest danger to the burgher's life and property. "The burning city" was so much on everybody's mind at the time that it even existed as a separate genre of painting in early modern Northern Europe.[27] Assuring "peace without," on the other hand, involved the watchman's task of alerting the population in case of an approaching enemy or horde of robbers from the surrounding – often unsafe – countryside. The gravity of these dangers to the community made the city draw strict rules for its night watchmen. Most importantly, the rules forbade the watchmen from compromising their responsibilities by falling asleep during their watch or bringing alcoholic beverages and women to sweeten their long, solitary hours up in the tower. Needless to say, over time quite a few watchmen had to be dismissed.[28]

---

24 For a general discussion of nocturnal life in the early modern city, see A. Roger Ekirch, *At Day's Close: Night in Times Past* (New York: Norton, 2005). The police measures typical of early modern German cities are detailed, for instance, in the case of Munich: "Curfürsl. Special Mandat die Tor-Sperre betr. 20 März 1747" and "Stadttorsperre und –öffnung," StdA München, Polizeidirektion, 20, 21.

25 Rolf Rosenbohm, "Die Straßensperren in den niederdeutschen Städten," *Lüneburger Blätter* 9 (1958): 21–38.

26 See, for instance, Gordon Craig, *The Politics of the Prussian Army 1640–1945* (Oxford: Clarendon Press, 1955), 3ff. Breslau's case is especially rich in terms of archival materials: "Erbauung eines neuen Soldaten Galgens in Oder Thore beym Ravelin," StA Breslau, Akten der Stadt Breslau, (1680) 12.219; and "Einrichtung der Laternen Wesens u. den Steuer Geld Einnahmen," StA Breslau, Akten der Stadt Breslau, (991) 11.530.

27 As can be seen in Frans Francken the Younger, *Gastmahl im Hause des Bürgermeisters Rockox*, ca. 1630/5, Alte Pinakothek, Munich.

28 For Breslau, see "Nacht Wacht Dienst," StA Breslau, Akten der Stadt Breslau, (985) 11.524. For a collection of instructions in Hamburg, see *Instruction für die Wächter an Thoren und Bäumen*, StA Hamburg (ohne Signatur).

Travelers and even locals who missed the gates' lock-out time (or had the strange notion of trying to enter the city during a *missa solemnis* on a major holiday, when the gates were also closed) were forced to seek accommodation at one of the inns in the suburbs or in a nearby tavern. As late as the 1820s, an English traveler would describe such a place just outside Vienna:

At ten o'clock the outer gate [of the inn] must be shut, whatever revelry may be going on within. It is a police regulation, and the police is watchful. Besides a body of men corresponding to our watchmen, the [city] streets are patrolled, all night long, by gens d'armes, both mounted and on foot. Street noise, street quarrels, and street robberies are unknown. It is only outside of the walls . . . that nocturnal depradations are sometimes committed; and, in such cases, robbery is not unfrequently accompanied with murder.[29]

The suburbs – for those cities that had them – often had the reputation of being unruly places. This is the origin of the English expression "beyond the pale" (beyond, that is, the palisades surrounding a town). They belonged legally to the countryside, not to the actual legal sphere of the city, and were consequently an unsafe and unstable social environment. In the suburbs of big, expanding cities such as Vienna or Berlin, the situation would steadily deteriorate from the second half of the eighteenth century onward, and the local gendarmerie would start raiding them frequently in search of "troublemakers." Such raids occurred so often in Berlin's suburbs in the late eighteenth and early nineteenth centuries that the authorities felt compelled to print out large numbers of blank report forms about a raid's possible outcomes in order to save the gendarmes precious time. Raids were held at ten o'clock in the evening, when "vagabonds" were expected to be playing and drinking in the local tavern, or at six o'clock in the morning, when they were supposed to be in deep slumber. The raid's aim was to arrest not only the troublemakers themselves but also their accomplices and helpers, of whom there was evidently no small number. As one regulation put it: "All local establishments as well as all houses and persons with any possible relation to, or communication with, these lawless persons should be thoroughly searched." Such searches were not to be limited to the taverns, therefore. "Stables, rooms, cellars, barns, gardens, courtyards, churches, and in general all other conceivable places where one might seek haven, should be thoroughly combed out," the regulation dictated.[30]

---

29 John Russell, *A Tour in Germany and Some of the Southern Provinces of the Austrian Empire*, 3rd ed. (Edinburgh: Longman, Rees, Orme, Brown, and Green, 1827), 2:221–22.
30 This particular quote is taken from "Die General-Vagabunden-Visitation, 1818–50," LA Berlin, A Rep. 038–01 Nr. 48.

Travelers had quite a few reasons, therefore, to refrain from roaming the city's surroundings at night and had to be very careful not to miss the gates' lock-out hour in the evening. This could force even the city's own sons and daughters (as Jean-Jacques Rousseau famously found out in Geneva) to spend the night in an open field or to look for a bed for the night in some suburban tavern or at the closest travelers' inn.[31] From there, together with the colorful dangers of such places, they could make out the nightly silhouette of the city's fortifications. From there, too, they could faintly hear – although not actually see – the watchman calling the hours from the church tower.

THE CITY AS AN ORGANISM

At daybreak, the city awakened.[32] For many early modern Germans such a statement was much more than a mere metaphor. The powerful legal philosophy of corporation theory, ubiquitous in central Europe throughout the late Middle Ages and the early modern period, perceived the city as an actual organism: it was both an independent, breathing individual and a limb or an organ of a larger being.[33] As the first of the two, it was called a corporation (from the Latin noun *corpus*, "body") and possessed its own limbs or organs (the guilds, the city councils, the city officers, etc.). As a corporation, the city also had the status of a legal person. It could sue and be sued in a court of law and had its own interests, views, and voice in many legal matters. "Look at the human body," explained one Strasbourg burgher to his fellow citizens in the sixteenth century, "how each member serves the whole. My eye sees for my feet, the feet walk and bear the whole body; the mouth eats for the belly, and the belly receives the food and distributes

---

31 Rousseau tells a story about his childhood years in Geneva, where, in a similar way to German cities, the city gates were closed every night: "I was caught out [of the city] twice, and found the gates closed on my return. The next day I was dealt with as may be imagined, and on the second occasion promised such a reception, if there should be a third, that I determined not to lay myself open to it." Jean-Jacques Rousseau, *Confessions*, trans. Angela Scholar (Oxford: Oxford University Press, 2000), 40–41.

32 This is an old biblical theme, of course (e.g., Isaiah 52:1). Compare also contemporary music: J.S. Bach, *Wachet auf, ruft uns die Stimme*, cantata, BWV 140.

33 See, most recently, Albrecht Koschorke et al., eds., *Der fiktive Staat: Konstruktion des politischen Körpers in der Geschichte Europa* (Frankfurt am Main: Fischer, 2007), esp. 78–88. Ideas about the metaphor of the body in other European countries during the early modern period are treated in Paul Archambault, "The Analogy of the Body in Renaissance Political Thought," *Bibliothèque d'humanisme et renaissance* 29, no.1 (1967): 21–53; and Leonard Barkan, *Nature's Work of Art: The Human Body as Image of the World* (New Haven: Yale University Press, 1975), esp. chapter 3.

Figure 3. Hans Burgkmair, *The Holy Roman Empire with Head and Limbs* (Quaternione-nadler), ca. 1530. *Source:* Erlangen, Grafische Sammlung der Universität, Hans Burgkmair (AH 216).

it to the whole body and its members. . . . We here at Strasbourg are all one body, and you and I are the members."[34]

A body with members itself, the city was also conceived as a member or "a limb" of a yet larger corporation or "body" such as a province (*Land*) or the Empire as a whole. Such larger bodies possessed not only individual members (such as the city) but also "a head." In the Empire, for instance, the head was the emperor (figure 3).[35]

In its role as a member or organ, the city was of vital importance to the existence and overall health or constitution of the body politic. This was

34 Quoted in Thomas A. Brady, *Ruling Class, Regime, and Reformation at Strasbourg, 1520–1555* (Leiden: Brill, 1978), 122

35 For the idea of the city as an organism see, most importantly, Richard Sennett, *Flesh and Stone: The Body and the City in Western Civilization* (New York: Norton, 1994). For the Holy Roman Empire as a living body, see Barbara Stollberg-Rilinger, *Das Heilige Römische Reich Deutscher Nation: Vom Ende des Mittelalters bis 1806* (München: Beck, 2006); and for its ceremonial practices, Barbara Stollberg-Rilinger, "Zeremoniell als politisches Verfahren. Rangordnung und Rangstreit als Strukturmerkmale des frühneuzeitlichen Reichstags," in *Neue Studien zur frühneuzeitlichen Reichsgeschichte,* ed. Johannes Kunisch (Berlin: Duncker & Humblot, 1997), 91–132. A classic study of the inner workings of small urban communities can be found in Walker, *German Home Towns,* 34–72.

Figure 4. The entrance to Frankfurt am Main from the south, ca. 1730. As in many other premodern German cities, entering Frankfurt entailed crossing several barriers. *Source:* Johann Baptist Homann, *Abbildung der Keys-Freyen-Reichs-Wahl-und Handelstadt Franckfurt am Mayn* (detail, 1730). Historic Maps Collection, Department of Rare Books and Special Collections, Princeton University Library.

Justi's opinion in the eighteenth century as it was the opinion of John of Salisbury in the twelfth century, Lucian's in the second century CE, and of course Aristotle in the fourth century BCE (in *The Republic*, Plato famously made the opposite analogy: the city is not like a body, but rather the human body is like a polis).[36] Justi, for instance, explained the role or place of the city in a state in the following way: "If one were to compare the moral body of a republic to a human body, then trade and the circulation of money would represent the blood circulation or the force of life itself." Furthermore, "one would have to consider the cities as the main or largest blood veins, which represent the actual engine that makes possible the entire movement."[37]

Like all members and persons in the hierarchical world of the Holy Roman Empire, the city had a political rank. The city could have a voice (a vote) in the Imperial Cities' Chamber (one of the three chambers in the Imperial Diet), in which case it would have the rank of an Imperial or free city. It could have a voice in a provincial diet only, in which case it would have the status of a provincial city or town. Or it could have an even lower legal standing, and exist as an independent legal person only in a smaller legal corporation such as a small princely state or a county. In order to assert its legal status, distinct privileges, and even its "honor," the city resorted to legal and political measures as well as to particular ceremonial practices. The walls played an important role in all these respects.

For a German living in the early modern period, the city was therefore a living, breathing organism. It was often even described in sexual terms – that is, imagined as a woman or a maiden (a virgin) – so "she" could also be "raped" and dishonored by having her walls "penetrated." This was an ancient metaphor, of course, but one still very prevalent in early modern Germany, so in many depictions of the destruction of Magdeburg during the Thirty Years' War, for instance.[38] Like all creatures, the city passed through natural cycles. It was sometimes healthy and sometimes ill; at times, it grew up and, like a plant, flourished while at others it grew old and declined. It was constantly changing and yet always the same. Little wonder, then, that the city also "awakened" every morning and "fell asleep" every night. Little wonder, too, that much like any other honorable person in Germany of the

---

36 John of Salisbury, *The Statesman's Book*, trans. John Dickinson (New York: Knopf, 1927), 258–263; Lucian, "Anacharsis," in *Lucian von Samosata sämtliche Werke* (Wien: Franz Haas, 1798), 4:338; Aristotle, *Politics*, Book I.

37 Justi, *Staatswirtschaft*, 491.

38 See, for instance, Werner Lahne, *Magdeburgs Zerstörung in der zeitgenössischen Publizistik* (Magdeburg: Magdeburger Geschichtsverein, 1931), 85–87.

time, the city also engaged in ceremonial practices when the time arrived to start the day.

The larger the city, the more elaborate were its morning rites. In smaller towns – where the city walls merely consisted of wooden fences, a series of hedges, or an enclosure of palisades – there was little sense in employing the same level of control and observation used in heavily fortified cities. But even in a typical German home town – where burghers knew each other very well and where, consequently, it was very difficult to pretend you were not who you were – one used the city gates and walls as important means for control and observation. "[Our] city walls are not meant to defend the city from an approaching army," explained one Coburg citizen in the mid-1780s, "[but] a lawless rogue is often much more dangerous than such an army."[39]

Nevertheless, in large, heavily fortified cities, morning rites were much more intricate than in the home towns. In Breslau, for instance, the gate-keepers woke up shortly before dawn and came down to the gate. Except for their commander, all gatekeepers had the key to one, single gate and could only inherit their posts when an older gatekeeper passed away. The keeper swore an oath to fulfill his job dutifully, to abstain from mingling with night watchers, and to let no one, no "women, children, relatives, acquaintances, or even superiors," distract him from his duties. His was the key to the city, and this key had to be safe.[40]

Other office holders soon followed.[41] According to several general instructions published by the Prussian government during the second half of the eighteenth century, such officers included soldiers in garrison towns and gate watchers elsewhere (to be distinguished from the night watch-ers), scribes (often Jews), and different types of customs officers. The last group was especially heterogeneous, as officers specialized in different types of customs (e.g., wine, beer, wood, foodstuff, etc.). The gate officers, dis-tinguishable from one another by different uniforms, would then occupy separate posts at the gate. The customs officer – dressed in green – would stand at the front together with the gate watchers, and the scribe occupied

---

39 "Berichtigung eines Aufsatzes im Kiel. Mag. II B. 2St. S. 186 die Thorpolicey in Coburg betreffend," *Journal von und für Deutschland* 10 (1785): 380–82.
40 "Acta generalia von der Combination der Expedition der Brel. Thor und Wasser Zöllner mit den Juden Thorschreibern und Thorstehern. Vol. I," StA Breslau, Akten der Stadt Breslau, (476) 11.016.
41 For the specific rules for Breslau, see "Acta specialia von den breslauischen Thorschlüssern oder sogenannt. Zircklern, derselben Bestellung, Besoldung, Vereidung u. Conduite. T. 2.," StA Breslau Staatsarchiv, Akten der Stadt Breslau, (1703) 12.242; "Koenigl. Preussische Accise Reglement," StA Breslau, Akten der Stadt Breslau, (1747) 12.286. About uniforms in Prussia in general, see Peter Kall, Harald Moritzen, and Lambert Frank, *Zolldienstkleidung einst und heute* (Bonn: Bundesministerium für Wirtschaft u. Finanzen, 1972).

a small office nearby. When all was ready, the gatekeeper would open the gate himself and immediately depart. The key's importance to the security of the city was so great that no burgher other than the gatekeeper (or his commander) would be trusted with it, day or night. At last, with the drawbridge lowered, the gate unlocked and unbolted, and all the gate officers in place, the city was open. The day could finally begin.[42]

THE CITY AND ITS BOUNDARIES

It was a part of the natural cycles of the city as an organ in a larger, pulsating body that it tended – to use Justi's metaphor – to "pump out" people and commodities in the morning and take them back in at sunset. It was a simple question of numbers. At dawn, many left the city to start the day outside the walls or to travel farther to a different city, town, market, or fair. "Turn thee about," writes Goethe in *Faust*, "and from this height/Back on the town direct thy sight.//Out of the hollow, gloomy gate,/The motley throngs come forth elate."[43] Later, at sunset, travelers and locals would crowd back into the safety of the city before the gates were closed. The bigger the city, the more marked this cycle was and the more mayhem ensued at the gate. Contemporaries would especially notice this movement shortly before lock out in the evening. As the city consumed more commodities and people than it sent into the bloodstream of the country, the traffic in a large city was more toward the city than out of it.

Travelers in the Holy Roman Empire would most likely leave early from the city or inn where they had spent the night, and start the day's journey to their next destination.[44] Such a journey in the German lands was a notoriously cumbersome affair. In the seventeenth and eighteenth centuries, there were over 1,000 more or less independent political entities in the Empire, including – among many others – great territorial states, free and Imperial cities, ecclesiastical territories and monasteries, smaller princely states, and even some Imperial free villages. Some of these entities were so small, claimed one eighteenth-century German writer half-jokingly, that

---

42 An interesting comparison with the case of late eighteenth-century Paris can be found in Louis-Sébastien Mercier, *Panorama of Paris: Selections from the Tableau de Paris*, ed. and trans. Jeremy D. Popkin (University Park: University of Pennsylvania Press, 1999), 47–49.

43 Johann Wolfgan von Goethe, *Faust: A Tragedy (First Part)*, trans. Bayard Taylor (Leipzig, Brockhaus, 1872), 34.

44 A general discussion of traveling to a fortified city as well as of this genre of travel literature can be found in Klaus Martin Hofmann, "Festungsstädte im Rahmen regional- und stadtgeschichtlicher Konzeptionen," in *Festung, Garnison, Bevölkerung: Historische Aspekte der Festungsforschung*, ed. Volker Schmidtchen (Wesel: Deutsche Gesellschaft für Festungsforschung e.V., 1982), 31–44.

they seemed to be made up completely of borders.[45] To a contemporary traveler, however, boundaries were no joking matter. Border controls were practically everywhere: on turnpikes, local roads, and bridges; at the entrance to canals; in mountain passes; in the middle of Germany's great rivers; and of course in and around towns and cities. "In the small district between Mainz and Coblenz, which, with the winding of the river [Rhine], hardly makes twenty seven miles," wrote one contemporary, "you don't pay less than nine tolls. Between Holland and Coblenz there are at least sixteen."[46]

The first border one would usually encounter upon approaching a major German city was its legal limit.[47] This limit could be quite far from the walls in the case of prosperous independent cities such as Nuremberg or Frankfurt am Main, which over the centuries had managed to subordinate a large territory to their control. In the case of Nuremberg, for instance, the city's territory included six smaller towns as well as dozens of market villages and other rural communities.[48] A city like Munich, on the other hand, was not a free city, and both sides of its legal boundary – although marking two separate legal spheres, city and countryside – were nonetheless under the overall sovereignty of the Bavarian Elector. In such a case, the city's legal boundaries enclosed a sphere known as the "peace of the castle" (one eighteenth-century milestone marking this boundary still exists today in Munich's English Garden).

In big or politically powerful cities, where the walls and legal boundaries did not converge, the latter were marked by one of two physical signs: milestones or dikes (*Landwehr*). Historically, the older of the two was the Landwehr: a long ditch flanked by a dike, trees, or hedges. Some dikes dated back to the early Middle Ages, when they served as signs of a territory's legal status as well as impediments to the movement of wild beasts and even an approaching army. In some cases, the Landwehren were exceptionally long, cutting the countryside for several dozens of miles. One Landwehr in southern Thuringia, whose remains are still visible today, stretched for almost forty miles. By the eighteenth century, however, these dikes did not

45 Quoted in James J. Sheehan, *German History, 1770–1866* (New York: Oxford University Press, 1989), 30.
46 Johann Kaspar Riesbeck, *Travels Through Germany, in a Series of Letters* (London, 1787), 3:284.
47 A general treatment of the history as well as prehistory of the concept of *Weichbild* (a city's legal limits) can be found in Ernst Kaeber, "Das Weichbild der Stadt Berlin seit der Steinschen Städteordnung," in *Ernst Kaeber: Beiträge zur Berliner Geschichte*, ed. Ernst Vogel (Berlin: Alter de Gruyter & Co., 1964). 234–376.
48 Richard van Dülmen, *Kultur und Alltag in der frühen Neuzeit*, 3 vols., vol. 2: *Dorf und Stadt im 16.-18. Jahrhundert* (München: Beck, 1990), 63.

usually correspond to the city's legal boundaries anymore and had been replaced by milestones.[49]

Three parts of the extended city became immediately conspicuous upon approaching a big and well-fortified city from afar: the suburbs, glacis, and fortifications.[50] The suburbs were often surrounded by a simple wall. They were sometimes as old as the city and, like exoparasites, fed on the city's fortified body. The suburbs' existence derived from the fact that while belonging to the economic sphere of the city, they belonged legally to the countryside. Consequently, the city had little or no legal obligations vis-à-vis its suburbs in such crucial matters as fire protection, poor relief, or even defense. Had the city possessed legal obligations to such a community, it would have had to defend it and therefore include it within its walls. In such a case, the suburb would be both physically and legally incorporated into the city – quite literally becoming a part of the city's very body or corpus – and would consequently cease to be a suburb.[51] Thus, while the suburbs of German cities began to expand rapidly in the second half of the eighteenth century, the cities themselves often remained the same size. German cities – unlike North American ones, for instance – did not simply expand into the surrounding countryside; rather, the population of the surrounding countryside increasingly "crowded" around certain cities.

The second conspicuous feature of a major seventeenth- or eighteenth-century German city was its glacis. The glacis was a slow, downward slope stretching from the city's fortifications toward the fields or suburbs around it. Its aim was to provide a field of fire for the city's gunners in case of an attack or a siege. For that purpose, it was either completely devoid of tall vegetation and man-made structures (as mandated by legal measures known as "radius laws" or *Rayon-Gesetze*) or it contained only objects that could be quickly demolished if necessary.[52] The word "glacis" was originally reserved for the artificial downward slope close to the fortifications themselves, but with time it came to describe the entire round, exposed belt or "no-man's-land" surrounding a fortified place and separating it from the suburbs.

---

49 For the origins and history of medieval fortifications in Germany, including *Landwehren*, see the collection of articles in Gabriele Isenberg and Barbara Scholkmann, eds., *Die Befestigung der mittelalterlichen Stadt* (Köln: Böhlau, 1997).

50 A good comparison between descriptions of German fortified towns in the eighteenth and nineteenth century is Hofmann, "Festungsstädte," 31–44.

51 Guido Helmig, "Die Befestigung der Basler Vorstädte und ihre Integration in den äusseren Mauerring," in *Die Befestigung der mittelalterlichen Stadt.*, ed. Isenberg and Scholkmann, 167–178.

52 For the case of Frankfurt am Main, see Albert Westerburg, *Ueber die rechtliche Natur der Frankfurter sogenannten Wallservitut, zugleich ein Beitrag zur Geschichte des deutschen Baurechts* (Frankfurt am Main: Ludwig Ravenstein, 1887).

Within the rings of the suburbs and the glacis stood the city's fortifications themselves, often under repair. In the early modern period, German cities often spent huge fortunes on the constant repair of their walls, work in which they usually employed the city's poor.[53] "When I perceived [Hamburg's] fortification I was amazed," wrote one seventeenth century observer, "[f]or it is almost incredible for the number of men and horses that are daily set on work about it. Besides, the work itself is so great that it is past the credit of report."[54] This traveler's astonishment derived in part from the fact that modern star-shaped fortifications could be so extremely intricate. They included ravelins (detached outworks), moats, dikes and ditches, drawbridges, bulwarks, ramparts, bastions, several lines of walls, gates, towers, magazines, and much more. An eighteenth-century field officer would have used many dozens of technical terms in order even to speak about the fortifications, let alone effectively command them. Within the modern fortification works stood the old medieval city walls. They were much simpler than the modern fortifications, containing only moats, gates, towers, and "curtains" (wall sections connecting every two towers).

Some sections of the medieval walls were inhabited or formed the outer walls of buildings. As such, the walls were a part of the city's living tissue. The towers, for instance, contained some of the city's most important institutions. Some housed the city's prison (*Hexen-* and *Diebtürme* – witches' and thieves' towers) or stored the wheat, barley, or gunpowder needed for the city's garrison. Others were inhabited or formed the outer walls of private houses. In the Imperial town of Schwäbisch Hall, for instance, one of the city towers was inhabited by the local executioner; in Berlin, parts of the walls belonged to the Charité, the city's biggest hospital; and in Frankfurt am Main, the medieval wall formed one side of the Jewish ghetto's enclosure.

In those German cities where they were allowed to live, Jews often settled right next to a part of the walls' inner side. This location was a manifestation of the Jews' equivocal position vis-à-vis the community: they were simultaneously insiders and outsiders. Sometimes Jews worked as clerks at the gate (as in Breslau or Berlin), and in some places they could enter the city only through a single entrance (the Rosenthaler Gate in Berlin).

---

53 The repairs in Berlin are well documented. See, for instance, "Die Reparatur und Unterhaltung der Landwehre bei den hiesigen Residenzen ingl. den neuen Graben in der Friedrichstrasse, darüber anzufertigende Brücke und neu zu erbauende Corps de Guarde auch die zur Fortificaktion gehörige Brücke," Br. LHA Potsdam, Rep. 2 B 71.

54 Quoted in Geoffrey Parker, ed., *The Thirty Years' War* (London: Routledge, 1998), 12.

It was anything but pleasant to live next to the walls' inner side. This part of the city was the most distant from the marketplace, and often housed not only the Jews but also the poorer sections of the population as well as the city's brothels (where these were allowed). Because the walls cast long shadows and often retained moisture, it was dark, wet, and slippery there.[55] With poor air circulation and no modern sewage systems, this part of the city also literally stank. If that was not enough, persons living right next to the walls also sometimes had a gunpowder storage tower looming right above their heads. Such a tower was a cause for great concern, as the whole structure could suddenly explode because of a force of nature or the carelessness of a single soldier.[56] When lightning struck the gunpowder tower in Breslau one day in 1749, the explosion not only broke the glass windows of churches hundreds of yards away but also killed many dozens of Jews living in its vicinity.[57] Worst of all was to live next to the walls when the city was bombarded during a siege, as the fate of the Jewish ghetto in Frankfurt am Main demonstrates all too well. The ghetto burnt down during several sieges in the eighteenth century, the last one in 1794. Because Frankfurt was defortified shortly thereafter, the ghetto walls were never rebuilt. In this case, as in others, the demolition of the city's physical boundaries implied a social restructuring as well.

Approaching the city by day, an eighteenth-century traveler would cross the suburbs and the glacis and advance toward the city gates through over- and underpasses in the fortification works. The gates were one of the city's busiest locations; they were spatially peripheral but economically and socially central, because all travel to and from the city had to pass through one of them. Some city entrances were very elaborate structures, containing not one but two or even three consecutive gates. At the gate, officers would charge entry fees and indirect taxes. Here, the guard would also examine travel documents and luggage – now and again searching the travelers' bodies, as well – admitting them or sending them away, sometimes quite brutally. When one Christina Bobingerin – a nineteen-year-old peasant from the area around Augsburg – tried to sneak into that city without permission in the sixteenth century, she was put in jail, whipped, and finally deported by the guards.[58] Almost two centuries later, things had

55 Goethe, *Gespräche*, 232.
56 For the reasons for and against keeping such a tower in Breslau, see "Der Bau der Koenigl. Pulver Magazine ausserhalb der Stadt," StA Breslau, Akten der Stadt Breslau, (1682) 12.221.
57 "Acta wegen des durch einen Wetterstrahl d. 21 Juni zersprengten Pulwer Thurm verursachten Schadens. T. 1," StA Breslau, Akten der Stadt Breslau, (1136) 11.675.
58 Christopher Friedrichs, *The Early Modern City* (New York: Longman, 1995), 214.

changed but a little. The gate watcher in Berlin, for instance, was instructed in the second half of the eighteenth century to "pay a special attention to the Jews approaching the gates, to let the locals in, and send back the foreign Jews."[59] Both Moses Mendelssohn and Salomon Maimon, the great Jewish philosophers, experienced the effects of these regulations personally when they tried to enter Berlin at the time.

On its external side, the gate was not unlike a combination of a modern checkpoint and a train station. It was often the location of a small market, where different types of people – peasants, playing children, and gate officers, but also beggars, thieves, and self-appointed preachers and prophets – would seek the money or at least the attention of passers-by.[60] One gets a glimpse into common scenes at the gate by reading what cities forbade the gate officers to do. The city of Hamburg, for instance, declared in one instruction that its gate officers and garrison troops should refuse bribes; abstain from stealing, insulting, or spitting on passers-by; avoid fights, duels, drinking, and gambling during their shift; and refrain from threatening anyone, including their comrades and even their officers, with their weapons (and yes, the instruction added, a dagger is also considered a weapon in this respect).[61] That such activities needed to be forbidden implies that they occurred often enough to draw the attention of the city government.

THE INVISIBLE CITY

Beyond its military, economic, social, and police roles, the gate also had an enormous symbolic function. It was the physical incarnation of the borders between the city and its adjacent countryside. As such, the gate always had two faces. For a traveler entering the city, it denoted the physical boundaries of the city corporation ("city-side"); for a traveler leaving it, the entrance to the adjacent territory ("countryside"). In its quality as a boundary, the gate (and the walls in general) belonged to more than one entity: the city on the one hand, its surrounding area on the other. At this convergence of boundaries, it was most appropriate to present the city's symbols, motto,

---

59 Heinz Knobloch, *Herr Moses in Berlin: Auf den Spuren eines Menschenfreundes* (Berlin: Der Morgen, 1979), 35.

60 Eighteenth-century travel accounts were often constructed along fairly rigid lines. See Wolfgang Griep and Hans-Wolf Jäger, *Reisen im 18. Jahrhundert* (Heidelberg: Winter, 1986). In order to overcome these often rigid narrative structures, I used customs and gate watchers instructions, letters of complaint regarding events at the gates, and other police documents (so, for instance, in the case of children playing near the walls: "Die Unterhaltung der Stadtmauer, Belegung von Pforten in derselben, Abbruch der Thore in Beeskow," Br. LHA Potsdam, Rep. 2 A, Nor. 1165).

61 "Revidire Kriegs-Artikel für die Garnison der Stadt Hamburg," StA Hamburg, A 480, 307.

or coat of arms. Through its "coat," "breastwork," and human officers, the city would "speak" to the persons approaching its walls, expressing its existence as a living being. Walking through the gate was, in the most literal sense of the phrase, a rite of passage.

Entering the city was much like entering a cathedral: a traveler walking through one of the city gates not only entered a place; he or she also performed a symbolic act. A cathedral's overall architecture represents the crucifix's body through the narthex, nave, transept, and chancel. Walking underneath the arch of triumph in its transept, chapels, altar, and ambulatory, a pilgrim reconstitutes Christ's body on the cross by the very act of visiting a basilica. The overall architecture of a city gate served a similar purpose: it made both visitors and locals perform symbolic acts vis-à-vis the city, acts that indicated and constituted the city's imperceptible presence as a living organism. Much as in religious ceremonies, the gate's rites not only described or indicated the city's symbolic form, they breathed life into it.

When a prince, bishop, or ambassador approached the city, it was at the gate that the urban community staged its welcome ceremonies. The first delegation had met the visitor earlier, near the city's legal boundaries. It was at the gate, however, that the entire city assembled to welcome its guest: the priests in their long robes (and, in Catholic towns, also carrying the local church's reliquaries); the garrison troops fully armed and in uniform; the gate watchers with the city's keys; and representatives of other members of the city, all performing their roles according to a strict protocol.[62] On an especially festive occasion such as an Imperial procession, heralds also sounded the trumpets; flags were planted on the walls and banners hung from windowsills; and the burghers, crowding along the procession's route, even cared enough (in the words of one contemporary description) to "wear clean clothes."[63] Even without such extraordinary ceremonies – when, for instance, a native of the city came back after a long absence – the gate served its function as a rite of passage. Goethe's Werther felt this way when he approached his old town after a long absence. "I approached the city," Werther/Goethe writes, "and on my way greeted all the old, familiar garden houses. . . . I walked in through the city gate, and felt, immediately and completely, like my old self again."[64]

---

62 Winfried Dotzauer, "Die Ankunft des Herrschers: Der fürstliche 'Einzug' in die Stadt (bis zum Ende des Alten Reiches)," *Archiv für Kulturgeschichte* 55, no. 2 (1973), 245–288.
63 *Kurtze Relation und Entwurff der Röm. Kayserl. Mayest. Leopoldi, zu Nürnberg gehaltenen Einzugs den 6. (16.) Augusti 1658* (Nürnberg: Johann Hoffmann, 1658).
64 Johann Wolfgang von Goethe, *Die Leiden des jungen Werthers* (Stuttgart: Reclam, 1999), 154–55.

The symbolic functions of the walls explain why even in small cities and towns the walls remained crucial for the city's self-definition long after they had stopped serving their original economic, defensive, and police functions. They were a basic element in the way every urban community constructed and asserted its presence: a manifestation of the idea of who or what the city was, its honor (*dignitas* in Latin). Thus, even in the small Saxon town of Königsbrück — which had never possessed actual gates, walls, or moats — one still called the two entrances to the city the Kamenzer and Schmorkauer Gates.[65] The gates and the walls were elements of a physical city, but they were also — to use Italo Calvino's poetic formulation — monuments of a *città invisibile*, an invisible city: the tangible form of every city's abstract idea of itself.[66]

A community, wrote Emile Durkheim, "is not constituted simply by the mass of individuals who compose it, the ground which they occupy, the things they use, and the movement they make, but above all by the idea it has of itself."[67] It is only too understandable, then, that historians have tended to look with suspicion on the old definition of the city as a fortified place. To reduce a city to one of its architectural elements seems like a basic misunderstanding of how the urban community functions and how it is perceived and experienced. It would be like equating a vineyard with its surrounding fence or collapsing the entire realm of human religious sentiment into a church's outer walls. The city was always much more than its physical features; it was, and it still is, a complex group of ideas.

Nevertheless, the city walls — as seen in the case of Königsbrück — were as much ideal or abstract structures as they were physical ones. They belonged to the idea of the city as much as to its visible side. Three main ideological components of the German city seem to have contributed to the symbolic (rather than physical) construction of the walls: the world of religion, the workings of human memory, and the symbolic cosmos of the Holy Roman Empire as a whole.

The city walls were part of the symbolic form of the city because of their biblical or religious connotations. In a world where the city was often perceived as a sacred community ("what else is a city," Erasmus once asked, "but a monastery?"[68]), the community's walls were an inseparable element in the religious imagination of the time and appeared in countless stories,

---

65 DSB II:115.
66 Italo Calvino, *Le città invisibili* (Torino: Einaudi, 1972).
67 Emile Durkheim, *The Elementary Forms of Religious Life*, trans. Karen E. Fields (New York: Free Press, 1995), 425.
68 Quoted from Brady, *Ruling Class*, 27.

works of art, and even reenactments of the Godly Word in the world.[69] They appeared in the description of the gates of Paradise with their eternally revolving sword in the story of the Original Sin; in Joshua's conquest of Jericho and the Land of Canaan; in Jesus' entrance into Jerusalem (a model for Palm Sunday processions and even royal entry ceremonies in some German cities), his passion and crucifixion, and in his legacy to the apostles in the form of the double key handed over to Peter.[70] Within such a symbolic world, the city was much more than a physical entity or even a body politic (*corpus politicum*); it was also a heavenly place, a model for social organization in general (St. Augustine), a *corpus mysticum*. No wonder that Luther, for instance, often used the metaphor of walls in his writings. In *To the Christian Nobility of the German Nation* (1520), he compared the papacy to a city surrounded by three rings of walls, and in his most famous choral, *A Mighty Fortress*, he followed the psalmist and compared God himself to a mighty, walled fortress, a "bulwark never failing." Indeed, the very crown of the Holy Roman Emperor represented the heavenly city (and therefore the Empire itself) by its octagonal shape, the "gates" in which its four plates were placed, and the setting of its gemstones, all alluding to the Book of Revelation and St. Augustine's *City of God* (figure 5).[71]

The invisible operation of the walls did not vanish with the destruction of the city's physical fortifications. On the contrary, it became all the more conspicuous. It was as if the symbolic form of the city came out of the shadows of the physical stones once the walls themselves had been destroyed. Such was the case, for instance, with the religious connotations of the walls. In Bonn – where in the early eighteenth century the peasants from the surrounding countryside helped demolish the city's walls – one poet commented that "What through trumpet blows in Jericho had happened/By that miracle, is all the world amazed//A different thing is what in Bonn has just transpired/When by sounds of peasants' horns the walls had just been razed."[72] Even a century later, one still finds a similar deployment of biblical imagery. When one Hamburg writer opposed the charging of fees

---

69 In early modern Northern Europe, it was customary to fix routes in cities and towns, modeled on Jerusalem's *via dolorosa*, to be used by locals in ceremonial processions on Good Friday. See Brad S. Gregory, *Salvation at Stake: Christian Martyrdom in Early Modern Europe* (Cambridge, MA: Harvard University Press, 1999), 56. Most important here were Corpus Christi and Palm Sunday.

70 Barbara Stollberg-Rilinger, *Des Kaisers alte Kleider: Verfassungsgeschichte und Symbolsprache des Alten Reiches* (München: Beck, 2008), 106.

71 Reinhart Staats, *Theologie der Reichskrone: Ottonische "Renovatio Imperii" im Spiegel einer Insignie* (Stuttgart: Anton Hiersemann, 1976), 24–32.

72 "Was durch Posaunenschall vor Jericho geschehen/Das ist ein Wunderwerk, bei aller Welt geacht'//Ein anders ist, was man bei Bonn jetzt hat gesehen/Daß eines Kühhorns Ton die Mauern fallen macht." My translation is not literal here. Quoted from Edith Ennen, ed., *Geschichte der Stadt Bonn in vier Bänden* (Bonn: Dümmler, 1989), 3:194.

Figure 5. The crown of the Holy Roman Emperor. By its octagonal shape, the "gates" in which the four plates are placed, and the setting of the gemstones, the Imperial crown represents the gates and walls of the heavenly Jerusalem. *Source:* Kunsthistorisches Museum, Vienna.

at his city's gates, he, too, composed a poem for the occasion. He claimed that charging fees at the gates was against the Bible itself. Hamburg might charge entrance fees at its gates, he wrote, "But when we climb to Heaven's door/From the earthly valley's floor/There Peter stands, no slave is he/He'd let one in and charge no fee."[73]

73 "Doch fliegen einst zum Himmelstor/Wir aus dem Erdenthal empor//Wird Petrus ja kein Pecus sein/Er läßt uns ohne Sperrgeld ein." My translation, from Wilhlem Hocker, *Opfer der Thorsperre: Local Lustspiel mit Gesang* (Hamburg: Tramburg, 1840), 59.

Apart from their religious connotations, the city's walls were also inseparable from the invisible presence of the city's past. They were *lieux de
mémoire*: places of memory.[74] After all, German cities had always been fortified. During the Middle Ages, walls – together with the city's market and
legal privileges – were the three prerequisites that turned a settlement into
a city. Strictly speaking, therefore, Munich, Freiburg, or Nuremberg – as
cities – had always possessed walls. Furthermore, the city gates, towers, and
walls were old, familiar faces for the burghers; they were part of the city's
genius loci. They stood around the city at one's birth and throughout one's
life, and they stood when crucial events in the city's history took place. The
Ulrepforte in Cologne reminded one of an important battle – the memorial
plaque still exists there today – and the Jerusalemer Gate in Büdingen (as its
name indicates) bore witness to the safe return from a historical pilgrimage.
The gates and the walls were in this respect often the only "witnesses" to
the city's history. At any rate, they were always witnesses to one's friends and
childhood games, one's family, culture, and home or *Heimat*. To demolish
the gates and walls would consequently be tantamount to dis-membering
the city, in the sense of both physically cutting or disjoining one of the
city's limbs or members from its body and in annihilating their functions as
places where the city's past was re-membered, where the present city was
symbolically connected with its traditions and its history.

Indeed, the city gates and towers had their own personalities. They had
individual names, sometimes so ancient no one could remember where they
had come from. In Hamburg, the twelve ravelins were named after Jesus'
disciples. In Dresden, parts of the star-shaped fortifications were named after
the planets. The walls in those cities were literally a part of the cosmology
or "metaphysics" of the city. To demolish them was almost unthinkable;
it meant (in the case of Dresden quite literally) to destroy a world. This
is why, as Katharina Elisabeth Goethe so beautifully put it, the "old wigs"
would have waited until the Second Coming before demolishing of their
own volition the city walls of Frankfurt. Time itself had to stop before such
an event could take place.

The walls belonged to the "invisible city" for a third and perhaps most
important reason. The city itself, as an organ in a larger body, also belonged
to an invisible world: the Holy Roman Empire and all of its organs or
members. Such a state of affairs was most evident in the case of a free or
Imperial city. The functioning of the Empire's whole body was visible –
in the form of the Imperial Diet – only to a select few. According to early
modern German political philosophers, it was only in the Imperial Diet,

---

74 For the concept of *lieux de mémoire*, see: Pierre Nora, "Entre mémoire et histoire," in *Les Lieux de
Mémoire*, ed. Pierre Nora (Paris: Gallimard, 1984), xv–xlii.

when all the members or organs of the Empire were physically present, that the Empire as a coherent body, "with head and limbs" (emperor and Imperial estates), became visible.[75] The Diet was then the Empire *in corpore*: "embodied" or physically "incarnated." "The sovereign princes and the estates constitute the Imperial body [*Reichskörper*]," wrote the important jurist Tobias Paurmeister in the early seventeenth century. "This body's head is the Emperor, and only when all members are present together in a *compendium representativum* can one say that the Empire [itself] has been assembled."[76]

Early modern political philosophers further stated that individual organs of the great pulsating body of the Empire were not distinguishable from their membership. A duke, for instance, was not only the individual who carried this title at a specific point in time. A duke was also all his ancestors and future descendents – in much the same way that kings, as human beings, always died yet *the* king never passed away. In such a world, external symbols of the intangible ideas of membership and rank were by no means superficial. They were of the essence because they were more durable than the specific person who carried them at a given point in time; they were how the invisible body of a king (invisible because it was always greater than the body of the crowned person), a bishop, or even the Empire as a whole made their presence known. "*Honor*," concluded one early modern legal theoretician, "*consistit in signis exterioribus.*"[77]

Likewise, the walls often stood more strongly as symbols than as physical barriers. Like the Imperial crown (modeled after Jerusalem's walls), a city's walls were external signs of an abstract idea, honor, or dignity (the city). This is why the burghers of Jena pleaded with their duke to leave their old honorable monument unharmed. Like a monarch's crown, the walls were always greater than their physical incarnation. They could change physically (compare a monarch) without ever changing substantially (compare *the* monarch or monarchy). They could even not exist at all, physically (Königsbrück), and yet still be very present. This is the reason why one sometimes spoke about the demolition of relatively new, modernized walls as if they had been built during the Middle Ages. The construction was indeed new, but it still bore the memory of the stones from the original

---

75 See, for instance, Johann Carl König, *Grüundliche Abhandlung von denen Teutschen Reichs-Tägen überhaupt und dem noch fürwährenden zu Regensburg insbesondere* (Nürnberg, 1738), 1:31.

76 Tobias Paurmeister, *De iurisdictione imperii Romani* (Hannover: Petri Ropfii, 1608), 2:1.

77 The quote is from Bartholomaeus Cassanaeus, a sixteenth-century scholar whose work appeared in new editions well into the seventeenth century. Stollberg-Rilinger, "Zeremoniell als politisches Verfahren," 95, n.13. My analysis of the importance and meaning of signs in the world of the Holy Roman Empire is influenced by St. Augustine's definition of signs in St. Augustine, *De Magistro*, 1.

walls and the rite of initiation that those walls once meant for a nascent city.[78] The city, consequently, was its actuality (its streets, houses, physical walls, and gates), but also an abstract idea. The gates and the walls, along with other urban institutions such as the town hall, were places where these two aspects of the city converged, places where stones had meanings and the meaning of living in a city was incarnated in stone.

In times of peace, the gates and walls were places where travelers and locals alike felt, recognized, and constituted the city. In times of war or political turmoil, the city's fortifications stood for the idea (by the mid-eighteenth century often little more than a mirage) that a city should be able to defend itself independently. Contemporary Germans called this idea *die Stadt in Waffen*, "the city in arms." Later chapters will demonstrate that in some (isolated) cases, urban fortifications possessed important military functions well into the second half of the nineteenth century. But the military revolution of the early modern period, coupled with the resulting changes in the art of siege and the science of fortification, made it increasingly clear that city walls were not sufficient by themselves for the defense of a city and that the community had to find additional ways to protect itself in times of war. Such practical considerations notwithstanding, the idea that a city ought to be able to defend itself independently was still very much alive in the second half of the eighteenth century. It might be tempting to ridicule the citizens of Frankfurt am Main, for instance, who well into the 1790s thought they could single-handedly defend their city from the French revolutionary armies.[79] More important, however, is not to ridicule but to understand. It was not only the actual military functions of the walls that were important to the citizens of the early modern city; it was also the abstract idea behind the military fortifications, the idea that in a time of need the city ought to be able to raise its arms and defend itself like any honorable person.

Within the mental universe of the Holy Roman Empire, the demolition of city walls was consequently much more than the destruction of purely military defenses. It was equivalent to a king wrecking his crown, to a bishop trashing his pastoral insignia, or to minor nobles – who were incidentally often addressed as *Veste* (literally, "His Fortress") – damaging their symbols of lordship. Such acts would be considered either as signs of madness or as

78 As, for instance, very often in "Der Abbruch der Stadtmauer sowie die Regulierung, Pflasterung und Unterhaltung der hierdurch frei werdenden Straßen, 1859–1882," LA Berlin, A Rep. 000–02–01 Nr. 1579.

79 "Verteidigungsmaßnamen der Stadt," ISG Frankfurt am Main, Kriegszeugamt, Nr. 5.

crimes against honor — that of the organ or member as well as that of the body politic as a whole.

The walls were important for the city's defense and public security but also related to the physical nature of the city and to the city as an idea. Even more significantly, they were a part of one's religious imagination; they related to the community's past, present, and future; and they belonged to the larger symbolic cosmos of the Holy Roman Empire. Walls were, in all these respects, an inseparable part of the life and honor of the city, an abstract idea that took a physical shape. To demolish the external signs of its personality, to destroy the stone-made borders of its community, was of course to deface the visible, physical city. At the same time, defortification also dealt a crushing blow to the invisible, intangible city: a painful blow to the city's symbolic rather than physical form. It was to dismantle (literally, to divest of a mantle or a cloak; to strip off a piece of clothing, covering, protection) the idea of the city. All of this explains why walls were still so fundamental to the city's definition of itself in the eighteenth century; why contemporaries felt a sense of magic when they looked at their transformed, defortified cities; and why the word "honor" appeared in so many contemporary descriptions of urban fortifications.

Defortification introduced, therefore, two interrelated sets of problems: the one practical, the other symbolic. On the one hand, the demolition raised a series of questions about the ability of the city to defend itself, finance itself, and control its population. It further raised questions about property, both in terms of the walls as a whole and of the fortifications' inhabited parts. Eighteenth- and nineteenth-century German burghers had to determine to whom the walls actually belonged, who was entitled to make decisions about their demolition, how defortification should be performed and by whom, and who should be allowed to profit by it. They also had to decide what would happen to the persons and institutions that had been related to the walls for so many centuries: where to relocate the magazines; what to do about the prisons; how to find new employment for all the different gate officers; and what to do with the exposed area around the city (including the glacis) after the walls were gone.

Beyond these practical issues, however, the community had to confront the assault on the walls' symbolic aspect, the assault on the invisible city. Not only the beauty of the city was at stake here but, and perhaps above all, its identity. Because the walls were *lieux de mémoire*, their demolition raised questions about the community's collective memory and its relation to its history. Because they served as external signs of the city's honor and membership in the Empire, the walls' demolition raised questions about the old mental universe of the Empire as a whole. And because the walls constituted both physical and symbolic borders between city and countryside, their demise raised questions about the city's very definition: questions such as where the city began and where it ended; who belonged to the city and who did not; and what differentiated the city from a big village once it was no longer a closed, protected place. In other words, in what respect could it still be called a city at all.

Contrary to depictions in so many modern history books, city walls never simply disappeared. Neither physically nor symbolically was such a disappearance ever possible. The city's population did not wake up one fine morning to find the gates, walls, towers, moats, and all the other fortification parts gone. Someone had to decide to demolish the walls and possess the political will and power as well as the financial means to execute such a plan. Nor did the city's population – and this was true not only during but also after the defortification – wake up suddenly to find all the walls' symbolic aspects completely eradicated from their minds. What was at stake, after all, was much greater than the visible city, greater even than the invisible city. What was at stake was the world to which the early modern German city belonged, the body of which it was a member or an organ, the mental universe in which city walls (figuratively and literally) made sense.

The city walls were both an urban construction and a monument of the political structure of central Europe in much the same way that personal armor simultaneously belonged to an individual and to his or her society, culture, and period. The cases of different city walls were consequently related to one another not only because they were similar or (as later chapters will show) because when the walls of one city fell there were immediate discussions in other cities about the event, discussions that often led to more demolitions. Above all, the cases of different city walls were related to one another because all German cities shared the same outside: they were all, to a greater or lesser degree, members of the same body. The story of the defortification of German cities between 1689 and 1866 is consequently at one and the same time the story of hundreds of particular cities, the story of the idea of what a city is or ought to be, and the story of the changing physical, political, and cultural landscape of German-speaking central Europe.

2

The French Model and the German Case, 1689–1789

It was at a time when the larger body of the Empire was slowly growing old that the fortified form of the German city also began to decline. The Empire did not cause the demolition of city walls directly. It was too loose a structure to cause such a fundamental transformation of its members; a transformation, furthermore, about which constitutionally it had little or no say. Rather, the slow weakening of the Empire and the first defortification waves of German cities were related to the fact that both Empire and city now faced a new political entity that undermined them. It was an entity that grew both inside and outside of the Empire and was fundamentally different from it. It was "a factory" or "machine" (Voltaire) rather than an organism; "an army with a state" (Mirabeau) rather than a "city in arms." Finally, it was an entity that saw differently and challenged the visible and invisible aspects of both city and Empire. It was the modern, bureaucratic, sovereign state.

The rising power of territorial states and the consequent disruption of the geopolitical environment of German cities affected different regions in Germany in different ways. The essential characteristic of the Holy Roman Empire – the environment or "habitat" of the early modern German city – was its variety: the diversity of its landscape and people and the richness of its governmental institutions, local customs, laws, and ideas. The Empire's political structure held this human diversity together by frustrating and absorbing opposing political wills. In the eighteenth century, the Empire's flexible political structure still absorbed much of the stimuli for change coming from territorial states. Consequently, in areas where especially French and Prussian influence was present or where these two countries engaged in open conflicts, the practices and symbolism of the walled city were often undermined. But in the majority of German cities – which were neither physically nor culturally close to such forces – the traditional, fortified form of the city remained intact.

The first stimulus for the transformation of the walled German city came from absolutist France. A significant element in this stimulus was direct: during the century that preceded the French Revolution, the armies of the Bourbon Monarchy were directly responsible for the demolition of many city walls in Germany. Even more important was the abstract model – rather than the concrete physical actions – set by the French Crown through its actions at home and abroad. Seventeenth-century France created a model for the relationship between the state and its cities that was markedly different from the one existing east of the Rhine, a model that entailed the defortification of the majority of the kingdom's cities. Germans from all walks of life reacted to the French model. Some German princes adopted parts of it in their residence towns; generals implemented it in the defenses of German states; and even simple burghers began to wonder why their cities were so different from French ones, why eighteenth-century French cities were usually defortified while German ones were not.

THE DIALECTIC FRENCH MODEL[1]

A plan to dismantle France's many urban fortifications was already under discussion in 1588 at the general diet of the French estates, the Estates General.[2] It would take three more decades, however, and a man as powerful and determined as Cardinal Richelieu – the chief minister to the king – to finally execute it. The first defortification waves in France took place in the context of the Wars of Religion and the noble revolts against the Crown, which often used Huguenot (French Protestant) fortress towns as their bases. At one point, Richelieu reportedly said, "France has two diseases: heresy and liberty." Subduing and demilitarizing the "free republics" of the Huguenots was meant to cure the two ills with a single medication.[3]

---

1 The following is based on Yair Mintzker, "The Dialectics of Urban Space under Louis XIV: The Example of Urban Defortifications During the Nine Years War, 1689–1697" (Paper presented to the annual meeting of the Society for French Historical Studies, Austin, Texas, 2007). An excellent recent overview of the history of fortified cities in France is Michael Wolfe, *Walled Towns and the Shaping of France* (New York: Palgrave Macmillan, 2009).

2 George-Marie-René Picot, *Histoire des états généraux considérés au point de vue de leur influence sur le gouvernement de la France de 1355 à 1614* (Paris: Hachette, 1872), 3:214–15, 321, 441–42; Fritz Textor, *Entfestigung und Zerstörungen im Rheingebiet während des 17. Jahrhunderts als Mittel der französischen Rheinpolitik* (Bonn: Ludwig Röhrscheid, 1937), 1:9.

3 Quoted in C.V. Wedgwood, *The Thirty Years War* (New York: New York Review of Books, 2005), 184.

The immediate impulse for the first demolitions was the case of the Huguenot city of La Rochelle. In 1629, Louis XIII's army finally managed to take this rebellious stronghold, which the king then immediately defortified. In the wake of the long siege of La Rochelle and in order to avoid such a long siege ever again, Richelieu ordered that defortification should not be limited to specific cases. "One needs to defortify," he wrote, "all the places which are not close to the country's frontiers, do not protect river passages, or do not allow the state to control important, mutinous cities."[4] Burghers, Richelieu implied, should not be allowed to rebel against the king and hide behind strong walls in doing so.

The scope of the defortification wave that followed Richelieu's order is not known with certainty because the execution of the 1629 edict was left to individual communes and provincial assemblies. Older estimates that as many as 600 French towns lost their walls in the 1620s and 1630s have recently been challenged, but that defortification took place in several hundred cities is still beyond doubt.[5] In the 1620s and 1630s, defortification took place in cities as different – and, at times, as distant – as Angers, Buis les Baronnies, Chantelle, La Rochelle, Loudon, Mévouillons, Montauban, Mortemart, Namur, and Nyons.[6] In the region of the Dauphiné alone, where the local assembly of notables ordered the defortification of the province's towns and chateaux in 1626 and then again after the siege of La Rochelle, dozens of cities and chateaux were affected. These included Livron, Vienne, Valence, Die, Embrun, Nyons, and Puymore. Other cities – such as Briançon, Crest, Grenoble, Montélimar, and Valence – did not physically demolish their walls in the seventeenth century but still neglected their fortifications to such an extent that by the end of the century they lost any military value.[7]

In the grand scheme of things, defortification was only one side of the coin, the other being the maintenance or strengthening of fortified places along the kingdom's borders. "One must fortify very strongly border towns," Richelieu wrote in the same defortification edict in 1629, "one

---

4 Denis-Louis-Martial Avenel, ed., *Lettres, instructions diplomatiques et papiers d'État du cardinal de Richelieu* (Paris: Imprimerie Impériale, 1858), 3:179–81.
5 Geoffrey Parker, *The Military Revolution*, 41–42; but compare Wolfe, *Walled Towns*, 137–141.
6 For the case of Montauban and other cities, see Michael Wolfe, "Walled Towns During the French Religious Wars," in *City Walls: The Urban Enceinte in Global Perspective*, ed. James D. Tracey (New York: Cambridge University Press, 2000), 337. Perhaps no other defortification is as famous as Loudun's. It served as a model for Aldous Huxley, *The Devils of Loudun* (New York: Harper, 1952) as well as for an opera, a play, and a movie by (respectively) Krzysztof Penderecki (*Die Teufel von Loudon*, 1969); John Whiting (*The Devils*, 1971); and Ken Russell (*The Devils*, 1971).
7 René Favier, *Les villes du Dauphiné aux XVIIe et XVIIIe siècles: la pierre et l'écrit* (Grenoble: Presses universitaires de Grenoble, 1993), 140–45.

should consider fortifying Metz and an advance on Strasbourg in order to have a possible entrance into Germany . . . and one should turn Versoy into a great fortress . . . to have, as it were, an open gate to Switzerland."[8] Fortified cities should exist in France, Richelieu implied, but only along the borders and in strategically important points in France's interior, thus creating a defortified, demilitarized interior and strong, fortified national borders. Most telling in this respect would be the case of Marseilles, whose walls were only partially demolished in the seventeenth century. Those fortifications that faced the north (read: France's interior) were demolished, while those walls that faced the sea (read: national borders) were maintained and even strengthened.[9]

The French Crown's defortification policies from the late 1620s onward were a direct attack on the old definition of the city as a fortified place. The ancient privilege of urban communes to defend themselves through fortifications was as important in the French context as it was in the German one. But Richelieu's language in his 1629 edict indicates the Janus face of the French attack on the definition of the city as a fortified place. At the very same time that he ordered or negotiated the demolition of so many city walls, Richelieu both called for the strengthening of other fortified cities and adopted the many qualities of the fortified city for the overall defense of the state. Strasbourg, for Richelieu, was "an entrance" and Versoy "an open gate"; one needs to open or build gates for France as a whole, the cardinal reportedly said on another occasion.[10]

A comparison with the situation in Germany is very telling here because it highlights the political dimension of what was happening in France. The political solution to the internal conflicts in post-Westphalia Germany was to retain the status quo by ensuring that no single member of the Empire would be strong enough to tip its delicate political balance. The ubiquity of urban fortifications in the Empire was the physical manifestation of this political equilibrium; a state of affairs in which the Empire, at least in theory, served as a political system that protected its members from each other. The French Crown, too, found itself confronted with internal conflict, but unlike the Empire, it solved the problem by creating one strong, sovereign, central power rather than by solidifying a precarious status quo. The defortification

8 Avenel, *Lettres*, ibid. On the same topic, see Gaston Zeller, *L'organisation défensive des frontières du nord et de l'est au dix-septième siècle* (Paris: Berger-Levrault, 1928), 29.

9 Junko Takeda, "Between Conquest and Plague: Marseillais Civic Humanism in the Age of Absolutism 1660–1725" (PhD dissertation, Stanford University, 2006), 131–32.

10 Pierre Grillon, ed., *Les papiers de Richelieu: section politique intérieure, correspondance et papiers d'état* (Paris: Pedone, 1982), 4:25.

policies suggested by Richelieu and followed throughout the rest of the seventeenth century went along the lines of this centralization policy. They meant to deprive most of France's cities of the means to militarily oppose the king's will – his undivided sovereignty – while strengthening France's position vis-à-vis its European neighbors.

The political language of sovereignty was the key issue here.[11] It was based on the idea that to ensure the smooth operation of a state – often imagined now as a great machine – there had to be a single, supreme will or "motor" of authority with a monopoly over the use of legitimate power and a final say in all legal and political matters.[12] In the sixteenth and seventeenth centuries, so plagued by religious and political strife, the language of sovereignty represented a radical solution to some of that age's most pressing issues. If the natural state of mankind was one of "the war of all against all," as some people now claimed, there had to be a supreme political authority to force the contesting parties to lay down their arms. This is why a "sovereign power" – as the natural law theorist Hugo Grotius wrote in the late sixteenth century – was by definition, "[a] power . . . whose Acts are not subject to the power of another, nor can by any Humane Authority be made void."[13] If nothing could challenge the will of the monarch, so the theory went, all contesting political views would disappear. They would all be subjugated to a single, central power: the king's sovereignty.

The new perception of centralized, sovereign royal power in France man-ifested itself physically in many ways: in the flocking of the French high nobility to the new center of power in Versailles; the architecture of royal palaces and their gardens; the creation of a huge standing army; and – most important for our story – the layout of the capital city itself. Because by 1671, the defortification of French cities had also reached Paris. At a time when it was still inconceivable for any German city to become defenseless, the French king moved his court to Versailles, demolished the ramparts of Paris, and laid out new, wide streets in their stead – the boulevard

---

11 Compare the wonderful description of a similar problem today in Wendy Brown, *Walled States, Waning Sovereignty* (Cambridge, MA: MIT Press, 2010), esp. 43-71.

12 About the state as a machine, see Barbara Stollberg-Rilinger, *Der Staat als Maschine: Zur politischen Metaphorik des absoluten Fürstenstaats* (Berlin: Duncker & Humblot, 1986). For a discussion of the role of sovereignty in absolutist France, see William F. Church, *Richelieu and Reason of State* (Princeton: Princeton University Press, 1972), 82ff. For sovereignty as a theory to combat political disorder, see Mack P. Holt, *The French Wars of Religion, 1562–1629* (New York: Cambridge University Press, 1995), 216.

13 Originally in *De iure belli ac pacis libri tres* (Paris: Buon, 1625). The English translation used here is from Hugo Grotius, *The Most Excellent Hugo Grotius, His Three Books treating of the Rights of War and Peace* (London, 1682), 1:37.

was born.[14] Nicolas de La Mare, who personally witnessed the defortification of Paris in the 1670s, commented later how all former masters of France, from Julius Caesar onward, strove to fortify Paris. "[But] everything changed in the reign of Louis XIV," he added. "The moats were filled, the gates demolished and triumphal arches erected in their stead, the streets enlarged."[15]

The second stage of the demolition of urban fortifications in France started shortly after the defortification of Paris. It is stated in one of the most important documents in French military history – the Marquis de Vauban's letter to War Minister Louvois from January 1673 – where the idea of the *pré carré* (the "square field") is first explicitly mentioned. Vauban wrote to the war minister:

> But seriously, Monseigneur, the king must think a little about creating a square field [of his kingdom]. I do not like this confusion of friendly and hostile places. You should keep one of every three of your fortified places; your people, as it stands, are tormented, your expenditures too high, and your forces overstretched; and it is almost impossible to keep all your fortresses in a good state and arm them properly. . . . Moreover, if, in the conflicts we so often have with our neighbors, we shall, God forbid, find ourselves one day in a minority, the majority of our fortified places will go as they came. This is why, either through a treaty or through military actions, Monseigneur, preach always the straight lines, not the circle, but the square.[16]

Vauban's plan to defend France's borders in a novel way had major consequences for France as a whole as well as for many of its cities. He not only suggested that internal fortifications should be demolished, strategic and financial considerations also led him to propose that now two of every three fortress towns on France's borders should be defortified. Otherwise, he claimed, the king might run into political and financial problems: residents of fortress towns would become frustrated by the presence of state troops, and military expenses would empty the state treasury.

Vauban's plan did not remain on paper. During the wars Louis XIV waged in the Franche-Comté in the second half of the seventeenth century (wars that ultimately led to the annexation of this Imperial province to France), the king and Vauban ordered the dismantling of the fortifications of most of the province's Decapolis or "Ten Cities" – the formerly Imperial cities in the area. The exception to this rule was the enlargement and

---

14 On the history of the boulevard, see Allan B. Jacobs, Elizabeth Macdonald, and Yodan Rofé, *The Boulevard Book: History, Evolution, Design of Multiway Boulevards* (Cambridge, MA: MIT Press, 2002).

15 Nicolas de La Mare, *Traité de la Police* (Amsterdam, 1729), 1:87.

16 Albert de Rochas d'Aiglun, *Vauban, sa famille et ses écrits, ses oisivetés et sa correspondance: Analyse et extraits* (Genève: Slatkine Reprints, 1972), 2:89.

strengthening of the fortifications of Besançon, which was then integrated into the fortification lines of the French monarchy as a whole.[17] Thus, for instance, the citizens of Colmar and Haguenau had to witness the demolition of their ancient walls in 1673 under the observant eyes of Louis XIV himself. For the humiliated burghers of Colmar, the defortification made their city, as they put it, "open to all to come and go, like a village."[18] Open, village-like cities but closed, fortified national frontiers: this was the essence of the French Crown's policies under Louis XIV. When that great monarch finally took Strasbourg in 1681, he struck a coin to celebrate not only the taking of the city but also the fact that France was now closed (or locked) vis-à-vis the Empire: *clausa Germanis Gallia*, it stated.

The symbolism of France's fortifications was important as well. The king's sovereignty extended throughout his lands and stopped only at the frontiers. In much the same way that the city walls symbolized the strength of the urban community, so, too, were the boundaries of the kingdom an excellent place in which to demonstrate the king's sovereign power.[19] Fortress towns were important elements in the symbolic construction of these boundaries. One contemporary writer put this idea as follows: "The quantity of artillery pieces placed on the ramparts [of a border-fortress], the well-supplied, orderly arsenals; all these *announce* the mightiness of the monarch."[20]

What was true along the borders was also true in the hinterland, although in a different way. Along the borders, the king announced his sovereignty through fortresses while in the hinterland he deliberately refrained from acknowledging any boundaries at all. This was the case in La Rochelle, but it was also the case in other towns and cities. In Marseilles, for instance, the Sun King deliberately avoided entering the city through the *porte réale* in 1660 (this was the traditional site of the king's royal entry into the city), preferring to make a new break in the walls to avoid an acknowledgement of the city's republican past.[21] In fact, from the 1660s and for over a century, no Bourbon monarch would have any elaborate entry ceremony into a

17 Colette Brossault, *Les intendants de Franche-Comté, 1674–1790* (Paris: Boutique de l'Histoire, 1999), 13; Léonce de Piépape, *Histoire de la réunion de la Franche-Comté à la France* (Genève: Mégariotis, 1881), 2:355–56.

18 Quoted in Christopher Friedrichs, *The Early Modern City* (New York: Longman, 1995), 24.

19 The classic discussion on the question of state building, national identity, and borderlands is Peter Sahlins, *Boundaries: The Making of France and Spain in the Pyrenees* (Berkeley: University of California Press, 1989).

20 My italics. Joseph de Fallois, *L'École de la Fortification ou les éléments de la fortification permanente, régulière et irrégulière* (Dresden: Goerge Conrad Walther, 1768), 45.

21 André Zysberg, *Marseille au temps du Roi-Soleil: La ville, les galères, l'arsenal, 1660 à 1715* (Marseille: Laffitte, 2007), 55ff.

French city. Such a ceremonial practice would have meant a recognition of France's internal boundaries, and the absolutist monarchy's very nature worked against such a recognition.[22]

From a practical perspective, the defortification of France's hinterland and the construction of a cordon of fortress towns along the kingdom's perimeter were very closely related. Once France's internal fortifications were gone, it had to better fortify its borders to prevent an invasion into the country's vulnerable interior, and once the country's external borders were strengthened, it was easier to continue to defortify the hinterland; the two processes relied on each other. Nicolas de La Mare recognized this full well. Louis XIV, he claimed, united the country like never before by establishing and fortifying the boundaries of France on every side: "The capital, which had been located close to the kingdom's frontiers in the past, is now at the very center of the kingdom. In this state of affairs . . . surrounded by the strongest fortresses anywhere in Europe, it has nothing to fear any more."[23]

Such practical considerations were undoubtedly crucial for the defortification of Paris and other French cities and towns. One should not, however, conclude from this that the demolition of the ramparts was a sign that the king no longer wanted symbols of his military power in his capital, as one historian has suggested.[24] The city walls had an immense physical presence ("visible city") but also a great symbolic power ("invisible city"); they had been an indispensable part of every urban community and remained an essential element in almost every lexical definition of the city in the seventeenth and eighteenth centuries. This is why it was exactly the absence of many urban ramparts in France that contemporaries found so conspicuous, why they felt that the lack of military defenses had to be explained.[25] Back in 1629, the demolition of the ramparts of La Rochelle was understood exactly along these lines. The point of the demolition, in the words of one eyewitness, was "to reduce to a village a place where the presumptuousness of the inhabitants led them to believe they were a [separate] republic."[26] The same was true in Paris. As the ramparts were replaced by boulevards – with the beautiful views they offered of the countryside, their cafés, and their street musicians – travelers and locals alike repeatedly commented on how these new streets, together with the new ceremonial gates that now led to the city, represented Louis XIV's greatness.

22 Simon Schama, *Citizens: A Chronicle of the French Revolution* (New York: Vintage, 1990), 57.
23 de La Mare, *Traité de la police*, ibid.
24 Colin Jones, *Paris: Biography of a City* (London: Allen Lane, 2004), 161.
25 Some common reactions to the defortification of Paris can be found in Leonardo Benevolo, *Die Stadt in der europäischen Geschichte*, trans. Peter Schiller (München: Beck, 1993), 170.
26 *Letres d'vn solitaire av Roy, princes, et seigneurs faisans la guerre aux Rebelles* (Poitiers: 1628).

Even La Mare, a thoroughly practical man, could not avoid the same conclusion. What was at stake in the demolition of the Parisian ramparts, he wrote, was not only military considerations but also the king's fame or *gloire*.[27] Demolishing his capital's ramparts demonstrated that the king no longer needed what practically every other prince in seventeenth-century continental Europe so eagerly sought: a fortified residence for a rainy day. The Sun King projected a different image: he was a stronger, more powerful monarch than any of his peers or predecessors. Their fortified residences showed their inherent weakness; his open capital demonstrated his power and glory. "And then Louis XIV reigned," wrote one late eighteenth-century author in a historical description of Paris, "and soon Paris's walls were no more. Its gates transformed into triumphal arches, its moats, filled up and planted with trees, became promenades. When one considers this great monarch, the noise he made throughout the world, his victories, his grandeur, his magnificence, his dignity ... it almost seems that Paris should have been even prettier under his reign."[28] "The capital of a great monarch's kingdom," Louis XIV is reported to have said himself, "should simply not be surrounded by ramparts."[29] The demolition of the Parisian ramparts, and later the layout of open German residence towns, did not undo the ostentatious display of military power in cities. On the contrary, they created a very ostentatious display of a new form of power: physically invisible, perhaps, but conspicuous and awe-inspiring nonetheless. In this case, as in so many other defortification stories, the absence of walls was an active, dynamic power; it was meaningful, not a simple nothingness.

Toward the end of the seventeenth century, the defortification policies of the French Crown also reached parts of the Holy Roman Empire. Louis XIV's politics of expansion on the left bank of the Rhine deprived the Empire of parts of its western provinces from the late 1660s onward. During the final war of the century, the War of the League of Augsburg (1688–1697), Louis's armies also occupied large parts of the Rhine Valley (especially the Palatinate), taking over some cities, defortifying others, and completely destroying other settlements, most importantly the fortress of Mannheim (November 1689). The brutal policies pursued by France in the Palatinate, and especially by one of its generals – Ezéchiel du Mas, Comte de

27 De La Mare, *Traité de la police*, ibid. Another example can be found in Edmé Béguillet, *Description historique de Paris* (Paris: Frantin, 1779), 64–65.
28 Germain-François Poullain, M. de Saint-Foix, *Œuvres Complettes* (Paris: Duchesne, 1778), 3:18.
29 Quoted in F. Bertout de Solières, *Les fortifications de Paris à travers les âges* (Rouen: Girieud, 1906), 13.

Mélac – have stirred much debate among French and German historians.[30] At stake in this debate were the reasons for the torched-earth policy ordered by the king and implemented so ruthlessly by his generals; a policy that in Mannheim "left not a single brick standing on top of another" and in Speyer left "not a single wall in the entire city intact."[31]

Both contemporaries and later historians spilled much ink on this brutal policy, trying to come to terms with its reasoning. The Comte de Mélac himself is reputed to have said upon receiving the order to destroy Pforzheim (just north of the Black Forest) that "it must be the devil himself who presides over the Council of War in Paris."[32] Vauban, too, was alarmed by the brutality and the logic of such an endeavor. He argued that defortification on such a scale was senseless, and suggested to War Minister Louvois that one must resort to political negotiations rather than brutal force in determining the fate of the Palatinate.[33] Modern historians raised similar questions about the overall logic of the French campaign in the Palatinate, some claiming that Louis XIV's actions during the war were nothing but a sign of his "spirit of destruction,"[34] others justifying it on strategic grounds. Such was the case of Louvois's nineteenth-century biographer Camille Rousset, for instance, who claimed that Louis XIV had sound strategic reasoning behind his actions. They represented an attempt to create an empty belt or "security zone" beyond France's fortification lines, Rousset claimed, a belt devoid of fortification but not necessarily devoid of inhabitants; a kind of glacis writ large.[35]

That the events in the Palatinate were traumatic to those who witnessed them is beyond doubt. Refugees from Speyer who found haven in Heidelberg and Frankfurt am Main in 1689 told the locals, sobbing, about the loss of life and property they had just endured: rapes, murders, and the total physical destruction of their city. The news was extremely sad and distressing to anyone who heard it.[36] Even Elisabeth-Charlotte, Louis XIV's relative on whose behalf the king based his claims to lordship over the province,

---

30 Camille Rousset, *Histoire de Louvois* (Paris: Didier, 1864), 4:158–59; Kurt Raumer, *Die Zerstörung der Pfalz* (München: Oldenbourg, 1930); Textor, *Entfestigung*, ibid.

31 About Mannheim, see Roland Vetter, *"Kein Stein soll auf dem andern bleiben." Mannheims Untergang während des pfälzischen Erbfolgekrieges im Spiegel französischer Kriegsberichte* (Heidelberg: Verlag Regionalkultur, 2002). A fascinating primary source about Speyer is *Eigentliche Beschreibung der Stadt Speyer/ Wie tyrannisch und unchristlich die Barbarischen Franzosen mit derselben Stadt und Innwohnern verfahren wird* (Nürnberg, 1689).

32 Quoted in Antoine Béthouart, *Le prince Eugène de Savoie: soldat, diplomate et mécène* (Paris: Perrin, 1975), 96.

33 Vetter, *"Kein Stein,"* source 41.   34 Raumer, *Die Zerstörung der Pfalz*, 100.

35 Rousset, *Histoire de Louvois*, 4:158–9; Raumer, *Die Zerstörung der Pfalz*, 98ff.

36 "Extract Schreibens auss Heidelberg, vom 1. Junii (1689)," in Wilhelm Harster, "Materialien zur Geschichte der Zerstörung der Stadt Speyer 1689," *Mitteilungen des Historischen Vereins der Pfalz*, vol. 14 (1889), 15.

thought the whole business a travesty. The events in the Palatinate, she wrote, "make my heart bleed, yet they [the king and his generals] are angry at my grief."[37]

The sheer brutality of the occupation of the Palatinate notwithstanding, it is crucial to repeat a point that the great urban historian Lewis Mumford recognized (but did not fully develop) a long time ago. Whether deliberately or not, France was slowly turning itself into a fortified city writ large; while demolishing many towns in its hinterland it also became the very "'City' that was to be defended."[38] Just like a walled town, France now had a demilitarized interior, it was surrounded by Vauban's cordon of fortress towns, and it created a glacis of sorts beyond its borders. The entire process was highly dialectic: it involved both destruction and construction, both an attack on the old fortified form of the city and its adaptation to the higher level of the state as a whole.

Such adaptation of the fortified city's form to the entire kingdom illustrates the great power that the fortified layout of the city held over contemporaries. This power was so great that even while demolishing the fortified character of many cities, the French Crown did not eradicate so much as raised this form onto the higher plain of the state. This was evident as early as in Richelieu's word choice in his edict from 1629, where he claimed that France needed gates and entrances and fortifications. It was evident, too, in what is still the most famous visual depiction of the idea of absolutism: the frontispiece prepared by the French artist Abraham Bosse for Thomas Hobbes's masterpiece *Leviathan* (1651).[39] Here (figure 6), the body politic is famously represented by the monarch himself and not, as in the Quaternionen Eagles characteristic of early modern Germany, as only one of its members. Drawing on the classical tradition of identifying any political body with the polis,[40] Bosse's state is also a fortified city writ large. Bosse's depiction of the relationship between city and state can also be interpreted in a different way, one in which the absolutist state does not only resemble the fortified city but, in the body of the monarch, also hovers

---

37 Charlotte-Elizabeth d'Orléans, *Life and Letters of Charlotte Elizabeth, Mother of Philippe d'Orléans* (London: Chapman and Hall, 1889), 32.

38 Lewis Mumford, *The City in History: Its Origins, Its Transformations, and Its Prospects* (New York: Harcourt, 1961), 360. Similar ideas, although never fully developed, can also be found in Joan E. DeJean, *Literary Fortifications: Rousseau, Laclos, Sade* (Princeton: Princeton University Press, 1984), 20–75; and Paul Virilio, *Speed and Politics: An Essay on Dromology*, trans. Mark Polizzotti (New York: Columbia University Press, 1986), esp. 13–14.

39 About Bosse's frontispiece to *Leviathan*, see Horst Bredekamp, *Thomas Hobbes visuelle Strategien* (Berlin: Akademie Verlag, 1999).

40 As, for instance, in Jean Bodin, *The Six Bookes of a Commonweale*, ed. Kenneth D. McRae (Cambridge, MA: Harvard University Press, 1962), 10.

Figure 6. Abraham Bosse, Frontispiece of Thomas Hobbes's *Leviathan* (detail, 1651). Source: Rare Books Division, Department of Rare Books and Special Collection, Princeton University Library.

threateningly above it – an even better representation of the dialectical relationship between state, crown, and city in the seventeenth century. After all, the simultaneous attack on the city's fortified form and its adaptation to the level of the state as a whole were the essential elements in French absolutist policies at the time.

Finally, the dialectics of urban form in seventeenth-century France can also be interpreted in a more technical sense, as demonstrated by the work of the early eighteenth-century engineer Louis de Cormontaigne, Vauban's most important follower. When Cormontaigne sat down to describe the best possible layout for a state, he based it on the same geometrical pattern used in planning contemporary fortresses. The primary difference between the layout of a fortress and Cormontaigne's fortified state was their scale; otherwise, although not identical, they were very similar indeed.[41] In Cormontaigne's case, the relationship between state and fortified city is not

41 "Cormontaigne," S.H.A.T. Paris-Vincennes, *Mémoires Historiques*, 1752.

political–metaphorical (Richelieu, Bosse) but military-technical. Drawing on the most advanced branch of military engineering at the time – the fortification of single cities – Cormontaigne adapted the same model for the defense of the whole state, probably using the very same technical tools to which he was accustomed in the planning of single fortified cities to the planning of the fortification of France's lines of fortification en masse.

The point is this: the French defortification policies of the seventeenth century amounted to both an attack on the old definition of the city as a fortified settlement and the adaptation of the fortified city's form onto the higher scale of the state. It was a model that was possible only in a country such as seventeenth-century France, where the king could force his conception of the overall defense of the state on his subjects and either compel or convince single cities to physically alter their centuries-old boundaries. It was also a model that related both to the physical and invisible aspects of the city's fortifications: to the physical aspect in the way the Crown changed the actual appearance of many cities and towns: defortifying many of them, while strengthening a selected few; and to the invisible aspect in the way the abstract form of the city served as the basic pattern for the state's defenses and in the way the Crown used the tension between the traditional form of the city and the open character of the capital to underline the new form of power it espoused: the king's indivisible, supreme political will or sovereignty.

FRENCH INFLUENCE ON GERMANY

France exerted a decisive influence on the demolition of many city walls in Germany in the century after 1689. Often, the French armies were directly responsible for the defortification of cities across the Rhine; at other times, it was the example they set through their policies at home that encouraged German princes to imitate them in their own neck of the woods. But the geopolitical environment in Germany was also quite different from that of absolutist France, and this environment prevented a replication of the French model in most parts of the country.[42] "Teutschland," wrote Johann Jacob Moser in the mid-eighteenth century, "wird auf teusch regirt" – the German Empire should be comprehended on its own terms.[43] Eighteenth-century travelers to the German states consequently recognized important French influence on the fate of city walls. At the same time, they also

---

42 Cf. Wolfe, *Walled Towns*, 159.
43 Johann Jacob Moser, *Von Teutschland und dessen Staats-Verfassung überhaupt* (Stuttgart, 1766), 550.

encountered a world where the events of the early defortification waves often unfolded in a different manner than in France.

As opposed to France, the early defortification waves in Germany were much more local in nature. They were influenced by the same power vector as in neighboring France: the rising importance of the absolutist state's military organs and political philosophy. Unlike France, however, this vector affected different regions in Germany in very different ways because there was no central bureaucracy that could envision – let alone implement – a general defortification plan. In the western provinces of the Empire – along the French border and in its vicinity – the forces of change were most evident and defortifications quite common. In regions under Prussian rule or influence, such forces were present but operated in a different way than in the west, leading more often to the loss of the walls' ancient symbolic meaning than to their actual demolition. And in the individualized country – the habitat of most German cities and towns – the effects of the rising power and political philosophy of absolutist states were very limited. During the eighteenth century, cities in this region hardly ever lost their walls. Eighteenth-century travelers to these three regions consequently encountered in them three distinct situations.

THE GEOPOLITICS OF THE RHINE BASIN[44]

The majority of defortification cases in eighteenth-century Germany took place along the Rhine and in its vicinity. It was in the basin of this great river that the threat to the old, fortified form of the German city first began to materialize, and it was here that the first attempts were made to face this threat by adapting the city's defenses to this new situation. Two factors determined these interconnected developments: one geographic the other political.

Today, as in the eighteenth century, the Rhine dominates the landscape of Germany's westernmost cities from the Swiss border in the south to the Dutch border in the north. Along most of its course, the river carves a deep valley through a mountainous terrain, dividing two thickly wooded ridges from one another. The western ridges stretch from the Vosges Mountains in the south to the Eiffel in the north, while those in the east extend from the Black Forest to the Westerwald. Several tributaries carve their way into the river through these ridges: the Bruche near Strasbourg, the Neckar near

---

44 This geopolitical analysis is based on French intelligence reports from the eighteenth century, most importantly S.H.A.T. Vincennes, Mémoires Historiques, 171, 1045, and 1746.

Mannheim, the Main in the vicinity of Mainz, and the Mosel near Koblenz. The river's valley is quite wide in the south (the area known as the Upper Rhine), and narrows to form a steep gorge from Bingen to Bonn (the Middle Rhine). North of Bonn, the Lower Rhine runs through the open plains of Westphalia and Lower Saxony, fans out into a delta in the Low Countries, and finally flows into the North Sea through several estuaries.

Throughout its course, the Rhine valley is marked by human activity: fields, vineyards, roads, villages, and towns. Indeed, several of Germany's most ancient cities are situated in the Rhine basin. Some, like Speyer, Mainz, and Cologne, were already fortified settlements in Roman times. Other famous cities along the river were founded or rose to prominence in the Middle Ages. This was the case of Freiburg im Breisgau, for instance, which was surrounded by a wall early in the twelfth century.

In the eighteenth century, as in earlier times, the Rhine basin's topography influenced the fate of many city walls by allowing any army advancing into Germany across the river only a limited number of routes (figure 7). In the Upper Rhine, there were five such conceivable entries, all lying along the river's tributaries, which break extensive openings in what contemporaries perceived to be "impassable mountains" or "impregnable lines" on the river's right bank.[45] The southern and most difficult of the paths led from Freiburg ("a large and well populated city, regularly fortified"[46]), up the sinuous Dreisam River, and through the high Black Forest, into the Neckar Valley in Swabia. Farther north, another route led from Strasbourg ("all round this Place there are some of the greatest and finest fortifications in Europe"[47]), across the Rhine to Kehl and Offenburg, and up the Kintzig River across the middle Black Forest. A much easier route than the first two also started in the vicinity of Strasbourg, and continued north of the Black Forest through Pforzheim in the direction of Stuttgart. A fourth advance path led from the Palatinate, across the Rhine near Mannheim (a city that was "entirely ruined, in the most barbarous manner" by the French back in 1689, but "seems to have recovered much of its ancient splendor" by 1745[48]), and through the Neckar valley into Hessen. Finally, just before the narrow gorge of the Middle Rhine, it was possible to traverse from Mainz ("a very strong Place, adorned with Churches"[49]), up the river Main to Frankfurt and beyond. In the eighteenth century, as in earlier times, cities

---

45 C. Bathurst et al., *The Modern Part of an Universal History, From the Earliest Accounts to the Present Time* (London, 1782), 27:288.
46 *The Theatre of the Present War upon the Course of the Rhine* (London, 1745), 167.
47 Ibid., 154.　　　　　　　　　　　　　48 Ibid., 179.
49 Ibid., 196.

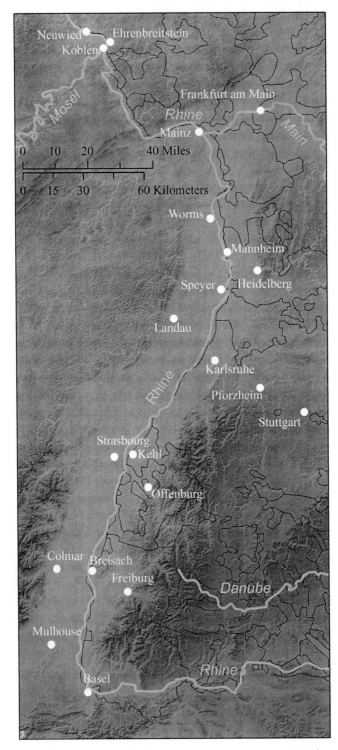

Figure 7. Topographical and political map of the Upper and Middle Rhine, ca. 1750.

located near these routes on the Upper Rhine were valuable strategic points, whether to an army advancing into Southern Germany or to an army trying to repel such an offensive. This is the reason Richelieu called one such city (Strasbourg) "an entry" or "a gate" into Germany.

The rest of the river's course can be divided into two different topographical–military environments. The steep gorge of the Middle Rhine allowed no feasible path of advance into the German hinterland. Cities located along this part of the river were spared the experience of large military campaigns in their vicinity, and therefore hardly any settlement here was forcibly defortified in the course of the eighteenth century. The German side of the Lower Rhine, on the other hand, is not flanked by substantial mountain ridges. This fact would make Westphalian and Lower Saxon cities very vulnerable to advancing French troops, as long as they found the means to safely cross the river.

The political environment in the German Rhine basin during the eighteenth century was as crucial for the fate of city walls as was the topography of the region. Most important here was the stark contrast between the homogeneity of power in France and the division of power in Germany. Throughout the eighteenth century, the French dominated the river's left bank from Huningue (just north of Basel) to Landau in the Palatinate. Following the Treaty of Ryswick (1697), the French withdrew from the territories they acquired east of the Rhine and from some lands west of it. Even after these concessions, however, they continued to have a powerful presence along the Upper Rhine, the star-shaped silhouettes of their mighty fortresses casting long shadows over the river's southern valley.

The political environment on the German side of the border was strikingly different. In the eighteenth century, the political map of this region was a patchwork quilt of small- and medium-size territories, Imperial cities, and ecclesiastical states. Baden was ruled by the Austrian Habsburgs alongside the Margraves of Baden. Down the river, the Palatinate was controlled by one line of the Wittelsbach dynasty, together with several ecclesiastical states and Imperial cities. And to the north, the plains of Westphalia and Lower Saxony were divided among the Prussian Hohenzollerns, the Welfs, and a multitude of other princes both ecclesiastical and temporal. Unlike France, then, there was no single political power that dominated the German territories of the Rhine basin and no unified fortification lines that could defend this region in its entirety in case of a French attack. Not only peaceful travelers but the French military intelligence, too, recognized this situation full well, and commented on it in reports whenever war seemed imminent.[50]

The defortification events in France unfolded along a relatively clear path. First, the state defortified smaller towns in the hinterland (e.g., La Rochelle); then, a cordon of fortress towns was erected along the state's exposed land borders; and finally, the kingdom's capital became an open city. A similar process took place in the German regions closest to France. First came the demolition of many local, ancient walls; then the construction of great fortresses in strategic locations; and finally, German princes followed the example of the Bourbons, and began to defortify their residence cities and towns.

UNDERMINING "THE CITY IN ARMS"

The Palatinate was to Germany what La Rochelle and other Huguenot cities were to France. It was not only the first German region to experience a major defortification wave; it was also an example and a warning to other cities about the likely consequences of an attempt to oppose a powerful territorial state. Even a century after Louis XIV's armies had left the area, the region's physical and cultural landscapes were scarred by their actions. Ann Ward Radcliffe, an Englishwoman traveling down the Rhine in 1794, was surprised by the scope of the destruction. Coming to the area from the north, she first visited the small town of Oppenheim (between Mainz and Worms), which "still bears the marks of the devastation, inflicted upon this country in the last century, more flagrant than could be expected, when the length of intervening time and the complete recovery of other cities from similar disasters are considered."[51] It was here, more than in any other part of Germany, that it became clear from the late seventeenth century onward that the rising power of territorial states was a harbinger of bad news for the old, fortified form of the German city.

Consider the city of Speyer, one of those cities defortified by the French in 1689. Before the War of the League of Augsburg, Speyer had been one of Germany's proudest Imperial cities, the seat of the Empire's highest legal court – the Imperial Chamber Court – and the meeting place of numerous Imperial Diets. Like all German cities, Speyer also possessed extensive city walls, and the Imperial coat of arms – a black, double-headed

---

50 S.H.A.T. Vincennes, Mémoires Historiques, 171, 1045, and 1746.
51 Ann Ward Radcliffe, *A Journey Made in the Summer of 1794: Through Holland and the Western Frontier of Germany* (London, 1796), 413.

eagle on a golden background – decorated its gates. Travelers to Speyer in the mid-eighteenth century found few indications of this great past. Indeed, they found the absence of the city's old monuments . . . well, monumental. "It was a flourishing city in the past and very populous," wrote one Frenchman in the 1770s, "but the French had razed it to the ground in 1689, and it hasn't recovered since."[52] The majestic Romanesque cathedral, the final resting place of eight medieval emperors and German kings, lay in ruins; large parts of the city were still uninhabitable, and the city walls, massive representative gates, and gate towers were mostly gone.[53] The devastation of Speyer was not only physical; it was also political and symbolic because in the wake of the war, the Imperial Chamber Court had to be permanently moved to another Imperial city – Wetzlar. So vast was the destruction that many of Speyer's inhabitants, who had fled the city during the war, never came back. They settled elsewhere, spreading horrific stories about the destruction of their city and the Palatinate more generally.[54]

In France, the events in the Palatinate caused quite a few prominent authors (including La Fontaine) to compose poems and epigrams in praise of Louis XIV's military successes.[55] From a German perspective, of course, the picture looked quite different. Many decades after the occupation of the Palatinate, Frederick the Great still remembered the events of the late seventeenth century, and invoked a comparison between French actions in the west and Turkish atrocities in the east in the late seventeenth century: "While the Turks besieged Vienna and Melac laid waste to the Palatinate, while houses and towns burned to ashes . . . while desperate mothers fled with their starving children from the ruins of their country – were sonnets to be composed and epigrams wrought in Vienna or Mannheim?"[56]

52 Antoine Augustin Bruzen de La Martinière, *Dictionnaire Géographique – Portatif, ou Description des Royaumes* (Paris, 1777), 666.
53 Wolfgang Hartwich, "Speyer vom 30jährigen Krieg bis zum Ende der napoleonischen Zeit," in *Geschichte der Stadt Speyer*, ed. Wolfgang Eger (Stuttgart: Kohlhamer, 1983), 5–133. Eighteenth-century depictions of Speyer, Worms, and other cities in the Palatinate can be found in Raumer, *Die Zerstörung*, esp. 337ff.
54 On emigration from the Palatinate, see Karl Scherer, ed., *Pfälzer – Palatines: Beiträge zur Volkskunde und Mundartforschung der Pfalz und der Ziellander pfälzischer Auswanderer im 18. und 19. Jahrhundert* (Kaiserslautern: Heimatstelle Pfalz, 1991). An important collection of sources about French atrocities can be found in Harster, "Materialien."
55 Jean de La Fontaine, *Œuvres de J. de La Fontaine*, ed. Henri Régnier (Paris: Hachette, 1892), 8:465–67. Two other examples are B. de Hautmont, *Ode à Monseigneur sur la prise de Philipsbourg* (Paris, 1688); and Barbier d'Aucour, *Ode sur la prise de Philipsbourg* (Paris, 1689).
56 Quoted in Gerhard Ritter, *Frederick the Great*, trans. Peter Paret (Berkeley: University of California Press, 1974), 49.

The physical ruination of cities like Oppenheim and Speyer was local in nature, but its cultural and political repercussions were widespread. If Paris was the best example for the defortification of a city by peaceful means, Speyer, Oppenheim, and other devastated cities in the Palatinate served as a constant reminder of the brutality of most contemporary defortifications. Throughout the eighteenth century, the actions of Louis XIV's armies in this region were evoked and debated. Whether one justified or condemned these actions, one fact was accepted by all: most urban communities could no longer oppose a strong territorial state by themselves. Consequently, not only the physical walls of Palatine cities were damaged; the very idea of the "city in arms" – a crucial component in the physical and symbolic construction of city walls – was undermined as well.

Eighteenth-century travelers in the Palatinate and adjacent territories discovered many cases similar to that of Oppenheim and Speyer. Farther downstream from Speyer in Heidelberg, Frankenthal, and Worms, the destruction caused by the War of the League of Augsburg was still evident in the mid-eighteenth century (in Heidelberg, it is still visible today). Worms alone had lost over forty towers, three massive representative gates, and most of its walls.[57] "Few of the [city's] present inhabitants can be the descendants of those who witnessed its destruction in 1689," wrote Radcliffe in the 1790s. Still, she was told stories of what had happened to the city a century earlier. "A column of Louis the Fourteenth's army had entered the city under the command of the Marquis de Bonfleur, who soon distressed the inhabitants by preparations for blowing up the walls with gunpowder. The mines were so numerous and large," she was further told, "as to threaten nothing less than the entire overwhelming of the city."[58] Similar stories were told in other regions along the river, from Kerpen in the north to Staufen and even Waldkirch (Baden) in the south. Although the walls of these urban communities would sometimes be repaired in the course of the eighteenth century, most urban fortifications in the Palatinate and the Upper Rhine would never possess a military function again. To have strong fortifications in these areas, concluded one scholar toward the end of the eighteenth century, made little sense: "Instead of security, they only bring to these lands the dangers of occupation by the enemy [and eventually] the complete devastation of the entire countryside."[59]

57 Gerold Bönnen, ed., *Geschichte der Stadt Worms* (Stuttgart: Theiss, 2005), 2:299ff. For a contemporary depiction of what Worms had lost during the French occupation of 1689, see Friedrich Soldan, *Die Zerstörung der Stadt Worms im Jahre 1689* (Worms: J. Stern, 1889), 52.
58 Radcliffe, *A Journey Made in the Summer of 1794*, 425.
59 GLA Karlsruhe, Abt. 65, Nr. 1443.

THE DIALECTICS OF STATE FORTIFICATIONS ALONG THE RHINE

The inability of most western German cities to oppose France single-handedly did not mean the complete abandonment of the old praxis to fortify cities. The situation here was similar to the defortification policies in France itself. The French Crown demolished the urban fortifications in the hinterland at the same time that it built massive cordons of fortress towns along the state's perimeter. In the eighteenth century, the same dialectical process was evident in the German territories of the Rhine basin. While a great number of urban communities were forced to see their walls demolished, a small number of strategically valuable cities, especially along the penetration routes into Germany, were now fortified more strongly than ever.

As in France, German military theoreticians recognized the importance of the question of urban fortifications for the state's defense and internal security. This is why, as in the rest of Europe, the construction and maintenance of fortress towns were important for most German princes and why they insisted that the Imperial Capitulations (the constitutional document negotiated between the electors and any newly elected emperor) would always include a clause about their right to do so independently of the Empire's institutions. The prime textbook on fortifications used by the famous école de Mézières (France's school of military engineering) expressed this significance in the following way: "All sovereigns, both ancient and modern, have made use of fortified cities and towns. . . . The Greeks, the Romans, and the Carthaginians had many such places. And at present all European princes, from the weakest to the mightiest, all possess fortress towns." "The Pope," the manual continued, "the [Holy Roman] Emperor, the King of France, the King of Spain, the King of Portugal, the Kings of Sweden and Denmark, the States of Holland, the Seigneury of Venice, as well as all other Italian princely states; all these states and princes still continue to build new fortress towns every day, laying them according to the changing [strategic] interests of their states."[60]

Princes and generals considered fortified cities crucial because they helped control the movement of people within the state's territory. Internally, fortified cities served as staging points for state troops, a place from which an army could march against mutinous regions, and to which it could withdraw if attacked. Even more important was the fortresses' role in the defense of the state from its external enemies. In the eighteenth century,

---

60 M. Maigret, *Traité de la sûreté et conservation des états, par le moyen des forteresses* (Paris: Esprit Billiot, 1725), 59.

strategically located, well-fortified towns could still block – or at least temporarily hold back – an army intending to advance into the country. This often brought large-scale devastation to single cities, and the events in the Palatinate were living proof of that. But it also allowed the state – which, unlike the single city, possessed strategic depth – to hold the enemy at bay while it mobilized its forces for a counterattack.

Even the Wittelsbachs – hardly a thoroughly militarized dynasty – fully recognized the importance of such places. Elector Maximilian I urged his successor in the seventeenth century to take special care of the land's fortified cities. Only thus, the elector claimed, "[one] would be able . . . to hinder a possible advancement of an enemy into the country [and] control the often restive burghers and state subjects, especially in the new territories the state had acquired." "These people," the elector added (meaning the burghers), "should not be trusted blindly until they come to completely forget their old masters."[61] Two centuries later, a general at the Wittelsbach court in Munich still echoed the same sentiment. "Fortified cities," he claimed, were the "fundamental columns on which the independence of the state is based."[62] Some military theoreticians, perhaps first and foremost among them Maurice de Saxe, objected to such a reliance on fortified cities for the defense of the state. Even Maurice, however, had to conclude that his arguments must fall on deaf ears: "Notwithstanding that what I have advanced is founded on reason, I expect hardly a single person to concur, so absolute is custom and such is its power over us."[63]

Travelers to the Rhine basin could recognize the effects of individual states' reliance on urban fortifications in the great fortress towns that still existed in this area in the mid- and late eighteenth century. One such fortress was Mannheim, which had been razed to the ground during the War of the League of Augsburg but rebuilt by the Wittelsbachs after 1715. Ann Radcliffe, who visited the city in 1794, mentioned the great palace in the city and the grandeur of "the numerous turrets and the fortifications." "The gates," she remarked, "appear to be defended by fortifications of unusual strength [and] beside two broad ditches, there are batteries, which play directly upon the bridges and might destroy them in a few minutes."[64] Farther upstream, on both sides of the Rhine, the presence of

61 Rainer Braun, "Garnisonsbewerbungen," in *Bayern und seine Armee: Eine Ausstellung des bayerischen Hauptstaatsarchivs aus den Beständen des Kriegsarchivs*, ed. Rainer Braun (München: Bayer. HStA, 1987), 217.
62 Ibid., 225.
63 Maurice de Saxe, "Reveries on the Art of War," in *The Art of War in World History*, ed. Gérard Chaliand (Berkeley: University of California Press, 1994), 588.
64 Radcliffe, *A Journey Made in the Summer of 1794*, 433, 444.

such fortresses was even more striking. On the western side of the river, under French control, stood the great fortresses of Vauban's *ceinture de fer*. Landau, approximately thirty miles southwest of Mannheim as the crow flies, was the northernmost point in this belt. It was followed (from north to south) by Wissembourg, Haguenau, Strasbourg, Selestat, Neuf-Brisach, and Huningue (just north of Basel). In the early eighteenth century, several fortresses on the right bank of the Rhine still rivaled the strength of the French fortresses: Kehl ("a very important post, upon the East Side of the Rhine, over-against Strasburg," remarked one observer[65]), Breisach, and Freiburg. So magnificent were some of these fortifications, noted one German traveler in 1740, that when you visit this area, "all conceivable types of fortifications built by Vauban, Cohoorn, and other famous engineers are laid out before your eyes."[66]

Finally, much like the French, the Germans also imagined cities and fortresses as creating a meta-fortress of sorts, defending a whole territory rather than a single city. The Habsburgs, for instance, called Freiburg and Breisach the *Vormauern* (literally, outermost fortifications) of Austria.[67] The Margrave of Baden warned in the 1690s that the fact that the French still kept Strasbourg was exceedingly dangerous: "For Germany, this city is nothing but a permanent insurance of peace; but for France it is an open gate for war, through which, whenever it chooses, it can break loose its power into the open country."[68] Most striking, perhaps, is Frederick the Great's self-description not only as "the first servant of the state," but also as its first gate watcher. The sovereign, Frederick wrote in his *Forms of Government and the Duties of Rulers* (1777), is "like a sentinel who watches unceasingly the neighbors of the state and the activities of its enemies."[69]

In his letter to Louvois, Vauban had urged the war minister to consider keeping one of every three fortified cities along France's borders. During the eighteenth century, a similar logic determined the fate of fortress towns on the right bank of the Rhine. Princes had to consider not only which fortresses to strengthen, but also which ones to demolish even when not directly attacked by an enemy.

65 J. Brindely, *An Introduction to the Art of Fortification* (London, 1745), 170.
66 Johann Georg Keyssler, *Neueste Reise durch Teutschland* (Hannover, 1740), 147.
67 GLA Karlsruhe, Abt. 65, Nr. 1443.
68 Aloys Schulte, *Markgraf Ludwig Wilhelm von Baden und der Reichskrieg gegen Frankreich, 1693–1697* (Karlsruhe: J. Bielfeld, 1892), 2:218–19.
69 Frederick the Great, "Forms of Government and the Duties of Rulers (1777)," in *The Foundations of Germany: A Documentary Account Revealing the Causes of Her Strength, Wealth, and Efficiency*, ed. J. Ellis Baker (London: John Murray, 1918), 21–22.

Consider the fortresses of Breisach and Freiburg in Breisgau, for instance. By 1740, Breisach was an Austrian fortress with a garrison of over 10,000 troops, which defended one of the advance routes from Alsace into Southern Germany. Its strong position overlooking the Rhine and its immense fortifications turned it, in the words of one French writer, into "one of the strongest fortresses in Europe ... the citadel of Alsace; the key to Germany."[70] When the War of the Austrian Succession broke out in 1740, the garrison troops in Breisach were badly needed by the Austrians elsewhere – against the invading Prussians in Silesia. Evacuating Breisach would have meant a guaranteed French occupation of this important fortress and its integration into the French fortification lines. Deeming Breisach too vulnerable, Empress Maria Theresa ordered the defortification of the city in 1741. So thorough were the Austrians in demolishing the fortifications, wrote the historian of Breisach in the nineteenth century, that when the French crossed the Rhine a few months after the evacuation of the fortress the city no longer had any military value: the once mighty fortress was now an open, defenseless settlement, "little more than a village."[71]

A similar event took place in neighboring Freiburg three years later. Toward the end of 1744, the French were forced to evacuate the Breisgau and fall back to their territories in Alsace. Now it was they who wanted to deny the Habsburgs a strong fortress. They mined the fortifications of Freiburg and blew them up in a series of explosions so immense that (in the words of an eyewitness) "all the houses round about the city and close to the fortifications were completely destroyed."[72] When the Austrian troops reentered Freiburg, they, too, found the city defenseless. From that time on, Breisach and Freiburg would remain defortified.

THE RESIDENCE CITIES: THE EXAMPLE OF KARLSRUHE

Defortifications in the western provinces of Germany were usually military in nature. Whether in the defortification of towns in the Palatinate in the late seventeenth century or further south in the Breisgau in the 1740s, the proximity of France's mighty army was the dominant cause of these events. But France's influence on urban fortifications on the German side of the Rhine was not restricted to its military actions and presence. The example set by the defortification of Paris and the king's move to Versailles was as

---

70 Louis Moreri, *Le grand dictionnaire historique* (Basel, 1731), 1:426.
71 DSB IV/2: 198; P. Rosmann and Faustin Ens, *Geschichte der Stadt Breisach* (Freiburg: Friedrich Wagner, 1851), 440–41.
72 StdA Freiburg, B 5 VI a Nr. 69.

Figure 8. Karlsruhe, ca. 1730. Source: Historic Maps Collection, Department of Rare Books and Special Collections, Princeton University Library.

crucial to the fate of urban fortifications in these areas as was the French military presence. One city where that was the case was Karlsruhe.

Karlsruhe's unfortified footprint, although not unique, was nonetheless the most famous adoption of the Versailles model to a west German city. In 1715, Margrave Karl Wilhelm of Baden-Durlach decided to move his court from the old city of Durlach, with its medieval outline and ancient walls, into a new residence town. Influenced by French taste, dress, literature, and political ideas – like so many other German princes of his time – he wanted to build "his own Versailles."[73] He laid his new residence town around his palace, from which avenues emanated in different directions. Here, symbolism and practical considerations went hand in hand. The prince's palace was visible from most parts of the city, while the wide avenues emanating from the palace helped supervise the new city's different parts. To see and be seen – one of the fundamental aims of any absolutist prince – found one of its possible solutions in Karlsruhe (figure 8).

73 In the nineteenth century, Wilhelm Heinrich Riehl had quite a few negative things to say about this practice. Wilhelm Heinrich Riehl, *Land und Leute*, 86.

As in other residence towns in the Rhine basin, Karlsruhe's unfortified footprint was not accidental but a result of a novel set of ideas about what a city ought to be, expressed in the founding document of the city in 1715.[74] With the aim of attracting newcomers to the city, settlers were granted land, free building materials, tax exemptions, and freedom of religion. Most of these privileges were not limited to the first generation of settlers. Much like Karlsruhe's potentially infinite avenues – stretching from the prince's palace in all directions – so, too, the settlers' privileges were not limited in time. The physical city was conceived as a grain from which an ever-expanding city would develop. This reflected the political idea behind Karlsruhe. As Carl Wilhelm himself put it: "It is the expressed and true will of the count to continue to expand these liberties, privileges, immunities, and exceptions, rather than to control or limit them."[75]

Karlsruhe and other princely residences in the Rhine basin represented a new conception of the city that was fundamentally different from the many walled towns around them. In the old cities, the walls stood for the city's independence, history, and legal, social, and political distinction from the surrounding countryside. In Karlsruhe, Neuwied (Middle Rhine), Ludwigsburg (Württemberg), and later in the century in bigger residences such as Hanover, Kassel (both defortified after 1763), and Koblenz (starting in 1777), the lack of walls was a physical expression of the political philosophy of sovereignty which eschewed political and physical distinctions other than the one between the prince and the rest of the population. These residence cities, through their potentially infinite avenues, were oriented toward the future (expansion, progress, openness) rather than toward the defense of the past and present (privileges, walls). They represented less the distinction between city and countryside (*Bürger und Bauer scheidet nichts als die Mauer*) and more the distinction between old and new. One traveler through the Middle Rhine in the 1790s connected all these threads to one another. Neuwied, he wrote, truly deserves its name. "It is a modern city . . . and Neu [German for "new"] compared with every other adjacent to the Rhine [because] it is not surrounded by walls."[76]

THE GEOPOLITICS OF THE NORTHEAST

Eighteenth-century travelers to northeastern Germany encountered a picture that would already be familiar to the reader in its broad lines. As in the

---

74 Robert Goldschmidt, *Die Stadt Karlsruhe: Ihre Entstehung und ihre Verwaltung* (Karlsruhe: Müllersche Hofbuchhandlung, 1915), 6.
75 The full Privilegienbrief can be found in ibid., 7.
76 "A Picturesque Description of the Rhine," *The Edinburgh Magazine*, vol. 6 (1795), 89.

Rhine basin, quite a few northeastern German cities had lost their ancient walls by the end of the century, cordons of fortress towns were built, and many a small Versailles was constructed. But while the eighteenth-century Rhineland demonstrates better than any other region in Germany what an external threat could do to the city walls, cities in the Prussian sphere of influence exemplify best what state protection most often meant. Here, as in the west, a changing geopolitical environment was crucial for the progress of the defortification waves.

Germany's northeastern provinces lie in the middle of the Northern Europe Lowlands, stretching from the foothills of the German Middle Uplands and the Bohemian Massif in the south to the Baltic Sea in the north. There is little in the way of topographical obstacles in this flat landscape, other than a series of great rivers which flow from south to north, through the plains, and into the North and Baltic Seas (so flat is the topography of these areas that even today Germans joke that in the north one can see a guest approaching one's town a week in advance). The Elbe and Saale form the western borders of these lands, the Oder and Vistula cross it in its center, and the Niemen River – in present-day Lithuania – marks its eastern boundary. Within these boundaries, the soil is often sandy and marshlands are a constant characteristic of the landscape. The harshness of the winters, the barrenness of the soil, the moving sands in some parts, and the thickly wooded pine forests in others all made human settlements in northeastern Germany rather difficult. As opposed to other parts of the country, the northeast was consequently only sparsely populated, and urban settlements a much rarer occurrence.

When contemporary Germans spoke about "the East Elbian territories," they alluded not only to a geographical region but also to a different social and political world. The nobility in the east, the Junkers, exercised control over the land but also over the manor as a social and economic unit. The East Elbian estates passed undivided from father to son, and were the basis of Prussia's military system, in which the Junkers served as officers and their peasants as foot soldiers (burghers in Prussia were denied any significant military role). This not only made the human landscape in the northeast less populated than other parts of Germany, it also made it much less urban in its culture and economy.[77]

During the seventeenth and eighteenth centuries, the great East Elbian lowlands witnessed the rise of Prussia. The Prussian ruling dynasty – the Hohenzollerns – managed to amass a large territory east of the Elbe

---

77 For the Prussian military system, see Otto Büsch, *Militärsystem und Sozialleben im alten Preußen, 1713–1807: Die Anfänge der sozialen Militarisierung der preußisch-deutschen Gesellschaft* (Berlin: de Gruyter, 1962).

unthreatened, as other states in Germany were, by other strong military forces such as the Habsburgs, France, or the Ottoman Empire. Prussia, more than any other contemporary state, was thoroughly militarized. Its second monarch, Friedrich Wilhelm I (1688–1740), was called the "Soldier King" for a reason; his son, Frederick the Great (1712–1786), was the most famous general of the century. Prussia was so heavily militarized that in 1752 (a year of peace!), nine of every ten talers in the Prussian budget went to cover the state's military expenses. Little wonder that Mirabeau reputedly called it "an army with a state rather than a state with an army."

Through a series of expansionist wars, the Hohenzollern dynasty succeeded in enlarging its territories almost five-fold by the end of the eighteenth century. Originally, it ruled over Brandenburg, a couple of enclaves in the west, and East Prussia (the latter, the real power base of the Hohenzollerns, lay outside the borders of the Holy Roman Empire). In the course of the seventeenth and eighteenth centuries, the Hohenzollern dominions expanded into Magdeburg and East Pomerania (1648), Silesia (1740–1763), and finally parts of Poland (1772–1795). By 1795, Prussia controlled most of the lands of the northeast, from the Niemen in the east, the foothills of the Bohemian Massif in the south, the Baltic and the southeastern end of the Jutland Peninsula in the north, to some lands on the Elbe's left bank and the enclaves along the Lower Rhine in the west. It was a vast and largely contiguous territory, which was less urbanized than most parts of Germany, more centralized, and more militarized. Between 1740–1786, it was also ruled by one of the great sovereign monarchs of eighteenth-century Europe, Frederick the Great. All these factors would play a major role in the fate of city walls in these lands.

THE DARK SIDE OF SOVEREIGNTY

Travelling to Prussia in the eighteenth century from any direction would mean encountering one of its numerous fortress towns. It was often stated at the time that Frederick the Great abhorred fortresses, believing that a decisive military action was much more likely to succeed through a pitched battle than by a series of sieges.[78] In the numerous wars he waged on his neighbors, Frederick exemplified this maxim repeatedly. He was a brilliant and ruthless strategist, who forced a numerically superior rival to its knees on more than one occasion. Even for Frederick, however, fortresses continued

---

78 As, for instance, Honoré Gabriel Riqueti, Comte de Mirabeau, *De la monarchie prussienne sous Frédéric le Grand* (London, 1788), 3:186–87.

to be crucial to the defense and internal security of his kingdom. Such a large territory as he now controlled needed cordons of fortress towns to block a possible penetration into its vulnerable, flat interior. Like the French Crown a century earlier, Frederick constructed and maintained a string of fortresses along the kingdom's perimeter, especially in those regions, such as Silesia, which were most strategically vulnerable.

In his political statement of 1752, Frederick emphasized the role of fortresses to his rule. Fortress towns, he wrote, "are the nails that connect the provinces to the king. In wartime, they are useful as staging points for any nearby army. They provide the troops with shelter, their mighty walls protect the army's supplies, the sick and wounded, and the ammunition magazines."[79] Of course, Frederick emphasized, one has to take into consideration a town's geopolitical location before choosing to turn it into a fortress: "Fortress towns, if built close to the borders, support any large army corps in the vicinity, whether the latter finds there its winter quarters, uses the fortress as a staging point for an offensive into enemy territory, or waits in it for the arrival of reinforcements from the hinterland."[80]

The similarity between the overall fortifications of eighteenth-century Prussia and contemporary France was unmistakable. Berlin, the capital, had already been defortified in the 1730s ("a mistake," Frederick the Great would later note in his political testament[81]). Along the exposed land borders of the realm and in some strategic points in the interior, Frederick and his father built or strengthened a long list of fortified places: Graudenz, Silberberg, Wesel, Magdeburg, Spandau, Glatz, Neisse, and Schweidnitz. These were augmented by a second line of fortified cities such as Breslau, Brieg, Cosel, Glogau, Pillau, Kolberg, and Küstrin as well as many garrison towns. Next to the numerous fortifications in the southeast, built and maintained by Austria against the Ottomans, eighteenth-century Prussia possessed the strongest cordons of urban fortifications anywhere in Germany.

As in France and the Rhine basin, the construction of fortresses in Prussia was accompanied by the defortification of other cities. Beyond Prussia's borders, Frederick was often involved in the defortification of cities he deemed too vulnerable to defend (e.g., Moers in the Rhineland, 1759[82]). At other times, Frederick would order the demolition of fortresses and urban fortifications in the hinterland, striving to save both money and

---

79 Quoted in Curt Jany, *Geschichte der preußischen Armee vom 15. Jahrhundert bis 1914*, 2nd ed. (Osnabrück: Biblio Verlag, 1967), 2:260.
80 Ibid.
81 Frederick the Great, "Political Testament (1752)," in *The Habsburg and Hohenzollern Dynasties in the Seventeenth and Eighteenth Centuries*, ed. Carlile Aylmer Macartney (New York: Walker, 1970), 341.
82 DSB III/3: 307.

military personnel for other, more important tasks (as in Peitz, Hamm, Lippstadt, and Minden[83]). There is reason to believe that unlike in bigger cities, defortification in such towns did not involve meticulous planning. Early in the next century, Michael Fuchs, a professor in the East Prussian town of Elbing (modern-day Elblåg in Poland), recalled how in early 1773 Fredrick the Great ordered the demolition of Elbing's walls, which the king deemed unnecessary for the defense of Prussia as a whole. The demolition proceeded from gate to gate and from wall section to wall section, but "without any regular plan," Fuchs wrote. The result left much to be desired. The fortification's bridges were demolished before the ditches were filled up, and consequently made the entrance to the town almost impassable, especially on rainy days. For a long time, the rubble from the demolished walls blocked some of the town's streets. Fuchs even suspected that an Elbing city council member, one Gottfried Gotsch, was involved in embezzlement: while selling the bricks from the walls to the highest bidder, he seemed to be keeping part of the money in his own pocket.[84] There was little here to suggest the same orderly defortification process as in residence towns, for instance.

The importance of such cases notwithstanding, the most significant development in eighteenth-century Prussia with regard to city walls related less to their physical demolition (such cases were at any rate rarer than in either France or the Rhineland, as Prussia's original territories were much less urbanized than other parts of central Europe). It related, rather, to the decline in their significance as symbols of urban independence and custom.

Because fortress towns were fundamentally important to the defense of Prussia, Frederick and his father strengthened the fortifications of their most strategically valuable cities and flooded them with garrison troops. In Berlin, there was one soldier for every five inhabitants; in Halle (Saale), the ratio was one to three; and in Potsdam, just outside Berlin, garrison troops outnumbered other residents by a ratio of four to one. One traveler to Potsdam in the 1750s found it to be a town of "considerable extent, and the buildings neat and regular." "But the town," he added, "seems to be entirely occupied by soldiers."[85] It would be a mistake to view the militarization of garrison and fortress towns as a purely Prussian phenomenon. In Bavaria, for instance, there were garrison towns already in 1716, and the Habsburgs were not left behind either. Before Breisach's defortification in 1741, for every one (civil) local resident the state stationed more than ten garrison

83 DSB III/2: 164, 224, 246; DSB (Neu) II: 390.
84 Michael G. Fuchs, *Beschreibung der Stadt Elbing und ihre Gebiete* (Elbing: Hartmann, 1818), 1:108–18.
85 Jonas Hanway, *An Historical Account of the British Trade over the Caspian Sea* (Dublin, 1754), 1:426.

troops in the city.[86] This is why, in the words of one eighteenth-century visitor, Breisach, "tho' a notable Fortification, is but a miserable Town."[87] The two characters of the town were interconnected.

The flooding of a city with state troops was not a happy moment for its residents. It almost always entailed the quartering of soldiers in the burghers' houses and brought great distress to the local economy. That was probably the reason the original name for garrison towns in some parts of the country was simply "occupations."[88] Composed of ex-convicts, deserters from foreign armies, vagabonds, and other outcasts, the garrison troops were often involved in theft, robbery, and even murder.[89] The spectacular punishments for desertion, for which the Prussian army was notorious at the time (and which the local population often had to witness), did not add to the popularity of the soldiers in the towns in which they were stationed.

Consider the events in the relatively small garrison town of Halle on the river Saale. The chronicler of the city enumerates some of the incidents involving the unruly garrison regiment stationed there in the course of the eighteenth century.

1763, July 12. From four to eight o'clock in the morning the city witnessed the most horrific execution in its history. Eighteen men of the newly arrived garrison regiment conspired to desert.

1768, April 26. A soldier, using his bayonet, stabbed the little son of a servant all over his body. Since the child did not eventually die, the man was not executed. He did have to run the gauntlet three dozen times, however, and was locked away for three years.

1771, August 30. Two men of the garrison troops, in whose tools were found gunpowder and bullets, confessed to have conspired to shoot their officer. They were brought to the gallows in the marketplace and hung.

1777, September 29. Private Becker of the garrison was executed by a firing squad outside the Schimmer Gate, after stabbing to death his non-commissioned officer.

1778, July 3. Last night, the garrison soldier Münch slipped into the Altermann's house, just outside the city, on the river, intending to rob the house of its valuables. He had heard before that the Altermanns would not spend the night in their house. As he broke into the house he found a little girl watching over her baby brother in a cradle. He immediately caught the girl, tied a rope around her neck, and tied her to the bed in the chamber. After stabbing her numerous times with his bayonet, of which wounds she quickly expired, he forced his way into a closet and stole the

86 Information about garrison strengths are taken from DSB III/2: 246; DSB VI/2: 197; and DSB (Neu) II: 400, 579.

87 Brindely, *An Introduction to the Art of Fortification*, 166.

88 *Besatzungen* in German. Braun, "Garnisonsbewerbungen," 217.

89 Many examples can be found in "Justiz und Polizei," Bayer. HStA KA, A XIII 4.

fifty talers hidden there. Finally, he put a burning lamp under the bed, made sure the house was on fire, and left the place [with the baby still inside].[90]

The presence of the unwieldy state troops in a city was one of the more dire consequences of its being a garrison or a fortress town. If that was not enough, the legal practices of the sovereign state made matters even worse. The preservation of city law was fundamental to the urban community. It was a fundamental component in, and expression of, its independence and its personality; it was part of the city's honor. In fortress and garrison towns, the practices of sovereignty dealt a crushing blow to this old perception of the city. The monarch was the ultimate and undisputed legal authority in a sovereign state, so he could suspend city law whenever he saw fit, and even suppress it altogether.

One common issue that was raised in garrison towns was the question of who would have control over the keys to the city gates. Turning over the keys to the garrison's commandant was a highly symbolic act to which most burghers strongly objected.[91] But perhaps nowhere was the infiltration of the state into the affairs of the city clearer than in a besieged city. During a time of war, a state often declared a state of siege in its fortified cities.[92] Such a legal decree entailed the replacement of the city's elected governing bodies by a state-appointed governor, the confiscation of private property and supplies for the troops, and even the evacuation of all nonmilitary personnel from the city and the implementation of strict military law for all remaining persons.[93] In short, a state of siege meant an almost complete suppression of all the burgher's most cherished liberties, even when the enemy ultimately refrained from attacking the city.

Maurice de Saxe, the famous German general in the service of Louis XV's France, drew important conclusions from this state of affairs. In the

---

90 Christian Gottlieb August Runde, *Rundes Chronik der Stadt Halle, 1750–1835* (Halle [Saale]: Gebauer Schwetschke Druckerei, 1933), 381–82.

91 For the cases of Nuremberg, Mainz, and Breslau, see, respectively: Bayer. HStA KA, MKr 9165; Geh. StA PK Berlin, III. HA, MdA Abt. I 10324; and StA Breslau, Akten der Stadt Breslau, (1702) 12.241.

92 For the connection between sovereignty and "state of siege," see, most importantly, Carl Schmitt, *Die Diktatur: von den Anfängen des modernen Souveränitätsgedankens bis zum proletarischen Klassenkampf* (München und Leipzig: Duncker & Humboldt, 1921) and Hans Boldt, *Rechtsstaat und Ausnahmezustand. Eine Studie über den Belagerungzustand als Ausnamezustand des bürgerlichen Rechtsstaates im 19. Jahrhundert* (Berlin: Duncker & Humboldt, 1967). A more recent study (based on Schmitt's argument) is Giorgio Agamben, *State of Exception*, trans. Kevin Attell (Chicago: Chicago University Press, 2005).

93 This practice would continue well into the nineteenth century. Concrete examples can be found in "Die Concurrenz und Verpflichtung der Civil-Autoritäten u. Communen in den Festungen u. Deren Bezirken bei Entstehender Einschließung un. Belegung," Bd. I 1809–1886 und Bd. II 1894–1914, GStA PK, HA I, Rep. 77 (Ministerium des Innern, Militärabteilung Sekt. 1, 2) 330a, Nr. 18.

spirit of Richelieu, Vauban, and Cormontaigne, Maurice also looked with suspicion at the attempt to fortify too many places. Like his predecessors, he, too, thought that only strategically located cities should be fortified. "Only few cities have been founded for these purposes," he wrote.[94] The most important reason one should be cautious about fortifying cities, however, was of a different nature. "Suppose you have stored food supplies for three months for the garrison," Maurice wrote around 1730:

After [the city] is besieged you find that they last only eight days because you have not counted on twenty, thirty, or forty thousand mouths that must be fed. . . . I imagine someone will say: 'I should expel the citizens who are unable to provide their own provisions.' This should be a worse desolation than the enemy could cause, for how many are there in the cities who do not live from day to day?

Complicating things even further was the question whether the enemy will tranquilly allow the inhabitants to leave a besieged city. No, Maurice wrote, "he will drive them back into the city. What will the governor do? Will he allow these unfortunates to die from hunger? Could he justify this conduct to his ruler? What can he do then? He will be forced to supply them with provisions and surrender in eight or fifteen days."[95]

Even in peacetime, the residents of a fortress town had to suffer certain limitations unknown in open or only weakly fortified cities. In order to provide the garrison's artillery with a free field of fire, restrictions were placed on the construction of buildings in the city's glacis. When, in rare cases, burghers were allowed to build houses or cultivate gardens in those areas, the state could still demolish them – without compensation – in case of a siege. Turning a city into a fortress or a garrison town perhaps strengthened its physical defenses, but it also deprived it of much of the meaning of being a city.

The relationship between the physical and invisible aspects of city walls in Prussia's fortress and garrison towns was therefore the exact opposite of that of open residence towns. In open residences, the absence of physical walls paradoxically underlined their invisible aspect. In Prussia's garrison and fortress towns – while the physical presence of the city walls became ever stronger – their association with the independence, prosperity, and honor of the city was almost completely eradicated. Raimondo Montecu-colli – lieutenant general and field marshal of the Habsburg armies – already observed in the late seventeenth century that "fortresses are the buttresses of the crown" and that the fact that "licentious" (i.e., free) nations, such as

---

94 Maurice de Saxe, "Reveries," 587.   95 Ibid., 587–88.

the English, disliked them only proved that point.[96] Jean-Jacques Rousseau, viewing the same developments a century later, agreed with Montecucolli's assessment but not with his conclusion. Rousseau must have expressed what more and more burghers realized when he wrote in the 1770s that "it is a bad idea for a free people to have fortress towns [because] everywhere, sooner or later, they will serve as nests for tyrants."[97]

MAKING THE HINTERLAND VISIBLE

Passing through the cordon of fortress towns lying along the state's perimeter, eighteenth-century travelers encountered the influence of one last element in Prussia's power structure – its bureaucracy – on the shape of city walls in the state's hinterland.

The Prussian bureaucracy was the most developed in contemporary Germany.[98] While the Hohenzollern armies ensured the state's ability to impose its will by force, it was the growing number of state officials that allowed it to maintain, supply, and use that force effectively. Such an apparatus was largely unique to territorial states, as the Empire and most cities did not possess similar devices. The Empire never developed a professional bureaucracy,[99] and cities (with some notable exceptions) often did not require such a complicated organizational structure. In a small- or middle-size city – unlike in a large state – everyone knew where everybody lived, people's identity was hardly ever a real problem (the community's size and its walls helped to guarantee that), and evading tax payments was a particularly dishonorable act that could lead to the loss of social standing and political rights.[100]

Unlike the requirements of the Empire and the cities, a professional bureaucracy was crucial for a state like Prussia. By collecting information about its subjects and by concentrating executive power in the hands of a small group of professionals, the state strove to make important decisions quickly and implement policies more effectively. With the information it

---

96 Raimondo Montecucolli, *Mémoires* (Strasbourg, 1735), 110–11.

97 Jean Jacques Rousseau, "Considérations sur le gouvernement de Pologne," in *The Political Writings of Jean Jacques Rousseau*, trans. C.E. Vaughan (Oxford: Blackwell, 1962), 2:490.

98 See, most importantly, Hans Rosenberg, *Bureaucracy, Aristocracy, and Autocracy: The Prussian Experience, 1660–1815* (Cambridge, MA: Harvard University Press, 1958).

99 For the case of cities, see Rosenberg, *Bureaucracy*, 7–8; for the failure of the creation of a standing bureaucracy in the Empire through its circles, see Karl Otmar von Aretin, *Das Alte Reich, 1648–1806* (Stuttgart: Klett-Cotta, 1993) 1:148–54.

100 A fine summary of taxation issues within the political culture of premodern Frankfurt am Main can be found in Karl Bücher, *Beiträge zur Wirtschaftsgeschichte* (Tübingen: H. Laupp'sche Buchhandlung, 1922), 332–44, 359–71.

collected, the bureaucracy facilitated large-scale conscription and maximized tax revenues needed to maintain the unprecedented size of the military. The standing army and the professional bureaucracy were two crucial buttresses, both supporting the emerging structure of the Prussian state.[101]

Considering city walls from their chambers (hence one possible root for the term used to describe their political philosophy – cameralism, from the Latin *camera*, "a room"), German bureaucrats perceived a slightly different picture from the one the generals saw.[102] Legally, cities had always been unique places. They had their specific privileges, traditions, laws, and monuments, and these – even when they bore close resemblance to those of other cities and towns – were always distinctive to them. This is why Johann Jakob Moser wrote in the mid-eighteenth century that "one cannot give any description of what a town is, or what town law is, that would be applicable everywhere in Germany."[103] This, too, is why Moser's legal treatise on German law ran in its final version to more than seventy quarto volumes. The ensuing administrative nightmare such a state of affairs caused state officials needs little elaboration.

The legal complexity was not the only element that obstructed the administration's view of the state's cities. In the mid-eighteenth century, large parts of central Europe were still not thoroughly mapped, and within cities houses were not numbered and people's identity – at least in large cities – very hard to ascertain.[104] When it came to important questions such as who lived where in the city, what political institutions and legal privileges were unique to it, and even what the state of the city's gates and walls was, the state was almost blind.[105] Such administrative blindness was mirrored in the terminology the bureaucracy used: it sought super*vision* (*Aufsicht*) over the city where it sent its *inspecteurs* (from the Latin *spectare*, "to see," "to watch").

The gate officers helped cast at least some light into the shadowy administrative landscape the state was facing. In those cities it manned with its men, the state could oversee the movements of people around the country.

---

101 This process was never simple or always successful. See, for instance, the discussion on the emerging information gathering attempts in the French case in Jacob Soll, *The Information Master: Jean-Baptiste Colbert's Secret State Intelligence System* (Ann Arbor: University of Michigan Press, 2009).

102 For a general treatment of how states "see things," see James C. Scott, *Seeing Like a State: How Certain Schemes to Improve the Human Condition Have Failed* (New Haven: Yale University Press, 1998).

103 Walker, *German Home Towns*, 173.

104 On this issue, see Anton Tantner, *Ordnung der Häuser, Beschreibung der Seelen. Hausnummerierung und Seelenkonskription in der Habsburgermonarchie* (Wien: Studienverlag, 2007).

105 An example from Prussia is "Bau von Torwachten in den Städten Osterburg, Werben, Seehausen, Arendsee, Arneburg," Br. LHA Potsdam, Rep. 2 S Nr. 11. One finds a similar situation in Bavaria even after the Napoleonic Wars in "Festungen, Band 1: 1825–44," Bayer. HStA KA, CI. 9 g 1.

It was able to catch deserters from the army, check the emigration from specific regions, and – as was especially evident in Prussia – even had some of the gate's revenues flow into its own coffers rather than to the city's.[106] Controlling the entrances to all of its cities at once also meant that the state could put in place general policies regarding its entire population. It was one thing to chase gypsies, beggars, and the insane across the countryside; it was quite another to order all cities to arrest them upon approaching their gates.[107] A similar procedure was sometimes adopted toward emigration. At a time when population was viewed by cameralists as one of the greatest assets of a state – it facilitated conscription and maximized tax revenues – emigration was a pressing problem, and the walls helped the state to check it. Thus, different states (and not only Prussia) ordered gate officers across the country to stop emigrants by refusing to accept their passports and even to arrest them and send them to workhouses. Such orders often involved very brutal practices and were most commonly enforced when travel across the country was easier after the spring thaw. In Bavaria, for instance, local authorities were repeatedly instructed to brand vagabonds with a special mark – like cattle – to facilitate their identification in the future.[108]

Journeying from the borders of the Hohenzollern territories into the hinterland, eighteenth-century travelers could witness the effects of these cameralist considerations. City walls in these regions were not fit to oppose a military attack, and whether because of their deliberate demolition or simple neglect, no one would compare their state to that of the great fortress towns that defended Prussia's borders. At the same time, provincial city walls in Prussia were still very much present in the eighteenth century and were maintained by the state to facilitate the bureaucratic and police functions it considered essential to its security. No wonder that Justi – perhaps the greatest cameralist of the eighteenth century – thought that, while only a few cities need to function as fortresses, all cities should be surrounded by walls.[109]

The clearest effects of these considerations could be seen in the metropolis. Contrary to the common belief that views the "disappearance" of city walls as the natural result of urban expansion, in the course of the eighteenth century rapidly expanding cities more often kept their walls than demolished them. Indeed, the police and economic functions of the walls

---

106 The situation in Prussia was especially grim from the burghers' perspective, as tax officials often literally governed these cities. Sheehan, *German History*, 59.
107 "Koenigl. Preussische Accise Reglement," StA Breslau, Akten der Stadt Breslau, (1747) 12.286.
108 Orders of July 31, 1757; July 14, 1762; and May 2, 1777, StdA München, Bürgermeister und Rat, Nr. 61/1.
109 Justi, *Staatswirtschaft*, 1:491.

in cities like Vienna, Berlin, or Munich were now more important than ever. They guaranteed at least some supervision over the growing flux of people into those cities, preserved the army's ability to isolate them in case of an insurrection, and helped tax persons and commodities entering or leaving the city. Large German cities therefore usually kept their walls in one form or another. In the west, Düsseldorf's fortifications were expanded to include the new suburbs in the 1770s; in Vienna, the inner city remained fortified while the outer suburbs were surrounded by a second wall (the so-called *Linienwall*, 1710); and in Berlin, which demolished its military fortifications in the mid-1730s, the city remained a closed place.[110] While the actual defense of the conglomerate of cities, suburbs, and villages Berlin now united was deemed to be both impossible and unnecessary, the entire city was surrounded by a strong customs wall, over eight and a half miles long and almost twenty feet high. In smaller Prussian cities the case was often similar, although on a much smaller scale.

As in the fortress towns, the continued existence of these city walls was accompanied by a marked decrease in their symbolic value to the community. It was now not the city's personnel who taxed travelers and defended the city; it was the state officers, dressed in a similar fashion in all cities and everywhere following the same tax and police regulations. Most importantly, the city walls often ceased to belong to the city: they were now officially state property.[111] There is no better indication for the changing relationship between burghers and their city walls than the growing number of reports about burghers trying to steal building materials from them. Such reports can be found in Prussian cities such as Breslau and Berlin, in small Bavarian towns such as Forchheim, and even in Hamburg.[112] In former times, such an act was not only dishonorable but also senseless, amounting to little more than stealing from oneself. In the context of the changing habitat of many German cities in the eighteenth century, with the growing presence of the state and the transfer of property rights over the walls into the state's hands, stealing building materials from the walls started to make

---

110 On Vienna's Linienwall, see Walfgang Mayer, *Der Linienwall: Von der Befestigungsanlage zum Gürtel* (Wien: Wiener Stadt- und Landesarchiv, 1986); on Berlin's customs walls, see Helmut Zschocke, *Die Berliner Akzismauer: Die vorletzte Mauer der Stadt* (Berlin: Story Verlag, 2007).
111 The issue of possession of the walls will be highly important once a decision is made to demolish them. As, for instance, in the case of Breslau: GStA PK, HA I, Rep. 77 (Ministerium des Innern, Militärabteilung Sekt. 1, 2) 263, Nr. 1.
112 "Die Diebstähle an den Königl. Festungswerken, Gebäuden und Materialen. 1812," Geh. StA PK Berlin, HA I, Rep. 77 (Ministerium des Innern, Militärabteilung Sekt. 1, 2) 330a, Nr. 14; "Forchheim: Tore, Wacht- und Torhäuser," Bayer. HStA KA, MKr 8046; "Varia von Diebereyen so an dem Wall und den Festungswerkend verübt sind," StA Hamburg, 111–1, Cl. VII, Lit. Cc Nr. 1 Vol. 4g 5.

sense. The walls ceased to be the city walls; they belonged to, and they primarily served, the state and its organs. Consequently, even when the city walls were not demolished – indeed, even when the walls were repaired and strengthened – their symbolic value was now fast diminishing. They used to stand for the city's independence, liberties, legal independence, and ability to defend itself. By the end of the eighteenth century, especially Prussian city walls lost many of these characteristics. In the fortress towns, they now announced the might of the monarch, not the city; became symbols of the city's subjugation to, rather than membership in, the state; indicated the constant danger of a state of siege and suppression of city law; and demonstrated how the old idea of the city in arms was little more than a fantasy in the new world of sovereign states, standing armies, and growing, centralized bureaucracies.

THE THIRD GERMANY

The geopolitical environment of the German city, the habitat in which walls had made sense, was thus subverted by emerging, strong territorial states. First in the west (France), then in the northeast (Prussia), the physical and symbolic aspects of the walls were undermined. The same was sometimes true in other parts of the country such as present-day Belgium, which in the late eighteenth century was still part of the Holy Roman Empire. Here, Joseph II – the Habsburg ruler of these territories – demolished the fortifications of many cities including Veurne, Ypres, Menen, Tournai, Mons, Charleroi, the citadel of Ghent, and Namur.[113] A traveler to this latter city in 1794 described how the area "was dismantled of a great part of [Namur's] fortifications." As in similar towns in the Low Countries, he added, "the feelings of the [local] people were so little consulted, that the walks and trees of the ramparts were at the same time insultingly injured and almost destroyed by the injudicious agents of the emperor." The purpose here as elsewhere was "to deprive the people of places of defense, when they remonstrated against grievances."[114]

All the developments described in this chapter were undoubtedly important. It was especially in the west and in the north, in areas under direct control or indirect influence of strong territorial states, that the origins of the movement to defortify cities can be found. But during the eighteenth century, most parts of the Empire were still only marginally affected by

---

113 Derek Beales, *Joseph II: Against the World* (Cambridge: Cambridge University Press, 2009), 373–74.
114 Robert Gray, *Letters During the Course of a Tour Through Germany, Switzerland, and Italy* (London, 1794), 467.

such states and the most urbanized parts of the Holy Roman Empire, the individualized country, were spared any significant defortification waves.

Late eighteenth-century travelers, coming from the west or the north, looked at these old urban communities with fresh insights. Some simply raised the question why cities in these regions could not be more like Paris and other French cities.[115] Christoph Friedrich Nicolai, visiting Southern Germany from Berlin in the late eighteenth century, found the continued existence of the ancient walls of cities like Nuremberg perplexing and illogical. They were "signs of the arbitrary attachment to old customs," he wrote, and sometimes "simply misanthropic."[116] One traveler to Coburg (Thuringia) in the mid-1780s went even further, claiming that the practices of protection in that city were ridiculous and outrageous. He argued that, with its walls and gate watchers, Coburg resembled Cairo, Baghdad, or Turkish towns much more than it resembled Paris or Berlin. He ridiculed what he viewed as the burghers' infantile perception of their walled city as a "paradise," defended by "seraphim" (gate watchers). Nothing could be further from the truth, he implied.[117]

Yet despite the verbal attacks against their ancient practices, most German cities – still unaffected by the practices of strong territorial states – continued to maintain their ancient walls. These continued to possess all the practical and symbolic aspects associated with the Holy Roman Empire, its defensive political culture, ceremonial practices, and symbols of communal honor. Faced by the allegation of travelers from other parts of Germany, burghers could only reply that the city walls made sense to them and that this, after all, was all that mattered.[118] Karl Theodor von Dalberg, the future Elector of Mainz, wrote in the 1790s that the Empire was perhaps similar "to an old gothic structure, which is not built according to all the rules of architecture." This building, however, he added, "gives one nonetheless a strong sense of security" and should therefore continue to exist.[119] A similar comment was sometimes made about the continued existence of city walls in these areas. They were perhaps not as effective as they had been in the past, but they still gave the burghers a sense of convivial comfort, *Gemütlichkeit.*

---

115 Johann Rautenstrauch, *Das neue Wien, eine Fabel* (Wien: Mößle, 1785), 33–35.
116 Christoph Friedrich Nicolai, *Beschreibung einer Reise durch Deutschland und die Schweiz im Jahre 1781,* (Stetting und Berlin: 1783), 1:200–01.
117 "Lästige Polizeianstalten vor Spaziergänger," *Kielisches Magazin* II (1784): 186–94.
118 A direct response to such allegations is "Berichtigung eines Aufsatzes im Kiel. Mag. II B. 2St. S. 186 die Thorpolicey in Coburg betreffend," *Journal von und für Deutschland* 10 (1785): 380–82.
119 Quoted in Heinz Duchhardt, "Dalbergs politische Publizistik," *Jahrbuch der Vereinigung 'Freunde der Universität Mainz'* 23/24 (1974/75): 59.

Even in the late eighteenth century, therefore, the walls remained crucial for the self-definition of the majority of urban communities in Germany. So much so, in fact, that when the Augsburg engraver Franz Xaver Habermann depicted North American cities such as Boston in the 1770s, he could not help imagining them as fortified settlements (they were not). To assume that cities could be defenseless anywhere – whether abroad or in Germany itself – seemed inconceivable both to Habermann and to his audience.[120] Even more cosmopolitan people than Habermann would often still defend the logic behind the maintenance of walls in so many German cities. As late as the mid-1790s, one English traveler to Cologne – despite the fact that he had been treated coarsely by the local gate watcher – still thought that the police measures the watcher implemented made sense. "Most of you, sons of liberty, I well know, revolt at these precautions, deeming them injurious to personal freedom," he wrote, addressing his British compatriots. "But surely an honest man cannot feel it a great hardship to be obliged to tell who he is, whence he cometh, and whither he goeth?"[121]

All this was soon to change in a dramatic way. In 1789, a revolution broke out in France, followed by a series of wars, and the final demise of the Holy Roman Empire. It was in this context of military, political, economic, and cultural crises that a massive defortification wave swept through the German lands. As opposed to the developments of the eighteenth century, this new defortification wave was general in its scope and rapid in its progression. It affected all parts of the German lands, connecting German cities to one another – Rhenish towns, Prussian, Austrian, and Bavarian cities, and towns and cities located in the individualized country – in a way they had never been connected before.

---

120 Franz Xavier Habermann, "Prospect von Boston gegen der Bucht am Hafen," in *The Changing Face of Boston Over 350 Years* (Boston: Massachusetts Historical Society, 1980), plate 9.
121 Thomas Cogan, *The Rhine: Or, A Journey from Utrecht to Francfort* (London: Printed by G. Woodfall for J. Johnson, 1794), 1:250.

PART II

A Perfect Storm, 1789–1815

3

The Great Defortification Surge, 1791–1815

Magnitude and General Characteristics

Among the many revolutionary transformations that swept across Western and central Europe between 1789 and 1815, one has largely escaped the attention of historians: the transformation of the majority of German cities from fortified to defortified places. Before the late eighteenth century, a relatively small number of German city walls had been demolished, and waves of defortification advanced slowly and unevenly, affecting German regions at different times and in various ways. The situation changed dramatically during the wars fought with Revolutionary, and later Napoleonic, France. What began as a series of small defortification waves in the eighteenth century swelled by 1800 into a massive defortification surge that progressed rapidly from town to town and province to province, eventually reaching some of the most distant corners of the German lands.

The magnitude of the defortification surge was not the result of a single development but of the simultaneous, combined effect of military, political, and social forces. Had these forces operated sporadically or in isolated locations, as they had during most of the eighteenth century, they would have had the same limited result. But during the twenty-six years that followed the French Revolution, all three forces coalesced to form a "perfect storm" that was much more powerful than the individual forces that brought it about. At first, the storm's gathering clouds only intensified the trends characteristic of the entire eighteenth century. By the late 1790s, however, the tempest finally broke, and it quickly gained such ferocious momentum that in the following years it would shake the very foundations of the world in which city walls had made sense and destroy hundreds of urban fortifications lying in its path.

Between 1789 and 1815, Germans neither counted the number of defortifications in their country nor charted their locations or looked for information about the kind of cities whose walls were being demolished. One should be cautious when attempting to do so today. No reliable information can be found about the defortification of some German cities, and to assign a specific date to the defortification of others can be problematic; in many places, the demolition of the walls was a gradual process that took many years to complete. With these caveats in mind, however, general statistics of defortification cases between 1789 and 1815 are still valuable. They allow the historian to sketch a general map of the defortification surge's scope, progress, and characteristics. And they both undermine some common explanations for the so-called disappearance of city walls in Germany and point out some likely causes for the surge's immense force and magnitude.

A QUESTION OF NUMBERS

The number of defortifications in Germany between 1789 and 1815 is staggering.[1] Prior to 1789, approximately only one of every five German cities had made substantial alterations to its fortifications, such as filling moats, demolishing central gates, and destroying long wall sections. By 1815, hundreds of additional cities had demolished their walls. Defortified cities, once a small minority in Germany, had become a clear majority.

A close examination of the defortification dates of German cities between the late seventeenth century and the late nineteenth century is quite revealing. In the late seventeenth century, there were approximately 1,500 cities with a population of over 1,000 inhabitants within the boundaries of the Holy Roman Empire. Of these, over 300 were not fortified (usually because of an advantageous topographical situation that made fortifications unnecessary), around 90 were very well fortified (strong fortress towns), and another 90 were reasonably well fortified. The rest, just shy of 1,000 cities, were surrounded by a complete enceinte (medieval city walls) but lacked modern fortifications (figures 9–10).

Most of Germany's fortified cities were concentrated in the individualized country (compare Figure 2, Chapter One). Within the boundaries

---

1 The most important source for the defortification statistics in this book is the multivolume encyclopedia of German cities, the *Deutsches Städtebuch* (DSB); and its Austrian equivalent, the *Österreichisches Städtebuch* (ÖSB): Erich Keyser and Heinz Stoob, eds. *Deutsches Städtebuch, Handbuch städtischer Geschichte*, 5 vols. (Stuttgart: Kohlhammer, 1939–); and Alfred Hoffmann, ed., *Österreichisches Städtebuch*, 7 vols. (Wien: Verlag der Österreichischen Akademie der Wissenschaften, 1968–). The DSB and the ÖSB contain entries on the architectural history of all cities currently in the German Federal Republic and parts of Austria as well as those cities located in the former German provinces of Silesia, Pomerania, and East Prussia. When the information in the DSB and ÖSB was insufficient, other secondary literature was consulted as well as sources from central state archives.

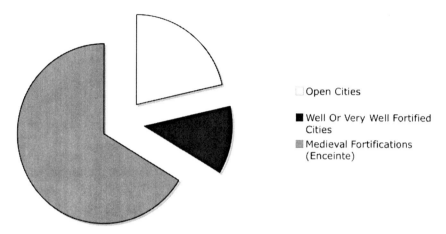

Open Cities

■ Well Or Very Well Fortified Cities

▨ Medieval Fortifications (Enceinte)

Figure 9. German cities by fortification types, ca. 1700.

of present-day Thuringia (6,200 sq. mi.), there were about eighty fortified cities in 1700, compared to only twelve within the boundaries of present-day Upper Austria (4,600 sq. mi.). Within the boundaries of present-day Saxony-Anhalt and Baden-Württemberg (combined area of about

Figure 10. Ysni (Swabia) in the seventeenth century. Ysni is an example of a home town surrounded by a simple enceinte. *Source*: Martin Zeiller, *Topographia Sveviae* (1660). Rare Books Division, Department of Rare Books and Special Collection, Princeton University Library.

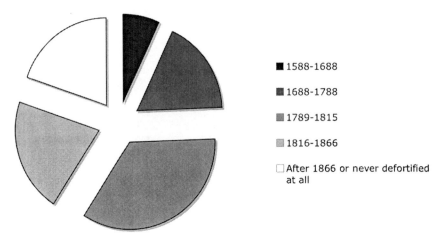

1588-1688

1688-1788

1789-1815

1816-1866

After 1866 or never defortified at all

Figure 11. Defortification cases by period.

22,000 sq. mi.), there were over 300 fortified cities in 1700 but within the boundaries of present-day Brandenburg, Berlin, and Mecklenburg-Vorpommern (combined area of 20,000 sq. mi.), there were fewer than 100. Indeed, of the approximately 1,200 fortified cities with a population of over 1,000 inhabitants in eighteenth-century Germany, over 900 were located in the individualized country, the belt stretching from Saxony in the east to the Palatinate and Baden in the southwest. Only one in every five fortified German cities was located within either the centralized country in the north (which was a Prussian sphere of influence) or in the south (which straddled the Austrian and Bavarian spheres). Thus, while in parts of the northern plains a traveler leaving a fortified city sometimes had to walk for over twenty miles before seeing another city's walls, in the individualized country, and especially in the southwest, the average distance between any two fortified cities was less than four miles.

The quality of information about the defortification of different cities is not always consistent. There are approximately 200 defortification cases for which no information can be found, and in about 100 more cases information is too scant to be useful. For the huge majority of fortified German cities, however – close to 900 out of about 1,200 cases – we possess either excellent information or just enough data to help paint a general picture of when and where defortification took place from the late seventeenth century onward (figure 11). All this information points to the importance of the defortification surge that took place around the year 1800.

Before 1688, defortification was a rare occurrence in the German lands. There are only sixty recorded cases of German cities that had defortified before then, mainly during the Thirty Years' War. Apart from rare cases, these cities repaired their walls after the war was over. In the century between 1688 and 1789, defortification of cities became both more common and more permanent. At least 150 defortification cases are on record for this period (a rise of more than 200 percent compared to the period 1588–1688). Many of these defortified cities never rebuilt their walls.

The period 1789–1815 saw an immense increase in defortification. During the twenty-six years that followed the French Revolution, approximately 350 city-wall demolitions occurred, an increase from an average of little less than 2 defortifications a year for the period 1688–1788 to over 13 a year for the period 1789–1815. Finally, between 1816 and 1866, 180 cities were defortified, an average of 3.5 defortification cases a year – more than in the eighteenth century, but substantially less than during the surge of the Revolutionary and Napoleonic Wars. All remaining walled German cities were either defortified after 1866 or kept their walls intact into the twentieth century.

The importance of the surge around 1800 is consequently twofold. First, it is the period with the highest spike in defortification cases. Neither before 1789 nor after 1815 were German cities defortified at such an accelerated rate. Second, during the Revolutionary and Napoleonic Wars, a major shift occurred from a situation in which close to 80 percent of all fortified German cities had kept their fortifications in one way or another (ca. 1788) to one in which most – over 60 percent – were defortified (ca. 1816). If one includes in these figures those cities that had not been fortified to begin with, the percentage of unfortified cities in 1816 rises to almost 70 percent of all urban centers in the German lands.

The difference between the defortifications of 1789–1815 and those of the preceding century is not only quantitative; it is also geographical. The defortifications of 1689–1789 (figures 12 and 13) tended to cluster along the French border in the west (in Baden, the Palatinate, the Rhineland, and Westphalia) and in the northern plains (Brandenburg-Prussia and Lower Saxony). The defortification surge of 1789–1815 was different (figure 14); it affected the west, but it also penetrated deep into the German heartland, the historic habitat of most fortified German cities. As opposed to the defortification patterns of the previous century, defortification during the Revolutionary and Napoleonic Wars eludes – at least at first glance – any general geopolitical characterizations: it affected cities in the north, south, east, and west, and in both the centralized and individualized countries.

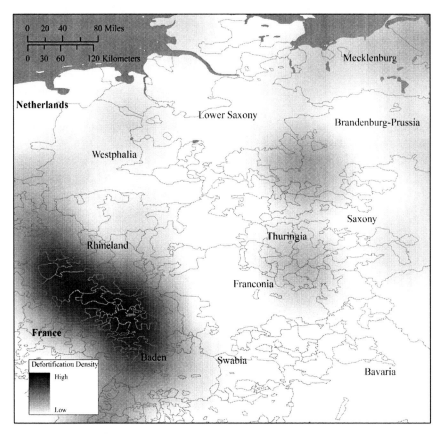

Figure 12. Defortification density in Germany, 1689–1715. During the last years of Louis XIV's reign in France, defortification in Germany took place primarily in the west, along the French border.

What is true in terms of the location of defortified cities between 1789 and 1815 is also true in terms of the size of their populace or a given city's expansion rate: defortification between 1789 and 1815 affected cities regardless of how they fit into such categories. Of the four dozen German cities with more than 10,000 inhabitants in 1800, 8 had already been defortified before 1789 (table 1). Between 1789 and 1815, twenty more large cities lost their walls (table 2):

Medium-size cities (with populations between 3,000 and 10,000 inhabitants) were affected as well. In the century before 1789, only one in every five medium-size cities in Germany was defortified. Fifty such cities

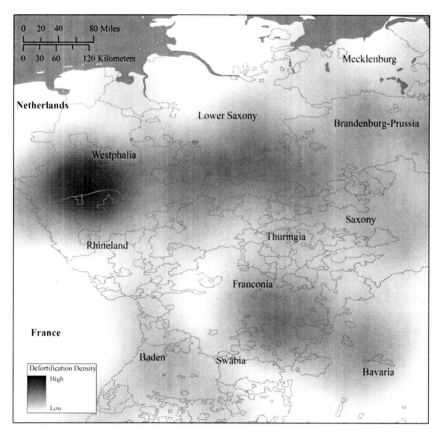

Figure 13. Defortification density in Germany, 1715–1789. In the course of the eighteenth century, defortification started affecting Northern Germany, especially Prussia itself and its sphere of influence.

demolished their walls before 1789 – mostly in the west – out of slightly fewer than 250 cities of similar size. Between 1789 and 1815, this number swelled to 120, close to half of all medium-size German cities. Twenty-five examples from across Germany demonstrate the scope of the defortification wave throughout these cities (table 3).

Even small towns (those with populations of 3,000 inhabitants or less) were defortified in great numbers during the wars. The data here are less complete than for larger cities because the defortification of German home towns usually progressed along different lines from those of larger cities. However, even a very partial list of defortifications in small German towns

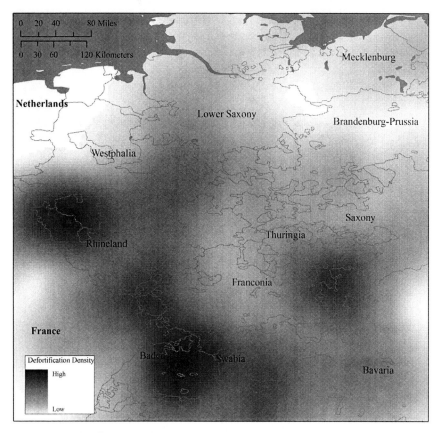

Figure 14. Defortification density in Germany, 1789–1815. During the defortification surge of 1789–1815, defortification affected almost all German regions.

during the Revolutionary and Napoleonic Wars shows the great number and wide geographical scope of this wave in the German home towns (table 4).

Beyond the sheer number and broad geographical scope of the defortification surge, the data highlight the great diversity of the cities affected by it. Defortification in the eighteenth century tended to take place in specific regions (e.g., the Palatinate) or affect a specific type of city (residences). Cities affected by the defortification surge during the Revolutionary and Napoleonic Wars escaped such specific categories, as all possible types of cities were defortified in great numbers around 1800. This included large cities, such as Hamburg; small cities, such as Nordenburg; independent cities, such as Bremen and Frankfurt am Main; cities belonging to

Table 1. *Defortification of Major German Cities During the Eighteenth Century (by population size)*

City	Year Defortification Started	Population (1800)
Berlin	1734	172,000
Leipzig	1763	33,000
Kassel	1764	18,000
Elbing	1772	16,000
Hanover	1763	15,000
Münster	1764	15,000
Halberstadt	1752	11,500
Bayreuth	1750	10,000

strong territorial states, such as Breslau or Landshut; residences, such as Munich; and fortress towns, such as Phillipsburg or Ulm.

What, then, incited this tremendous impulse to defortify cities? Why did defortification penetrate so deeply into the German hinterland and affect so many types of cities by 1800? Who supported the demolition of the old

Table 2. *Defortification of Major German Cities Between 1789 and 1815 (by population size)*

City	Year Defortification Started	Population (1800)
Hamburg	1804	130,000
Breslau	1807	65,000
Dresden	1809	61,000
Munich	1791	50,000
Frankfurt a/M	1804	40,000
Bremen	1802	35,000
Braunschweig	1802	28,000
Aachen	1793	24,000
Stuttgart	1806	22,000
Lübeck	1804	21,000
Düsseldorf	1801	20,000
Linz	1800	19,000
Mannheim	1799	18,000
Regensburg	1809	18,000
Würzburg	1804	16,000
Ulm	1800	13,000
Hanau	1806	12,000
Stralsund	1808	11,000
Chemnitz	1810	11,000
Flensburg	1792	10,000

Table 3: *Examples for Defortification of Middle-size German Cities Between 1789 and 1815 (by population size)*

City	Year Defortification Started	Population (1800)
Nordhausen	1800	8,400
Landshut	1800	7,500
Esslingen	1795	7,000
Bautzen	1796	6,000
Pirmasens	1790	6,000
Amberg	1796	6,000
Heilbronn	1804	5,600
Nördlingen	1808	5,600
Straubing	1810	5,400
Glückstadt	1814	5,200
Gießen	1805	4,500
Ingolstadt	1800	4,500
Pirna	1811	4,400
Zwickau	1798	4,200
Greiz	1802	4,000
Radevormwald	1802	4,000
Kirchheim /T	1811	3,900
Verden	1815	3,700
Freising	1803	3,500
Hameln	1808	3,500
Tuttlingen	1803	3,500
Oettingen	1813	3,500
Friedland	1800	3,400
Kulmbach	1793	3,300
Kempten	1803	3,200

city walls in this period, and for what reasons? The general data about the defortification surge cannot provide answers to all these questions. When examined closely, however, they do point out the direction in which such answers could – and could not – be found.

TRADITIONAL EXPLANATIONS AND THEIR APPLICABILITY TO THE DEFORTIFICATION SURGE

The general statistics about defortification between 1789 and 1815 call into question two of the traditional explanations for the impetus to defortify cities: level of industrialization on the one hand and size and expansion on the other. The more problematic of these two explanations is that of industrialization. By 1816, over 60 percent of all German cities had already been defortified, at least two decades before the 1835 opening of the first

Table 4. *Examples for Defortification of Small-size German Towns Between 1789 and 1815 (by region)*

Region City	Year Defortification Began
Upper and Lower Austria	
Baden	1805
Braunau	1805
Poysdorf	1814
Baden	
Pfullendorf	1808
Phillipsburg	1800
Sinsheim	1812
Württemberg	
Aalen	1812
Bad Mergentheim	1795
Balingen	1809
Bopfingen	1803
Giengen an der Brenz	1810
Herrenberg	1807
Leonberg	1813
Marbach	1811
Schwaigern	1812
Sindelfingen	1801
Sulz	1794
Weinsberg	1805
Swabia (Bav.)	
Kaufbeuren	1805
Mindelheim	1806
Bavaria	
Aichach	1804
Erding	1801
Landsberg	1806
Osterhofen	1810
Pfaffenhofen a. d. Ilm	1807
Pfreimd	1800
Schwandorf	1800
Hessen	
Friedberg	1792
Hochheim am Main	1812
Wiesbaden	1803
Ziegenhain	1807

(continued)

Table 4 *(continued)*

Region City	Year Defortification Began
Franconia	
Hersbruck	1800
Königshofen i. Grabfeld	1803
Kronach	1804
Lichtenfels	1813
Spalt	1809
Staffelstein	1792
Weißenstadt	1810
Wunsiedel	1800
The Rhine Provinces	
Alzey	1808
Essen-Werden	1809
Oberlahnstein	1810
Ratingen	1807
Remscheid-Lennep	1815
Solingen	1807
Vallendar	1807
Lower Saxony and Westphalia	
Attendorn	1812
Lüdenscheid	1800
Neheim	1807
Northeim	1815
Rinteln	1806
Winterberg	1791
Saxony, Anhalt, and Thuringia	
Bischofswerda	1813
Dommitzsch	1814
Leutenberg	1800
Roßwein	1806
Waltershausen	1808
Brandenburg, Mecklenburg, and East Prussia	
Calau	1794
Nordenburg	1789
Seestadt Pillau	1796
Stavenhagen	1791

railway line in Germany and the industrialization of most parts of central Europe. Industrialization could not have caused the defortification of most German cities for the simple reason that it usually took place after the demolition of the walls had begun.

Population size and expansion rate are also problematic explanations for the changing boundaries between city and countryside in Germany in the late eighteenth and early nineteenth centuries. The defortification surge around 1800 affected a wide range of German cities. Some, like Munich (1791), Hamburg (1804), and Breslau (1807) were large, expanding cities with populations of 50,000–130,000 inhabitants. Many other defortifications took place in considerably smaller cities. The town of Rinteln (Lower Saxony, def. 1806) only had 2,000 inhabitants in 1800. Vallendar (Palatinate, 1807), Kronach (Upper Franconia, 1804), Erding (Upper Bavaria, 1801), and Sinsheim (Northern Baden, 1812) were of a similar size. Not only were these towns small, they were also not appreciably expanding around 1800.[2] Freising is the most extreme case in this respect: shortly before the city's defortification in 1803, its population actually dropped from 6,000 inhabitants to about 3,500.

Urban expansion as a general explanation for the defortification surge is problematic for another reason. While several rapidly expanding cities did demolish their fortifications around 1800, not all expanding cities did so. Vienna, the largest German metropolis, retained its walls until the second half of the nineteenth century, as did Cologne and Mainz. The most extreme example here is Berlin, which had already been defortified in the mid-1730s. In the next century and a half, Prussia's capital would expand more rapidly than any other urban center in central Europe, but instead of marking a final end to the city's closed character, expansion seems to have caused the opposite development. In the 1770s, Berlin was surrounded by new, eleven-mile-long customs walls, which remained intact until the 1860s. For all these reasons, urban expansion is at best only a partial explanation for the main defortification surge, although it might still prove important in some specific cases.[3]

If industrialization and expansion are both problematic categories in analyzing the main wave of defortifications in Germany, so, too, is the strength of a given city's fortifications. One of the three common historiographical claims about defortification argues that it was the military uselessness of urban fortifications that brought about their demolition. In view of the data about the defortification surge, this argument is by no means as problematic as the other two. After all, the great defortification surge took place during a

---

2 Vallendar grew from 2,000 inhabitants in 1767 to only 2,115 more than a century(!) later (1877). Erding grew from 1,700 (1796) to 1,803 (1812) and Sinsheim from 1,705 inhabitants in 1798 to 1,746 in 1809. Kronach's population even declined in this period, from 2,447 in 1790 to 2,369 in 1811. Source: DSB, IV.2:152–3; IV.3:441; V.1:312; V.2:176.

3 See also the discussion in Karl-Klaus Weber, "Stadt und Befestigung: Zur Frage der räumlichen Wachstumsbeschränkung durch bastionäre Befestigungen im 17. und 18. Jahrhundert," *Die alte Stadt* 22, no. 4 (1995): 301–21.

general war when new tactics were used and more modern weapons tested. This military argument, however, also raises some intriguing questions. If the military uselessness of the walls was the main reason for defortification, why not demolish the walls of the more weakly fortified cities first? With the gradual increase in firepower during the eighteenth century, weaker fortifications should have been found useless earlier and demolished before stronger ones. The data do not support this pattern: both strong and weak fortifications were demolished before 1815 (and, indeed, before 1789). Some such walls, like Mannheim and Phillipsburg's, were immensely impressive. Other fortifications, like Breslau, Ulm, and Frankfurt am Main's, were perhaps not first rate, but still strong. And many other fortifications were little more than simple enceintes of the Middle Ages. This was the case in Pfullendorf (Baden, 1808), Calau (Brandenburg, 1794), and Pillau (Mecklenburg, 1796), to name just a few examples. At least at first glance, the military usefulness of many cities' fortification systems does not appear to be a good metric for ascertaining the causes of the entire defortification surge.

The need to treat the argument about the city walls' supposed uselessness with caution also arises from a second trend in the general statistics: the fact that between 1789 and 1815, while hundreds of German city walls were demolished, others remained intact. At times, two neighboring city walls had very different fates. In the west, Mannheim lost its walls in 1799, but the walls of neighboring Mainz remained intact. In Franconia, the walls of Wunsiedel (1800) and Spalt (1809) were demolished, but those of Weißenburg were only partly affected. And in the east, the walls of Breslau were blown up in 1807, but those of other Silesian cities escaped the wars without a scratch. In fact, some urban fortifications, like Mainz, Cologne, and Ingolstadt's, were even strengthened during this period. What was the point of keeping, or even strengthening, any city walls if all of them were completely useless? Why spend the money and the manpower to construct and maintain a useless defense?

Part of the answer to these questions must be sought in the many non-military functions that city walls had served throughout the Middle Ages and the early modern period. Even if the walls proved useless in defending a town or a city, they were still important to the urban community in many other ways. To treat the demolition of city walls in purely military terms is therefore to fail to see what city walls meant to German burghers until about 1800, and how burghers and foreigners alike reacted to defortification on the ground. Stressing the supposed uselessness of urban fortifications around 1800 also causes one to overlook those groups of people who still perceived the walls to be valuable for military purposes, and who therefore helped keep at least some of them intact. Most importantly, overstressing the uselessness of fortifications around 1800 might cause one to miss that most fundamental (and paradoxical) fact about urban fortifications around 1800. Burghers did not simply perceive the walls to be useless at the time; in many cases, as we shall see, they now viewed the continuing existence of urban fortification as an imminent threat to their old way of life.

The experience of war in the two and a half decades following the French Revolution is undoubtedly fundamental to an analysis of the great defortification surge in Germany. It is far more important than either industrialization (which is largely irrelevant) or urban expansion (which is marginal, but could prove important in some cases). Even the experience of war, however, should be treated in a nuanced way. It would be a mistake to treat the defortification surge in absolute terms, as if – at one point in time – all types of urban fortifications ceased to serve any purpose. Far more useful is to pose a more complex set of questions: Exactly when and where were urban fortifications deemed useless or even dangerous in the years around 1800? By whom? Under what political and military circumstances? Two final trends in the data provide most important clues about the answers to these questions.

First, the surge in the demolition of German city walls was widespread around 1800, but it was not ubiquitous, at least not in Germany's territorial states. There we find a mixed picture: a dramatic surge of defortification cases that nonetheless did not affect all cities. By 1815, individual German states had substantially fewer fortified cities within their borders, but without exception, all of them still had at least some. Where defortification was ubiquitous during the Revolutionary and Napoleonic Wars was in Germany's remaining independent city-states. On the eve of the French Revolution, Germany still hosted several dozen Imperial free cities, but by the end of the Napoleonic Wars only four – Frankfurt am Main, Hamburg, Bremen, and Lübeck – remained so, and all four had been defortified. In the past, a city's ability to defend itself ("the city in arms") had been a crucial component of guaranteeing its liberties, but during the wars with France, the last remaining independent German cities lost their defensive systems and would never attempt to rebuild them in the same way again. This distinction between territorial state and independent city is fundamental to an understanding of the defortification surge around 1800. It draws one's attention to the fact that the defortification surge marked the end of a long process, which entailed the slow overtaking of the monopoly of using military force from independent cities by territorial states. The roots

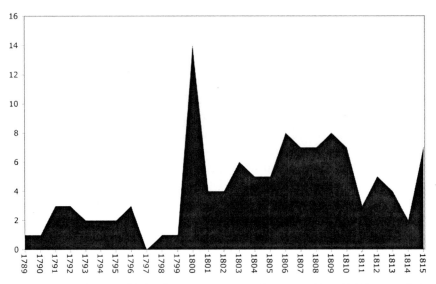

Figure 15. Distribution of defortifications in Germany by year, 1789–1815 (106 examples).

of this process can be found in the seventeenth and eighteenth centuries, but its climax and conclusion should be dated to the Revolutionary and Napoleonic Wars. City and territorial state, which in the past shared much in common, were now clearly moving along different trajectories: the one losing some of its ancient privileges; the other taking them on itself.

If the fundamental distinction between city and state shed light on the larger political context of the great defortification surge, so, too, does the issue of how the defortification surge unfolded within the timeframe of the Revolutionary and Napoleonic Wars (figure 15). Indeed, of all the trends in the data, this is the most arresting. Of the 106 cases represented in the tables above, only 17 cases (16 percent) occurred before 1799, while an overwhelming majority of 89 (84 percent) took place in the next 16 years. When one includes all known defortification cases between 1789 and 1815, the trend is only slightly less clear. Out of 250 well-documented defortification cases between 1789 and 1815, 198 took place between 1800 and 1815 (79 percent), compared to only 52 between 1789 and 1799 (21 percent). This is a difference between an average of 5 defortifications a year for the period 1789–1799 and an average of more than 12 for 1800–1815.

The distinction between the defortification cases before and after 1799 is geographical as well as quantitative. In the last decade of the eighteenth century, defortification cases continued to cluster in the same areas as in the eighteenth century: in the vicinity of the French border (Aachen, 1793;

Mannheim, 1799) and in a strong territorial state's hinterland (Munich, 1791; Nordenburg, 1789; Stavenhagen, 1791; Pillau, 1796). In the sixteen years after 1799, defortification spread to new regions such as Franconia, Thuringia, and Württemberg, regions which had been largely unaffected by previous defortification waves.

That such a dramatic surge in defortification cases began around 1799 should give one pause: it seems to take place "at the wrong time." On the one hand, the 1799 spike in defortification took place long enough after the outbreak of the French Revolution that no immediate connection can be drawn between the two. On the other hand, the spike happened long enough before some of the great battles between Napoleon, Austria, and Prussia (in Ulm, Austerlitz, and Jena-Auerstadt, 1805–1806) or the final dissolution of the Holy Roman Empire (1803–1806) to be directly connected with these developments. This is the point where an analysis of the data about defortification between 1789 and 1815 reaches its limits, the point where numbers are suggestive but provide no further help. The great defortification surge around 1800 was surely related to the experience of war more than to industrialization or expansion; it progressed in two distinct stages divided by the year 1799; it had something to do with the distinction between city-state and territorial state; and it affected most – although not all – of the walled cities and towns in the German lands.

The demolition of so many city walls after 1799 was much more than a purely statistical phenomenon. Defortification was sometimes traumatic, often highly dramatic, and almost always contested. Following the defortification of their towns and cities, German burghers had to redefine themselves and reimagine their communities. An understanding of the great defortification surge and the perfect storm that caused it must therefore go beyond statistics alone and closely examine defortification cases, underlining their human, rather than general or statistical, dimensions. The following two chapters will do just that: they will explore the defortification of several German cities both before and after the dividing line of 1799, turning from the desk of the weatherman – who follows the storm's progress from a comfortable distance – to the regions, cities, and people directly hit by its devastation.

4

The Road to Lunéville, 1791–1801

In the beginning of the defortification surge there was an intensification of older trends. Between 1791 and 1801, the motivation for the demolition of city walls in Germany stemmed from absolutist politics on the one hand and from a reaction to the slow changes in the art of war on the other. Such developments were not novel; they had shaped the outer appearance of some German cities ever since the late seventeenth century and of many French ones since the reign of Louis XIII. During the 1790s, however, these developments became more pronounced and consequently threw the entire controversy over defortification that had been building up until that point into sharp relief. The nature of the controversy, the kind of people who took part in it, and the arguments most commonly deployed in it can be seen most clearly in three places: the events behind the defortification of Munich (starting 1791); common reactions to the experience of war and occupation in parts of western Germany in the 1790s; and the defortification of Ehrenbreitstein (near Koblenz) in 1801.

Apart from exemplifying old trends, the developments of the 1790s are important for two additional reasons. Munich was the largest city to begin losing its walls in the 1790s, and Ehrenbreitstein, along with several other fortresses along the Rhine, was one of the strongest fortresses in Europe. A detailed examination of the defortification of these cities allows one to test the influence of urban expansion (Munich) and advances in military technology (Ehrenbreitstein and the Rhine fortresses) on the fate of city walls. What the previous chapter could only suggest through general defortification statistics is substantiated in the cases of these cities through a close reading of official documents and eyewitness accounts. Finally – and perhaps most importantly – because the events of 1791–1801 bridge the transition from the eighteenth century into the nineteenth, they help start to explain a fundamental fact about defortification in Germany: the demolition of urban fortifications – still limited up until the late 1790s – became ubiquitous by the time of the signing of the Peace Treaty of Lunéville between the Empire and France in 1801. The events of the decade after 1791 start to explain, in other words, why the years around 1800 represented such a watershed in the long history of walled towns and cities in the German lands.

MUNICH, 1791–1799: THE EFFECTS OF ABSOLUTIST IDEALS[1]

Ten years before the defortification of Munich began, a local professor, Lorenz von Westenrieder, described the city's gates and walls.[2] Munich, he explained to his readers, was surrounded by two lines of fortifications. The inner line was a typical medieval wall, with a covered path on top of it that stretched along the entire wall. Between the first and second (outer) fortification lines of the city, several *Zwinger* – outer wards or concentric castles – were located. Beyond the Zwinger was a large, deep moat filled with water that dated back to the time when Munich had been surrounded only by its medieval walls. Finally, beyond the medieval walls, the Zwinger, and the first moat were Munich's modern fortifications, the bastions and long stretches of low-profile walls, and past them yet another moat. Nine massive gates led into the city: the Neuhauser, Herzogenstadt, Schwabinger, Neuveß, Wurzer, Isar, Schiffer, Anger, and Sendlinger. Quite a few documents from the second half of the eighteenth century pointed out that Munich's fortifications were not properly maintained.[3] Westenrieder paid little attention to that. He enjoyed the general view of the city, its canals, and fortifications, and he especially recommended to his readers "the cool, fresh, and healthy air" of Bavaria's capital.[4]

There is little reason to doubt that most Müncheners shared Westenrieder's positive evaluation of their city's walls, at least before 1799. But Munich's fortifications, together with the traditions and privileges they represented to the burghers, had also powerful enemies. Indeed, around the time that Westenrieder described Munich, the city gates welcomed two horse-drawn carriages carrying the men who would instigate the city's

1 Munich's case, together with Vienna's, is the best-documented defortification story available today. See Peter Grobe, *Die Entfestigung Münchens* (München: München Stadtarchiv, 1970), and Hans Lehmbruch, *Ein neues München: Stadtplanung und Stadtentwicklung um 1800* (Buchendorf: Buchendorfer Verlag, 1987). Lehmbruch published many of the documents relating to Munich's defortification, including the magnificent collection in "Demolierung der Festugswerke," Bayer. HStA München, Gl. Fasz. 2756/Nr. 973.
2 Lorenz Westenrieder, *In München Anno 1782* (München: Süddeutscher Verlag, 1970), 14–16.
3 Bayer. HStA KA, C 132, 137.   4 Westenrieder, *In München Anno 1782*, 15.

defortification. The first came in 1778, transporting the new Bavarian Elector, Karl Theodor, from his lands in the Palatinate. The second arrived seven years later, carrying Sir Benjamin Thompson (later Count Rumford) to Karl Theodor's residence city on the Isar, where he would serve as the elector's close advisor in the following years.

The confrontation between the representatives of the Munich citizenry and some state officials on the one hand, and Karl Theodor and Rumford on the other hand focused on the question of defortification from April 1791 onward. On April 6, "a large number" of citizens assembled at the house of Johann Anton Miller – a member of Munich's city council – and demanded explanations from Karl Theodor about the demolition of the Neuhausertor, one of Munich's city gates.[5] What, they asked, was the overall purpose of the work on and around this gate? Repairing, strengthening, or changing single gates was of course nothing new, and therefore no cause for alarm, as early modern fortifications were constantly under repair. The work on the Neuhauser Gate, however, seemed to Miller and his fellow city representatives to be more than just the repairs on a single city gate. Miller summed up the group's concerns later that day in a letter to the elector: "The [work] entails the razing of all the wall sections next to the gate."[6] What was afoot?

Rumors were spreading, Miller reported to the elector, "that other parts of the walls surrounding the city will be eventually demolished." Was this rumor true? "If this happens," Miller warned, "then in a case of a war (heavens forbid!) the safety of the prince himself will be threatened. A prince, whose residence, treasury, and archives are in the city, as are the state archives and registrars, and the houses and property of the nobility and the citizenry." Surely, the elector would want to avoid such destruction. If a war does come about, "or even if any small army or brigade approaches the city, all these [unprotected properties] will have to face the utmost dire prospects, such as the one the city of Bamberg faced during the seven-year long Prussian war by General Mayer, and the city of Berlin by Generals Haddik and Lacy."[7] What, then, were the elector's intentions? What was the true purpose of the work on and around the Neuhauser Gate?

The group assembled at Johann Anton Miller's house in early April 1791 had many reasons to be worried, and the issue of the work around the

---

5 "Protocoll, so gehalten den 6ten April 1791," Bayer. HStA, GL 2756/973.
6 Lehmbruch, *Ein neues München*, 410–11.
7 "Eingabe der Repräsantanten der Münchner Bürgerschaft an den Kurfürsten, 6. April 1791," quoted in Lehmbruch, *Ein neues München*, 410–11.

Neuhauser Gate was only one of them. Throughout the previous fourteen years, Elector Karl Theodor remained an outsider and an unpopular ruler in his residence city, and his relationship with the local population remained tense.[8] Coming from the branch of the Wittelsbach family that ruled the Palatinate, Karl Theodor inherited the Bavarian lands in 1777, after the last member of the Bavarian Wittelsbachs died childless. Back in the Palatinate – where Karl Theodor had spent much of his childhood and adult life – he had been a popular, enlightened ruler: founder of the local academy of sciences, sponsor of Mannheim's famous theater, patron of the arts, and a political reformer. Implementing reforms in Munich turned out to be a very different story. From the very beginning, Karl Theodor disliked the city, while the Münchners disliked him and his "enlightened ideas." Felix Lipowsky, Karl Theodor's biographer and admirer, found the local reactions to Karl Theodor's "good deeds" to be shameless and especially "ungrateful."[9] From the perspective of the burghers, the situation looked different. In one complaint letter sent to the elector in 1786, Munich's magistrates claimed that Karl Theodor's reforms emptied the state's coffers, caused inflation, threatened corporative (including guilds') independence, and overfilled the local (princely) administration with unqualified foreigners.[10]

One of the foreigners the magistrates were complaining about was Rumford, who had come to Munich in 1785 at the invitation of the elector.[11] A Massachusetts native, Rumford had fled North America after siding with the British during the American Revolution, and moved in the late 1770s to London, where he was warmly received and even knighted and where he began a series of experiments on heat and gunpowder that would earn him fame as a scientist. In 1785, he accepted Karl Theodor's invitation, moved to the Bavarian capital, and started to overhaul the state according to his understanding of enlightened political philosophy: herding the throngs of the poor that crowded Munich's streets and public places into newly created workhouses; reorganizing the Bavarian army to ensure that soldiers were better fed and treated more humanely by their officers; taking care of

---

8 About Karl Theodor, see Felix Joseph Lipowsky, *Karl Theodor, Churfürst von Pfalz-Bayern* (Sulzbach: Seidel, 1828); about his government, see Caroline Gigl, *Die Zentralbehörden Kurfürst Karl Theodors in München 1778–1799* (München: Beck, 1999); and about Bavaria's history during Karl Theodor's reign more generally, see Andreas Kraus, *Geschichte Bayerns: Von den Anfängen bis zur Gegenwart* (München: Beck, 2004), 341–69.

9 Lipowsky, *Karl Theodor*, 175.   10 Ibid., 175–79.

11 On Thompson, see W.J. Sparrow, *Count Rumford of Woburg, Mass.* (New York: Thomas Y. Crowell, 1965); and Sanborn C. Brown, *Benjamin Thompson, Count Rumford* (Cambridge, MA: MIT Press, 1979).

state finances and administration; improving the state highways; and even (re)introducing the potato to the local diet.[12]

Even before Rumford's arrival, the elector and the Bavarian estates and corporations had found themselves on a collision course. Within a year of Karl Theodor's arrival in Munich, he was already trying to leave the city by negotiating an exchange with Austria of his Bavarian lands for Habsburg territories in the Low Countries and along the Rhine. These negotiations not only proved unsuccessful but also led to the War of the Bavarian Succession in 1777–1778 and to tensions between the elector and the local population in Munich that would endure for the next twenty-one years. After Rumford's arrival in Munich, the situation deteriorated further. In 1788, three years before the work on the Neuhauser Gate began, Karl Theodor and Rumford already sought to demolish some of the economic boundaries between Munich and its surrounding areas. Aiming to fight high unemployment rates in some of Munich's suburbs – especially in Au and Haidhausen, just across the Isar – the elector released an edict allowing the inhabitants of Munich's suburbs to work in the city. The magistrates and guild members in Munich were outraged because the edict overruled their monopoly over manufacturing and the labor market in the city. On September 27, 1788, a deputation of the magistrates, headed by Munich mayor Ludwig von Reindle, had an audience at the elector's palace. The tension, distrust, and threatening atmosphere during the audience can be felt even from a distance of over two centuries. After a long speech, in which he listed the city's complaints against the elector, Reindle assured Karl Theodor that "the city council guarantees that no one would hurt the elector."[13] What he wanted Karl Theodor to understand, of course, was that some people did want to physically harm their prince if he, the elector, did not put a stop to his reformist agenda.

Following this implicit threat from Reindle and the rest of the deputation members, Karl Theodor left Bavaria and moved back to the Palatinate for a year, fearing for his personal safety. He returned to Munich a year later, but once again had to suffer insults from Munich city council members, who now used the events of the French Revolution to further threaten their elector and undermine his attempts to reform the state along enlightened lines. What happened in "other nations" (i.e., France), the city council declared in a brochure dated July 26, 1790, could also happen in Munich.[14]

---

12 Some of Thompson's works have been published in Benjamin Thompson, *Collected Works of Count Rumford*, ed. Sanborn C. Brown, 5 vols. (Cambridge, MA: Belknap, 1970).
13 Lipowsky, *Karl Theodor*, 186–87.
14 Richard Bauer, *Geschichte der Stadt München* (München: Beck, 1992), 255.

The city council understood little of the events in France: in Paris, the revolutionaries were at first busy demolishing boundaries – the Bastille and the customs walls of the 1780s – while the Munich magistrates were trying to keep economic, social, and physical boundaries intact. Be that as it may, the fact that Miller welcomed the other city representatives to his house and not to the city hall was directly related to the city council's earlier threats. Karl Theodor, fed up with such insults, disbanded the council shortly after the publication of the threatening brochure on grounds of lese majesty. This is why, apart from the complaints about the work on and around the Neuhauser Gate, Miller started his letter of April 6, 1791, by mentioning his "great pain" about "the emptying out of the role of the magistrates in this city" that the rule of Karl Theodor entailed.[15]

The elector and Rumford's reformist agenda affected Munich's fortifications even before April 1791. Upon his arrival in the city, Rumford was highly alarmed by the state of the local garrison. The soldiers were poorly clothed and fed, and they lacked any real attachment to the city or the state. He did his best to change all of this. He raised the soldiers' pay, improved their training, and even allowed them to plant gardens in the vicinity of the city walls in order to supplement their rations and instill in them a sense of attachment to their place of service. Within a few years, Munich's glacis was filled with these soldiers' gardens and, after 1787, with what would be Rumford's most important addition to Munich's cityscape: the English Garden. The English Garden was one of the largest urban parks in late eighteenth-century Europe. Originally built by Rumford for military drills, it turned very quickly into one of the city's most popular promenades and radically changed the appearance of the city's immediate surroundings to the north.[16]

By 1791, after all the political turmoil of the preceding fourteen years, Karl Theodor knew a thing or two about his subjects. Exactly when he made his decision to turn Munich into an open city is unknown. Initially, he did not publish a defortification edict, and his private conversations with Rumford were left undocumented, perhaps deliberately. The political context was crucial here: anticipating the local population's reaction to the transformation of their ancient cityscape, the elector refrained for four long years from releasing any official proclamation about the purpose, and indeed the very existence, of Munich's defortification.[17] This princely silence is

---

15 "Protocoll, so gehalten den 6ten April 1791," Bayer. HStA, GL 2756/973.
16 On the history of the English Garden in Munich, see Pankraz von Freyberg, *200 Jahre Englischer Garten München* (München: Knürr, 1989).
17 Rumford, as opposed to the elector, did speak about the defortification publicly. See Lehmbruch, *Ein neues München*, 17.

telling in and of itself: it was part of the elector's attempt to move forward with the defortification as quickly as possible before dealing with opposition from the burghers. Karl Theodor's aim, in short, was to have the burghers face a fait accompli.[18] This is what Miller and his colleagues realized in April 1791, which is why they were alarmed by the transformation of the Neuhauser Gate and immediately protested it.

Karl Theodor's concealment plan enjoyed only a limited success. The work itself could not, of course, have been kept a secret for long. Defortifications were highly visible processes, and once the workers had assembled and the Neuhauser Gate and its adjacent wall sections were reduced to rubble, the population was indeed alarmed. The level of emotion in the correspondence between the elector and the surprised and distressed city representatives shows that both sides knew from the start that the issues at hand went far beyond the mere transformation of one single city gate. Rather, they constituted a continuation of the ongoing contestation over the nature of the city and over the relationship between the prince, the city, and the Bavarian estates.

In their first letter to Karl Theodor, Miller and his colleagues contested the military logic of any attempt to defortify Munich. Soon enough, other groups in the city would share this concern and raise further objections to the demolition. Ten days after Miller sent his letter, on April 16, 1791, the estates of Lower and Upper Bavaria also inquired at the court about the reasons behind the work on the Neuhauser Gate. "We never pay much attention to rumors running around the population," the estates wrote to the elector, "and we are aware of the fact that Munich, because of its topographic position and the new developments in the art of war, is no longer a place that can be considered to be a strong military fortress." At the same time, the estates added, if the intention behind the work around the Neuhauser Gate was the complete defortification of Munich, one should pause to think about it. Even if Munich could no longer serve as a strong fortress town, "the walls [are] still crucial to any residence city because of their role as an ornament, as a sign of the city's honor, and as a guarantor for the security ... of the entire population at least against local attacks, vagabonds, bands of deserters, and any general commotions in the land."[19]

The estates did not stop at symbolic or even police-related arguments. For them, an important argument against defortification was also a jurisdictional one. In their letter of April 16, 1791, the estates reminded the elector that it was they, the estates, who had borne the great cost of the construction

18 Ibid.   19 Ibid., 411.

of Munich's modern fortifications back in 1612 (the same outer walls that Westenrieder described in 1782). It was therefore only just and proper that they would be consulted before any substantial changes were made to them.[20] Next to military and symbolic claims, such a jurisdictional argument was one of the oldest claims against state intervention in the question of urban fortifications. If the construction and maintenance of the walls were funded by local corporations, the decision to pull down or even only transform any part of them should be exclusively within their power.

It did not take long for Karl Theodor and Rumford to respond to such claims. The elector's passionate response to the burghers and estates' demands, dated May 9, 1791, mirrors the old hostility between the ruler and Bavaria's corporative bodies. In his response, the elector pursued a mixed strategy. He continued to conceal the nature of the work that he and Rumford were already executing around the Neuhauser Gate. "It must be clear," the elector dictated, "indeed, absolutely clear, to the representatives of the citizenry, that these rumors, these fairy tales [of the complete defortification of Munich] were hoaxes by agitators whose only motive was to inflame the city's citizens by spreading false information from ear to ear." The agitators' aim, he claimed, was not to stop the repair of a single city gate. Rather, "their only aim was to stop the good and useful steps of the sovereign of the people in order to supply his subjects with better food, to regularize trade, to denounce the best intentions of our government, and to obscure the best intentions under which we work for the well-being we strive to achieve for Bavaria and the Bavarians."[21]

The elector did not stop at that. He also rejected the political and legal issues raised by Munich and Bavaria's various representative bodies. It is simply a "baseless claim," he wrote, that the estates had contributed to the construction of the modern fortifications in 1612. At any rate, in the event of a military campaign, Munich's fortifications would only bring harm by attracting the enemy to the city, unnecessarily prolonging the war and widening the scope of its destruction.[22] With the city walls intact, he wrote, "an attack on the city would have far more horrible consequences and the citizens would suffer a more significant loss of property and a more devastating fire [than if the walls were gone]."[23] The arguments about the city's outer appearance and honor in the wake of defortification were also highly debatable. If what the citizens really wanted was to defend their property and protect the honor of their city, the best way to do so would

---

20 Ibid., 412.   21 Ibid.
22 Ibid., 412.   23 Ibid.

be not to maintain the walls but rather – paradoxically – to demolish them. Additionally, because of his "mild government" of Bavaria, Karl Theodor claimed he had no reason to fear an uprising and that therefore keeping Munich's walls intact was not an urgent priority for him.

Soon enough, Rumford joined the debate as well. In three articles he published (anonymously) in the local Munich newspaper *Der Baierische Landbot* between mid-April and mid-December 1791, he called for the reasonable discussion of the defortification issue. "Nothing saddens one more," begins the first of these articles, "than when the good intentions of a prince . . . are deliberately misrepresented." The burghers opposing the transformation of the Neuhauser Gate based their opinions on rumors and not on reason, the article concluded. Look around you, Rumford continued in another article a few months later, and decide for yourselves whether it makes sense to keep the fortifications of the city. The city walls "can serve only as an example for how *not* to defend a modern city." Use your faculty of reason, Rumford called on Munich's burghers, and do not be carried out by your emotions or traditions. One can almost hear Kant's call *sapere aude* in the text.[24]

The elector's letter and Rumford's articles were received by the estates and the city representatives with alarm. The elector completely disregarded the issue of the actual work, devoting his attention not to what had been taking place in and around the Neuhauser Gate but to "certain agitators" who wished to convince others that this demolition was but the first in a series. His evasion of the issue was itself cause for alarm. But Karl Theodor did not stop there. His answer was not as saturated with enlightened ideas about public good and the use of one's reason as were Rumford's articles. But still, in his letter to the estates, he alluded to "Bavaria" and the "Bavarians" rather than to Munich and its inhabitants. He did not even pay lip service to the city by claiming that the work was being done for Munich's sake rather than the state's. The language of the burghers and the elector were incompatible here: the Münchners and the Bavarian estates expected an answer addressed to the corporations (city and estates), while Karl Theodor spoke in a condescending manner and as "the sovereign of the people" rather than the head of the old corporative political order. He employed arguments founded on a political language that stemmed, as he himself did, from outside the city. In his world, there were rulers and subjects but no corporations (such as cities, guilds, or estates). Apart from a single gate, the

24 Ibid., 412–16.

walls of Munich were still physically standing in 1791; but discursively, in the elector's very language, these communal boundaries were already gone.

In the face of the opposition party, Karl Theodor and Rumford could continue the demolition of parts of Munich's fortifications in the years after 1791 only very slowly and without the financial assistance of any of the city or Bavaria's corporative bodies. Complicating things even further was the fact that even the elector's own military advisors, assembled at the Electoral War Council, objected to defortifying Munich as late as 1794 and even 1795.[25] "Munich was never a fortress of the first order," the council wrote to the elector in one typical letter, "but it has always been a place that could defend itself from small groups of soldiers or from bandits. The latter, especially, are known to cause the greatest damage during a conflict.... We kindly ask," the council concluded, "that in the future, as in the past, one will have to ask for a special permission to use the walls or the glacis for the construction of new buildings."[26]

The lines in the defortification controversy in Munich were now drawn, save one last group of individuals. On the one hand stood the corporative bodies in Munich and Bavaria and even the elector's own military advisors, who raised a series of objections against the defortification of Munich and managed to slow down the process considerably. On the other hand stood Karl Theodor and Rumford who, even six long years after the work had begun, managed to transform only the Neuhauser Gate (which was the elector's own private property and therefore easier to demolish), and begin work on only one other city gate of the remaining eight. The defortification of Munich was still very far from being complete. That the demolition work managed to proceed at all had to do with the support of one last group that joined the debate about the city's defortification. Paradoxically, this group – just like the opposition party – consisted of Munich burghers.

Dismantling any wall section – let alone the defortification of an entire city – undermined the traditional political and social order in the city. These had been the traditional grounds for opposing defortification before 1800. If a city like Munich lost its walls and became an open city, Karl Theodor would not have to publish a new edict about the right of suburban residents in Au and Haidhausen to work in the city, for instance, because they could do so at will. What was true for a corporation, however, was not necessarily true for all of its members. With the walls gone, the area of the former fortifications could be turned into real estate property, one could more easily access one's gardens just outside of the walls, and one wouldn't have

---

25 Ibid., 353–54.   26 Ibid.

to pay certain oppressive taxes (to the city and to the corporations) as in the past. As members of corporations, Munich burghers stood to lose a lot from defortification; as individuals, they could still profit from it.

Quite a few Münchners took advantage of the new circumstances after about 1793. They came from all walks of life: servants, carpenters, gardeners, butchers, merchants, actors, and even some court officials.[27] The defortification allowed all these people to make changes that had hardly been possible before: to build new houses, stalls, and sheds outside the walls; to add floors, rooms, and whole living sections to their houses; and to take down wall sections themselves. Many of them are known by name: the court actor Franz Xaver Heigle, who was granted a small section of the city walls for his personal abode; the Countess of Aretin, who – after a long struggle – managed to acquire a small wall section for her house; and Mr. Stuckbohr, Mrs. Perglas, and even Privy Councilor Huber, who all acquired new property in and beyond the old fortification lines.[28] The number of such persons should not be exaggerated, however. Because of the opposition of the Electoral War Council, acquiring parts of the walls or any area in the glacis was still a long, complicated, and expensive affair until 1797. All such requests were consequently documented, totaling less than twenty a year for the period 1791–1797. Furthermore, there is no indication that a shortage of housing in the city played a substantial role in the defortification debate of the early and mid-1790s and drove people to seek property outside the walls. Had that been the case, Karl Theodor, Rumford, and other supporters of the demolition of Munich's fortifications would have surely used such a state of affairs to advance their arguments.

Thus, despite Rumford and the elector's orders on the one hand, and the profit some individuals hoped to gain from Munich's defortification on the other, the demolition of Munich's massive fortifications progressed very slowly in the 1790s. The reasons were many. Munich's walls stretched for well over two miles, were surrounded by ditches, and had close to twenty ravelins and nine massive gates (several of them double gates). The demolition of all these structures could not have been accomplished in just a few years. Another impediment was legal. Karl's Gate (the new name given to the transformed Neuhauser Gate) was the elector's personal property, but other gates and wall sections were not. Before the demolition of such structures could start, the state had to find money to purchase them out of its own coffers (the estates would not pay for the defortification), and this

---

27 "Baugenehmigungen in Festungsbereich, 1794–8," Bayer. HSt A KA, C 1, Nr. 136–38.
28 Ibid.; also "Demolirung der Festungswerken," Bayer. HStA Gl 2751/911 and "Hofkriegsrat Akten," 2747/870.

process took time.[29] Finally, there were some important developments in the city's political habitat after the mid-1790s that caused even Karl Theodor and Rumford to reconsider their position.

When he responded to Miller's letter back in 1791, Karl Theodor claimed that because of his "mild government" of Bavaria, he had no reason to fear an uprising and that therefore keeping Munich's fortifications intact was not an urgent police priority. By 1796, however, with the War of the First Coalition against Revolutionary France (1792–1797) well underway, Karl Theodor feared once again for his personal safety and left the city. This time, the elector's flight was not due to threats by his own estates but rather to his fear that Bavaria would turn into a theater of operations for Austrian, and perhaps French, troops.[30] Left behind to prepare Munich for a possible involvement in the war, Rumford changed his mind about the defortification and used the walls to hold off some small formations of Austrian and French troops who had indeed appeared just beyond the Isar. In this engagement, the soldiers' gardens in the city's glacis were destroyed, and the city's gates were strengthened, bolted, and locked. Finally, in 1798, Rumford left his post indefinitely due to intrigues in the Bavarian court. A year later, Karl Theodor, who had in the meantime returned to Munich, died after suffering a stroke (the happy Munich citizenry celebrated the occasion for several days). The defortification of Munich, which had so heavily depended on the will of these two individuals, seemed to have reached an impasse, with the city and estates on the verge of a victory that would turn back the clock and return the city walls to their former glory.

As it turned out, Rumford's dismissal and the elector's death caused only a temporary pause in the defortification of Munich. In the first decade of the nineteenth century, the defortification efforts were actually accelerated, this time with the support of Munich's burghers. Already in 1803 one finds a description of the Karl's Gate as a positive "ornament" of the city, in complete opposition to the reactions to the new gate in the 1790s.[31] From that point, the other gates would also be demolished in rapid succession. The Witches' Tower was demolished in 1803, the Jungfernturm a year later, the Kaufinger Gate in 1807, and a long stretch of the medieval city walls (including large parts of the Schwabinger Gate) in 1808.[32]

29 Lehmbruch, *Ein Neues München*, 35–36.   30 Kraus, *Geschichte Bayerns*, 361–62.
31 Lorenz Hübner, *Beschreibung der kurbaierischen Haupt- und Residenzstadt München* (München, 1803), 1:242.
32 Helmuth Stahleder, *Erzwungener Glanz: Die Jahre 1706–1818* (München: Dolling und Galitz, 2005), 570.

The reason for the radical change in the burghers' opinion about the defortification is not as well documented as their original opposition; often, general consensus leaves a much shorter paper trail than discord does. What is clear, however, is that Münchners did not live in isolation and that they were very much aware of what was taking place in other parts of Germany during those years. Especially significant here was the misery of burghers in other fortified cities, who suffered the consequences of siege and occupation in the early years of the Revolutionary and Napoleonic Wars. Their misery, it seemed, was fast approaching Munich as well. "You proud Munich," one contemporary wrote in 1805, "the day of your last judgment is come when no brick is left on the other, when stones from your walls are toppled down and carried away, and the entire city is hidden behind the multitude of soldiers on the streets."[33] In view of such imminent destruction, the elector's earlier argument that fortified cities might suffer more during a war than defortified ones suddenly made sense and was embraced by the Münchners themselves.[34]

The two stages of the defortification of Munich are important for the general story of the defortification of German cities for two interrelated reasons: one political the other emotional. As the defortification statistics of 1789–1815 suggest, the events in Munich during the 1790s did not break from the general practices of the eighteenth century. In Munich, the debates were intense, and the opposition to, and support of, defortification were phrased in passionate terms. However, in Bavaria's capital in the 1790s the opposing parties were still the traditional ones: the prince and at least one of his advisors advocated the demolition of the walls while the local corporations opposed it. There is little here to suggest a marked watershed in the overall process of the defortification of cities in Germany.

The second important aspect of Munich's case is the arguments deployed by both sides in the debate between Karl Theodor and his estates in Munich and Bavaria. Munich's walls did not simply disappear following the city's expansion (a term used neither by the elector nor by the local population in the early stages of the controversy), nor were the walls viewed by all as militarily useless when the defortification began. The arguments used in the defortification debate were primarily of a political nature, a contestation of opposing jurisdictions (city, estates, prince), competing political cultures (enlightened absolutism versus corporative political culture), and contending military logics (the walls' military usefulness versus

33 Joseph Richter, *Original Eipeldauer Briefe* (Wien, 1805), 17.
34 Lehmbruch, *Ein neues München*, 22.

their harmfulness). Demographic growth and a need for new quarters out-side the city were not the main issue in the 1790s even in Munich, the largest city to be defortified during this decade. When they finally changed their minds, Münchners were in all probability less concerned with hous-ing and much more with the strategic situation of the country vis-à-vis Revolutionary, and later Napoleonic, France.

WAR AND FORTIFICATIONS IN THE WEST, 1791–1801

The actions of absolutist princes like Karl Theodor in Munich were the first cause for the collapse of German city walls between 1791 and 1815, although these actions were limited in scope and, in 1790s Munich, had only limited ramifications. The second and much more puissant cause was the military conflicts between German states and Revolutionary, and later Napoleonic, France.

The political situation between France and its neighbors to the east began to deteriorate after Louis XVI's failed attempt to flee Paris in June 1791. With a growing numbers of French aristocratic émigrés in Germany (especially in Mainz), and with the French royal family's safety in jeopardy (Marie Antoinette was Emperor Leopold II's sister), war seemed imminent. In April 1792, France took the initiative and declared war on Austria. A few weeks later, Prussia got involved, too, and in the following year, the Imperial Diet declared a general Imperial war against the French Republic. In the following several years, Germany's western provinces witnessed many military campaigns: French forays into Germany's western and southern provinces and counterattacks by, among others, Austrian, Prussian, and Hanoverian troops.[35]

Of all the many scourges brought about by war, the actual bombardment of his city was the burgher's worst nightmare. Living in a bombarded city had never been easy. In the early modern period, a bombardment usually came after many months or even years of siege and deprivation, and the usual practice of besieging armies was to allow soldiers to loot property, burn down houses, and even rape women after the walls had been breached.[36] Before the late eighteenth century, Thomas A. Brady has recently reminded

---

35 For the military situation in Germany's western provinces in the 1790s, see, most importantly, T.C.W. Blanning, *The French Revolution in Germany: Occupation and Resistance in the Rhineland, 1792–1802* (Oxford: Clarendon Press, 1983).

36 See, for instance, the series of engravings "Représentations des actions les plus considérables de siège d'une place," ca. 1730, HGM Wien.

us, "[t]o plunder a village was routine [but] to sack a great city was a soldier's dream."[37] Such practices allowed the underpaid, undernourished soldiers a way to direct their anger at someone other than their commanding officers who, on their part, used the promise of looting at the end of a successful siege to keep soldiers in line during the siege's long, harsh months. They also made clear to the burghers the possible consequences of resisting the besieging army, thus putting more pressure on them to open their city's gates and surrender without a fight.

By the late eighteenth century, the surrender of a city or a fortress no longer necessarily implied the brutalities of earlier times, but the devastation that contemporary sieges entailed was still substantial. During the Revolutionary and Napoleonic Wars, artillery officers often directed their shells less at the fortifications themselves than at the city's buildings, supply magazines, and churches located behind them. The rationale for these tactics was that creating a break in the strong fortifications was much more difficult than setting fire to the city itself, a practice that meant to make the life of the local garrison so unbearable that it had no choice but to surrender. This is why in many contemporary depictions of sieges the projectiles are seen flying over the walls rather than at them.

The bombardment of a city was an awe-inspiring scene, which civilian spectators frequently came to observe (from a safe distance). "We watched this terrible spectacle," wrote Goethe in his diary about the bombardment of Mainz by Prussian troops in the summer of 1793:

The night was absolutely clear and full of stars, the bombs seemed to vie with the heavenly lights, and there were moments when it was really impossible to distinguish between the two.... The ascending and descending of the incendiary bombs was something new to us; for though they threatened at first to reach the very firmament in a flat circular curve, they always reached a certain height and then fell again on a parabolic path, and soon the rising flames showed that they had reached their target.[38]

Jacob Walter, a foot soldier from Württemberg, felt the same way:

If anyone would or could be an onlooker at frightful explosions, he could get the finest view at a fortress attack, which is a more remarkable sight by far than a battle on a field.... The bombs and grenades crisscrossing in the air in such great numbers, all floating like balls of fire in the air and exploding or bursting in the

---

37 Thomas A. Brady Jr., *German Histories in the Age of Reformations, 1400–1650* (New York: Cambridge University Press, 2009), 388.
38 Johann Wolfgang von Goethe, *From My Life*, eds. Thomas P. Peine and Jeffrey L. Sammons (New York: Suhrkamp, 1987), 757.

air or on the ground with a small cannon report, the slow ascent of each shell, the fast descent, often also a collision of them in the air – all this is a sight of moving beauty.[39]

Although beautiful from a distance in the dark of night, the results of such bombardments were horrendous the following morning. Goethe, in Mainz, enumerated some of the buildings damaged by the attacks: the bombardment set ablaze Mainz's famous cathedral, adjacent burgher houses, the Jesuit church, the Benedictine monastery, the city hall, and other public buildings. One day, a cannonball made a direct hit on the ammunition factory in the city and the entire building exploded, causing shock waves that broke windows and toppled chimneys halfway across the city. In another instance, the mills on the Rhine were damaged beyond repair and the Dominican church went up in flames. "Was not such a sight," Goethe sighed, "a sign of the sad situation we were in, that in order to save ourselves and more or less recover our position, we had to resort to such means?"[40]

The destruction caused by the frequent military campaigns in the west and the direct bombardment of German cities had both physical and symbolic consequences. "It is unusual," wrote one contemporary, "to be able to walk away from all this destruction and to find a peaceful place, where one can simply sit down, calmly, under the shadow of a tree."[41] In a letter sent to the Imperial Diet in 1797, one local count in western Germany described the effects of the continuing war on the lands and villages closest to the border with France:

The location of this county on the main road between Frankfurt and Cologne, in the vicinity of the Rhine, not far from Koblenz and Neuwied . . . brought about a sad state of affairs. Ever since the coming of the Prussian troops to this area in 1792, we have witnessed seven – or, when one includes the very latest movements in the area – eight military campaigns, heavy contributions, as well as frequent looting, fire, and plagues. Villages were deprived of whole hordes of cattle, either when these were driven away by the enemy or killed by the recurrent plagues. In the course of the military actions, two of the most important villages here were completely burned to the ground, and whole districts had to deliver their harvests to the enemy. The situation is all the more difficult because Imperial troops are stationed in our vicinity, and what the inhabitants did not lose to the French armies

39 Jacob Walter, *The Diary of a Napoleonic Foot Soldier*, ed. Marc Raeff (New York: Doubleday, 1991), 16.
40 Goethe, *From my Life*, 758.
41 A. Klebe, "Beobachtungen eines Reisenden in den untern Rheingegenden," *National-Chronik der Teutschen*, February 3, 1802.

they had to deliver to the Imperial troops, whose provisioning partially depends on these supplies.[42]

No less important than the physical destruction in Germany's western provinces were the symbolic consequences of both the bombardment and the occupation of some of the country's most famous cities. First among those was Mainz, the city whose bombardment Goethe so beautifully described (and bemoaned) in 1793. The writer Johann Joseph von Görres, a native of the Rhine Valley, saw in the French annexation of this old Imperial city a symbol for the imminent collapse of the Empire itself. "On December 30, 1797," he famously wrote, "the day of the transfer of Mainz [to France], at three p.m., the Holy Roman Empire, at the ripe old age of nine hundred and fifty-five years, five months, and twenty-eight days, fully conscious and consoled with all the sacraments, died peacefully and piously as the result of a total paralysis and attendant apoplexy."[43] A few years later, in 1799, Johann Christian Ludwig Fresenius of Frankfurt am Main viewed the situation in a similar way. He compared the French occupation of Mainz and several other cities along the Rhine with the amputation of a limb from the body politic of the Empire.[44]

At first glance, Görres and Fresenius's descriptions of the close connection between the annexation of Imperial cities to France and the death of the Empire as a whole might seem hyperbolic. Why, after all, should the loss of a single city be an omen for the general decline of the Empire? The answer to this question is crucial to an understanding of what happened to German cities during the Revolutionary and Napoleonic Wars. The Empire, as we saw in a previous chapter, was figured in the contemporary imagination as a living organism, and the health or constitution of this body was dependent on the health of its organs, among them Imperial cities. To annex an Imperial city, and an important city like Mainz at that, was tantamount to a deadly attack on (à la Görres) or the amputation of (Fresenius) the Empire as a whole, much in the same way that an attack on the Empire as a whole was bound to affect its cities. Empire and city, body and organ: neither could survive without the other. The demise of single German cities and the general demise of the Holy Roman Empire were consequently bound together in contemporary descriptions of the wars and

42 Burggraf von Kirchberg, *Pro-Memoria von Seite des Burggrafen von Kirchberg des Landesherren der Grafschaft Sayn-Hachenburg an die Reichsversammlung* (1797). BSB, Munich.

43 Karl Otmar von Aretin, *Heiliges Römisches Reich 1776–1806* (Wiesbaden: F. Steiner, 1967), 1:349ff.; Sheehan, *German History*, 242.

44 Johann Christian Ludwig Fresenius, *Reichsfriede, Deutschland, Frankfurt: Neujahrgeschenk für deutsche Mitbürger* (Frankfurt am Main, 1799), 13–14.

their aftermath. This symbiotic connection between city and Empire would also affect contemporary descriptions of the demolition of city walls.

Generals, as the old saying goes, always prepare for the last war, and this was certainly true in the case of German staff officers and fortress commandants in the 1790s. Their first instinct was still to resort to eighteenth-century methods, which entailed both a strengthening of certain fortresses and the demolition of unnecessary ones along the lines of the "French model." German states and individual cities made such preparations almost everywhere throughout the 1790s. Frankfurt am Main hired a new general to command its garrison, enlisted more soldiers, inspected and ordered more ammunition for its guns, and rebuilt parts of its walls.[45] Other cities along the Rhine and in the vicinity of possible penetration routes from France into Germany did the same: Düsseldorf, Mannheim, Cologne, and Ehrenbreitstein (across the Rhine from Koblenz), to name just a few. Cases of strengthening a city's fortification are also reported far from the main theater of operations in the west; in Pillau, for example, and in Brieg on the Oder River.[46]

Travelers to cities located along the French-German border in the 1790s encountered a sudden fortification frenzy. On the French side of the border, massive attempts were made to repair and strengthen border fortifications. In Sedan, for instance, the local magistrates organized a special festival for the "Defense of the Fatherland." The festival (taking place, not coincidentally, at the same time as the old Corpus Christi festival, which used city walls as props or a stage for its processions) included the actual rebuilding of the fortifications by local patriots.[47]

On the other side of the border, in Germany, things were not much different. Goethe, a native of Frankfurt, described the territories along the Rhine in those years in *Hermann und Dorothea* (1798):

> How I welcomed, with joyous surprise, the floods of the Rhine stream,
> When from my travels I came once again to the shores of our river!
> Always it seemed to me grand, and uplifted my mind and my spirits;

---

45 "Akten aus dem Nachlasse des städtischen Kommandanten und Obersten Edlen von der Planitz betr. ihm gewordene militärische Aufträge in Sachen des reichsstädtischen Kontingentes, der Armierung der Festungswerke, der Beschaffung von Waffen und Munition u.a.," ISG Frankfurt am Main, Revolutions- und Befreiungskriege, Nr. 65; and "Verhandlungen mit Landgraf Wilhelm von Hessen Kassel in Wilhelmsbad und Bockenheim betr. Vertheidigung des rechten Rheinufers und Beitragsleistung der Stadt zu diesem Zweck," ISG Frankfurt am Main, Revolutions- und Befreiungskriege, Nr. 81. Other examples are Hamburg and Bremen, "Protokolle des Fortifications-Departements," StA Hamburg, 111–1, Nr. V, Vol.7; and Herbert Schwarzälder, *Geschichte der freien Hansestadt Bremen* (Bremen: Röver, 1975), 1:510–25.

46 Kurt Burk, *Handbuch zur Geschichte der Festungen des historischen deutschen Ostens* (Osnabrück: Biblio, 1995), 43, 116.

47 Timothy Tackett, *When the King Took Flight* (Cambridge, MA: Harvard University Press, 2003), 160.

Yet I never could dream that so soon its beautiful borders
Would be used as a wall to defend ourselves from the Frenchmen,
And its broadspreading bed would become an impassible barrier.[48]

Adopting the French model in the 1790s entailed not only the strengthening of certain fortresses but also the demolition of those fortifications deemed too expensive or not sufficiently important for the overall defense of individual states. While Prussia strengthened some of its fortresses, it demolished others, especially in the east. This was the case of Calau, for instance, in 1794, and of Thorn and Posen a year later. Such policies were also adopted in the Bavarian residence. In the 1790s, the Bavarian government ordered the strengthening of state fortresses, especially those closest to France in the Palatinate.[49] General inspection of all state fortifications was ordered, a new supervisor for the state's fortresses was appointed, and considerable sums of money were allocated for refortification projects. It was at this very time, however, that the Bavarian government also ordered the defortification of its capital, Munich. The defortification cases of the 1790s and the simultaneous fortification frenzy in the west were two sides of the same coin: they were policies that attempted to economize the defense of single states by maintaining a smaller number of well-fortified cities instead of a large number of weakly fortified ones. In this respect, less was thought to be more.

It is easy to forget that even in the first stages of the Revolutionary Wars such measures could still be effective. The siege of Mantua, during Napoleon's First Italian Campaign, lasted eight months, and Napoleon never managed to take Acre (Palestine) two years later. The experience along Germany's western border with France during the Wars of the First Coalition (1792–1797) proved the same point. The siege of Mainz by French troops, which began in December 1794, lasted almost a whole year and ended in the defeat of the French besiegers under Jean-Baptiste Jourdan. The same was true in the case of Ehrenbreitstein, a fortress that successfully withstood no less than four different sieges between 1795 and 1799.

The importance of fortresses during the campaigns of the 1790s is also demonstrated by the clashes between French, Prussian, and Hanoverian troops in Northern Germany. At the early stages of the Flanders Campaign of 1793–1795, three French armies withheld an attack of the anti-Revolutionary Coalition by relying, at least partly, on their fortresses

---

48 Johann Wolfgang von Goethe, *Hermann and Dorothea*, trans. Daniel Coogan (New York: Frederick Ungar, 1966), 17–19.
49 "Antheil am 1. Reichskrieg gegen Frankreich," Bayer. HStA München, Abt. IV, B 267 I–IX.

in northeastern France. When the French counterattacked, however, the Coalition forces could no longer rely on the old "barrier fortresses" in this area, which had been demolished by Joseph II only a few years earlier. The result was the occupation of the Austrian Netherlands by France and the establishment of a pro-French Batavian Republic there in 1795.

The comparison between Northern Germany and the Empire's border with France along the Rhine is striking. As opposed to the exposed areas in the north, in the Middle and Upper Rhine – where German fortresses were still largely intact – France was unable to stage a general invasion deep into Germany, although some small-scale expeditionary forces did cross the river and fought against Austrian, Hessian, and other German troops. This is the reason for the skirmishes outside Munich in 1795, for instance, which caused a halt in Munich's defortification. Even during the War of the First Coalition, however, a general invasion of Germany's southern and middle parts proved beyond the ability of the French. Five years of intensive campaigns in the region by five different Revolutionary armies led nowhere. Strong fortresses stood in France's way like a bone in the throat. Not surprisingly, despite the sufferings of the local population, German states did not demolish their western fortresses at this point in the conflict.

In 1797, just two years before the defortification spike in Germany, the situation changed dramatically. Napoleon Bonaparte, a young artillery officer who knew a thing or two about siege warfare – he had successfully besieged Toulon in 1793 – was appointed commander of France's Army of Italy, and proceeded to invade the Italian peninsula. Although he failed at first in taking the strong fortress of Mantua, he managed to defeat the Austrians in successive battles from the spring of 1796 until early January of the following year. Especially devastating to the Habsburgs (who controlled Northern Italy), was their defeat in the Battle of Rivoli (January 14–15, 1797) and the fall of the fortress of Mantua shortly thereafter. Only now did the full scope of Napoleon's achievement become apparent. His army found itself only 100 miles from Vienna, with no substantial Austrian forces blocking its way to the Austrian capital. A breakthrough in the war, which had been going on for almost five years, was suddenly achieved. The defense of Germany in general and Austria in particular was staged along the Rhine. But now, with Napoleon's detour through Italy threatening their rear, the Habsburgs had no choice but to sue for a ceasefire. The fortified frontier along the Rhine became irrelevant.

Bonaparte's First Italian Campaign brought a halt to the fortification frenzy along the Rhine, as strengthening fortresses along the river no longer made any strategic sense. Defeated by the French, many German states were now considerably weaker than they had been during the preceding several years. Prussia had already signed a separate peace treaty with France in 1795, and following Bonaparte's Italian Campaign, the Habsburgs surrendered large territories to the French in the Treaty of Campo Formio of October 1797.[50] Some of the treaty's secret clauses stipulated the extension of France's frontiers all the way to the Rhine at the same time that Austria was compensated for its territorial losses in the west by (illegally) giving it territories further inland, in Germany. Even those German states that aligned with Napoleon were more dependent on French goodwill for their survival than on their own political and military powers. Under such circumstances, states lacked both the resources and the will to continue fortifying certain cities as they had done in the previous few years.

The final stroke in the fundamental transformation of the strategic situation in Germany's western and southern provinces came about between 1799 and 1801. In 1799, another war broke out between France and the European powers, including Austria. As in 1796–1797, Bonaparte invaded Italy and defeated the Austrians in the rightly famous Battle of Marengo (June 1800), threatening the Habsburg's lands once again from the south and east. Unlike during the Wars of the First Coalition, the weakened Rhine frontier collapsed. In the wake of Campo Formio, many Austrian troops had to be pulled out of the Rhine fortresses, and the French Army of the Rhine under Jean Victor Marie Moreau invaded Southern Germany and defeated the forces of a combined Bavarian-Austrian army in December 1800 at the Battle of Hohenlinden, about twenty miles east of Munich. In the Peace of Lunéville (February 1801), which concluded this campaign, France's extension of its borders all the way to the Rhine was once again acknowledged, as were its territorial gains in Italy. Most importantly for the fate of urban fortifications in Germany, however, was Clause VI in the treaty: although France agreed to withdraw from all its acquisitions on the right bank of the Rhine, it did so "under explicit condition that all the fortresses its armies [would] evacuate, would remain in the same state as at the time of their withdrawal."[51] The implications of this clause, less evident in the final text of the treaty than in its preliminary draft, were nonetheless clear: if France were to demolish any fortifications, German states would not

---

50 For instance, Lunéville, Article vi; Campo Formio, Secret Articles 1, 13; James Harvey Robinson, ed., *The Napoleonic Period*, vol. 2/2: *Translations and Reprints from the Original Sources of European History* (Philadelphia: University of Pennsylvania Press, 1895), 3–13.

51 A. du Casse, *Histoire des négociations diplomatiques relatives aux Traités de Mortfontaine, de Lunéville et d'Amiens* (Paris: Dentu, 1855), 10:326.

be allowed to rebuild them.[52] Soon enough, the French Army of the Rhine proceeded to blow up the fortifications of German cities along the river: Mannheim, Düsseldorf, Wiesbaden, Ehrenbreitstein, and a host of smaller fortresses and castles. Napoleon even considered defortifying Mainz, but then changed his mind. After all, Mainz – located on the Rhine's left bank – had been annexed to France, and its fortifications – as opposed to those cities from which France was about to withdraw – could still be useful to the French Republic.

EHRENBREITSTEIN, 1801

The consequences of the campaigns in Italy in 1796–1797 and 1799–1800 as well as the successful invasion of Southern Germany in the fall and winter of 1800 were not restricted to the closed rooms of peace negotiations or high politics. They were felt clearly and sometimes painfully in a series of cities and towns along the Rhine and in Southern Germany. During the campaign of 1800, for instance, Jean Victor Marie Moreau and his army captured the important fortresses of Phillipsburg, Ulm, and Ingolstadt. Because at this point the war was far from over, Moreau decided to defortify these three fortresses in order to deprive the Austrian and Bavarian armies of strong bases from which to attack his forces. Local burghers could neither oppose Moreau, nor did they always wish to do so; the experience of war, sieges, and occupation in the previous few years made sure of that. This was the case in Ulm, for instance, where the burghers' reactions to the defortification of their city were described by the man of letters Johann Gottfried Pahl:

On October 13, Moreau published his order that the fortifications of Ulm, Phillipsburg, and Ingolstadt be demolished and, moreover, that they be demolished in such a way that would make it all but impossible to reconstruct them later. For the German patriots in the city, the annihilation of the fortifications was a deeply humiliating event, a demolition of the bulwarks of the Empire, whose construction cost so many millions. But the inhabitants of Ulm received the news with great joy because it demolished not only the fortifications, but also their concerns and fears [of additional sieges and bombardments], and opened, as it were, a view into the city's future.[53]

War fatigue played an important role in this decision, then.

Ulm was not an isolated case. In several other cities, local government officials who were either the instigators of defortification or had collaborated with the French in defortifying fortresses tried now to convince

---

52 Cf. the preliminary formulation in ibid., 10:430–31.
53 Johann Gottfried Pahl, *Geschichte von Schwaben* (Nördlingen: Beck, 1802), 338–39.

citizens to celebrate rather than bemoan the loss of their city walls. Their reasons echoed those of Pahl's in Ulm. In Mannheim (defortified in 1799), a special song was composed to celebrate the defortification of the city that emphasized the "patriotic" aspect of the demolition.[54] In Munich, Maximilian I (Karl Theodor's successor) argued along similar lines that by finally completing the defortification of Bavaria's capital, he performed a patriotic act. "*Bürgerliche Liebe ist die stärkste Mauer*" (figure 16), reads one of Maximilian's proclamations: the burgher's love of his city is the strongest wall — stronger, that is, than the actual, physical city walls themselves.[55] One could demolish the physical walls of a city, Maximilian implied, without demolishing their invisible aspect: the burgher's love and loyalty to his community.

Official propaganda notwithstanding, the demolitions of 1799–1801 were hardly ever simple, one-sided, "joyful" affairs. Just like Pahl's patriots in Ulm, who viewed the defortification of their city as a humiliating act, burghers in other cities often looked at the destruction of their cities' defenses with sadness and at times outright indignation. Perhaps no better example for this can be found than in the case of the important fortress of Ehrenbreitstein, whose defortification is documented well enough to allow one a penetrating look into the causes and significance of defortification around 1800 as well as into common burghers' reactions to it.

Ehrenbreitstein, it was believed in the eighteenth century, had been originally built in the eleventh century and substantially strengthened in the seventeenth century (we now know it had a much longer history, dating back to prehistoric times). It contained both the fortress itself, which "crowned" (as contemporaries put it) the massive rock overlooking Koblenz from the other (right) side of the Rhine and, just beneath it and closer to the river, a palace as well as a small town called Thal-Ehrenbreitstein.[56] The fortress's immense strategic and symbolic importance derived from its location opposite Koblenz, where the Moselle joined the Rhine. "The fortress," one British traveler in the 1790s described Ehrenbreitstein, is considered "one of the keys of Germany towards France and . . . consists of several tiers of low walls, built wherever there was a projection in the rock capable of supporting them. Above these tiers, which are divided into several smaller parts, is built the castle, covering the summit, and surrounded by walls more regularly continued, as well as higher." In the fortress itself, there

54 Peter Ritter, "Gesellschaftslied, gesungen bei Schleifung der Festung Manheim 1799," BSB, 2 Mus.pr. 1722–29.
55 Lehmbruch, *Ein neues München*, 214 (Abb. 207).
56 Johann Kaspar Risbeck, *Briefe eines Reisenden Franzosen über Deutschland* (Paris, 1784), 2:347.

BÜRGERLIEBE DIE STÄRKSTE MAUER.
1801.

Figure 16. The burgher's love is the strongest wall (1825). *Source:* Münchner Stadtmuseum, Sammlung Graphik/Plakat/Gemälde, M I / 3078.

were several buildings, towers, and a large number of garrison troops. "It seems impregnable," wrote the traveler, and as far as Koblenz was concerned, it "is therefore the real defense of the city."[57]

The events of the Wars of the First Coalition brought Ehrenbreitstein to the forefront of the conflict. After the Battle of Valmy in September 1792,

57 Ann Ward Radcliffe, *A Journey Made in the Summer of 1794 through Holland and the Western Frontier of Germany* (London: G.G. and J. Robinson, 1796), 289–91.

Austrian and Prussian troops began a general withdrawal from territories deep in France. As the war came closer to Ehrenbreitstein, a new commandant arrived in the fortress that made it his job to strengthen the fortress's walls and supply magazines. Two years later, in the summer of 1794, the situation deteriorated further. A combined French army of 90,000 men managed to beat the Coalition forces in Fleurus (Austrian Netherlands, between Charleroi and Brussels), and decisively changed the strategic situation in the north. The Austrian Netherlands were occupied by France, and soon enough the Dutch Republic would also collapse. Outflanked in the north, the Coalition forces started a general withdrawal from the left bank of the Rhine. By October 23, 1794, the Austrians evacuated Koblenz, moved their artillery pieces and ammunition across the Rhine to Ehrenbreitstein, and destroyed the bridge connecting the fortress with the city. The only thing preventing the French from crossing the river and penetrating deep into Germany was Ehrenbreitstein.

Four years and many a cannonade later, Ehrenbreitstein still stood, defiant, in the face of a general French invasion of central Germany. But Bonaparte's Italian campaign in 1796–1797 and the rapid collapse of Imperial institutions in the following years brought about a situation in which the tactical success of defending the fortress amounted to few strategic advantages. Already in the wake of Bonaparte's First Italian Campaign, the Austrian army withdrew both troops and supplies from Ehrenbreitstein and transferred them farther to the east; with Vienna itself threatened, it had little choice in the matter. Imperial troops counted now for even less than purely Austrian ones because the Empire qua Empire (as opposed to some of its individual members) withdrew from the war completely. Ehrenbreitstein's garrison could count on no one to supply it and help it keep opposing French bombardments. The final scene came in January 1799 when, a little over a year after signing the Treaty of Campo Formio, the Austrians finally withdrew from Ehrenbreitstein, taking with them some, if not all, of the fortress's light artillery pieces and ammunition. The fortress was finally in French hands.

French engineers and military personnel stormed the fortress not with weapons but with maps, drawings, and fortification manuals, in an attempt to assess the strength of this defiant place. Some were impressed by what they saw in Ehrenbreitstein but others were disappointed, and an order was now given to strengthen the fortifications once again. The burden of these works fell on the peasants from the surrounding countryside. Then, after Lunéville, the French changed their minds once again because they were about to evacuate the right bank of the Rhine and withdraw across the river to Koblenz. The treaty was signed in early February 1801, and already a month later the works for the defortification of Ehrenbreitstein were underway. The French had no qualms about the local population's reaction to the demolition, nor were they interested in the beauty of the place after its walls were razed. In the wake of Lunéville, France's sole objective was to demolish as many German fortresses as thoroughly and as quickly as possible before turning them back into Austrian hands.

How the blowing-up of Ehrenbreitstein's fortifications proceeded can be glanced in French military manuals.[58] First, one had to find the right location for the mines and then dig a tunnel (known as a "gallery") toward that area. When, for economy's sake, the gallery led to more than one mine, its forks created smaller galleries or "branches." Once the location of the mine had been reached, engineers worked to create a large enough space beneath the walls for the planting of the mines themselves. These spaces were known alternately as "chambers" or "ovens." Then the charge was placed inside the chamber. It was made up of a varying number of gunpowder boxes, depending on the depth of the chamber and the material the explosion had to work its way through. The average amount of gunpowder needed to blow up fortifications laid on loose earth was about forty pounds per mine; sand was more resistant to such a blast and demanded about fifty pounds of explosives; and to work its way through solid rock (as in Ehrenbreitstein), a mine had to contain at least seventy-five pounds of gunpowder per chamber. Once the gunpowder boxes had been brought down to the chamber through the galleries (a process known as "charging"), the chamber was blocked from the gallery with wooden boards, bricks, sacks of sand, and other materials so that the blast would work itself up through the fortifications and not through the gallery. When all was ready, the charges were ignited through a fuse known as a "sausage" – elongated leather sacks filled with gunpowder that ran from the chamber all the way to the gallery's entrance – and the walls were, literally, undermined.

Some seventeenth- and eighteenth-century engineers (including during the Napoleonic Wars) worked to develop a "science of demolition" through mathematical calculations and empirical experiments. This was little more

---

58 For the methods employed by military engineers to blow up fortifications, see Maximilian von Traux, *Die beständige Befestigungskunst* (Vienna: Fritsch, 1817), esp. 453ff.; Karl von Decker, *Die Artillerie für alle Waffen* (Berlin: Mittler, 1816), 247ff; and the entry in Diderot's encyclopedia: "Mine," *Encyclopédie, ou dictionnaire raisonné des sciences, des arts et des métiers*, eds. Denis Diderot and Jean le Rond D'Alembert (University of Chicago: ARTFL Encyclopédie Projet [Winter 2008 Edition], ed. Robert Morrissey, http://encyclopedie.uchicago.edu/ , 10:529-33).

than wishful thinking. The substantial differences in size and materials between any two fortification systems made demolition with mines into an art rather than a science, to be wielded differently in different situations. Be that as it may, the ultimate purpose of the operation was always the same. "In order to blow up a wall section," one contemporary manual for military engineers explained, "one should place the mines under the fundament of the wall in such a way that, through the blast, the whole construction will be thrown into the air and be shattered into pieces upon falling back on the ground."[59] A good explosion, the manual further explained, is one in which one sees no explosion at all on the surface. The blast should demolish the walls' foundations in a way that would make the entire construction collapse upon itself. "Use too few explosives, and the walls will only crack; use too many, and bricks and stones will fly in all directions."[60] To appreciate the magnitude of what was about to take place in Ehrenbreitstein, one only needs to keep in mind the fact that French engineers anticipated the need for about 30,000 pounds of gunpowder for the mines, and this was only one, isolated fortress.

Such a defortification method made sense to French military engineers. "In the French [i.e., Napoleonic] Wars," one military theoretician explained after the war, "the French used such methods wherever they could: in Fort-Louis, Tarragona, Padua, Verona, Tortona, Schweidnitz, Breslau, Vienna, Raab, Scharnitz, Gratz, Spielberg, and Hüningen," among others.[61] It was a simple, quick, and cheap method to use when one had no legal or political considerations to take into account. Moreover, as it was in the very foundations of the fortifications that the blast took place, any reconstruction efforts in the same location became all but impossible.

Joseph Anton Lucas, a Koblenz burgher who kept a journal describing daily events in his city and Ehrenbreitstein, crossed the river in early April 1801 to witness the demolition itself. Later that day, reflecting on the events he had just witnessed, he wrote:

The peace treaty of Lunéville has finally decided the fate of Ehrenbreitstein.... A large crowd assembled to witness the blowing-up of the fortress. The French officers, who were assigned the demolition task, marked with red flags those parts of the fortifications that were about to be annihilated. Just before the explosion, they fired a warning shot from one of their cannons, so as to give one final warning to people living in the vicinity.

59 Von Traux, *Die beständige Befestigungskunst*, 246.   60 Ibid.
61 Karl von Decker, *Die Artillerie für alle Waffen*, 468. Other famous examples are those of Turin and Brussels.

The preparations completed and the mines charged, it was time to get down to business:

Then the mines exploded. Within a single moment one could see those walls prostrate on the ground, which for many centuries had so bravely withstood harsh weather, barbarism, and heroism. Even the hope to have beautiful ruins in the vicinity of Koblenz proved to be misplaced – one can see so little now of what previous generations experienced here.

Lucas then went on to enumerate some of the "casualties" of the defortification:

The Johannis Tower, which withstood a first blast, surrendered to a second French mine, and had to pay for its arrogance [of withstanding the first mine] by being completely annihilated by the second. Another tower, on the south side of the fortress, was a true monument of ancient times – it was originally built in the year 1166 and was therefore over six hundred years old when it fell. In a few moments, it turned into nothing but dust and debris, and only a tiny part of its walls has survived.[62]

Lucas, whose description of the demolition of Ehrenbreitstein is filled with the attribution of anthropomorphic qualities to the fortress's walls ("the city as an organism"), concludes his description by reflecting on the demolition's wider strategic and symbolic significance. "Who can watch the rubble [of Ehrenbreitstein] without feeling a deep sense of sadness?" he asks rhetorically. "Who cannot feel the humiliation of Germany? With Ehrenbreitstein demolished, no fortress will defend our fatherland in case the enemy decides to cross the river once again and march into the hinterland. The fall of Ehrenbreitsten annihilates also the security of Northern Germany . . . we have only our field armies to defend us now!"[63] Beyond his emotional reaction to the demolition of Ehrenbreitstein, Lucas presents here a succinct description of the strategic chain reaction taking place all around him, a description that only lacks its first cause. This chain reaction started with Bonaparte's Italian campaigns, led to Lunéville, continued with the demolition of the Rhine fortresses, and ended with the opening up of Germany to a general land invasion by the French.

The local population in and around Ehrenbreitstein and Koblenz often lacked the bird's-eye view of people like Lucas. Its concerns were perhaps more down-to-earth, but they were substantial nonetheless. Even before the explosions took place, the remaining ammunition, firearms, furniture, and foodstuff left in the fortress had to be evacuated. The burden of this work fell, as it so commonly did, on peasants from the surrounding areas. Already

---

62 Quoted from A. Klebe, "Beobachtungen," Ibid. 63 Ibid.

on February 26, 1801, the French Brigadier General Lorge ordered 150 blacksmiths and 20 wagons from the nearby village of Runkel to help in the demolition of the fortress.[64] Less than a week later, on March 3, authorities in Koblenz were asked to provide the French army with local carpenters and other laborers to prepare for the demolition. It is in the best interest of Koblenz to find volunteers for such a job, Lorge wrote on that occasion, because "since the war began, the city [of Koblenz] had suffered much" from the existence of Ehrenbreitstein across the Rhine. When only few volunteers presented themselves the following day, Lorge began to force the local population to assist in the transportation of materials from the fortress (before the demolition) and debris (afterwards). Burghers and peasants not only from Koblenz and Runkel but also from Ehrenbreitstein-Thal, from the nearby village of Winningen, and from other nearby places were ordered to take part in the clean up.[65]

The inhabitants of Ehrenbreitstein-Thal were especially affected by the defortification of the fortress in their town. The French cared little about the future of the town and castle (as long as those remained defortified), and some Koblenz burghers – such as Lucas – might have watched the demolition with sadness. For Ehrenbreitstein-Thalers and even for some burghers in Koblenz, however, their very existence – economically and politically – was at stake here. Already on March 8, 1801, with rumors circulating in Koblenz and Ehrenbreitstein-Thal that the French were eager to demolish not only the walls of Ehrenbreitstein, but also some of its public buildings, worried burghers sent a letter to Lorge, pleading for mercy:

It is with surprise mixed with the most urgent concern that we hear that an order has been given for the demolition of all the buildings beneath the fortress. These buildings, which have nothing to do with the fortifications nor can ever be employed for such a purpose, have to be demolished now, with the rest of the fortifications. . . . Please consider the deplorable situation of the inhabitants of this town, inhabitants who, after having suffered six long years of bombardments have to witness not only the destruction of the fortress but also of their livelihoods both now and for the future.[66]

In emergency meetings, petitions, and personal letters directed at Lorge, burghers in Koblenz and especially in Ehrenbreitstein kept making the point again and again in the following few weeks. "*Citoyen Général!*" reads one

64 LHA Koblenz, 342,003.
65 "Abstellung von Arbeitskräften aus der Mairie Winningen zum Abbruch der Festung Ehrenbreitstein," LHA Koblenz, 655,047 Nr. 186; and "Entfestigung Ehrenbreitstein 1801," StdA Koblenz, 623 Nr. 1451.
66 "Nachrichten über das Schicksal der Festung Ehrenbreitstein und deren Umgebung 1799–1802," LHA Koblenz, 1C Nr. 9391.

of them, for instance, "it would not – it could never be! – the intention of a government so just to demolish, in a time of peace and without the least advantage to the French Republic, the resources of a people pauperized by the events of the preceding war . . . we evoke your humanity, *Citoyen Général!*"[67]

What was especially upsetting to these petitioners about the whole situation was the fact that – as in 1790s Munich – at the very same time that the community was trying to convince General Lorge to change the defortification plan, some individuals were trying to profit from it. These individuals were eyeing some of the building materials of the soon-to-be-demolished buildings, which they were planning to use in expanding their personal homes. These are simple "acts of vandalism," Ehrenbreitstein-Thalers called them in one letter to Lorge.[68] Thankfully, as far as most burghers were concerned, Lorge found their concerns "just and reasonable," and ordered that at least some of the buildings in the castle and town not be harmed.[69]

Despite the modification in the French plans, the extent of the demolition was still very wide indeed. The Peace of Lunéville dictated that the Austrians had no right to rebuild the fortresses (including Ehrenbreitstein) that the French had demolished after February 1801. French military personnel consequently had the right to cross the river and inspect these fortresses later to be assured of Austrian compliance with the treaty. On June 3, 1801, Charles Chavellot and Courlet Vregille, two of the military engineers who assisted in the demolition in April, crossed the river from Koblenz with a mandate by Lorge to inspect the ruins across the river. The account they sent to Lorge of what they had seen that day is the most detailed description in existence of the defortified fortress. "We have been to the fortress of Ehrenbreitstein [today] and have surveyed, successively, all the fortifications of that place as well as all the buildings in its vicinity," they began their account. What they saw in the former fortress pleased them greatly: "The two ravelins, the two half bastions, the old walls, the courtyard, the artillery batteries, the towers . . . are completely destroyed. . . . The same is true for the arsenal, the old military hospital, the commandant's lodgings, the water cisterns, then also the gunpowder magazines, the supply storage rooms, and the barracks." After exiting the former area of the fortress itself, Chavellot and Vregille also examined the surrounding buildings. "The walls themselves are gone," they reported, "as are the glacis and the forward

67 Letter from March 8, 1801, LHA Koblenz, 1C Nr. 9391.
68 Letter from March 9, 1801, LHA Koblenz, 1C Nr. 9391.
69 Letter from March 10, 1801, LHA Koblenz, 1C Nr. 9391.

bastions." Buildings in the town itself were still largely intact, but "the paths leading from the town to the fortress have vanished." All constructions of any military value in Ehrenbreitstein "*sont ruinés absolument*," they concluded their report.[70]

What Chavellot and Vregille inspected from up close in the early summer of 1801 was also visible from afar to later travelers along the Rhine. Perhaps most famous among them was Lord Byron, who traveled through the Rhine Valley a few years after Ehrenbreitstein's defortification. Byron, too, was well aware of the story behind the demolition of the fortress in the wake of Lunéville, the "Peace" that "destroy'd what War could never blight":

> Here Ehrenbreitstein, with her shattered wall!
> Black with the miner's blast, upon her height
> Yet shows of what she was, when shell and ball
> Rebounding idly on her strength did light;
> A tower of victory! from whence the flight
> Of baffled foes was watch'd along the plain:
> But Peace destroy'd what War could never blight,
> And laid those proud roofs bare to Summer's rain –
> On which the iron shower for years had pour'd in vain.[71]

Not without its romantic touch, Byron's poem reiterates Lucas's experience of the demolition back in 1801. Placed next to all the other descriptions of Ehrenbreitstein and other fortresses' defortification up to 1801, it emphasizes once again the often forcefully emotional reactions to the demolition of fortifications typical of that stage in the great defortification surge of the Revolutionary and Napoleonic Wars. Some observers (Chavellot and Vregille, for instance) viewed it with satisfaction; others viewed it as an opportunity to make a quick buck. Many other reactions, however, were saturated by a deep sense of sadness and humiliation, and they repeatedly referred to fortresses, cities, walls, and gates as living things ("The Johannis Tower *surrendered*" wrote Lucas; "*her* shattered wall," "*her* strength," and "*proud* roofs," Byron continued[72]). For this latter group of observers, the demolition was not only the demolition of military functionality, of the ability of a particular fortress, city, or even Germany as a whole to defend itself. It was also a painful blow to the very notion of the city as an organism, a demolition of the city or fortress's living tissue, the annihilation of one of

---

70 Report from Koblenz, 14 Praireal, An 9, LHA Koblenz, 1C Nr. 9433.
71 Quoted from George Gordon Byron, *Byron: Selected Poetry and Prose*, ed. Donald A. Low (New York: Routledge, 1995), 46.
72 My italics.

the elements that made the fortified city into the kind of organism it had been during the Middle Ages and the early modern period.

The demolition of Ehrenbreitstein also illuminates the strategic justifications for the demolition of German fortifications by the French. Had such fortification been useless, they would not have withstood, as Ehrenbreitstein did, several sieges in the 1790s. Had they possessed no strategic or tactical value, they would not have been demolished. French officers blew up Ehrenbreitstein's walls because they were useful, or at least could potentially be useful, to the Austrians.

The defortification of Ehrenbreitstein was not an isolated or unique case. Later during the Revolutionary and Napoleonic Wars, the Grande Armée decisively contributed to the defortification of German cities. French divisions conducting campaigns in Germany frequently inflicted severe damage on urban fortifications. Regensburg's ancient walls were heavily damaged during a battle between French and Austrian troops in 1809, and the walls of Tuttlingen (Württemberg, 1803) and Bischofswerda (Saxony, 1813) suffered similar fates. In other cases, the French forcibly defortified cities after a battle or a peace treaty. This was the case in Phillipsburg, Ulm, and Ingolstadt in 1800–1801 as well as in Hanau in the west (1806), Marienburg in East Prussia (1807), and Gratz and several other Austrian fortresses after the Treaty of Schönbrunn in October 1809. The French, one observer wrote about the case of Gratz, "razed everything to the ground, even the prison in the fortress, and were willing to spare only one tower and even that only after receiving a large sum of money from the local population." In Brunn, he continues, "as the fortifications were blown up, the entire city was shaken.... The French seem to spare nothing."[73]

Even when the Grande Armée did not target wall sections, it often caused great damage to city gates. This was so in the case of the small city of Alzey (Palatinate), whose gates were blown up to facilitate the march of the Grande Armée through the city in 1808,[74] in Sinzig (Palatinate, 1797), Bunzlau (Silesia, 1813), and most importantly in Vienna (October 1809). In the latter case, it seems that the French were especially careful not to damage nearby houses with their explosions. "They took especially good care to calculate the amount of gunpowder to be used so that only the bastions themselves – and not the entire length of the walls – would be demolished," reports one observer. "Still," he continues, "small, adjacent

---

73 Aemilian Janitsch, *Merkwürdige Geschichte der Kriegsvorfälle zwischen Oesterreich und Frankreich im Jahr 1809* (Wien: C. Gräffer, 1809), 233–34.
74 The information about Regensburg, Tuttlingen, Bischofswerda, Phillipsburg, Hanau, Marienburg, Alzey, Sinzig, and Bunzlau was taken from the relevant volumes of the DSB.

gardens, a promenade, and Duke Albert's Riding School were damaged, and the explosions caused a tremor equivalent to a small earthquake."[75]

By the first decade of the nineteenth century, defortification in Germany was no longer the result of the first wind of change – the decisions of absolutist monarchs like Karl Theodor in Munich to create an open residence in the face of burghers' opposition. The Grande Armée was pushing for defortification of many cities now in what can be seen as a continuation of the same policies pursued by Louis XIV and Louvois over a century earlier, although on a much grander scale. That the number of defortification cases in Germany started to rise so rapidly after 1799 was the direct result of French actions.

It would be a mistake, however, to view the case of Ehrenbreitstein (or any other great fortresses along the Rhine, for that matter) as just another example of defortification, one among many; its importance was much greater than that. With the rendering of the Rhine fortresses irrelevant from a strategic point of view, the evaporation of any general Imperial war effort, and the weakening of Austria (Bonaparte's Italian campaigns, Campo Formio, Lunéville), Bonaparte and his generals managed to demolish fortresses that for well over a century prevented an overall invasion of Germany's hinterland by French forces. With these fortresses gone, the classic penetration routes into Germany's interior were finally open. Lucas, in Koblenz, understood this well, as did Fresenius in Frankfurt, Görres further north, and – as the next chapter will demonstrate – practically anyone who viewed the progression of the wars from a strategic point of view at the time. To paraphrase Louis XIV's strategic evaluation of the Nine Years' War a century earlier, "Germania" now became "Galliae aperta" – Germany became open to France.

With the demolition of the Rhine fortresses, the experiences of war, bombardments, and occupation became a potential danger to any German city and not only, as in the previous century, to those cities located along the country's western borders. For the first time since the wars had begun, German cities far from the main theaters of operation of the 1790s had to make a decision about their own fortifications. Should they continue to maintain them? Should they be allowed to be demolished by the French? Should they be demolished by the cities' own burghers in an attempt to at least spare themselves the horrors of bombardments and perhaps avert their occupation? That the number of defortification cases in Germany rose so dramatically after about 1799 was certainly the result of French

75 Janitsch, *Merkwürdige Geschichte*, 233.

actions in Ehrenbreitsten and elsewhere. But, as the next chapter will show, it was also the result of the fact that by 1801, with Germany's western fortified barrier open, an increasing number of burghers were resigned to the fact that in order to save themselves from bombardment their city walls had to be demolished. In the process, these burghers created some of the most remarkable defortification documents in the entire history of the defortification of German cities in the eighteenth and nineteenth centuries.

5

Collapse, 1801–1815

In the wake of the Peace of Lunéville, the Rhine lost much of its strategic value. Ever since Richelieu's assessment of the military situation along France's northeastern borders in the 1620s – and even after the devastation of the Palatinate during the War of the League of Augsburg – German fortresses located along the river continued to check the strategic penetration routes leading from France into the German hinterland. By 1801, however, with the left bank of the Rhine securely in French hands and the German fortresses along its right bank defortified, Germany was finally open to France: the dreams of Richelieu, Louvois, and Louis XIV had finally come true.

The strategic dimensions of the conflict between France and its eastern neighbors changed after Lunéville. In the 1790s, the conflict had been conducted mainly along a line (the Rhine); after 1801, it covered a large surface (southern, central, and northwestern Germany). Even the names given to the French armies along the country's eastern borders indicated this development. Back in 1793, the main French army in the northeast was called the Army of the Rhine; by century's end, it would be called the Army of Germany (soon enough, there would also be an Army of the Danube). The wars, waged mostly in Germany's western and southern provinces up until that point, were about to touch the lives of practically every inhabitant of Germany, wherever he or she happened to live.

The reactions of burghers to the military campaigns in Germany were by no means the same everywhere. As many studies have shown, there was no single "German" reaction to the events of the Revolutionary Wars.[1]

---

1 See, for instance, the new collection of essays in Alan Forrest, Karen Hagemann, and Jane Rendall, eds., *Soldiers, Citizens, and Civilians: Experiences and Perceptions of the Revolutionary and Napoleonic Wars, 1790–1820* (New York: Palgrave Macmillan, 2009).

Some Germans were appalled by what was happening, some welcomed the French with open arms (at least at first), and others had yet to make up their minds. But on the ground, in cities as distant as Frankfurt am Main in the west, Hamburg and Bremen in the north, and Breslau in the east, a dramatic change was taking place with regard to the fortifications of individual cities. The walls of individual cities – a majority of burghers in all the major German cities had come to agree – had to be torn down because, under the new circumstances, they threatened the lives of the burghers much more than they protected them. The unprecedented scale of the defortification surge in Germany after 1800 consequently did not derive only from absolutist princes' actions (e.g., Munich) or direct actions of the French Revolutionary armies (Ehrenbreitstein). In many cities, defortification after 1800 would be the result of the active participation of burghers in the demolition of their ancient city walls.

FRANKFURT AM MAIN, 1801–1807

In 1801, the year of the Peace of Lunéville, an imaginary funeral procession took place in Frankfurt am Main involving a colossal body the likes of which had never been laid to rest before.[2] It was a somber day, and all the deceased's friends came to say their farewells. They were many: a priest, a music director with his troupe of musicians, pallbearers, friends, and family members. Wrapped in black mourning shawls, they stood around the freshly dug grave, playing mourning music, singing dirges to the accomplished life of the deceased, and reflecting on the temporality of all living things.

It was no ordinary funeral, and the deceased was no ordinary person. In fact, it was not a person at all, but rather one of Frankfurt am Main's gate towers – the Brückenturm (Bridge Tower) – which had overlooked the bridge connecting Frankfurt with Sachsenhausen, the neighboring settlement over the river Main. The priest, musicians, pallbearers, and friends who participated in the funeral were no less strange than the deceased. They were the towers and gates of the city of Frankfurt who came to pay their last respects to their old companion: the first victim – though not the last – of Frankfurt's changing cityscape.

---

2 The following is taken from "Der alte Frankfurter Brückenthurn wurde abgerissen im August 1801, der jüngere, der Sachsenhäusser war geboren 1345 und starb 1765," His. M. Frankfurt am Main, Grafische Sammlung, C 03129. All translations are mine.

The Pfarrturm (literally, "Priest's Tower"), serving as the priest and accompanied by trumpets and clarinets, opened the ceremony by singing:

> Adieu, I wish to tell thee
> Friend Brückenturm, and rest in peace,
> Thy long tenacious life
> Has found its last eclipse.
> Now standing all around thee
> We mourn and contemplate,
> That soon enough, we too,
> Shall suffer the same fate.[3]

The music director, the Katharinenturm (Katharine's Tower), accompanied by flutes, horns, and a bassoon, continued the eulogy:

> Through loyalty connected
> And sobbing over thee,
> In mourning clothes all shrouded,
> Around thy grave are we.
> The Holy Roman Empire
> In all its history,
> Has not so grand a corpse admired
> As thine is, previously.[4]

The Nikolaiturm (Nikolai's Tower), serving as the bassist, added his own farewell, to the accompaniment of trumpets:

> I too must grieve for thee
> Thy passing ties my hands,
> Soon will I too appear
> With thee in far-off lands.
> From this collapsing world
> I shan't depart with pain,
> Who knows where up in heaven
> We two shall meet again.[5]

---

3 Valet will ich dir geben/Freund Brückenthurn! gut' Nacht!//Du hast dein zähes Leben/Nun hoch genug gebracht.//Wir steh'n an deinem Grabe,/Und denken, daß uns spät//Noch zu betreffen habe/Daß uns auch so geht. Ibid.

4 Geknüpft durch Freundschafts-Bande,/Und weinend stehen wir,//Gehüllt in Trauer-Gewande/An deinem Graben hier.//Im Ganzen deutschen Reiche/Ist es noch nie geschehen,//Daß man solch eine Leiche/Wie diese, hat geseh'n. Ibid.

5 Auch ich muß dich beweinen,/Dein Abschied macht mich weich.//Bald werd' ich auch erscheinen,/Bei dir in deinem Reich.//Aus diesem Weltgetümmel/Werd' ich mit Freude gehn,//Wer weiß in welchem Himmel,/Wir uns einst wiedersehn.

After several more such eulogies, Frankfurt's gates and towers engraved an epitaph on the tombstone and draped it with a black mourning shawl. The epitaph read in part:

Here, dear reader, rest the remains of the Brückenturm, in whose honor these lines were composed. He was born into this world seven hundred years ago . . . and from the chronicles we learn that he was ill only very seldom. He used to move in a very exclusive society and showed little politeness to foreigners. On his deathbed he fought for a long time for his life, until being brought here, his final resting place. With him the old saying is fulfilled: he dug a grave for others, and fell himself inside. His body is gone, but his soul, his true fundament, lives on. You, who are passing upon this spot, should know: he served the city well.[6]

The description of this imaginary funeral procession, published in Frankfurt in 1801, was probably composed on behalf of Frankfurt's city council. It contains several motifs that should already be familiar to the reader: the attribution of anthropomorphic qualities to the city's gates and towers ("he was born seven hundred years ago," "thy long, tenacious life"); the perception of the gate as much more than its physical "body" ("his body is gone, but his soul, his true fundament, lives on"); and the dramatic sense of loss once the city's old monuments were demolished ("grief," "mourning," "sobbing"). The frontispiece of the poem further underscores these characterizations (figure 17). It is divided into three parts. The first, entitled "Leben" ("life"), portrays the Brückenturm when it was still alive and well; the second, "Tod" ("death"), shows the demolition itself; and the third, entitled "Grabmal" ("gravestone") shows the burial of the gate. The description also discloses an important clue about how the building materials of gates, towers, and wall sections were disposed of after their demolition: the debris was often used to fill up the moat surrounding the city, creating a flat area for new buildings or public and private gardens. This was the pun in the epitaph: "He dug a grave [*Gruben* in German, which sounds like *Graben*, "a moat"] for others and fell himself inside."

Most importantly, the description of the Brückenturm's death and burial opens a window into one important reaction to the demolition of city walls during the Napoleonic Wars. While the gate's long life is described as "impolite to foreigners" (it was on the Brückenturm, Goethe reminisced in *Poetry and Truth*, that the skeleton of an early seventeenth-century rebel was still on display in the late eighteenth century[7]), a sense of real grief

6 Ibid.
7 Johann Wolfgang von Goethe, *The Autobiography of Goethe; Truth and Poetry: From My Life*, trans. Parke Godwin (New York: Wiley and Putnam, 1846), 130–31.

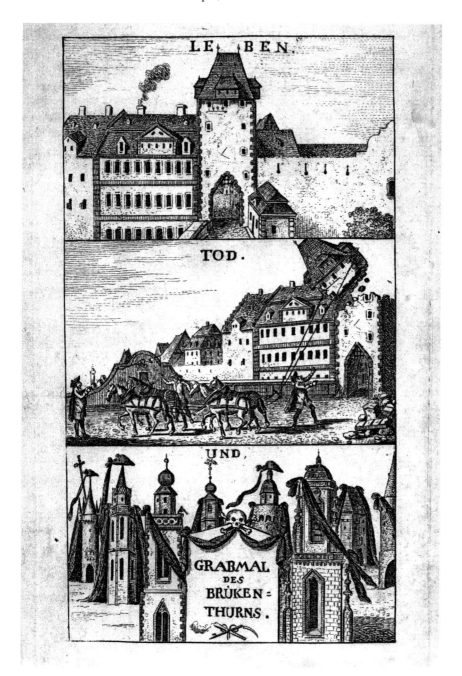

Figure 17. *Life, Death, and Gravestone of the Brückenturm. Source*: Historisches Museum Frankfurt am Main, Grafische Sammlung, C03219a-b.

saturates the description, and the demolition decision is depicted in the epitaph as the result of a long, hard struggle: "On his deathbed he fought for a long time for his life." Above all, a deep melancholy hovers over the poem, a melancholy whose scope extends well beyond the demolition of one gate tower. The demise or collapse the gates and towers mourn, as the Nikolaiturm puts it, is not of a single tower, not even of all of Frankfurt's other towers and gates, whose destruction is described as imminent: "We mourn and contemplate//that soon enough, we too/shall suffer the same fate". Rather, it is the demise of a larger "collapsing world" from which, the mourning gates feel, old monuments like themselves would depart soon and with joy: "From this collapsing world, I shan't depart with pain."

The defortification of Frankfurt, which would follow closely on the demolition of the Brückenturm in 1801, was indeed closely related to the collapse of the old political order in the city's habitat. Like Munich and Ehrenbreitstein's cases, Frankfurt's defortification was inseparable from the larger events in Germany at the time. But unlike the other cases discussed so far, the forces that brought about the demolition of Frankfurt's walls were not related at first to absolutist ideas nor did they involve French officers undermining and blowing up the fortifications. Rather, they were related to the dire political and military straits in which the city found itself by 1801 and to an active participation of the burghers in the demolition decision and its execution. The first wind of change contributing to the perfect storm of 1789–1815 originated in the centralized country, the result of absolutist ideas: that was Munich's case. The second and fiercer wind consisted of the direct actions of the Grande Armée; it toppled the walls in Ehrenbreitstein and other cities along the Rhine and in the south. The third wind came from German burghers directly, stirred by their realization that their ancient walls now threatened their city's safety rather than protected it. This was Frankfurt's case, and, as will become evident soon, it was the case of other cities as well.

Frankfurt's fortifications, though not first-rate by the standards of the day, were nonetheless a valuable strategic asset and recognized as such by all contesting parties.[8] "Frankfurt has gates and walls," explained one English visitor in the early 1790s, "but the magistrates do not oppress travelers by a military examination at their entrance."[9] Still, "the fortifications are laid

---

8 "Verteidigungsmaßnamen der Stadt," ISG Frankfurt am Main, Kriegszeugamt, Nr. 5; "Akten aus dem Nachlasse des städtischen Kommandanten und Obersten Edlen von der Planitz betr. ihm gewordene militärische Aufträge in Sachen des reichsstädtischen Kontingentes, der Armierung der Festungswerke, der Beschaffung von Waffen und Munition u.a.," ISG Frankfurt am Main, Revolutions- und Befreiungskriege, Nr. 65.

9 "Description of the city of Frankfort am Main," *The Lady's Magazine* 27 (June, 1796): 247.

out in a regular way. They consist of an enceinte, thick [modern] walls, eleven strong bastions, and wide moats. The burghers spent seventy two years bringing them to their present, beautiful condition."[10] The city lay not far from the French border, on one of the strategic penetration routes from the Rhine Valley into central Germany, the one leading from Mainz, up the river Main, into Hessen and Franconia. What this location meant and what consequences it implied was something Frankfurters would learn all too well during the 1790s and early 1800s. It was an experience that would lead to the city's decision to finally demolish its walls a couple of years after Lunéville.

Frankfurt's case was typical of Germany's western provinces, which from the outset of the military conflict between France and German states were located in the war's main theater of operations. In October 1792, one month after the Battle of Valmy, Frankfurt was occupied by French revolutionary troops led by the Comte de Custine (1740–1793), better known to his soldiers – thanks to his dominant facial characteristic – as Général Moustache. Facing a strong combined army of Prussian and Hessian troops, Custine ordered a partial withdrawal from the territories on the right bank of the Rhine in the fall of 1792, but he also left a garrison at Frankfurt, ordering the local commandant to set the city ablaze should he be forced to surrender it. Custine's revolutionary sentiments notwithstanding, his orders seemed very similar to Louis XIV's tactics in the Palatinate a century earlier.[11] Frankfurt's guild members, attempting to subvert Custine's plans, helped the German troops reenter the city by spiking the cannons on the walls (thus rendering them useless), the same cannons that had belonged to the city before the French used them for their own purposes.

In 1792, the immediate threat to Frankfurt's existence was averted, but the city's troubles were far from over. 1796 brought the threat of another French occupation. The Prussians had already signed a separate peace with Paris in Basel in the previous year, but the Austrians were still in the war, and Frankfurt lay in the path of the opposing armies. In less than a year, the city saw Prussian troops enter it to guarantee its safety only to leave shortly thereafter; an Austrian occupation that led to a French bombardment; a French occupation, followed by demands for huge contributions from the

10 Heinrich Sebastian Hüsgen, *Getreuer Wegweiser von Frankfurt am Main und dessen Gebiete für Einheimische und Fremde* (Frankfurt am Main: Behrensche Buchhandlung, 1802), 69.

11 About the Comte de Custine's campaigns in Germany, see Jean Louis Camille Gay de Vernon, *Mémoire sur les opérations militaires des Généraux en Chef Custine et Houchard, pendant les années 1792 et 1793* (Paris: Firmin Didot Frères, 1844), esp. 70–97.

local population; and another Austrian occupation, after another French withdrawal.[12] All of this, remember, took place within a single year.

Frankfurt, like Mainz and many other German cities, suffered several bombardments in the 1790s, one of which destroyed the Judengasse, Germany's oldest ghetto. "Our days are awful," wrote one Frankfurter at the time, "days the likes of which our city has never witnessed in its entire history. One hundred and fifty houses in the city are now little more than heaps of smoldering ashes, many more have been damaged by fire. All our great efforts have proved futile in avoiding these calamities."[13] Beyond the actual devastation of a siege, what characterized life in Frankfurt at the time was the constant fear of the possibility of a bombardment. One day in July 1796, a rumor that the French were approaching Frankfurt once again made its way around the city. Crowds of burghers fled to one of the city gates, making sure they could immediately escape in case of another bombardment. The rumor proved false; the fear, however, was very real.[14]

Apart from the actual or possible bombardment of the city, Frankfurters had to deal with the war contributions demanded of them by the different garrison troops stationed in their city. The French occupying army in Frankfurt demanded the supply of many articles, plus truckloads of money. In the course of the *annus calamitatis* of 1796 – and above and beyond cash payments – the city delivered to the French 127 cannon of various calibers; 27 mortars; 3,398 rifles; 445 swords; 200 daggers; and 14,288 gulden worth of gunpowder. The requisitions were not limited to military supplies. The French demanded and received everything from boats, ships, and anchors to pots, pans, carriages, ropes, wood, straw, bread, books, and maps. When they wanted to celebrate, as was the case on August 1, 1796, the French also ordered large quantities of plates, cooking utensils, wine bottles, beer kegs, beer glasses, and food. Perhaps the French celebrated that night; the local population certainly did not.[15]

The first impulse of the authorities in Frankfurt, as in many other places in Germany during the 1790s, was to revert to the practices of previous centuries and strengthen the city's fortifications. In the early 1790s, the city hired a new general to command its garrison, enlisted more soldiers, inspected and ordered more ammunition for its guns, and rebuilt parts of

---

12 Waldemar Kramer, *Frankfurt Chronik* (Frankfurt am Main: W. Kramer, 1987), 242–43.
13 Letter from July 14, 1796, in "Verhandlungen mit Österreichischen und Französischen Militärbehörden betr. den Kreig um Frankfurt und die Übergabe der Stadt," ISG Frankfurt am Main, Revolutions- und Befreiungskriege, Nr. 130.
14 Ibid.
15 "Verhandlungen betr. Lieferungen aller Art an die Franzosen," ISG Frankfurt am Main, Revolutions- und Befreiungskriege, Nr. 122.

the city's walls.[16] This strategy, it turned out, was not just unsuccessful but attracted opposing armies to Frankfurt's strategically located fortifications ever more strongly, threatening the property of the citizens through bombardments and requisitions. The consequences of the strengthening of the fortifications in terms of property loss were staggering.

Johann Christian Ludwig Fresenius had already warned his fellow Frankfurters back in 1791 that their insistence on keeping the fortifications might bring harm to the city rather than protect it. Eight years later, he reiterated his warnings. The walls, he wrote, were useless in defending the city: "Usefulness? Not at all," he wrote. The walls only bring "one disadvantage after another." In the past, it made sense to surround oneself with strong fortifications. "But now, in this day and age, with the huge standing armies of the great European powers, fortresses are useless [for communities like Frankfurt].... They only manage to draw great armies to a city."[17]

For Fresenius, even more annoying than arguments in favor of keeping the military fortifications of Frankfurt were nonmilitary arguments supporting the idea that the city walls should be maintained and even strengthened. One such argument was related to Frankfurt's honor. Because Frankfurt was the historical host city of the election and coronation of German emperors, some of Fresenius's fellow burghers thought it both a dishonor and breach of the city's Imperial obligations to demolish its fortifications. How else could Frankfurt protect newly elected emperors in the future? How could it hope to continue to hold its obligations, stated in the Golden Bull of 1356, to host the conclave of the electors upon the death of an emperor? Fresenius ridiculed such arguments. With or without the walls, he wrote, Frankfurt can no longer hope to protect any Imperial assembly. One needs to live in the present, he implied, not in a distant past that bore no resemblance to the city's situation in 1799.[18]

Few took heed of Fresenius's original warnings in 1791. Not a single discussion took place in either the city council or in the senate about the demolition of the fortifications in the following decade. Reiterating his arguments in 1799, Fresenius's text is a response to this inactivity, full of bitter and sometimes outright nasty language directed against his fellow burghers who, even after several years of war and devastation, still would not seriously consider his calls for the city's quick defortification. That Fresenius

---

16 "Akten aus dem Nachlasse des städtischen Kommandanten" and "Verhandlungen mit Landgraf Wilhelm von Hessen Kassel in Wilhelmsbad," ISG Frankfurt am Main, Revolutions- und Befreiungskriege, Nr. 81.
17 Johann Christian Ludwig Fresenius, *Reichsfriede, Deutschland, Frankfurt: Neujahrgeschenk für deutsche Mitbürger* (Frankfurt am Main, 1799), 28–29.
18 Ibid., 35.

spent so much effort attacking arguments in favor of keeping the walls intact implies that such arguments were common and powerful enough to draw his attention and ire. His voice, in short, was still a lonely one in 1799.

All of this does not mean that Frankfurters lived in a completely imaginary world and did not realize the magnitude of the events they were witnessing. Documents from the second half of the 1790s depict common burghers' reactions to the wars that are full of despair, anxiety, and sadness about the city's fate. Frankfurters knew that their city was in a tough spot, but they were also realizing, albeit slowly, the futility of defending it by themselves. They had few options left. The resulting anxiety and despair surfaced repeatedly in internal correspondence among the city's government officials from 1796 onward. "Our sad fate," is how one official begins a letter to his fellow Frankfurters; "Our circumstances are sad beyond measure," writes another official.[19]

After 1800, such sentiments found their way into a public sphere that had become more accommodating to Fresenius's arguments. The local poet Johann Isaac von Gerning echoed the thoughts of more and more of his fellow Frankfurters when he wrote in 1802 that "it is to be wished that, at a time of a future general peace, the steaming moats and the walls will disappear, and in their stead will be built pleasant, useful parks, much in the same way as in Aschaffenburg, Leipzig, and many other places. The events of 1796 have demonstrated [to us] how much destruction can be avoided by such means."[20] That Frankfurt's gates "spoke" about their coming destruction in their dirges to the fallen Brückenturm in 1801 was not an isolated incident, then. The Brückenturm's eulogy reflected the penetrating agony and melancholy of contemporary Frankfurt: it was a poetic formulation of the idea that the old world the fortified city had inhabited for so many centuries was rapidly collapsing. It also reflected the opinion of a growing number of people who understood now that the walls must go, although as Gerning put it, such a demolition was expected to take place not in the middle of the present war but later, "at a time of a future general peace."

Beyond the discussions and sentiments of the Frankfurters themselves, there was of course the issue of French policies vis-à-vis the city. Indeed, the first concrete push for the defortification of Frankfurt came from Napoleon and officials at his ministry of foreign affairs. Already in 1800 (a year before

19 Most importantly in "Verhandlungen mit Österreichischen und Französischen Militärbehörden betr. den Kreig um Frankfurt und die Übergabe der Stadt," ISG Frankfurt am Main, Revolutions- und Befreiungskriege, Nr. 130.
20 Johann Isaak von Gerning, *Skizze von Frankfurt am Main* (Frankfurt am Main, 1800), 12.

the demolition of the Brückenturm), Bonaparte urged Frankfurters to consider the close relationship between the fate of their city and the larger military developments in Germany. "Your interesting city," he wrote to Frankfurt's magistrates, "surrounded by different armies, can hope to find an end to its woes only through the establishment of a general peace [in Germany]."[21] Trying to defend the city independently, Bonaparte implied, would be the wrong way to go. This was not yet a call for Frankfurters to demolish their walls, but it was a first step in that direction. If Frankfurt's woes would only end with a general peace in Germany (Napoleon), and if a general peace in Germany would render the fortifications superfluous (Gerning), then the demolition of the walls would signify that peace had finally been achieved and Frankfurt's woes were over.

Then, in November 1802, the city's delegate to Paris reported back to Frankfurt about a conversation he had at the French ministry of foreign affairs, in which his French colleagues urged him to consider the actual defortification of Frankfurt.[22] The city was politically neutral, the French officials explained to him, and as the last war had shown, the fortifications were not only useless in defending Frankfurt but in fact threatened the life and property of the burghers in the event of a general conflict between the great European powers. Better to defortify the city, the French officials urged the delegate, than to keep its fortifications intact. The French suggestion was not altruistic, of course. From a strategic-defensive point of view, a defortified Frankfurt would deny France's enemies a staging point for an attack on French-occupied Mainz. The same was true from an offensive perspective: with Mainz in their possession and Frankfurt defortified, there would be nothing preventing the Grande Armée from using the Main valley as its main penetrating route into Germany. Either way, it was in France's best interest to see the walls of Frankfurt demolished.

Back in 1799, Fresenius had realized that Frankfurt's own strategic interest would also benefit from the demolition of its fortifications. With what he termed "the amputation of Mainz" from the Empire's body, Frankfurt remained the main obstacle to the advance of French troops up the river Main, which meant that the city and its surrounding area would soon become a primary target for the opposing forces in the conflict.[23] To avoid this fate, Frankfurt had to render itself strategically negligible. Three years

---

21 Napoléon Bonaparte, *Correspondance de Napoléon Ier*, ed. J.B.P. Vaillant (Paris: Impr. Impériale, 1858–1869), 6:letter 4671.
22 Rudolf Jung, "Die Niederlegung der Festungswerke in Frankfurt am Main 1802 - 1807," *Archiv für Frankfurts Geschichte und Kunst* 30 (1913): 125.
23 Fresenius, *Reichsfriede*, 13–15.

after Fresenius published his analysis, and in light of the report of their delegate in Paris, the authorities in Frankfurt began to see the matter in a similar light. "We are in favor of the demolition of the militarily useful parts of the city's fortifications," the senate ordered its delegate in Paris to tell the foreign ministry there, "but intend to do so only very cautiously."[24]

As far as the larger political situation in Germany was concerned, much had changed between 1799 and late 1802. In the years immediately after the Peace of Lunéville, it became increasingly clear that the constitution of the Empire was about to undergo a fundamental transformation. In 1802, the text of the resolution of the special committee of Imperial delegates assembled in Regensburg to discuss major changes in the Imperial constitution was already at hand (its final form would be published in February 1803). The resolution was a combination of a special agreement between France and Austria reached in June 1802 and article VII of the Peace of Lunéville. According to the Imperial resolution, the number of Imperial cities would be reduced from about fifty to only six (including Frankfurt), the remaining Imperial cities would be left to fend for themselves, and the cities' old obligation to contribute to the military defense of the Empire would be officially terminated. One of the arguments for the maintenance of Frankfurt's walls that Fresenius so passionately attacked in 1799 was related to their symbolic value and Frankfurt's obligations vis-à-vis the Empire. With these obligations about to disappear and the bonds that connected Frankfurt to the body politic of the Empire quickly falling apart, the opponents of defortification lost an important argument. Even the author of the eulogy of the Brückenturm, who certainly valued the symbolism of Frankfurt's gates and walls, did not use such an argument to call for their maintenance. The entire political and symbolic world to which the walls had belonged was collapsing. By 1801 even he recognized that although this collapse is to be mourned, it should not – it could not – be reversed.

By early December 1802, the city's senate had accepted the idea that Frankfurt should be defortified, but once again cautioned that any kind of demolition must proceed very cautiously. "We need to figure out a way of demolishing the fortifications bit by bit, but without losing their important functions as civil [rather than military] defenses," urged one senator. "The demolition should not be executed hastily," added another, as "it entails great costs to the city."[25] In Ehrenbreitstein, defortification could proceed quickly because it was executed by French officers who cared little for the

---

24 Jung, "Die Niederlegung der Festungswerke," 126.
25 Ibid., 125–26.

city's past or future. In Frankfurt, however, the defortification was the community's own decision. It was not enough to decide to blow up the walls, gates, and towers; one also had to carefully consider the police, financial, and symbolic consequences of such actions.

During the months that followed the senate's first defortification decision, little progress was made in terms of the actual demolition of Frankfurt's fortifications. Three different reports were written about possible defortification policies, each attempting to strike a delicate balance between four needs: to dismantle the military fortifications while continuing to safeguard the wall's police functions; find a new way of dealing with sewage (formerly, the city's sewer system depended on canals that were fed by the moats); find creative ideas for financing the defortification; and guarantee the city's enduring beauty.[26] To find answers for the complex set of questions a general defortification plan had to solve, the senate sought the advice of foreigners. In June 1803, for instance, the construction director of the city suggested contacting Lieutenant Colonel Johann Heinrich Müller, a lecturer at the University of Göttingen, who had planned the defortification of Hanover in 1763 and Braunschweig in 1802. At another point, the senate sent a delegation to Mannheim to learn more about how that city had been defortified in 1799. The original reasons for the defortification of Frankfurt, the way contemporaries experienced it ("this collapsing world"), and the way they thought about how to execute it – in all these respects Frankfurt's defortification was closely linked to the larger political and military context of the times. What happened to the urban organism was inseparable from what was happening in, and to, the city's habitat.

The transformation of the political order around Frankfurt also affected the pace of the defortification works. At first, the demolition progressed not at all and later only very slowly. The senate reached its original defortification decision in late 1802, but the city council agreed on a plan only in April of 1804, and it took five more months before it assembled the first group of workers. An advertisement in a local newspaper on September 13, 1804, called for anyone interested in a daily wage of twenty-four kreuzer to come to the city's construction office between nine and twelve o'clock in the morning during the following three days and sign up for the job.[27] The response was, to put it mildly, rather disappointing. The first group of workers consisted of one inspector and only about sixty men. Three months on, not a single part of the walls had been completely demolished.

---

26 The main principles of the reports (now lost) can be found in Jung, "Die Niederlegung der Festungswerke," 132–36.
27 *Frankfurter Frag- und Anzeigungsnachrichten*, September 13, 1804.

A contemporary estimate calculated that at this slow pace, the defortification would take ten more years and a gargantuan amount of money.[28]

What accelerated the defortification of Frankfurt were, once again, political developments. Toward the end of September 1805, with a French invasion of Germany seemingly imminent, the city council changed the original defortification plan, which called for the demolition to proceed one section at a time, and decided to demolish the strongest parts of the fortifications first, regardless of their location. Then, in November, the senate called on all Frankfurters to participate in what it called "patriotic demolition." Rather than auctioning off parts of the fortifications as the original defortification plan demanded, the senate called for a complete and quick demolition of the walls. "Since our city had the misfortune to be bombarded in the last military campaign," the senate resolution stated, "we need to make sure its fortifications are reduced to its old [medieval] city walls." The issue was not only military, the senate's resolution emphasized, but also political. "It has been recently agreed upon," the resolution read, "that all remaining Imperial cities would be militarily neutral. It is consequently our duty . . . to protect our city through the destruction of the fortifications."[29]

Johann Christopher Berndt, a local artist, left to posterity a colored engraving of how this "patriotic demolition" was executed (figure 18). In the background, workers demolish a small gate and flatten the earthen walls with pickaxes, sledgehammers, and shovels. In the foreground, the materials from the demolished fortifications are carried in wheelbarrows to fill the moat, a process supervised by a man dressed in green with his hands in his pockets, sitting in front of a makeshift table spread with bread and wine.

There was one last twist in the story. While the defortification was underway, the political habitat of Frankfurt deteriorated even further. The French invasion of Germany Frankfurters so dreaded in the early fall of 1805 did take place, ending in humiliating Austrian defeats in Ulm and Austerlitz in October and the creation of the Confederation of the Rhine under Napoleon's protection the following year. By early August 1806, the Empire itself – the old habitat of the walled German city – formally ceased to exist, and the political map of Germany was radically transformed. It now contained three main political entities: a still-defiant Prussian kingdom, soon to be attacked by Bonaparte, in the northeast; the newly created Confederation of the Rhine, allied with France and with Frankfurt as its capital, in the west and south; and the Austrian lands, reduced and

28 Jung, "Die Niederlegung der Festungswerke," 147.
29 Reproduced in its entirety in ibid., 151.

Figure 18. Patriotism of the Frankfurt burghers by the demolition of the walls (1805).
Source: Historisches Museum Frankfurt am Main, Grafische Sammlung, C00718.

humiliated after Napoleon's great victories during the autumn and early winter of 1805, in the southeast.

Once again, the city's external form was molded by these developments. True, the Brückenturm had already been demolished in 1801, and urged by the French, the city senate had ordered the demolition of Frankfurt's main wall sections from 1802 onward and even began the actual demolition work in the fall of 1804. But it was only after 1806 that the work was completed and the fate of the area of the former fortifications finally decided. The moving spirit behind this last stage of the defortification was Karl Theodor Maria von Dalberg, the prince-primate of the Confederation of the Rhine, who made Frankfurt the Confederation's capital.[30]

Dalberg's political solution for those large sections of Germany that had been abandoned by both Prussia and Austria was to neutralize the French threat by forming an alliance with Bonaparte. The rapid defortification of Frankfurt under Dalberg was a local manifestation of the prince-primate's larger political solution for the majority of the Empire's territories: the creation of a disarmed "Third Germany" (third because it was not in the

---

30 About Dalberg, see John G. Gagliardo, *Reich and Nation: The Holy Roman Empire as Idea and Reality, 1763–1806* (Bloomington: Indiana University Press, 1980), 206–26, 265–89; and Konrad Maria Färber, *Kaiser und Erzkanzler: Carl von Dalberg und Napoleon am Ende des Alten Reiches* (Regensburg: Mittelbayerische Druckerei- und Verlags-Gesellschaft, 1988).

Austrian or Prussian spheres of influence), unable and unwilling to protect itself militarily and aligned with France. Although at first he was slightly hesitant about the magnitude and expenses of the work, Dalberg quickly changed his mind and hired the architect Jakob Guiollett, who had already planned the defortification of Regensburg in 1802, to draw up the plans and supervise the defortification of Frankfurt. Guiollett's main idea (which he published in a treatise in 1806 and executed with the help of the landscape architect Sebastian Rinz[31]) was to transform the fortification area into a long promenade and series of public parks in the English style. Travelers to Frankfurt witness the products of Guiollett's defortification plan to this day. They can also visit Guiollett's monument, erected in the architect's honor by Eduard Schmidt von der Launitz in 1837 at the place where one of the old bastions had stood.

What in Munich during the preceding decade caused heated strife between the prince and the burghers, and what onlookers at Erhenbreitstein found so humiliating, became the basis of a new agreement between prince and population in Dalberg's Frankfurt. The walls had to go, both prince and city magistrates agreed, not because they were useless but because they were politically and militarily harmful. The walls had to go because their absence protected the city and the Third Germany in general much more effectively than their presence.

The defortification of Frankfurt made one thing quite apparent. In the wake of the collapse of the Rhine fortresses, single cities located farther inland – even those as wealthy as Frankfurt – could no longer realistically expect to defend themselves from strong armies. Although fortress towns would continue to be important to German states well into the nineteenth century, city walls stopped serving their original function of defending the city. A solution to the city's predicament, as Napoleon suggested in 1800 and Gerning reiterated in 1802, had to be found not within the city, through walls and ravelins and bastions and moats, but beyond the city, in a reconfiguration of its political habitat. Fresenius suggested as much in 1799 when he wrote that Frankfurt would be defended not through its walls but "through the creation of a new political constitution for Germany."[32] In the wake of Lunéville, Frankfurt's civil authorities slowly came to the same conclusion.

Historians Rudolph Jung and Björn Wissenbach have argued that the defortification of Frankfurt was viewed as a positive development by its

---

31 Jakob Guiollett, *Bemerkung über die Schleifung hiesiger Festungswerke* (November 5, 1806). ISG Frankfurt am Main.
32 Fresenius, *Reichsfriede*, 40.

burghers.[33] Certainly, some viewed it in this way. A year after Guiollett began the methodical defortification of Frankfurt, Katharina Elisabeth
Goethe – mother of the famous poet – viewed the demolition of Frankfurt's
walls and gates with enthusiasm. In a letter Goethe sent to her son on July
1, 1808, she concentrated on what she viewed as the extremely positive
social and political consequences of the defortification. It is worthwhile to
quote this letter now at length. "In this time of year," she wrote:

Frankfurt is crowded with foreigners – it's like the migration of nations during the
Middle Ages. We have guests even from Norway, and they are all dumbfounded
by the beauty of the city and especially of its surroundings. The old walls were
demolished, as were the old gates, and a park now surrounds the entire city. It is all
really like magic – one cannot even imagine how it had all looked before – our 'old
wigs' would have surely waited until the Second Coming before daring to do such
a thing of their own volition. As soon as a single ray of sun cuts its way through the
clouds everyone assembles outside the gates, Christians, Jews, all mixed together in
the most beautiful order one can imagine, it is the most touching spectacle one can
imagine. And all this is done without any costs to the city whatsoever! The terrain
where the old walls had once stood was sold to local burghers. Some bought a great
deal of land while others only little, and they all build on their lots to their hearts'
content![34]

Björn Wissenbach, especially, used other positive evaluations of the
defortification to imply that the process in Frankfurt was uncontested and
perceived with much enthusiasm by contemporaries. He quotes Johanna
Schopenhauer (mother of the famous philosopher), the novelists Alexandre
Dumas and Jean Paul, and the historian Anton Krischer to support this
argument, although all these authors (unlike Katharina Elisabeth) described
the state of the defortified city as it was many years after the demolition of
the walls.

Documents from and about the actual time of the defortification present
a much more ambivalent picture. The eulogy of the Brückenturm in 1801
swelled with sadness over the collapse of Frankfurt's old cityscape and waxed
nostalgic for the lost world to which walls, gates, and towers had belonged.
Bettina von Arnim commented later that, with the demolition of the walls,
she suddenly felt cold and out of place in her native city, "as if a comforter
was brutally ripped off my bed in the middle of winter."[35] Even Katharina
Elisabeth and Fresenius's texts, when read against the grain, attest to a

33 Jung, "Die Niederlegung der Festungswerke," 159–60; Björn Wissenbach, *Mauern zu Gärten: 200
   Jahre Frankfurter Wallanlagen* (Frankfurt am Main: Societätverlag, 2010), 27.
34 Katharina Elisabeth Goethe, *Briefe an ihren Sohn Johann Wolfgang, an Christiane und August von Goethe*
   (Stuttgart: Reclam, 1999), 287.
35 Bettina von Arnim, *Dies Buch gehört dem Könige* (Frankfurt am Main: Inselverlag, 1982), 146.
   Originally published in 1843.

powerful antagonism to the demolition by the majority of Frankfurters (Fresenius in 1799) or Frankfurt's more conservative circles (Goethe in 1808).

Perhaps most important in this respect is a short description of the demolition published by Friedrich Siegmund Feyerlein in the same year Katharina Elisabeth rejoiced over the demolition of the walls. "The burghers now," Feyerlein wrote about the progress of the demolition in 1808, "have to destroy the works of their own hands" – the very walls, that is, that had been built by their forefathers.[36] "In these so dangerous times," he added, "so many beautiful, ancient things are being destroyed, even by us." Perhaps one cannot fight against it, Feyerlein meditated, but as a writer, "I still wish to erect a small monument in writing for all those towers and gates" that are being so ruthlessly demolished.[37] A deep melancholy saturates his subsequent description of the city walls' history, a far cry from Katharina Elizabeth's optimistic evaluation.

HAMBURG AND BREMEN: THE EXISTENTIAL CRISIS OF TWO FREE CITIES

While the defortification of Frankfurt was still underway, events proceeded in a rather similar way 300 miles to the north, as the crow flies, in the Hanseatic cities of Bremen and Hamburg. Of the two, Hamburg was better fortified in the late eighteenth century. The city's fortifications were constructed in the early seventeenth century by the great Dutch military engineer Johann van Valckenburgh. They included twenty-two bastions, thirteen ravelins, six major land gates, and an unusually wide moat. Next to these were also various outer works, lairs, guardhouses (sometimes as many as five per bastion), barriers, bridges, and a glacis so huge that it "seemed to vanish only in the distance."[38] The most thorough observer of Hamburg's physical appearance in the late eighteenth century, Jonas Ludwig von Hess, called Hamburg's walls "unusually tall and thick." He estimated that the entire built area of the city – a little over 30 million square Hamburger feet – was only one and a half times larger than the area occupied by the fortifications – over 20 million square feet, excluding the glacis. This ratio of 1.5:1 is equivalent to modern New York City being divided into two parts: Brooklyn and Queens as residential areas and Manhattan, Staten Island, and the Bronx combined as the area for the city's fortifications.[39]

---

36 Friedrich Siegmund Feyerlein, *Ansichten, Nachträge und Berichtigungen zu A. Kirchners Geschichte* (Frankfurt am Main, 1809), 1:147.
37 Ibid., 182.
38 Jonas Ludwig von Hess, *Topographisch-politisch-historische Beschreibung der Stadt Hamburg* (Hamburg: Bachmann und Gundermann, 1796), 1:34.
39 Ibid., 1:4–5, 33–68.

Some of Hamburg's walls were inhabited by locals (as, for instance, on the inner side of the Casparus Bastion), and all were manned by city officers. At the end of the eighteenth century, Hess wrote, Hamburg possessed its own (paid) army, comprised of one regiment or ten companies of infantry, one company of artillery, and one company of dragoons (mounted infantry). Next to the professional soldiers was a city militia, composed of 317 volunteers divided into 55 squads. These were further supplemented by the night watchers (60 men every night), who kept an eye on the locked gates, maintained law and order on the city's nocturnal streets, and could be used as firefighters in case of a catastrophe. All these buildings, fortifications, and men, Hess reminded his readers, were originally meant to "put any enemy on hold, whether he comes by sea or by land."[40]

Even Hess, who devoted close to forty pages of his topographic study of Hamburg to just a general description of the city's fortifications, was unsure about their military purpose. "That the city of Hamburg is fortified and protected on all sides by walls, helped it, in the last [i.e., seventeenth] century, on more than one occasion," he wrote. "Nowadays, however, when both the art of the attacker and that of the defender had changed so much, we cannot see in the walls a sure means of defending the city.... The inhabitants of Hamburg," Hess concluded, "will have to rely more on their relationships with other political powers than on their high, thick walls, if they wish to protect themselves from external threats."[41]

Carl Gottlob Küttner, who visited Hamburg in the summer of 1797, had an even stronger view than Hess. As opposed to other cities that neglected their fortifications over the years, Hamburg's fortifications were in good condition, Küttner reported. Even so, he wrote, "when you look at them, you realize immediately that they can function only in peacetime.... This city can no longer be, in this day and age, a strong fortress, it should never even consider using its fortifications to defend itself from an enemy." "The only thing that Hamburg's inhabitants can expect from their walls," Küttner concluded, "is to serve them in their police roles or offer locals and foreigners alike a wonderful view of the city's surroundings."[42]

During the 1790s, Hamburg's senate took no notice of such calls. On the contrary, the reaction of city authorities to the political storm's gathering clouds during the Wars of the First Coalition was to strengthen, not demolish, the walls. On March 30, 1795, for instance, the senate ordered the strengthening of the fortifications "without which the defense of the city

40 Ibid., 1:33.   41 Ibid.
42 Carl Gottlob Küttner, *Reise durch Deutschland, Dänemark, Schweden, Norwegen und einen Theil von Italien* (Leipzig: Göschen, 1797), 1:29.

would be impossible."[43] Such measures were meant to kill two birds with one stone. Because the repairs and constant modernization of Hamburg's fortifications were traditionally done by some of the poorer laborers in the city, repairing the fortifications provided these laborers with much needed employment, at the same time keeping the city's defenses up to date. In the first decade of the Revolutionary Wars (1792–1802), the works on the fortifications proceeded rather slowly, partly because laborers could find more attractive jobs elsewhere. But when the situation became more threatening after about 1801 (as in Frankfurt), the repairs of the fortifications began to pick up steam. In December 1802, there were still only 6 poor laborers employed in repairing the walls; exactly a year later there were over 200 of them.[44]

As in Erhenbreitstein, Frankfurt, and a host of other German cities, the geopolitical situation of Hamburg and its sister Hanseatic cities in the north changed dramatically in the early years of the new century. With the Empire's western borders breached by the French, military campaigns began to take place closer to home, around Hamburg, Bremen, and Lübeck. Anticipating a French invasion of Northern Germany, Prince Carl of Hessen occupied Hamburg in March 1801 without a shot being fired, and in June 1803, the French themselves marched through Hamburg's city gates. Events in the less heavily fortified city of Bremen, about seventy miles southwest of Hamburg, proceeded along similar, if not identical, lines. After the occupation of the Low Countries by France in 1795, Hanoverian-British troops forced their way into the city with the intention of using its fortifications in the defense of Northern Germany. The Hanoverian soldiers would stay in the city, with some interruptions, for six years. In 1801, in the aftermath of Lunéville, Bremen's very independence was threatened. It was feared that like most other Imperial cities, a nearby territorial state would annex the city and deprive it of its independence. Luckily, this danger was averted, but in April 1801, only two months after the peace treaty was signed in Lunéville, parts of Bremen's territory were occupied by Prussian troops. During all this time, no local person thought seriously about using the fortifications in the defense of the city.[45]

Of the two cities, Bremen was the first to react to the situation by demolishing its military fortifications. True, there were voices calling for the

---

43 Quoted in W.L. Meeder, *Geschichte von Hamburg: Vom Entstehen der Stadt bis auf die neueste Zeit* (Hamburg: Wörmer, 1839), 2:443.
44 Mary Lindemann, *Patriots and Paupers: Hamburg, 1712–1830* (New York: Oxford University Press, 1990), 45, 184.
45 Herbert Schwarzwälder, *Geschichte der Freien Hansestadt Bremen* (Bremen: Röver, 1975), 1:515–47.

defortification of the city even before Lunéville. A poem composed by an anonymous Bremer in 1800 entitled "On the Walls" was a call for the demolition of all "medieval" constraints, suffused with religious imagery: "Deliver us Lord of this world of torments/From weapons and wars and from life in camp tents//From fortresses big and from fortresses small/Surround only hell with a moat and a wall."[46] But it was only the political and military situation three years later that brought about actual steps in this direction. On March 30, 1803, some local burghers asked the city's senate to consider the demolition of Bremen's fortifications. The senate took a whole month to respond, but on April 30 it ordered that the city be defortified, although the demolition work, it noted, "should proceed cautiously, from year to year . . . and concentrate at first on the modern fortifications [i.e., not the old city walls themselves] and the glacis."[47] The logic behind this step was not stated clearly in the official order, but two of the participants in the deliberations of the Bremen senate in April 1803 later shed light on them. Christian Abraham Heineken, one of the four mayors of Bremen at the time (the city was ruled by four mayors, each representing one of the four Bremer districts), explained in his diary that the senate considered a fortified Bremen too lucrative a staging place for Prussian and Hanoverian troops camping in the city's vicinity. The senate, Heineken wrote, had assumed that without the walls such armies would leave Bremen alone.[48] Liborius Diedrich von Post, another mayor who attended the senate meetings in April 1803, was more specific. The defortification of Bremen was meant to "turn it into an unusable tool for any party in the ongoing military conflicts" in the region, whether Prussian, Hanoverian, Danish, English, or French.[49]

The progression of the demolition works in Bremen began very slowly and cautiously. First, there were some financial obstacles, as the sums of money needed for the demolition of the entire fortifications area were calculated to exceed 150,000 gulden, not an insignificant sum for a city distressed by war. Complicating things further was the disorganized nature of the demolition. The filling up of the moats, for instance, was supposed to take place by encouraging individuals to load their carts with dirt and placing them on one of the bridges that extended over the moats. Then, having emptied the contents into the ditches, the burghers were instructed

---

46 "Erlös uns, o Herr der geängsteten Welt/Vom Kriege, von Waffen und Lagergezelt//Von Festungen gross und von Festungen klein/Die Hölle nur möge befestiget sein!" J.G. Kohl, *Denkmale der Geschichte und Kunst der Freien Hansestadt Bremen* (Bremen: C. Ed. Müller, 1870), 61. My translation.
47 "Bürgerconventzprotocoll de 1801 April 23 bis 1805 August 30," StA Bremen P-9.d.3.a.13: 65, 73–75.
48 StA Bremen, 2-P.1.268;106–07.   49 StA Bremen, 2-P.1.265;295d–296.

to receive a special note from the gate watchers that they could then redeem in one of the city's offices.[50] This was no way to organize a demolition on such a scale, nor did the red tape involved encourage many people to come forth and help fill up the moats.

Political considerations further slowed things down. Even in 1803, several senators still opposed the demolition of parts of the fortifications and tried to put stumbling blocks in its way. In May 1803, over a year after the original defortification decision by the senate, several senators still argued against the demolition. They mentioned the need to compensate individuals who inhabited parts of the old walls and the damage done to the city's honor by the demolition of the ancient fortifications. They even challenged the military logic behind the demolition. "There is a real dilemma here," a member of the opposition party said in one of the meetings of the special fortifications committee of the senate. If the logic behind the defortification is to deprive Hessian and Prussian troops of a valuable strategic asset, he argued, then beginning to demolish the walls would "instantaneously attract them to the city in an attempt to prevent this from happening." "These people [i.e., the senators] raise the most ridiculous counter-arguments against the demolition," retorted a senator from the other party in this argument. "They mention the most irrelevant arguments one can imagine against the demolition."[51] The following decision to continue the demolition was reached only by a small margin. Evidently, "old wigs" who would rather wait until the Second Coming before demolishing their beloved city walls were not a Frankfurt specialty; they existed in Bremen as well.

Seventy miles away, some Hamburg burghers took notice of the events in their sister Hanseatic city on the Weser. In June 1803, eight days after the French marched into Hamburg, several private individuals tried to convince the city's senate to undertake Hamburg's defortification as well.[52] One Hamburg senator reported how the burghers "held the continued existence of the fortification to be highly dangerous" for their own safety and urged the senate to undertake "the demolition as quickly as humanly possible." The group of burghers' main argument was a replica of Karl Theodor's arguments in Munich back in the early 1790s and the senate in Bremen's a year before: if Hamburg's walls were left intact, Hanoverian

---

50 "Bekanntmachung, 15 August 1803," StA Bremen, 2-P.2.f.6.b.1.d, p. 43e.
51 "Extract aus den Ratprotocollen der Geheimen Deputation, 21. Mai 1803," StA Bremen 2-P.2.f.6.b.1.d.
52 For a general description of Hamburg's history during the Revolutionary and Napoleonic Wars, see Burghart Schmidt, *Hamburg im Zeitalter der Französischen Revolution und Napoleons (1789–1813)*, 2 vols. (Hamburg: Verein für Hamburgische Geschichte, 1998).

and especially Prussian troops would be attracted to the city's strategically located fortifications – now occupied by the French – and cause massive destruction of property.[53]

Even now, Hamburg's senate refused to grant such requests. A year earlier, in response to a similar suggestion, a local newspaper claimed that "only foreigners" can think seriously about the demolition of Hamburg's fortifications. "Who has the right," the newspaper rhetorically asked, "to suggest to an Imperial city that it should give up its privileges to fortify and defend itself?... Such a fundamental metamorphosis of the city is simply out of the question."[54] Writing in response to the concerns raised by the group of burghers in June 1803, a majority in Hamburg's senate still opposed the demolition, although it employed weaker language than before. "The time has not yet arrived to undertake such a project," it wrote, "although in more peaceful times the senate should definitely consider this request."[55] Still, the keyword here was "consider" (and only in peacetime), by no means "accept."

It was only in the following year that Hamburg's senate reluctantly accepted the need to defortify the city. It was early October 1804, and the suggestion came once again from local burghers. As before, the group suggested that "anything and everything that could bring about the siege of this city should be demolished."[56] Unlike their earlier request, the burghers now took other factors into consideration as well. They acknowledged the fact that the walls had many police and financial roles. The demolition should proceed in such a way, they consequently wrote, "that our internal and nocturnal security would be left unaffected, and that the customs and other city revenues [related to the walls] would be secured." Such an idea was more acceptable to the senate than the earlier suggestion to simply demolish all the fortifications. Realizing the danger in keeping Hamburg fortified, but also reassured by the burghers' resolution to retain all the other roles of the fortifications, the senate finally conceded. In its resolution of October 18, 1804, the senate stated its reasons for the defortification decision clearly: "Realizing how greatly disadvantageous are Hamburg's fortifications under the current political circumstances, as well as how urgent it is to transform

53 "Protokolle des Fortifications-Departements," January 1803. StA Hamburg, 111–1, Cl VIII, Nr. V, vol. 7:33–35.
54 *Hamburg und Altona: Eine Zeitschrift* 4 (1802), 354–59.
55 "Protokolle des Fortifications-Departements," January 1803. StA Hamburg, 111–1, Cl VIII, Nr. V, vol. 7:33–35.
56 Meeder, *Geschichte von Hamburg*, 443–45.

them in such a way as to prevent the city from undergoing a siege, we hereby order that any or all parts of the fortifications that might bring about a siege of the city should be demolished immediately."[57]

As in the cases of Munich, Ehrenbreitstein, Frankfurt, and Bremen, it was not expansion or the alleged complete military uselessness of Hamburg's walls that caused the senate to finally order the city's defortification in 1804. Rather, it was a set of political circumstances. Learning of events in other German cities, Hamburg aimed to evade the consequences of siege and bombardment. "It is better to demolish our walls with spades and axes . . ." wrote one Hanseatic burgher about the logic behind the defortification of Hamburg, Bremen, and Lübeck in the first decade of the nineteenth century, "better, that is, than to have our churches and houses demolished by bombs."[58] Defortification, in such a case, was a preventive act undertaken without any prince ordering the demolition of the walls or any actual bombardment of a city. It was an act that recognized that cities could no longer protect themselves through walls and moats and bastions, but also that urban fortifications were still extremely useful for large state armies; otherwise, there would be no reason to demolish them.

In late 1804, the demolition in Hamburg was already underway. A writer for the *Allgemeine Zeitung* reported on December 28 that "500 daily workers are engaged in the defortification of the city. The ravelins have already been razed, and now the workers demolish the inner walls as well."[59] But having rejected for so long the idea that Hamburg should be defortified, the senate was unsure about how to proceed. This is where Bremen came back into the picture; after the somewhat slow progress with its own defortification, the city hired the architect Christian Ludwig Bosse and the local landscape architect Isaak Altmann to plan the new area around the city. Bosse and (especially) Altmann's solutions for the re-planning of the fortifications of Bremen were ingeniously simple: instead of completely demolishing the entire fortification works, they ordered the physical demolition of only the old (medieval) city walls in the city. The thick ramparts of the modern fortifications were left more or less intact, although Altmann turned them into an elevated park with the moat serving as a kind of pond surrounding the entire city. Such a plan saved millions for the city. In 1805, Hamburg's

57 Resolution from October 18, 1804, in Peter David Lohmann, ed., *Rath- und Bürgerschlüsse vom Jahre 1801 bis zu Ende des Jahres 1825*, vol. 1 (Hamburg, 1828). See also W. Meeder, *Geschichte von Hamburg*, 2:444–45.

58 J.U., *Ueber die Entfestigung Lübecks* (Lübeck: Rohdensche Buchhandlung, 1838), 7.

59 *Kaiserlich und Kurbayerisch priviligierte Allgemeine Zeitung*, December 28, 1804.

special fortification committee, impressed by Altmann's work in Bremen, invited him to Hamburg to help plan its defortification as well.

The information exchange between Hamburg and Bremen was not a one-way street. Architectural considerations notwithstanding, Bremen's authorities still wanted to learn from Hamburg's experience, especially about the police measures taken in the wake of its defortification. This was the purpose of a letter sent on May 8, 1805, by the Bremen *Syndicus* (city official) Eelking to Hamburg's senate. "Since even there [in Hamburg] the demolition is underway, I would like to inquire as to several issues," Eelking wrote. "Do you still have gate watchers at the entrances to the city, even after the demolition? If yes, do you use professional soldiers for this purpose or only the local militia? Are they standing there both day and night? What kinds of uniforms do they wear?"[60] Questions of honor were also on his mind, as when he inquired whether the gate watchers had to pay respect to burghers upon their entrance to the city.

The response of Hamburg's senate to Eelking's inquiries six days later makes clear how seriously the Hamburg authorities took the police role of the gate watchers even after the transformation of the military fortifications had began. "Yes," a lieutenant in the local burgher militia responded to Eelking, "the entrances to the city are still guarded here day and night, by professional soldiers during the day and by the local militia at night." "The burghers," the lieutenant continued, "do not wear uniforms, except for their commandant, who wears here, as before, a gray uniform, a triangular black hat, and a sword. When burghers enter or leave the city, the guards present their weapons to them."[61] While the military fortifications were transformed into a promenade, then, Hamburg kept intact many of the policies that helped distinguish it from its surroundings in years past. Hamburg (like Bremen) was a demilitarized city now, but not necessarily an open one. This was the consequence of the suggestions made by the burghers back in October 1804 and adopted by the senate the same month, but it was also a condition for adopting the defortification resolution in the first place.

Even with Altmann's expert help, Hamburg's actual defortification was not complete by the end of the first decade of the nineteenth century. Three factors contributed to the delays. First, the magnitude of the work was such, according to the senate's fortification committee, that it would take as many as six years to complete. Further complicating things were

60 "Herrn Syndici Eelking von Bremen Anfrage wegen Demolierung unseren Festungswerks," StA Hamburg, 111–1, Cl VII, Lit. Cc Nr. 1, vol. 3a 5.
61 Ibid.

the many legal questions about property rights in and around the former fortifications. One such legal dispute, typical for those years, concerned one Christian Friedrich Fromann. Fromann's house was adjacent to the walls and had been damaged during the demolition. Reaching a compensation agreement with him took the senate over two years.[62] Finally, there was the enormous cost of hiring workers to execute the defortification plan. In 1804, Hamburg's senate estimated that the demolition would take at least 6 years and its total costs would exceed 360,000 gulden. To cover these expenses, the city sold artillery pieces and building materials from the walls to the highest bidder. Such transactions were supposed to raise about 240,000 gulden – still a far cry from covering all the expenses associated with the defortification.[63]

Nevertheless, by the summer of 1805, much work had already been accomplished and many of the physical obstacles that had once separated Hamburg from its surroundings were gone. Some who opposed the defortification at first discovered that its aesthetic consequences were not bad, after all. One Lübecker later recalled the events in his own town, when he witnessed "with the amazement of a child" the demolition of the city walls. Yes, the walls had been beautiful in their own way, he wrote, "But can't something else replace them now, which would also be pretty in its own way?"[64] Reactions in Hamburg and Bremen, at least in some circles, were similar. "It is like witnessing a second Genesis," wrote one Hamburg poet in August 1805. "The entire landscape surrounding the city lies before us now, and the view, which in the past had been blocked [by the walls], stretches, happily, into the distance."[65] Marcus Theodor von Haupt, in Bremen, shared the same sentiments. What Altmann achieved here, he wrote in 1810, was "romantic . . . charming" and even "magical."[66]

Having found an aesthetic, honorable, and even – police-wise – compatible solution to the defortification of Bremen and Hamburg, the senates of these cities were still far from finding a political solution to their cities' dire straits. Indeed, between 1804 and 1806, the political and military position of Hamburg and its sister Hanseatic cities continued to deteriorate. The consensus in Hamburg's senate, for instance, was that the military and political situation in Germany threatened the very existence of the city. By the word "existence," Hamburgers did not refer to the city's footprint, though

62 "Differenz zwischen L.K. und Fromann," StA Hamburg, 111–1, Cl. VII, Lit. Cc Nr. 1 vol. 4g 12.
63 "Die Befestigung und Entfestigung Hamburgs," *Sonderbeiträge zum Hamburger Adressbuch* (1929): 62.
64 J.U., "Ueber die Entfestigung Lübecks," 7.
65 *Privilegirte wochentliche gemeinnützige Nachrichten von und für Hamburg*, August 7, 1805.
66 Quoted from Herbert Schwarzwälder, ed., *Bremen in alten Reisebeschreibungen, Briefe und Berichte von Reisenden zu Bremen und Umgebung, 1581–1847* (Bremen: Temmel, 2007), 279.

it, too, could have been affected by a bombardment if the walls had been kept intact and the Grande Armée or any of the opposing armies in Northern Germany elected to besiege and bombard the city. Instead, "existence" referred to what the first chapter of this book called the invisible city – the sum total of all the traditions, laws, privileges, and external relationships that made Hamburg into what it was: a free Imperial city. The existence of the city was now in jeopardy, it was agreed, because the military situation in Germany and the upcoming dissolution of the Empire pulled the rug out from under what it had meant to live in Hamburg for hundreds of years.

With the publication of the Imperial Delegation Resolution of 1803, Hamburg, Bremen, and Lübeck (along with Frankfurt, Nuremberg, and Regensburg) retained their status as free Imperial cities. Their neutrality in the ongoing conflicts in Germany was even recognized by all opposing parties. But three years later, in early August 1806, sixteen Imperial members declared that "the very ties, which up until now had connected us to the body of the German Nation, are null and void."[67] Five days later, Emperor Francis II dissolved the Empire itself. Using the same language that characterized the political vocabulary of the Empire throughout the early modern period – the "organic language" of body politic, head, and members or organs – Francis declared that "the ties that up until now have bound us to the body politic of the German Empire are hereby dissolved."[68] This did not come as a complete surprise. A host of late eighteenth-century thinkers, let alone early nineteenth-century observers, thought this process inevitable. Inevitable or not, however, the consequences of the dissolution of the Empire for cities like Hamburg and Bremen were grave and threatening. Surely, they could not defend themselves independently any longer. Their defortification in the preceding few years was a recognition of this state of affairs. But defortification was not a solution to a problem so much as a recognition that a problem existed. What would be the future of Germany's free cities, then? How could their existence be guaranteed?

In some cases, the story was relatively simple. Of the fifty-one Imperial cities that existed on the eve of the French Revolution, only six retained their free status by 1806, a number that would dwindle further to only four (Hamburg, Bremen, Lübeck, and Frankfurt) by the end of the Napoleonic Wars in 1815. The huge majority of formerly Imperial cities were incorporated into German states; they were now Bavarian, Wurrtembergian, Hessian, and so forth. The situation in the remaining free cities was

---

67 Barbara Stollberg-Rilinger, *Das Heilige Römische Reich Deutscher Nation: Vom Ende des Mittelalters bis 1806* (München: Beck, 2006), 7.
68 Ibid.

different. The dissolution of the larger body of which they had been members signified an end to their ancient allegiances. But a new constellation
in their habitat – a new environment that would define what kind of cities
they were – had yet to be formed.

A month after the dissolution of the Empire, Hamburg, Bremen, and
Lübeck sent delegates to a general conference of the Hansa cities in Lübeck.
The main agenda for the conference, as the Lübeck delegate to the conference put it, was to consider "the consequences, for the Hanseatic cities,
of the dissolution of the Holy Roman Empire."[69] The Hanseatic cities, he
explained, were no longer obliged to follow the decisions of the Imperial
Diet or the Imperial courts, and they owed no allegiance to the emperor. At
the same time, they also ceased to be protected by Imperial institutions, laws,
or armies and the emperor ceased to serve as the guarantor of their peace
because there was no longer a Holy Roman Emperor to defend any city.
"With the unraveling of the constitution of the Empire," said Johann Smidt,
Bremen's representative in the conference, "a new [political] situation for
the Hanseatic cities must be found."[70] On the symbolic level, Hamburgers,
Bremers, and Lübeckers had to decide what their cities actually were after
they had ceased to be Imperial cities. On the political-military level, all
three cities had to find ways to survive the current political storm. "We
need to gain the support of all the important forces in Germany," Smidt
observed. "But even if we achieved this, we should not conclude that our
cities would be safe from all further storms. To guarantee our existence,
we need to be always on our guard against attempts to intervene in our
internal affairs. . . . Only in this way can we hope to remain a recognized
and respected asylum of peace and quiet in the middle of the storms of this
world. . . . It is this character of our cities that we need to rescue from the
debris of the Holy Roman Empire all around us."[71]

It was above all Smidt, Bremen's representative in the Hanseatic conference of September 1806, who understood the full scope of the dramatic
change that transformed the Hanseatic cities' geopolitical environment. "A
state can guarantee its independence through several means," he wrote during the conference. "It can try to accomplish it through its own independent
military strength, it can try to do so through an alliance with other states so
that their combined strength is sufficient to deter enemies from attacking

69 "Protokolle der hanseatischen Conferenzen, September 1806," StA Hamburg 111–1, Cl. I, Lit. Pb
   Vol. 8b Fasc. 30bP:3.
70 "Verhandlungen der Hansestädte über Möglichkeiten ihre Unabhängigkeit und Neutralität zu
   bewahren; Darunter unter Doss. 4 Protokoll der Hanseatischen Konferenz der Jahren 1806, 1806–7,"
   StA Hamburg, 111–1, Cl. I, Lit. Pb Vol. 8b Fasc. 30b.
71 Ibid.

it, or it can do so by guaranteeing that it would not be in the interests of other states to find any advantage in attacking it."[72] In light of the brittle balance of power in Northern Germany after the Empire's dissolution and the Napoleonic campaigns in Germany, Smidt urged the Hanseatic cities to strive to retain their independence through the third of these options. The paradox of Hamburg and Bremen's fortifications (Lübeck had never been as heavily fortified) now became particularly evident. By 1806, the most important aim of the Hanseatic cities, as Smidt understood it, was to "retain their sovereignty within their walls and in their territories."[73] But this very sovereignty was possible only through neutrality in the ongoing conflicts in Northern Germany, and an important way of demonstrating this neutrality was by demolishing the cities' fortifications. To retain their sovereignty "within their walls," the Hanseatic cities had to demolish them.

Art historians tend to emphasize the architectural and aesthetic consequences of the defortification of Hamburg, Bremen, or any other city during the Revolutionary and Napoleonic Wars. There is a good reason for this: hundreds of German cities underwent a radical physical transformation during those years, and their appearance changed dramatically in the process. But one should not let aesthetic factors overshadow the main issue at stake in this transformation. Defortification in independent cities like Hamburg, Bremen, or Frankfurt had grave military and political consequences. Having to choose, to paraphrase an old Yiddish saying, between contracting both cholera and typhus or only cholera, these cities understandably chose the latter. "We have experienced plundering to our satisfaction," wrote one observer sarcastically after the war. "Let us at least save ourselves from bombardment!"[74] In 1806, the defortification of the remaining independent German cities did not signify a solution to all their woes, then. At least in theory, it was meant to eliminate one (military) threat while conceding that a whole range of (political) issues was still unresolved.

THE ROAD TO THE EAST, 1805–1807

That Johann Smidt used the metaphor of a storm in his description of the Hanseatic cities' strategic situation was no coincidence. "Gathering clouds," "a great storm," or "tempest": such metaphors appeared frequently in contemporary descriptions of Germany's plight from the fall of the Rhine fortresses onward. Already in 1799, Bonaparte alluded to a "tempête qui

---

72 Ibid.
73 "Aphorismen des Hern. Sen. Smidt," StA Hamburg, 111–1, Cl. I, Lit. Pb Vol. 8b Fasc. 30b.
74 J.U., *Entfestigung Lübecks*, 7.

semblait devoir anéantir l'empire germanique."[75] Six years later, when Dalberg examined the Empire's political situation, he used similar metaphors. "Opposing powers from Southern, Northern, Eastern, and Western Europe coalesce now in Germany," he wrote. As a consequence, "such a fight has surged, the likes of which has rarely been seen in the annals of man. Every German in his right mind wishes and hopes that, facing this storm, the old constitution of the Empire would still survive."[76] Even from a distance of seven decades, Theodor Fontane continued to deploy the same imagery: his first novel, set in Prussia just before Napoleon's invasion of Russia in 1812, is simply called "Before the Storm."

Indeed, by 1806 – after it had affected the west, south, and north – the war was about to affect eastern German cities as well, Prussian ones included. The early stages of the wars in the 1790s left these cities and towns largely untouched, partly because Prussia had already pulled out of the War of the First Coalition in 1795, partly because the French strategic breakthrough in Italy still lay in the future. John Quincy Adams, American ambassador to Prussia and future U.S. president, described the situation in one Prussian province around 1800 in his remarkable *Letters on Silesia* (published a few years later, in 1804). Garrison troops in Silesian towns, Adams wrote, behave in the most inhospitable manner imaginable. In Glatz, he reached the city gates at eleven in the evening, "and found that they had been shut at ten, after which they never admit anybody into the town. We were obliged to take up our quarters at an inn without the walls, and come into the city in the morning."[77] In Schweidnitz, he was subjected to the most "tedious and disgusting examinations" by four different officers before he could enter the town. "Who are you?" the officer repeatedly asked Adams, and compelled him to give an account of his entire life and adventures. "When you come to the [Prussian] fortresses, you have to run through a whole gauntlet of them," Adams wrote about such officers, "as if the soldiers meant to take there a full indemnity for all the opportunities of vexation which had been denied them."[78]

The garrison troops he met during his trip to Silesia were not only inhospitable, they were relics of a distant era, ignorant of anything that lay

75 Napoléon Bonaparte, "Exposé de la Situation de la République. Message au Sénat et au Corps Législatif (Paris, 20 février 1803)." Quoted from Napoléon Bonaparte, *Correspondance de Napoléon I, publiée par Ordre de l'Empereur Napoléon III*, eds. Henri Plon and J. Dumaine (Paris: 1861), 8:219.

76 "Regensburg, vom 11. Nov.," *Frankfurter Kaiserl. Reichs-Ober-Post-Amts Zeitung*, November 15, 1805.

77 John Quincy Adams, *Letters on Silesia: Written During a Tour Through That Country in the Years 1800, 1801* (London: Printed for J. Budd, 1804), 197.

78 Ibid., 201–02.

beyond their own neck of the woods. "You might naturally take [a typical Prussian soldier] for a Roman legionary in the days of Plautus," Adams commented. These people could not even grasp how an ambassador like himself could not have a "von" in front of his family name. Where (or what) the United States was remained a mystery to them.[79]

Soon enough, this isolation would change dramatically. By the late summer of 1805, Napoleon, frustrated by his inability to subdue Great Britain, turned east, toward Germany. In late August, he began moving close to 200,000 troops from Boulogne (20 miles south of Calais, along the English Channel) to Strasbourg. He then crossed the Rhine and marched, north of the Black Forest, toward the Danube Valley. There was no need to make a detour through Northern Italy this time, as the roads from the Upper Rhine into Swabia were unprotected after the defortification that followed Lunéville.

In October 1805, shortly after hearing of the devastating defeat of his fleet at Trafalgar, Bonaparte met the Austrians near Ulm (October 16–19), then Austerlitz (December 2), and forced the dissolution of the short-lived Third Coalition against him. In the Treaty of Pressburg, signed three weeks after the battle of Austerlitz, Austria had to reaffirm the Treaty of Lunéville, concede further territories to Napoleon's allies Bavaria, Württemberg, and Baden, and pay an indemnity of 40 million francs. Now, in command of much of central Europe but with his fleet decisively defeated by the British, Napoleon resorted to economic pressure in the hope of subduing England, his last major foe. In November 1806, he created the Continental System, a total embargo against English merchandise by a Napoleon-dominated Western Europe. In an important sense, this blockade brought the "French Model" of the early modern period to its climax. Not only was a state a fortress, as in Louis XIV's France, now all of Western Europe was to become a fortress of sorts, with its gates shut against trade with Great Britain.

The effects of this first version of "Fortress Europe" (alas, it would not be the last) were felt in German cities very acutely after 1806. Especially cities lying in the vicinity of the North Sea, including Bremen and Hamburg, were first forced to participate in the blockade (with catastrophic financial consequences for them[80]), then annexed to France in 1810 as part of a newly created French *département*. Hamburg was even refortified by the French, which used the city as a fortress as their soldiers were retreating from the disastrous Russian campaign of 1812. Thousands of burghers had

---

79 Ibid., 202.
80 For the effects of the blockade on Hamburg, see, for instance: StA Hamburg, 111-1, Senat, Cl. I, Lit. Pb Vol. 8b Fasc. 30b.

to flee Hamburg, and many more lost their property during the siege's many artillery duels. What Hamburgers feared intuitively in 1804–1806 had become a bitter reality for them a decade later.

Even before the official proclamation of Napoleon's Continental System, however, it affected the situation further to the east. When Prussia joined a new coalition against Napoleon only months after the Austrian defeat in Austerlitz, it fared no better than its longtime enemy to the south. The Prussian army lost the twin battles of Jena and Auerstedt on October 14, 1806, and Friedrich Wilhelm and his family fled to Memel, in East Prussia. Indeed, when Bonaparte officially proclaimed the creation of the Continental System he did so from occupied Berlin. Behaving as if nothing was happening beyond their town walls was no longer an option for Prussian burghers and garrison troops. Perhaps, in the past, they had shown little interest in exploring the world themselves. But by late 1806 and early 1807 – after Jena-Auerstedt – with Napoleon in Berlin and the Prussian king in distant Memel, the world had come to them. This was the case, for instance, in Silesia's capital, Breslau.

BRESLAU, 1807

In 1806, Breslau belonged to the second line of state fortresses maintained for Prussia's overall defense. The city had six main gates and six smaller ones, eight military barracks (including one on the walls themselves), no less than fifteen guardhouses in or near its gates, one enceinte, two lines of modern walls, two lines of moats, and a multitude of ravelins and bastions.[81] It was perhaps not the best-fortified city in Prussia, but its fortifications were impressive, nonetheless.

In the wake of Jena-Auerstedt, a siege of the city became imminent because what Napoleon had in mind was no less than the complete defortification of Silesia, except, perhaps, for the fortress of Glogau.[82] Even before the first French troops had reached Breslau, a state of emergency was declared in the city. In late October, gate watchers were ordered to close the gates earlier each evening and stricter police measures were implemented. A month later, with the arrival of French troops expected any day, the gates were to remain closed throughout the day, allowing entrance to the city

---

81 Johann Adam Valentin Weigel, *Geographische, naturhistorische und technologische Beschreibung des souverainen Herzogthums Schlesien* (Berlin: Hamburgische Buchhandlung, 1802), 6:106; "Breslau," S.H.A.T. Vincennes, Article 14.
82 Bonaparte, *Correspondance de Napoléon Ier*, 14: letter 11863.

only once every hour for a few minutes each time. Shortly afterward, a state of siege was declared in the city.[83]

The general orders of King Friedrich Wilhelm III regarding the issue of martial law and state of siege decrees are a good summary of the practices used by all sides in fortified cities during the wars, including Breslau. The order stipulated, among other things, that all city and state authorities had to provide requisitions of all types for the maintenance and defense of the fortress (article 1), and that the fortress commandant had the authority to put all magistrates, soldiers, and civilians under his direct command (article 3). The order further stipulated that any person posing a threat to the defense of the fortress could be punished by a court-martial, and that all property and foodstuffs in the city could be confiscated without compensation if judged necessary for the maintenance of the garrison troops (articles 4 and 7). Finally, the king ordered that attempts to convince the commandant to surrender the fortress – and even mere complaints about the measures necessary for its defense – were rebellious acts that should be dealt with in the most severe way possible (article 10). In such cases, the local population could be expelled from the city and stripped of its property without compensation.[84]

As with the walls of all other German cities, Breslau's fortifications were originally built for the defense of the city itself. By 1806, however – after almost seventy years of Prussian control (Silesia was annexed to Prussia in the 1740s) – little was left of the idea of the city in arms here. Breslau's walls were armed and maintained for the defense of Prussia, not the protection of the city. The local magistrate in Breslau made this state of affairs very clear in a proclamation to the city's inhabitants on the eve of the French siege. Breslau's defense, the proclamation stated, was not the business of the burghers, but of the state alone.[85] "The peaceful burgher," the proclamation continued, "should have nothing to do with the defense of the city. The state does not demand your participation [in the defense] at all."[86] The 6,000 men of the garrison, 208 cannons on the walls, and huge quantities of gunpowder and ammunition were meant to help the defense of Prussia, not Breslau.

---

83 Günther Gieraths, *Breslau als Garnison und Festung 1241–1941* (Hamburg: Helmut Gerhard Schulz, 1961), 30.
84 "Die Concurrenz und Verpflichtung der Civil-Autoritäten un. Communen in den Festungen u. Deren Bezirken bei Entstehender Einschließung un. Belegung. Bd. I 1809–1886, Bd. II 1894–1914," GStA PK, HA I, Rep. 77 (Ministerium des Innern, Militärabteilung Sekt. 1, 2) 330a, Nr. 18.
85 Ibid.   86 Ibid.

The French, too, paid little respect to Breslauers both during and after the siege, which was ordered by Napoleon himself, who reckoned it would take only four days.[87] In early December 1806, when the siege had already proved far more difficult than he had anticipated, Bonaparte ordered Marshal Louis-Alexandre Berthier – the commanding officer of the besieging French army – to "demolish, without losing a single hour, all the fortifications [of Breslau], except for the citadel,"[88] an order Berthier followed to the letter a month later. For Napoleon, Berthier, and their men, the siege and defortification of Breslau were technical matters. They had no sentiments respecting Breslau's history or cityscape, nor were they obligated – as the Prussian government and Breslau's local magistrates were, at least in theory – to ensure the safety of the city's inhabitants.

The first casualties of the siege were the suburbs, of which Breslau had five (the Sand-, Ohlauer-, Schweidnitzer-, Nicolai-, and Odervorstadt). During the Napoleonic Wars, the city's suburbs were the first places to suffer the devastation of a siege. Even in a relatively small town like Lindau (Swabia), the consequences of a siege in the city's surroundings were dire. One foot soldier from the Württemberg regiment that occupied the city in 1809 described how, once the regiment was inside the city, "the trees standing in the gardens [around the city] were cut down by the thousands, along with the beautiful box hedges which stood there tall and beautiful like walls, and the rest of the buildings were completely torn down, so that they would not be a hindrance to the shelling. This inflicted damage of 1 million florins on the city."[89]

In a large, expanding city like Breslau, the damage in the suburbs was even greater. Over the last few decades of the eighteenth century, the city's five suburbs expanded, and many Breslauers had property outside the walls: houses, shops, vegetable gardens, stalls, stables, and much more. Because Breslau was a state fortress, the Prussian government made clear that in case of a siege, the suburbs and gardens adjacent to the walls would be demolished in order to create a field of fire for the fortress's artillery batteries.[90] In early November 1806, the city's suburbs were set on fire by the Prussian garrison, causing damages in the millions and inciting a compensation

---

87 Bonaparte, *Correspondance de Napoléon Ier*, 14: letter 11368.
88 Ibid., 14: letter 1386.
89 Jacob Walter, *The Diary of a Napoleonic Foot Soldier*, ed. Marc Raeff (New York: Doubleday, 1991), 23.
90 Copies of these orders can be found in "Die Besetzung der Festung Breslau im J. 1807 durch die Franzosen," GStA PK, HA I, Rep. 77 (Ministerium des Innern, Militärabteilung Sekt. 1, 2) 263, Nr. 1.

dispute between burghers and government that would continue for many years.[91] When the first French troops arrived on the scene a few days later, they completed what the Prussian garrison troops had started. "Almost all the houses in the suburbs fell victim to the scorching flames," wrote one observer. "We experienced some horrible nights here, when the devastating fire raged [in the suburbs] without interruption. The horrible spectacle lasted for almost two weeks...and even to the very last moment, the poor inhabitants of the suburbs tried to rescue their possessions from their homes. They succeeded in doing so only as far as the danger from the flying projectiles allowed them to."[92]

The loss of the suburbs was not a foregone conclusion. During the Revolutionary and Napoleonic Wars, not all large German cities witnessed such destruction. True, in order to use artillery for its defense a city had to create a field of fire for it, which meant the demolition of the suburbs. But a city's commandant or his superiors could always opt for the surrender of a fortress if the price in terms of property and human life was too high. This, for instance, was the resolution reached in Vienna – the largest contemporary German city – after the Austrian defeats in Ulm and Austerlitz. The military theoretician Georg Heinrich von Berenhorst meditated on the reasons for the rapid and seemingly effortless French occupation of the city in 1806, which he found baffling. "There is only one other royal city in Europe," Berenhorst wrote, "which is as fortified as Vienna, and that is Copenhagen. But as soon as the enemy pitched its camp in front of Vienna's city gates, he was able to march in as a conqueror." The reason for this, Berenhorst continued, was simply lack of courage. "The memory of the resistance of the forefathers against Suleyman [the Great, the sixteenth-century Ottoman Sultan] seems to have been completely erased from the minds of their descendents. What was the reason for constructing and sustaining the high and strong walls of the city, the carefully planned ramparts, yes, even the long wall sections by which the entire southern part of the city was protected?"[93] Berenhorst had to conclude that the impetus for Vienna's surrender was not purely military, but had to do with the changing mentality of the Viennese, especially with the attitude toward the city's suburbs. "And then a sigh is heard," Berenhorst wrote in reply to such sentiments, "'Oh, the beautiful suburbs!' If, during a time of such distress, the only things that can be heard are sighs, then one thing is for

91 Ibid.   92 *Breslauische Erzähler* 8 (1807), vol. 2: 21.
93 Georg Heinrich von Berenhorst, *Annalen des Krieges und der Staatskunde* (Berlin: Himburg, 1806), 2:184–86.

certain. That it is completely unnecessary to maintain such high walls with so much money."[94]

Unlike Vienna (or Berlin, for that matter), Breslau was not spared the horrors and devastation of a siege by its own ruler. Apparently, some cities were more important to monarchs than others. As soon as the first bombardment began on December 10, 1806, people evacuated the top floors of buildings and looked for haven in stone-built cellars across the city. "A strange stillness descended on the city," one eyewitness reported, "no sounds of joy could be heard, no clock tower marked the hour, no rattling of wagon's wheels pierced the silence of the streets. Only the unceasing roar of the guns and the sounds of explosions when projectiles hit their targets broke the silence." "Horror and death surrounded us constantly," he continued. "Not a single day passed, nor a single night, when we did not hear about the death of neighbors and loved ones, whom the Angel of Death struck down in the most horrifying ways. . . . The city resembled an open grave in which 50,000 people awaited their deaths."[95]

In January 1807, with large parts of Breslau's fortifications damaged beyond repair and the garrison's food rations running dangerously low, the Prussian commandant was finally forced to surrender the city. The French marched through the gates. A few days later, they blew up the fortifications and Breslau ceased to be a fortified city.[96] In Munich, Frankfurt, Bremen, and Hamburg, plans were drawn before and during the demolition of the walls. There was a serious debate about, and often several conceptions of, how the city should look in the wake of defortification. In some cases, even those people who originally opposed defortification found the defortified city aesthetically pleasing. Breslau, along with a series of other cases, presented a different case.[97] A French military map of Breslau dating from shortly after its defortification makes very clear the French attitude toward the demolition of the walls: the walls were simply erased from the map, as if that was all the defortification entailed.[98]

Thus, in 1807, one did not find in Breslau a "charming landscape" (Bremen, Hamburg) or witness a "most touching spectacle" (Goethe in

---

94 Ibid.   95 *Breslauische Erzähler* 8 (1807), vol. 3:34.

96 As shown in the correspondence with the authorities in Berlin after the French occupation. GStA PK, HA I, Rep. 77 (Ministerium des Innern, Militärabteilung Sekt. 1, 2) 263, Nr. 1.

97 "In the French [i.e., Napoleonic] Wars," one military theoretician explained after the war, "the French used such [defortification] methods wherever they could: in Fort-Louis, Tarragona, Padua, Verona, Tortona, Schweidnitz, Breslau, Vienna, Raab, Scharnitz, Gratz, Spielberg, and Hüningen," among others. Karl von Decker, *Die Artillerie für alle Waffen oder Lehrbuch der Gesammten reinen und ausübenden Feld- und Belagerungs-artilleriewissenschaft* (Berlin: Mittler, 1816), 468. Other famous examples are those of Turin and Brussels.

98 S.H.A.T. Vincennes, article 14, "Breslau."

Frankfurt). "The Nicolai Gate Tower stood erect for over three hundred years," wrote one Breslauer in late 1807, "when it fell victim to the general demolition of the fortifications. This tower, which several months ago still weathered the upheavals of the times, is no more. In its ruins we see a clear proof for the temporality of all earthly things."[99] "The city," concluded another Breslauer later, "surrounded by the debris of its demolished walls, gave one the impression of a devastated place."[100]

Some sentimental reactions notwithstanding, Breslauers reacted to the siege and the subsequent defortification of their city in three major ways. The first was a call for compensation from the central government. The siege in the winter of 1806–1807 caused the burghers a tremendous loss of life and property, both inside and outside the city walls. But it was not for Breslau's sake that the burghers suffered. It was, after all, the state government that took over the defense of the city from the hands of its inhabitants and the state army that decided to defend Prussia by utilizing Breslau's fortification and burn the city's suburbs in the process. Burghers consequently flooded the government in Berlin with letters demanding that the state bear the financial burden of the property lost. As one group of burghers wrote to Berlin during the long correspondence about this matter, "A fortress is maintained for the defense and benefit of the entire province. It is only fair, therefore, that the entire province would participate in covering the damages of a bombardment."[101]

Another reaction of burghers to the circumstances of those years was a surge in the theft of building materials from the remains of the walls. Such cases of theft were ubiquitous in Germany in the 1790s and 1800s. It was common in small towns like Forchheim (Bavaria),[102] in middle-size cities like Augsburg,[103] and big cities like Breslau. The thieves left no written documentation of their actions, of course, but state officials often commented on these incidents with alarm. A secret letter directed to the Prussian ministry of interior in 1812 details the sorts of incidents prevalent in what was left of Breslau's fortifications. "The theft of building materials from the fortification works and buildings have gained unprecedented dimensions in this city," reported the royal commandant and the military engineer to the minister of interior. "We would like to mention in particular that at present no door, lock, or hinge is safe from theft. Any conceivable object

99 *Breslauische Erzähler* 8 (1807), vol. 8:555.
100 Henrich Steffens, *Was ich erlebte* (Breslau: Joseph Max, 1843), 7:8.
101 "Die Besetzung der Festung Breslau," GStA PK, HA I, Rep. 77 (Ministerium des Innern, Militärabteilung Sekt. 1, 2) 263, Nr. 1.
102 "Forchheim: Tore, Wacht- und Torhäuser," Bayer. HStA KA, MKr 8046 and 9605–74.
103 "Augsburg: Stadtthore, Thürme," Bayer. HStA KA, MKr 7791.

made of iron has already been stolen from the debris of the fortifications works around the city. Even the locks we used to prevent people from entering adjacent buildings are now lost, and we had no choice but to nail up all doors and gates."[104]

Apparently, it was not only the inhabitants themselves who engaged in such acts. "It would be in vain to order the garrison troops to keep an eye on the fortifications," the commandant and military engineer continued their letter. "Since the troops themselves are suspect of taking part in the thefts. Even the palisades surrounding the fortifications works are gone now, stolen by the inhabitants of the suburbs who were probably also responsible for taking the large iron chains that blocked the entrance to the city from different directions. We fervently ask for your assistance in allowing the strictest punishments for such offences."[105]

With large parts of the walls blown up, Breslau's suburbs reduced to charred badlands, and Prussia's army defeated, the Prussian government resorted to creative solutions to counter the situation in the city. It was forced to accept the fact that Breslau was no longer a state fortress and find a way to reattach and "re-endear" the burghers to the state if it wanted to effectively oppose the Grande Armée in the future. The solution here, as in other contemporary Prussian cities and towns, was to compensate the burghers by granting them the rights to use the terrain as well as the remaining structures of the fortifications as they saw fit. In July 1809, Friedrich Wilhelm made this decision official for Breslau with a proclamation. "Under the current circumstances," the king ordered, "the rebuilding of Breslau's fortifications is out of the question. I have therefore decided to transfer the property rights over the remains of the fortifications to the burghers of the city as a sign of my good will and as a form of compensation for their losses during the war. I have now made this decision official, with the understanding that the exact decision as to the new buildings to be constructed in the terrain of the former fortifications would be decided upon by a combined committee of both military and civil authorities."[106]

There was more than a little disingenuousness in this order: most parts of the walls were already gone and the burghers were already taking building material from the walls without the king's permission. The important point was this: whereas a typical eighteenth-century defortification such

---

104 "Die Diebstähle an den Königl. Festungswerken, Gebäuden und Materialen. 1812," GStA PK, HA I, Rep. 77 (Ministerium des Innern, Militärabteilung Sekt. 1, 2) 330a, Nr. 14.
105 Ibid.
106 "Die Besetzung der Festung Breslau," GStA PK, HA I, Rep. 77 (Ministerium des Innern, Militärabteilung Sekt. 1, 2) 263, Nr. 1.

as Munich's was an open act of aggression by the prince against the burghers, Breslau's defortification was utilized by Friedrich Wilhelm and his government as a marker of a new contract between state and burghers. Friedrich Wilhelm accepted his responsibility vis-à-vis the burghers, although legally he did not have to do so. The legal measures of the eighteenth century explicitly stated that the construction of buildings and gardens in the suburbs was risky, and that in case of a siege the state would be entitled to demolish any or all structures in the suburbs without compensation to the property owners. What the order of 1809 did, then, was to reattach the burghers to the Prussian king. This was not done by allowing the burghers to participate once again in the defense of their city, by turning the clock back to the sixteenth or seventeenth centuries. Rather, it was done by compensating the burghers materially for their strife and property loss. Such a form of compensation was not restricted to Breslau; it would be repeated in other Prussian towns that took Breslau's case as their primary model.[107]

Last but not least were the debates about the overall plan for the empty areas vacated by the fortifications. It was one thing to order that the exposed belt around the city would serve the city's inhabitants and not the state; it was quite another to decide exactly how to do so: where to lay new streets, what to do about the gates and moats, and whether to use the newly created area for commerce and residential buildings or as a promenade and public park.

The debates about Breslau's future footprint took place both in the chambers of the city's magistrates and publicly in the local press. Following Friedrich Wilhelm's grant of the old, largely demolished fortifications to the city, the general inspector of buildings, Johann Friedrich Knorr, was given the task of re-planning the area. His plan foresaw turning the old fortifications into a series of promenades and public parks, the integration of the old moats into the parks, and the complete demolition of all the old gates. Despite the bitter opposition of some people – including the director of the local academy of arts, Carl Daniel Bach, and magistrates such as Carl Ferdinand Langhans, who had some radically (and some have said fantastic) ideas about what to do with the vacated area – Knorr managed to push his plan through. But as the works progressed slowly between 1815 and 1821, the debates between Knorr and his opponents never completely subsided,

---

107 The Prussian ministry of the interior collected all relevant materials concerning Breslau's case, assessed them, and used them as a template for similar cases. This is why, as opposed to most defortification cases, the issue of the compensation of Breslau's burghers was not handled on the provincial level but by the highest echelons of the Prussian government in Berlin.

and Knorr (not an easy man to interact with) was not reappointed to his position when his term as the general inspector of buildings was over in 1821. What was at stake in this dispute were surely different aesthetic views of the city's future, but very likely also the enormous potential for the creation and selling of real estate in place of, and around, the demolished fortifications.[108]

That the public was also interested in the issue of the re-planning of the city is clear. "It seems to us that a matter of so great importance to all of Breslau's inhabitants should be discussed publicly," proclaimed one article in the *Schlesische Provinzialblätter* in 1814 in response to the secret dealings of the city council. "The general will of the inhabitants is therefore to receive the detailed plan of the new works, on the basis of which the debate can continue." All of this, continues the author, is of the utmost importance because so far all one can see around the old city is work here and there, "and in many places we see the construction of unpleasant wooden barriers, which cause us to believe that this newly-created, magnificent space [of the demolished fortifications] would shortly disappear."[109] Other journalists continued the debate by disputing the idea that the decision about the city's new footprint should be made by the public and not (as was in fact the case) by a small group of experts.[110] At times, writers concentrated on more specific issues, such as the kind of vegetation that should be used for the creation of shaded boulevards around the old city.[111] In many of these articles, a curious word appears over and over again: the area of the old fortifications and even the city itself are suddenly described as "spaces." The final chapter of this book will come back to the importance of the appearance of the term "space" in defortification debates. Suffice it to say at this point that this appearance signifies a fundamental shift in the way locals spoke about their cities in the transition from the eighteenth to the nineteenth centuries. The city, or at least one of its parts, was no longer perceived as an organism; it was an abstract, open, perhaps even geometric phenomenon, an area (rather than a living thing) that can be planned, manipulated, filled in.

---

108 Gerhard Scheuermann, ed., *Das Breslau-Lexikon* (Dülmen: Laumann Verlag, 1994), 1:809–10.
109 "Breslau's abgetragene Wälle und deren Verschönerung," *Schlesische Provinzialblätter* 60 (1814): 324–28. Italics in the original.
110 "Die Berge gebären! – die Wälle fallen!," *Schlesische Provinzialblätter* 61 (1815): 433–39; and "Gedanken über die Verschönerung Breslau's, in Hinsicht der abgetragenen Wälle," *Schlesische Provinzialblätter* 60 (1814): 423–31.
111 "Ueber die Bepflanzung öffentlicher Lustörter mit Bäumen, mit Rücksicht auf Breslau's Verschönerung," *Schlesische Provinzialblätter* 60 (1814): 503–10.

1815: AN END AND A BEGINNING

The following chapter, which will concentrate on the effects of the defortification surge on the cases of fortresses, home towns, and metropolises between 1815 and 1848, will also have more to say about the events of 1791–1815. The cases of smaller urban communities, Mack Walker's famous "German home towns," especially still need to be discussed. It is time, however, to draw some general conclusions about the character of the great defortification surge, about its causes, and about common reactions to it.

One of the most important characteristics of the defortification surge was its scope. Travelers to Germany around 1815 could still see vestiges of the old walls in many cities and towns. In a minority of cases, the walls managed to survive the great storm of the previous twenty-four years; in others, the demolition of the fortifications was a project of such massive scale that it would take many more years to complete. But by the summer of 1815, after Wellington and Blücher had defeated Napoleon at Waterloo, the German urban landscape was already radically different from what it had been before the 1790s. Defortified cities, which up until the Revolutionary and Napoleonic Wars had been the exception in the German lands, had become the norm.

The defortification surge was massive in numerical terms, but it was also unprecedented in its geographical scope. Between 1689–1789, defortification was concentrated in specific areas (along the Rhine and in the north) or affected only certain types of cities (princely residence towns). The defortification surge of the Revolutionary, and especially the Napoleonic, Wars affected all German regions and all types of cities: fortresses and residences, free cities and home towns, northern cities and southern ones, cities located in Germany's western provinces and those located in the east. The surge of 1789–1815, unlike previous defortification waves, was a general, nationwide event.

Although the defortification surge was a general phenomenon, there were clearly huge differences in its instigation and progress. The geopolitical, military, and social contexts of different cities and the physical differences between any two systems of fortification made this inevitable. Sometimes the local absolutist prince demolished city walls (Munich); in other cities, it was the French who blew up urban fortifications (Ehrenbreitstein, Breslau); and in a third group of cities, it was the burghers themselves who decided to defortify (Frankfurt am Main, Bremen, Hamburg). In fact, it was the diversity of defortification's instigators that allowed the surge to swell to such huge dimensions.

It is still common to credit the Napoleonic experience for rendering the construction and maintenance of fortresses obsolete. But had fortresses possessed no military value, the burghers of Munich would not have objected to the elector and Rumford's plans; Frankfurters would not have sought to defend their city in the 1790s by means of their walls; Hamburgers would not have felt a need to quickly raze their ancient fortifications after 1804; and the French army would not have blown up Ehrenbreitstein's walls in 1801 and Breslau's six years later. Far from confirming the simplified argument that urban fortifications played no role during the Revolutionary and Napoleonic Wars, these cases underline the continuing strategic importance of state fortresses.[112] The principal motivation for the demolition of so many city walls in Germany in the transition to the nineteenth century was not their supposed uselessness but their potential usefulness. This is conspicuously evident in cities defortified both by the Grande Armée and by local burghers. The former wanted to deprive German states of their ability to defend themselves; the latter did their best to avoid the horrors of siege and occupation.

Another important conclusion one should draw from the case studies discussed here relates to the decline of the ancient idea of the city in arms. Although fortresses could still be useful to large state armies, the ancient idea that the urban community should be able to defend itself had become a thing of the past. How a city should be defended in the future depended, now more than ever before, on the urban organism's situation within its geopolitical habitat. This is one reason defortification was not only – and perhaps not even primarily – a military event but a political one, too. Bonaparte himself emphasized this point in his letter to the magistrates of Frankfurt am Main in 1800; the senate in Hamburg made it clear in its defortification decision of 1804; and Friedrich Wilhelm commented on it in the wake of the defortification of Breslau. We also saw how the method and pace of defortification depended on political considerations. When the political circumstances of the city worsened, defortification was often accelerated (Munich, Frankfurt, Hamburg), and while the French could allow themselves to simply blow up fortifications (Ehrenbreitstein, Breslau), local governments had to adopt a far more cautious and slower method (Munich, Hamburg, Bremen, Frankfurt).

Diversity and uniformity were closely related to one another during the defortification surge: it was the very diversity of instigators that allowed

---

112 Napoleon's concerns regarding fortresses in Germany are evident, for instance, in his published letters. See: Bonaparte, *Correspondance de Napoléon Ier*, 14: letters 11354, 11368, 11386, 11407, and 11586.

the surge to reach its unprecedented dimensions. The same relationship between diversity and unity is evident in common reactions to defortification in those years, reactions that were simultaneously diverse and uniform. Some Germans, especially in the early stages of the defortification surge, experienced a deep sense of grief, melancholy, and anxiety when they watched the demolition of the ancient symbols of their cities' history, traditions, and honor. This was the case in Munich, Ehrenbreitstein, and Hamburg, and it was most eloquently expressed by the dirges over the "death" of the Brückenturm in Frankfurt am Main in 1801. The demolition was viewed by such observers as a sign of the general collapse of the world of the Holy Roman Empire, the old world in which city walls had made sense. These reactions make clear that defortification was much more than a military event or even a political moment. It was also a highly emotional experience for contemporaries whose writings reflected the fact that the old perception and definition of the German city were rapidly dying away.

As the wars drew on, more and more burghers reacted to defortification in a positive way. Already in Mannheim (1799) and Ulm (1800), some locals celebrated rather than bemoaned the demolition, and in subsequent years an increasing number of Germans would follow in their footsteps. Such sentiments were expressed most eloquently by Goethe's beautiful letter to her son and in the description of the defortified Gotha in 1810, which was quoted in Chapter 1. Such joyful reactions to defortification were of course very different from the anxiety or ambivalence expressed by other contemporaries, but the joy, confusion, and anxiety all expressed a fundamental, unified insight: an appreciation of the fact that the old conception of the city was collapsing and a new era in the history of the city was about to begin. For some, this was a sad moment, while for others it was a sign of the new opportunities created by defortification, be they aesthetic (Gotha), social (Frankfurt), or political (Ulm, Munich, Breslau). The unifying theme of these diverse reactions, however, was the same: a basic consensus that defortification marked a watershed in the history of the city, a point in time that divided a "before" from an "after," an "old city" from a "new city."

In the wake of defortification, the widening gap between the present and past explains the paradoxical phenomenon of the romanticizing of the walled city. It is, of course, a phenomenon that is still with us today. At first, to romanticize the walled city seems like a contradiction in terms. German Romantics, before they turned toward nationalism (and some, like Eichendorff, even thereafter), were not preoccupied with walled urban communities but with the individual, with nature, with the seeming infinitude of the sea, the forest, the night, and the universe itself. "Refugee in the world that I am, I have no home," wrote the young Friedrich Schlegel to his friend Novalis;[113] "When God decides to show his favor/He sends one into the wide, wild world" and "Travel further, I shall not ask/where the road is leading," adds Eichendorff.[114] This opposition of man and the infinite was perhaps most elegantly depicted in that most famous of all romantic paintings, Kaspar David Friedrich's *Wanderer over a Sea of Fog* (1818). No wonder, therefore, that the Romantics did not prefer to live in the seclusion of walled cities; they did not seek to turn the clock back and actually live in the Middle Ages. (The only exception seems to be Hölderlin, who spent the last thirty-six years of his life in one of the old gate towers in Tübingen. He did not do so, however, out of choice, but was forced into this protected lifestyle after suffering a nervous breakdown.) How can all of this be squared with the fact that almost all German Romantics described and idealized the walled city, a monument that belonged to a world of communal honor, restrictions, and locality – the opposite, in many ways, of what they believed in, at least at first?

The explanation for this paradox lies in the widening temporal gap between the urban world of the early nineteenth century and the fast-disappearing world of the walled city. For the Romantics, the modern city seemed inorganic; it was, to E.T.A. Hoffman, for instance, a populated yet "desolate space," a place without a soul.[115] The premodern walled city was perhaps near at hand physically, but it was also far away temporally. This was well expressed by Ludwig Tieck, one of the earliest German Romantics, who in the 1790s traveled to Franconia with his friend Wilhelm Heinrich Wackenroder. The two friends wandered through the province and visited Bamberg, Bayreuth, and Pommersfelden. They viewed the old city of Nuremberg and listened to the night watchman calling the hours from his tower during the night. With its walls and towers resembling sails and masts, Nuremberg seemed to them like a stranded, majestic ship from a bygone era, a kind of Noah's Ark miraculously saved from a lost, submerged world. Tieck even translated this temporal distance into a physical one in his recollections from that trip. Franconia, with all of its walled cities,

---

113 Max Preitz, ed., *Friedrich Schlegel und Novalis: Biographie einer Romantikerfreundschaft in ihren Briefen* (Darmstadt: Gentner, 1957), 139.

114 Joseph von Eichendorff, *Der Frohe Wandersmann* (1823) and *Frische Fahrt* (1841).

115 E.T.A. Hoffmann, *Poetische Werke in sechs Bänden* (Berlin: Aufbau Verlag, 1958), 6:281–88. Compare also Joseph von Eichendorff's critique of the modern city as a machine in *Ahnung und Gegenwart* (1815). Joseph von Eichendorff, *Werke in einem Band* (München: Carl Hanser, 2007), 605.

"is a place so unexplored," he wrote, "that one might have assumed it is in Africa or Asia."[116]

For Tieck, Weckenroder, and many other Romantics, although walled cities were still present in some parts of early nineteenth-century Germany, they were also far, far away; they became ephemeral and melancholic. They seemed to have vanished into the infinitude of the past, just like medieval castles and knights, witches and fairies. Achim von Arnim famously wrote in 1820 how "We leaf [now] through an old calendar, where the engravings reflect the foolishness of bygone eras. But how they seem to us now to represent a magical, fabulous world!" "How richly full," he continued, "was the world then, before the general revolution . . . had brought down all the old forms! It seems as if centuries had passed since that time, and only with difficulty do we recall that our youth still belonged to it."[117] This perceived temporal gap between the modern and the old was exactly what made the romanticizing of city walls possible. Because they belonged to the old, submerged world of the past, the walls acquired a romantic, magical, and ephemeral aura. Because they no longer belonged to the contemporary world, the walls could be projected onto an imagined distant place (Tieck's Africa and Asia), to that faraway-ness that was so quintessentially romantic. In a nutshell: fading into the past, the walled city could be romanticized because just like the trees of a huge forest, waves of the ocean, or shadows of the night, it, too, now belonged to a seemingly endless entity – the past with all of its roaming ghosts.

By 1815, then, German cities seemed to be on the verge of a new era. The old idea of the city as a fortified, protected place had passed into a different world, just like Frankfurt's Brückenturm. Most German cities were now open, oriented toward an uncertain future that no contemporary could precisely predict. German cities were yet to be industrialized; the opening of the first German railway line was twenty years to come. But with a clear break in the city's history and its habitat dramatically transformed from an ancient empire into a central Europe disenchanted with its old political culture, a new period in the history of German cities and the idea of the German city was about to begin. Beyond all the many important aspects of the defortification surge, this was perhaps its greatest consequence: the acceptance – whether mournful, joyful, ambivalent, or romantic – of the fact that German cities would never quite be their old selves again, that

---

116 Ludwig Tieck, *Schriften in zwölf Bänden*, ed. Manfred Frank (Frankfurt am Main: Deutscher Klassiker Verlag, 1985), 2:18.
117 Achim von Arnim, *Isabella von Ägypten und andere Erzählungen* (Zürich: Manesse Verlag, 1959), 315.

defortification represented not only a physical break in the city's footprint but also a temporal break in its long history. In 1815, one did not have to count defortification cases, as a previous chapter had done, to realize the magnitude of the change. Evidence for it was present everywhere: in the south, west, north, and east, in Munich, Ehrenbreitstein, Frankfurt, Bremen, Breslau, and many hundred similar cases. Even in Hamburg, which in 1815 was still surrounded by walls (the ones the French erected during their retreat from Russia in 1813), a dramatic change had taken place. Richard Boyle Bernard, an Irish M.P. who traveled to Hamburg just after the French evacuated the city in 1814, could not have expressed it any better when he wrote, considering the relationship between Hamburg and its ancient walls, that "Hamburg has recently afforded a melancholy example of the evil which walls may bring upon a city."[118]

118 Richard Boyle Bernard, *A Tour Through Some Parts of France, Switzerland, Savoy, Germany and Belgium* (Philadelphia: Edward Earle, 1815), 190.

PART III

After the Deluge, 1815–1866

6

Restoration's Boundaries

Fortress, Home Town, Metropolis, 1815–1848

In *Elective Affinities*, Johann Wolfgang von Goethe's characters reflect on the meaning of change in early nineteenth-century Germany. As opposed to many contemporaries who see their period as the age of "Great Men," Goethe's characters feel that the events of the Napoleonic Wars – including the demolition of city walls – have transcended the contribution of any single actor, even one as "great" as Napoleon Bonaparte himself. "As life draws us along," meditates Charlotte, the novel's heroine, "we think we are acting of our own volition, ourselves choosing what we shall do and what we shall enjoy; but when we look more closely we see they are only the intentions and inclinations of the age which we are being compelled to comply with."[1] Charlotte's interlocutor, a schoolmaster, agrees with her. Men, for the schoolmaster, do not shape their era; it is the age that shapes men. "If a son's youth happens to coincide with an age of transition, you may be sure he will have nothing in common with his father," he says. "If the father lived in a period in which there was a desire to acquire property and to secure, limit, and enclose it and to fortify one's pleasure in it through seclusion from the world, then the son will try to expand, open out, spread abroad and unlock the gates."[2] "Whole ages are like this father and son you have described," Charlotte agrees:

[W]e can scarcely imagine the days in which every little town had to have its walls and moats, every manor house was built in the middle of a marsh, and the meanest castle was accessible only by a drawbridge. Even the bigger cities are now taking down their walls, the moats even of the castles of princes are being filled in, the towns are now nothing more than big villages [*große Flecken*] without defenses, and when you travel around and see all this you might think universal peace had been

1 With some minor changes, the following quotes are based on Johann Wolfgang von Goethe, *Elective Affinities*, trans. R.J. Hollingdale (Harmondsworth: Penguin, 1971), 217–18.
2 Ibid., 217.

established and the Golden Age to be at hand. . . . Do you think, my friend, that we could go back from this state of things to another, earlier state?[3]

As Goethe wrote these lines in 1808, the great defortification surge had already affected almost every corner of the German lands. In its wake, Charlotte's disbelief in the possibility of a return to an earlier state of affairs – when cities were closed and fortified and their walls, moats, drawbridges, and towers dwarfed their surroundings – seemed justified. Perhaps a Golden Age was not at hand. The suffering caused by the wars, the sheer misery and fear and anxiety – all of which, as Chapter 5 argued, contributed to the surge's magnitude – had guaranteed that. But to turn back the clock on the events of the previous twenty years seemed all but impossible. Could the walls really be rebuilt? The cities turned back to closed, protected places? Were not the Napoleonic Wars, which witnessed the death of the idea of the city in arms in Germany, also the swan song of the walled, closed German city?

Goethe's novel provides an unexpected answer to Charlotte's question, a reply that might surprise a reader used to the idea that the demolition of city walls was an uncomplicated, linear development. "Why not?" the schoolmaster replies to Charlotte's question with a question of his own. "Every state of things has its difficulties, the restricted as much as the free. . . . As soon as shortages occur, self-restriction at once returns. Men who are compelled to make use of their land again erect walls around their gardens to secure to themselves its produce." "Believe me," he finally adds, "it is quite possible that your son will turn his back on all your parklands and retire again behind the grave walls and among the tall lime-trees of his grandfather."[4]

Goethe's characters are of course fictitious, but the scenarios they outline – Charlotte's disbelief in the possibility of turning back the clock and the schoolmaster's different opinion about the matter – seemed to be very real options after 1815. When the Napoleonic Wars were over, German burghers and states had the choice of either accepting the new reality created by the wars, including the opening up of hundreds of cities, or attempting to restore the political and physical boundaries of the world Bonaparte had done so much to destroy. During the three decades after Waterloo, one can find realizations of both these potential courses of events: cities that remained open and cities that were refortified. Of Charlotte and the schoolmaster's proffered scenarios, however, it was the latter's that dominated in the years immediately after 1815. The old political universe of the Holy

3 Ibid., 218.   4 Ibid.

Roman Empire and its fortified cities was not recreated. But in the case of city walls, much was done to reverse the trends of the massive defortification surge of the previous two decades. Great fortresses were repaired, rebuilt, or even erected anew; many German home towns remained closed to the outer world; and even in Germany's most rapidly expanding cities – Vienna, Berlin, Hamburg, and Munich – some form of physical separation between the city and its immediate surroundings persisted or was even strengthened. There is good reason to believe that Charlotte's son, as the schoolmaster had suggested, was indeed more likely to live in a closed, protected city in 1828 than his mother had been two decades earlier.

The reasons behind attempts to turn back the clock and reestablish the old, closed character of many German cities between 1815 and 1848 were political. They were not, as both Charlotte and the schoolmaster suggested, the result of the abstract forces of the times, if one is to understand such an expression to mean forces devoid of any human agency. All too often, historians have attributed the demolition of city walls to such abstract, impersonal forces: economic, technological, or demographic forces that caused the walls to disappear over time. It was, however, not technology or the economy or even expansion that erected or demolished city walls. It was rather human beings that at times (though not always) deployed economic, technological, and demographic arguments. The nature of decisions to erect or demolish urban fortifications remained as fundamentally political after 1815 as it had been throughout the long history of city walls in German-speaking central Europe.

The essentially political nature of the events in German cities after 1815 explains a curious fact. "Restoration," the term most frequently used to describe the political systems that emerged in many German states after 1815, corresponds directly to practices on the ground concerning the German city's physical boundaries. Restoration was not merely an architectural metaphor for a political ideal. In the case of German city walls, restoration was also an actual, physical event.

The political concerns that shaped the discussions about German city walls between 1815 and 1848 related to three types of cities: fortresses, home towns, and metropolises. The need for security, both external and internal, and the question of property were two leitmotifs that appeared in discussions about all such cities. But while the general set of concerns was similar, the relative weight of specific issues was different in each type of city. In fortresses, the main concern was the defense of states from external threats; in home towns, discussions about city walls revolved around questions of property and the community's self-definition; and in metropolitan areas, the maintenance of walls was above all a reaction to concerns about states' internal security – the fear that states might lose control over their rapidly expanding urban population and be toppled from within.

FORTRESSES

In most military histories of the nineteenth century, fortresses occupy a marginal place.[5] It has become almost a cliché to describe Napoleon's campaigns as a watershed in military history, when the open maneuver replaced the static wars of absolutist monarchs and the great annihilation battle took the place of the siege warfare of preceding centuries. One historian even claims to know the exact year, month, and even day when this transformation of military history happened.[6] At first glance, the German case seems to corroborate these "watershed" narratives. During the Napoleonic Wars, the ancient idea of the city in arms was dealt a mortal blow in Germany, the Prussian fortresses surrendered to Bonaparte's army one after the other (with the symbolically important exception of the fortress of Kolberg), and the old cabinet wars of the eighteenth century were replaced – at least in popular imagination – by a new model of "people's war." Goethe himself is often cited to support the watershed narrative. Long after the end of the Napoleonic Wars, he reminisced about the "Cannonade of Valmy" (1792), writing that "[f]rom this place and from this day forth begins a new era in the history of the world."[7]

The famous British caricaturist James Gillray (1757–1815) had depicted the collision between the old and new ways of waging war along such lines as early as 1805 (figure 19). On the left-hand side of Gillray's caricature, General Mack – the commander of the Austrian forces in Ulm – obese, outfitted in outdated dress, wearing a periwig, and prostrate on the ground, throws aside his sword and presents to Napoleon the keys to the fortress. Behind him stand the medieval towers and walls of Ulm's fortifications. On the right-hand side of the caricature, sits a young, self-assured Bonaparte, sword in hand, perched atop a war drum and surrounded by his personal guard. The sky above the French army on the right is pierced by *tricolors*; on the ground before Napoleon lies a recumbent Imperial flag. In Gillray's

---

5 Some examples are John Keegan, *A History of Warfare* (New York: Knopf, 1993); Geoffrey Parker, *The Cambridge History of Warfare* (New York: Cambridge University Press, 2005); and Archer Jones, *The Art of War in the Western World* (Urbana: University of Illinois Press, 1987).
6 Martin Van Creveld, *Supplying War: Logistics from Wallenstein to Patton* (New York: Cambridge University Press, 1977), 40–42.
7 David Bell, *The First Total War: Napoleon's Europe and the Birth of Warfare as We Know It* (Boston: Houghton Mifflin, 2007), 131.

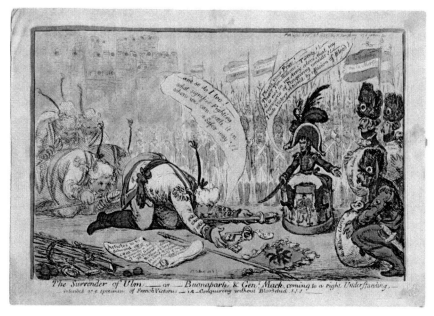

Figure 19. James Gillray, *The Surrender of Ulm – or, – Bonaparte & General Mack, coming to right understanding* (1805). *Source:* Anne S. K. Brown Military Collection, Brown University Library.

caricature, Mack and Austria represent the outdated, fortified, and dishonored world of yesteryear while Napoleon and the Grande Armée stand for the new, open, and modern world of warfare.

When military history is narrated in this dualistic fashion of old versus new and fortifications versus openness, the reestablishment of dozens of fortresses in post-Napoleonic Germany makes little sense. It can perhaps be interpreted only as an expression of the romantic nostalgia for the lost world of the Middle Ages prevalent in early nineteenth-century Germany, not unlike the reasons historians ascribe to some princes' decisions to construct neo-gothic castles in the country during the long nineteenth century: Löwenburg in Hessen-Kassel, Franzenburg near Vienna, and that most famous of all German tourist attractions, Neuschwanstein in Bavaria.[8]

A deeper examination of the military and political conclusions that German states drew from the Napoleonic experience reveals a much more equivocal picture. Let there be no mistake about it: by 1815, the idea of the city in arms was dead. No single German city could reasonably

8 Cf. James J. Sheehan, *German History, 1770–1866* (New York: Oxford University Press, 1989), 391.

hope to defend itself only by moats, walls, and artillery. Indeed, after 1815, Hamburg, Lübeck, Bremen, and Frankfurt am Main – the only four independent German cities still in existence – remained defortified and would never try to erect military defenses again. But while the defense of single cities through strong fortifications was ruled outdated, the defense of the state through fortresses was still very much alive. In a city, there was little difference between the tactical and strategic levels of war: between the level of the battle or siege on the one hand, and the level of the war as a whole on the other hand. For a city, to be on the losing side of a siege was by definition to be on the losing side of the war. But for a large territorial state there existed a fundamental difference between tactics and strategy. A large territorial state could still survive the loss of a single battle or a few fortresses, regroup its forces, and live to fight another day. Even after 1815, states could still use fortresses to secure their borders, block or delay an invading army, or keep the military magazines secure. If the state's defensive system were planned wisely, the loss of a few fortresses would by no means imply the end of the war.

The clearest theoretical formulation of the continued importance of fortresses in post-Napoleonic Germany can be found in Carl von Clausewitz's famous treatise *On War* (1832). Clausewitz witnessed many of the events of the Napoleonic Wars up close. In 1793, while still a young ensign in a Prussian regiment (he was only thirteen at the time), he participated in the siege of Mainz. He later participated in the battles of Jena and Auerstedt (1806) and became involved in planning the reforms in the Prussian army led by his patron, Gerhard von Scharnhorst. In 1808, Clausewitz left for Russia and witnessed Napoleon's defeat during the campaign of 1812, before finally returning to Prussia. Clausewitz, in short, enjoyed a privileged position from which to view and reflect on the Napoleonic Wars. *On War*, though published posthumously, contains many of the theoretical foundations that guided the Prussian army during the reforms and the Restoration years.[9]

Clausewitz defined war through politics, force, and human will. War was the "continuation of politics by other means."[10] It was not an isolated phenomenon, divorced from other state actions, but rather the forceful pursuit of the state's political objectives once diplomacy had failed, a phenomenon

---

9 On Clausewitz's life as well as about his overall influence on the Prussian army, see Peter Paret, *Clausewitz and the State: The Man, His Theories, and His Times* (Princeton: Princeton University Press, 1976). On Clausewitz's continuing influence on the Prussian army, with some important reservations, see Michael Howard, "The Influence of Clausewitz," in Carl von Clausewitz, *On War*, trans. Michael Howard and Peter Paret (Princeton: Princeton University Press, 1976), 27–44.

10 Clausewitz, *On War*, 87.

he equated with a wrestling contest between two giants (states), where each tries to force the other to bow down to his own will.[11] To achieve such a superiority of will in the geopolitical context of the early nineteenth century, Clausewitz advocated the annihilation of the opponent's military forces in a single battle and the occupation of the opponent's "center of gravity," which was usually the capital.[12] The first of these principles aimed at quickly depriving the opponent of the means to achieve his political objectives by force while the second targeted the very heart (the capital) of the opposing state: it targeted the ability to have a political will at all. The seizure of the capital was therefore especially important if "it is not only the center of administration but also that of social, professional, and political activity" in the state.[13]

That Clausewitz underlined the idea of the "battle of annihilation" did not mean that he also gave up the idea of a fortified frontier or even fortified towns located in the state's hinterland. Fortresses were not, and could not be, the main means of forcing the opponent to follow one's will. They could, however, still be crucial for the management of the military in peacetime and for both defensive and offensive operations in wartimes. In *On War*, Clausewitz concedes that "[t]he time is past when mere enclosures and fortifications, without any other military preparations, protect a locality against a tide of war that inundates the whole country."[14] But he rejects the tendency of some of his contemporaries (we shall come back to them later in this chapter) to completely "discard the notion of using fortresses for the immediate protection of the population and property of the towns."[15] Even if fortresses and walled cities should not be as numerous as in previous centuries, they remained, in Clausewitz's opinion, crucial to a country's defense system.

Clausewitz advanced no fewer than eleven reasons for the continued strategic and tactical importance of urban fortifications. Fortresses, he wrote, were important as secure depots for the army, defenses of certain cities and towns, obstacles to an invasion of one's own territory, and convenient resting points for troops moving up and down the marching line – along with being important in many other respects.[16] Though no longer the sole means of waging war, they still had a crucial role to play in the military constitution of a strong territorial state. Fortresses, Clausewitz wrote, are "the knots that hold the web of [state] strategy together."[17]

11 Ibid., 75.
13 Ibid., 596.
15 Ibid., 394–95.
16 For the entire discussion of Clausewitz's views on fortifications, see Ibid., 393–403.
17 Ibid., 394.

12 Ibid., 595–600.
14 Ibid., 393.

The maintenance and even rebuilding of fortresses after 1815 was not only a consequence of abstract theoretical maxims; they were also related to a commonly held interpretation of the reasons for the Grande Armée's successes during the Revolutionary and Napoleonic Wars, an interpretation far more equivocal than the watershed narrative one finds in so many military histories. The previous chapter already noted how the military theoretician Georg Heinrich von Berenhorst interpreted the refusal of the Viennese to defend their city and the consequent surrender of Vienna in 1805. For Berenhorst, these events were a sign of a lack of will and motivation, not a sign of the absence of logic behind the construction and maintenance of urban fortified defenses per se. He was by no means alone in this view. In 1797, Gerhard von Scharnhorst made a similar claim in his essay "The Development of the General Causes of the Success of the French in the Revolutionary Wars and Especially in the Campaign of 1794"[18] (brevity in titles was not much in vogue then). Scharnhorst claimed that beyond the geopolitical context of the wars and the opposing armies' strength and training, it was above all the motivation of the single soldier that brought about French successes in the campaigns of the early and mid-1790s.[19] The wars were not a clash of different technologies but of different worldviews, a collision of what Scharnhorst called "different national characters."[20] For Scharnhorst, as for Berenhorst several years later, the events of the wars were determined more by will and character than by anything else.

Almost ten years later, in December 1806, one finds the clearest expression of this interpretation of the Revolutionary and Napoleonic Wars in the reaction of Prussia's King Friedrich Wilhelm III to the collapse of his fortresses in the previous two months. Far from occupied Berlin and with little information about the state of his army, Friedrich Wilhelm wrote down his thoughts about the current situation of his kingdom in the Declaration of Ortelsburg (December 1, 1806).[21] Under the current circumstances, the king acknowledged, "it is impossible to distinguish the false from the true, rumors from facts," hence impossible to draw clear conclusions about the reasons for the "almost total dissolution" of the Prussian field forces. The reasons for the collapse of the Prussian fortresses in Stettin, Küstrin,

18 Gerhard von Scharnhorst, "Entwicklung der allgemeinen Ursachen des Glücks der Franzosen in dem Revolutionskriege," in *Scharnhorst: Ausgewählte militärische Schriften*, ed. Freiherrn v.d. Goltz (Berlin: Schneider, 1881), 192–242.
19 Ibid., 195.   20 Ibid., 206–10, 224–28.
21 Christopher M. Clark, *Iron Kingdom: The Rise and Downfall of Prussia, 1600–1947* (Cambridge, MA: Harvard University Press, 2006), 312; About Friedrich Wilhelm III more generally, see Thomas Stamm-Kuhlmann, *König in Preussens grosser Zeit: Friedrich Wilhelm III, der Melancholiker auf dem Thron* (Berlin: Siedler, 1992).

Spandau, and Magdeburg, on the other hand, were clear. The surrender of these fortresses was a scandal "without precedent," the king wrote, and all their commandants should be summarily executed.[22] Neither the strength of the Grande Armée's artillery nor the supposed shortages of provisions or ammunition or training nor – more important – the very idea of fortresses as means of defense were to blame for the capitulation of the fortresses. Rather, a combination of a lack of devotion to king and country and simple cowardice had brought about these scandals. In private, Napoleon thought in similar terms about the capitulation of Prussia's fortresses. They surrendered, he noted at the time, not because they could not fight against his army but because they lacked the will to do so.[23]

After 1815, theoretical formulations about the importance of fortresses (as in Clausewitz) went hand in hand with this common interpretation of the experience of the Napoleonic Wars. This combination of theory and experience explains why after 1815 Prussia rebuilt many, if not all, of its fortresses, and why in 1815 one Bavarian general could still assert that "fortresses are the pillars on which the security of the state is based."[24] This same combination also explains why even in France a decision was made after 1815 to build new fortresses[25] as well as why, as the representatives of the German states assembled in Vienna to discuss the creation of a new confederation of German states that would maintain its own army "based on the newest form of military theory," they decided to order the construction of several fortresses for the defense of the new confederation.[26]

What types of fortresses were maintained, repaired, and rebuilt in Germany after 1815? How many fortresses existed in Restoration Germany, and what did they look like? Between the Congress of Vienna and the Prussian victory over the Austrian army in Königgrätz (1866), German fortresses were of several types. A handful of federal fortresses stood along the French-German border in the southwest. They were manned by contingents of different state armies (e.g., Prussia, Austria) and placed under

22 GStA PK, HA VI, NL Friedrich Wilhelm III, Nr. 45/I.
23 These notes were reprinted in Napoléon Bonaparte, *De l'importance des places fortes. Notes de Napoléon sur un écrit du Lieutenant-Général Sainte-Suzanne* (Paris: Moreau, 1826).
24 Rainer Braun, "Garnisonsbewerbungen," in *Bayern und seine Armee: Eine Ausstellung des bayerischen Hauptstaatsarchivs aus den Beständen des Kriegsarchivs*, ed. Rainer Braun (München: Bayer. HStA, 1987), 217.
25 For the history of discussions in France between 1815 and the mid-1840s, including the decisions of the Saint-Cyr committee to rebuild fortresses after Napoleon's overthrow, see Éléonore-Bernard-Anne-Christophe-Zoa Dufriche de Valazé, *Des places fortes et du système de guerre actuel* (Paris: Leneveu et Riant, 1845), esp. iii–xv.
26 "Grundgesätze der Kriegsverfassung des Deutschen Bundes vom 9. April 1821," in Ernst Rudolf Huber, ed., *Dokumente zur deutschen Verfassungsgeschichte* (Stuttgart: Kohlhammer, 1978), 1:119.

the overall command of the German Confederation, the loosely struc-
tured organization of German states founded at the Congress of Vienna
in 1815.[27] A much larger number of fortresses, called "state fortresses,"
belonged directly to territorial states. These were usually ranked according to their strategic significance. Fortresses located in especially important strategic locations, normally along the state's borders, were known as
"fortresses of the first line"; others, maintained in the state's hinterland,
were "of the second line." Finally, there were the weakly fortified garrison
towns that were not fortresses per se, but were often better fortified than
towns that did not host a garrison. All these types of fortified cities can
also be ordered hierarchically. Federal and some state fortresses had national
importance, as they helped defend the German Confederation as a whole.
State fortresses, as their name suggests, were usually meant to defend a single
territorial state. And fortified garrison towns had a local significance: they
housed local regiments whose purpose was not to defend the country as a
whole but to keep an eye on public order in a given city, town, or province.

The idea of converting existing fortresses to federal ones and of constructing new federal fortresses from the ground up was conservative in the
military-theoretical sense, but unprecedented in political and legal senses.
Throughout the thousand-year existence of the Holy Roman Empire, the
Empire had never possessed fortresses under its direct command. That was
the result of the legal basis of the Empire. Free cities and single territorial
states had the right to construct, maintain, or even demolish fortifications
as part of their rights of sovereignty, while the Empire as a whole was not a
sovereign body and had no jurisdiction over such matters.

At least on paper, the newly created German Confederation was meant
to secure both the smaller and bigger German states that survived the
Napoleonic Wars.[28] The opening articles of the Vienna Final Act (1820)
stated that "[t]he German confederation is a . . . society of German states,
aimed at securing single members both internally and externally, as well
as Germany as a whole."[29] This society or confederation of states allowed
for different members to have separate internal policies but foresaw a common foreign policy that would guarantee the security of all its members
together.[30] As part of the military constitution of the Confederation, the

27 On the history of the military policies of the German Confederation, see Jürgen Angelow, *Von Wien
   nach Königgrätz: Die Sicherheitspolitk des Deutschen Bundes im europäischen Gleichgewicht, 1815–1866*
   (München: Oldenbourg, 1996); and Elmar Wienhöfer, *Das Militärwesen des Deutschen Bundes und das
   Ringen zwischen Österreich und Preussen um die Vorherrschaft in Deutschland, 1815–1866* (Osnabrück:
   Biblio, 1973).
28 See also Sheehan, *German History*, 393ff.   29 Huber, *Dokumente*, 91.
30 Ibid.

Congress foresaw the creation of a federal army, composed of contingents from the Confederation's different members as well as the construction of several federal fortresses. In the course of the Confederation's existence, its army never quite materialized. Its major branches (infantry, artillery, and cavalry) were supposed to be mobilized from different state armies only in wartime, and Germany did not experience another major war for several decades after Waterloo. The situation of the federal fortresses was different. They could not be hastily built after hostilities had already begun, but had to be maintained in peacetime as well. This is why, despite the overall weakness of the federal army, five federal fortresses were indeed constructed and maintained until 1866.

The first three federal fortresses – Mainz, Landau (Palatinate), and Luxemburg (which was part of the Confederation) – were manned within a few years after 1815.[31] These fortresses had not been substantially damaged during the Napoleonic Wars, and their conversion to federal fortresses after 1815 entailed only minor repairs. In the early 1840s, Rastatt and Ulm were added to the three original fortresses. Both cities had been defortified during the Napoleonic Wars, but their possible strategic importance was not forgotten. Once the funding for their reconstruction became available, Ulm and Rastatt's fortifications were rebuilt according to the latest fashion in military fortification.[32]

In peacetime, the number of garrison troops in federal fortresses was limited, but in case of a war they could be substantially strengthened. Mainz, for instance, had a standing garrison of 7,000 troops (divided equally between Austria and Prussia), but in wartime its garrison could have been strengthened to over 20,000 soldiers.[33] In Ulm, the situation was similar; around mid-century, the city hosted a garrison of 5,000 troops, but in case of war that number could have reached as many as 20,000.[34] In the 1860s, a decision was reached to construct a sixth federal fortress in the northern city of Rendsburg (Schleswig-Holstein), a decision that only the outbreak of the Prussian-Austrian war of 1866 prevented from being executed.[35] All of this suggests the continued importance assigned to fortresses in general, and

---

31 On the general history of the federal fortresses, see Angelow, *Von Wien nach Königgrätz*, 57–64.
32 For a closer examination of Ulm's case, see Otmar Schäuffelen, *Die Bundesfestung Ulm und ihre Geschichte: Europas grösste Festungsanlage* (Ulm: Vaas, 1980).
33 Friedrich Schütz, "Provinzialhauptstadt und Festung des Deutschen Bundes (1814/16–1866)," in *Mainz: Die Geschichte der Stadt*, eds. Franz Dumont, Ferdinand Scherf, and Friedrich Schütz (Mainz: Zabern, 1998), 377.
34 Wienhöfer, *Das Militärwesen des Deutschen Bundes*, 65–66.
35 Ibid., 65.

federal fortresses in particular, long after the supposed dramatic watershed in military history the Napoleonic Wars had signified.

What was true for the German Confederation as a whole was also true in individual German states. At different times in the nineteenth century, Bavaria maintained nine fortresses: in Forchheim, Ingolstadt, Passau-Oberhaus, Rosenberg, Rothenberg, Wülzburg, Würzburg-Marienburg, Nuremberg, and Germersheim (Palatinate).[36] The vast Habsburg lands were protected by several massive fortresses and many smaller ones. These included cities as far as Peterwardein (Petrovaradin) in the Balkans, Trento (Trient) in Northern Italy, Krakau and Przemysl in Galicia, Komorn in Hungary, Olmütz (Olomou) in Moravia (in the present-day Czech Republic), and Linz. Prussia maintained by far the greatest number of state fortresses, using them especially, as Clausewitz had suggested, along its land borders in the east and west. In the east, nineteenth-century Prussia maintained the fortresses of Glatz, Glogau, Neisse, Schweidnitz, and Silberberg (Silesia); Kolberg, Küstrin, and Stettin (Pomerania); and Pillau, Memel, and Königsberg (East Prussia). In the state's interior, there were fortresses in Spandau (near Berlin), Magdeburg, and Minden. In the west, Prussia fortified its border with fortresses in Wesel, Cologne, Koblenz, and Saarlouis. Even Ehrenbreitstein was refortified after the war, despite the great damages inflicted on it during the defortification of 1801. These last five fortresses were for all practical purposes a continuation of the line of federal fortresses in the southwest. The line started in Wesel in the north and extended up the Rhine through Cologne, Koblenz-Ehrenbreitstein, Mainz, and Landau to Rastatt.

The point in listing all these fortresses is not to overwhelm the reader but to demonstrate three important points. First, that although Germany's four remaining independent cities refrained from rebuilding their military defenses after the end of the Napoleonic Wars, single states continued to rely on their fortresses for their defense well into the nineteenth century (and indeed sometimes into the twentieth century as well).[37] In the decades after Waterloo, the idea of the city in arms was dead, but the idea of state fortresses was still very much alive.

The long list of federal and state fortresses in nineteenth-century Germany proves another important point. The particular interpretation of the Napoleonic experience in Prussia, combined with formulations of military

---

36 Information is taken from DSB except for Austria's case; see Mörz de Paula, *Der Österreisch-Ungarische Befestigungsbau, 1820–1914* (Wien: Stöhr, 1997).

37 Article 42 of the Treaty of Versailles (1919) stipulated the destruction of some of Germany's last great fortresses in the west.

theory, were not abstract statements but principles that directly affected practices on the ground.[38] That Prussia continued to maintain fortresses at all after the collapse of 1806–1807 can be explained only through the particular interpretation of the Napoleonic experience in the Hohenzollern monarchy. The Prussian army viewed urban fortifications as very important indeed, as long as fortress commandants and garrisons had "the right spirit." But although Prussia continued to maintain, repair, and even construct new fortresses after 1815, its fortresses were no longer as numerous as in the preceding century. To have a small number of well-maintained fortresses as a part of a larger strategic plan for the defense of the state was exactly Clausewitz's recommendation in *On War*.

Finally and perhaps most importantly for our story, the continued existence and persistent reconstruction of fortresses in nineteenth-century Germany shows the weaknesses of any linear, uncomplicated description of the demolition of urban fortifications in the nineteenth century. In some cases, no doubt, this was true. Breslau and Mannheim's fortifications, to name just two examples, were not rebuilt after the Napoleonic Wars. But a long list of other fortresses were maintained and repaired, and in the cases of some cities (e.g., Ulm, Rastatt, Linz, Ehrenbreitstein), they were even rebuilt after 1815. The overall process of the defortification of German cities, in short, was much less linear and much more contested than is commonly assumed.

Contemporary Germans were well aware of the nonlinear history of urban fortifications. In Hamburg, several treatises were written shortly after the wars arguing against any attempt to refortify the city.[39] There was, of course, no reason for publishing such treatises unless the fear that someone might attempt to turn back the clock in this regard was very real. Even visitors to German cities in the early decades of the century commented on the many reversals in decisions concerning city walls. When the satirist Carl Julius Weber visited Ulm after the wars had ended, he wrote in his diary how "at the end of the last century, Ulm was fortified by the Austrians, who demanded great contributions from all the Swabians. Then Ulm's fortifications were demolished by the French after the battle of Hohenlinden, but Mack refortified the city shortly thereafter. . . . Then the fortifications were demolished once again. And now, finally, Ulm is threatened once

---

38 Klaus T. Weber, ed., *Was ist Neuere Befestigung?*, vol. 1: *Quellen für die Festungsforschung* (Berlin: dissertation.de, 2002), 15.

39 *Ist es nützlich und ausführbar, Hamburg zur Festung zu machen?* (Hamburg: Perthes und Besser, 1814); *Über Befestigung und Bewaffnung grosser Handelsstädte* (n.p., 1814); *Ist es gut und nothwendig, Große und Handelsstädte zu Festungen zu machen?* (Berlin: Societätsverlag, 1815).

again by plans to turn it into a fortress. The least of the disadvantages of such a development would be the complete destruction of all the vegetable gardens around the city."[40]

When visitors such as Weber approached a fortress, they could see elements that went back in time hundreds of years, but could also observe some marked differences from the fortifications of the pre-Napoleonic era. As before, construction of buildings in the fortress's surroundings was restricted. Prussian law stipulated 3 concentric circles around a fortress, the first stretching for 600 yards and the other 2 for about 400 yards each. In each of these three concentric zones, different building regulations were enforced, from the zone closest to the fortress's walls, where hardly any buildings were allowed, to the zone farthest away from the fortifications, where only minor restrictions applied.[41] Needless to say, such restrictions caused many disputes between the state and local burghers.[42] Another legal measure that affected the fortress's surroundings was the stipulation that gunpowder magazines be stored in one of the most distant parts of the fortification works.[43] Such restrictions were not novel; eighteenth-century fortresses, too, were usually surrounded by a glacis, and the danger of the accidental explosion of magazines was as old as European use of gunpowder itself.

The fortress's actual fortifications were very different from the kind of medieval walls and towers depicted in Gillray's caricature of Mack's surrender at Ulm. Though the fortification's overall height – measured from the bottom of the moat – could be substantial (about three stories, or twenty feet, in Ulm), the deep moats fronting them made them appear only slightly above ground from afar. If the three concentric zones around the fortress were meant to provide an unobstructed field of fire for the fortress's guns, the low profile of the walls guaranteed that enemy guns would not be able to target them easily. Large parts of the walls of the fortress of Ulm, still in existence today, show such a low profile: long wall curtains pierced at the top by a series of small, plain windows and interrupted every few dozen yards by strong bastions. Because the fortress's walls were not able (or meant) to hold an army indefinitely, they were usually shorter in total length and simpler

40 Carl Julius Weber, *Deutschland oder Briefe eines in Deutschland reisenden Deutschen* (Stuttgart: Hallberger, 1834), 265.
41 "Allerhöchste Kabinetsorder, 30. September 1828," in *Gesetzsammlung für die Königlichen Preußischen Staaten* (Berlin, 1828), 119–30.
42 See, for instance, Thomas Tippach, "Die Rayongesetzgebung in der Öffentlichen Kritik," in *Die Stadt und ihr Rand*, ed. Peter Johanek (Köln: Böhlau, 2008), 213–34.
43 "Pulvermagazine (1817)," in Weber, *Was ist Neuere Befestigung*, 1:49.

in overall appearance than the huge constructions Vauban, Coohorn, and their followers had raised in the seventeenth and eighteenth centuries.[44]

It is one of the paradoxes of nineteenth-century fortresses that while they were immensely strong they were also much less visible than traditional urban fortifications. Medieval and early modern city walls were conspicuous objects. They functioned not only as military defenses but also as signs of the city's honor: physical manifestations of the abstract idea of the urban community's existence as a living, noble person. The visibility of city walls was consequently one of their most important characteristics.

It is true that some nineteenth-century fortresses in Germany were still very visible, especially if they were located in places that dominated the surrounding topography. John Forbes, an Englishman traveling through Bavaria in late 1855, commented on the construction of the fortress of Oberhaus (near Passau): "On the very summit of this lofty ridge, and exactly at its terminal or eastern point, the fortress and castle and barracks of Oberhaus, are erected and constitute a striking object, conspicuous in every direction."[45] Ideally, however, a nineteenth-century fortress was supposed to be as inconspicuous as possible, because the military–architectural logic behind the construction of fortresses was to make the enemy visible (by way of the exposed zones around the fortress) while keeping oneself invisible (by means of the low profile of the walls and the simple, unornamented wall curtains). Indeed, in 1820 King Friedrich Wilhelm III of Prussia felt things had gone a bit too far in this direction. "Although I approved in the past," he wrote, "following the advice of the ministry of war, that the Prussian national colors of white and black should not be painted on fortresses' drawbridges, barriers, and similar buildings – since these can be of disadvantage to the garrison in case of a siege – I hear with great discontent that also in other parts of the fortresses one now avoids using such colors."[46] A fortress commandant's reason for refraining from displaying the national colors was directly related to this question of invisibility. The fortress's whole purpose was to cover the presence of its troops while facilitating the discovery or uncovering of the enemy. It is no coincidence at all that the prime example for the use of the German noun "cover" (*Deckung*) in Grimm's German dictionary (1860) was related to "a fortress."[47]

---

44 For a thorough discussion of the differences between early modern and nineteenth-century fortifications, see Weber, *Was ist Neuere Befestigung*, 7–19.
45 John Forbes, *Sight-Seeing in Germany and the Tyrol in the Autumn of 1855* (London: Smith, 1856), 134.
46 "Farbe," in Weber, *Was ist Neuere Befestigung*, 1:53.
47 "Deckung," in *Deutsches Wörterbuch*, eds. Jacob Grimm and Wilhelm Grimm (Leipzig: Hirzel, 1860), 2:894.

Another important difference between nineteenth-century fortresses and those of earlier periods was the construction of many towers and fortified positions away from the fortresses' walls.[48] Such towers and fortified positions were meant to keep the enemy's field guns away from the fortress itself for as long as possible. Because the entire purpose of building a fortress was the delay of the enemy, the fact that such towers and positions could not hold up for long was of little consequence. Fortresses were meant to hold the enemy at bay so that one's own forces could be mobilized and engage the enemy in a pitched battle.

Finally, inside the fortress itself, one could witness a physical separation of garrison troops from local population. Traditionally, garrison troops were quartered in local burghers' houses. In a typical nineteenth-century fortress, at least in theory, soldiers were supposed to be housed in separate barracks. As late as 1857, the mayor of Magdeburg (a Prussian fortress) complained about the garrison troops in the city. "In 1817," he wrote, "there were 31,529 inhabitants in the city (excluding garrison troops); in 1855, however, there were already 55,229 souls here and 5,000 troops, most of whom are quartered in burghers houses, because there aren't enough barracks in the fortress."[49] This might have been true. But the very fact that one could complain about such a state of affairs at all is indicative of a major difference from earlier times. At least theoretically, civilians and fortress troops were not supposed to live in the same quarters.

The strategic importance, number, and physical form of German fortresses in the first half of the nineteenth century exemplify the mixed nature of Restoration politics. In terms of the fortification policies of the German Confederation as a whole and the strong territorial states that composed it, Restoration politics contained both old and new elements. Old policies included the recognition of the strategic importance of fortresses and maintenance, repair, and even new construction of dozens of federal and state fortresses. New policies included the shaping of a new strategy that no longer relied solely on fortresses, policies that demanded some substantial changes to fortresses' physical appearance, legal basis (e.g., the construction of federal fortresses), numerical reduction, and changed internal organization. Ultimately, therefore, both scenarios outlined by the interlocutors in Goethe's novel – Charlotte and the schoolmaster – contained a grain of truth as far as nineteenth-century fortresses were concerned. The politics of restoration did manage to turn back the clock on some of the

48 Important examples are Ulm, Linz (Austria), and even Brussels.
49 Bernhard Mai, "Das befestigte Magdeburg," in *Magdeburg: Die Geschichte der Stadt 805–2005*, eds. Matthias Puhle, Peter Petsch, and Maik Hattenhorst (Dössel: Stekovics, 2005), 502.

developments of the Napoleonic Era, but they also had their limitations in practice.

The first of the paradoxes in the history of city walls in nineteenth-century Germany is that while dozens of German fortresses were restored and their walls strengthened, such fortresses also became less visible than the walls of the typical eighteenth-century German city. The cases of many German home towns – small and middle-size cities that were neither metropolises nor state fortresses[50] – demonstrate a second paradox in this history, one that in many respects represents the exact opposite of the case of nineteenth-century fortresses. In the decades after the Congress of Vienna, home towns' walls gradually lost much of their physical components: parts of the fortifications were completely demolished; long sections of the walls were reduced in height; new gates were opened; and many stones from the old fortification works were transported elsewhere. The diminished size of the home towns' walls, however, did not make them less visible. For states, burghers, and even travelers, it was exactly the reduced, pierced walls of nineteenth-century home towns that were the most visible city walls in contemporary Germany.

The region known as the Third Germany, stretching from the mountains of Saxony in the east to the Upper Rhine valley in the southwest, had traditionally been composed of extremely diverse geographical and political landscapes, in which over three-quarters of all German walled cities were located. During the Middle Ages and the early modern period, these lands constituted the very heart of the Holy Roman Empire, the lands where its legal and political principles were most clearly prevalent. The huge number of Imperial and other cities in these regions was one physical manifestation of the political culture of the Empire, while the fortified silhouette of such cities was yet another. The final collapse of the Empire and the political culture that sustained it during the Napoleonic Wars consequently affected the Third Germany and its fortified cities more than any other region in Germany.

In the territorial agreements reached during and immediately after the Napoleonic Wars, large parts of the Third Germany fell to Bavaria, which formed them into four new administrative regions: Bavarian Swabia and

---

50 For a discussion on the definition of a "home town" in the German case, see Mack Walker, *German Home Towns: Community, State, and General Estate, 1648–1871*, 2nd ed. (Ithaca: Cornell University Press, 1998), 1–9.

Upper, Middle, and Lower Franconia. The four new provinces were at the very heart of the Third Germany, about halfway between Saxony in the east and Baden in the southwest. They were home to some of medieval Germany's most famous cities: Würzburg, Bamberg, Nuremberg, and Rothenburg in Franconia and Nördlingen and Kempten in Swabia.

The economic decline of these cities had already begun in the seventeenth century during the Thirty Years War,[51] but it was not until the perfect storm of the Napoleonic Wars that the decline had become a political one as well. In the 1790s, almost all the Imperial cities listed in the peace treaties of Westphalia were still free; after 1815, not a single city remained so in either Franconia or Swabia. Within just a few years, such cities found themselves not at the heart of the German lands but in an important sense at their most distant margins. In an age that emphasized progress, Franconian and Swabian home towns seemed stuck in a distant, medieval past; in an era of unprecedented migration to metropolitan areas, they remained small and undeveloped; and in an age of strong territorial states, they were located as far from the state's bureaucratic center (Bavaria's capital, Munich) as one could imagine. In brief, while the geographical location of nineteenth-century Franconian and Swabian cities and towns had not changed, their political and cultural roles in the nineteenth century placed them at the very edge of the "known world." Exploring the developments in such home towns is different from exploring those of fortresses, metropolitan areas, or even large free cities like Frankfurt am Main or Hamburg. It is to look at the regions most directly affected by the collapse of the political culture of the old empire, at cities and towns that had a markedly different historical trajectory during the nineteenth century from those of fortresses or large cities.

Much as in Prussia, where the reform movement of the 1800s brought about the promulgation of a new Cities Ordinance in 1808, so, too, in Bavaria did the government at first try to tether its new subjects to the Crown by means of new political measures. In the case of city walls, both the Prussian and Bavarian governments resorted to similar measures during the wars. In Breslau and other Silesian cities, the Prussian government allowed burghers to use the newly vacated terrain around the city as compensation for burghers' material losses during the siege and occupation of their cities in 1806 and 1807. In January 1804, the Bavarian government – already in control of much of Franconia and Bavarian Swabia – did the

---

51 For a discussion of the economic decline of one early modern German home town, see Terence McIntosh, *Urban Decline in Early Modern Germany: Schwäbisch Hall and Its Region, 1650–1750* (Chapel Hill: University of North Carolina Press, 1997).

same. It allowed cities, as long as they did not serve as fortresses or garrison towns, to drain their moats and demolish their walls without the need for further governmental approval.[52] That this order assumed provincial cities would want to demolish parts of their walls allows us a first glimpse into the changing mentality of home towns' burghers; that the decree further stipulated that cities and towns were allowed to demolish the walls in order to "make for an easier connection between burgher houses inside the walls and gardens and buildings outside the city" is a first clue as to why burghers might want to do so.[53]

In Franconian and Swabian home towns, just as in the case of fortresses in Germany as a whole, the years immediately after 1815 saw an attempt to maintain what was left of the old world and at times even turn back the clock on many of the novel developments brought about by the Napoleonic Wars. One example of the maintenance of traditions was the question of a city's local officers. When Bavaria took over the former Imperial city of Weißenburg (Middle Franconia), it did not eliminate the strict police measures implemented in the town by over 100 gate watchers and other city officers. Rather, it laid off a small minority of the city officers and retained the majority at their jobs, paying them now from the state's coffers rather than the city's.[54] Sometimes, previous state measures that represented a departure from traditional city life were completely reversed. Special entry fees into cities were abolished in Bavaria in 1803 but reintroduced in some cases after the war, and while Bavaria abolished the requirement of all travelers to carry passports in 1809, it revoked this same edict in 1826.[55]

After 1815, the effects of the reintroduction of traditional police measures on the experience of travelers in Franconian and Swabian towns were unmistakable. During the wars and in their immediate aftermath, travelers often commented about the "magical transformation" of cities from closed to open places. In the 1830s and 1840s, however, it was a leitmotif of travel accounts to describe German home towns in almost antithetical terms: as closed, restricted, "medieval" places.[56] William Howitt, an Englishman traveling in Germany in the 1840s, could not but reflect after visiting such places, "How continuously has the traveler occasion to curse the spirit of

52 Edict of January 4, 1804, in *Churbayerisches Regierungsblatt* (München, 1803).
53 Ibid.
54 For the changes in Weissenburg during the Napoleonic Wars, especially in relation to the question of city officers, see Reiner Kammerl, "Die Reichsstadt Weissenburg an der Wende zum 19. Jahrhundert," in *Das Ende der kleinen Reichsstädte im süddeutschen Raum*, eds. Rainer A. Müller, Helmut Flachenecker, and Reiner Kammerl (München: Beck, 2007), 288–319.
55 Edict of January 14, 1803, *Churbayerisches Regierungsblatt* (München: 1803); edict of February 7, 1826, *Regierungsblatt für das Königreich Bayern* (München, 1826).
56 For similar descriptions by inhabitants of such cities, see Sheehan, *German History*, 485.

monopoly and restriction! At every town-gate the poor countryman has to curse it too, as his corn bags are bored through and through with a great pointed iron, to see if he has concealed anything contraband in it."[57] Reading such descriptions, one should keep in mind that these conditions were not necessarily results of the old, "medieval" spirit of restriction of the burghers, as Howitt and his contemporaries often assumed. Rather, they were the consequence of police measures implemented in many German home towns in the decades after Waterloo, controls that a few decades earlier had been less frequent and more relaxed.

A similar attempt to turn back the clock took place with regard to the question of city walls. In 1804, the Bavarian government allowed the demolition of city walls with some minor restrictions, but in 1826 that edict, too, was revoked (Prussia's government did the same four years later).[58] As part of the politics of restoration pursued by Munich, for instance, the government now wanted to investigate the physical conditions of as many city walls as possible before allowing their demolition. The reason for this reversal was not the protection of national patrimony but rather the state's decision to enlarge some existing fortifications, create new fortresses, and keep others intact so that the relevant city could house a garrison.[59] It is no coincidence that, after 1826, the ultimate decision of whether to allow a city to demolish its walls was left to the military, and that the officers sent to some of Bavaria's most remote cities to report on the state of city walls were not architects or historians but military engineers.[60]

Thus, while in many cases a home town's walls became more visible for travelers because of the reimplementation of passport control at the city gates or because such travelers had come from cities that had already been defortified, the walls of the nineteenth-century home town became increasingly visible to the state as well. Munich wanted to know – and sent its agents to ascertain – the physical condition of walls in different places, and it prohibited towns from demolishing their walls without the government's explicit approval. Bavaria attempted to better "see" the condition of its home towns' walls and collected in the process what amounted to the most thorough general information to date on city walls' physical

---

57 William Howitt, *The Rural and Domestic Life of Germany* (London: Longman, Brown, Green, and Longmans, 1842), 386.

58 For Bavaria, see the decree of January 12, 1826, in *Regierungsblatt für das Königreich Bayern* (München: 1826); for Prussia's case, see *Gesetzsammlung für die Königlichen Preußischen Staaten* (Berlin, 1830), 113.

59 See, especially, Rainer Braun, "Anfänge der Denkmalpflege," in Braun, ed., *Bayern und seine Armee*, 240–49.

60 Many such reports have survived in Bayer. HStA KA, C 2, 3, 10. See also Braun, "Anfänge der Denkmalpflege," especially 244ff.

condition throughout Germany.[61] As the demolition of city walls was now prohibited without the state's explicit approval, a large number of petitions by local communities and individual burghers for permission to demolish parts of the walls flooded local, provincial, and state administrators. The state, consequently, knew much more about its home towns' walls than ever before.

The state and burghers had often stood on opposite sides of the debate over demolishing city walls. In the eighteenth century, it was usually the state that advocated defortification and local burghers who opposed it. In the decades after 1815, this situation was reversed. The cases of many Franconian and Swabian home towns demonstrate that after 1815, it was the state that restricted the demolition of cities' and towns' walls while local burghers often urged the government to defortify their cities. Indeed, sometimes burghers went about destroying parts of their cities' walls in defiance of explicit state decrees.

Why did the central government in Bavaria feel a need to prohibit burghers from demolishing their cities' and towns' walls? After all, for centuries walls had been the most recognizable aspect of German cityscapes, the expression of the urban community's honor and self-rule, a crucial component of what it meant to live in a city. What, then, was at stake for the burghers in the demolition of Franconian and Swabian city walls, and why did they so frequently oppose the central government's anti-demolition decrees?

Consider the new Bavarian provinces of Bavarian Swabia and Middle Franconia. Historically, these were two of the most densely urban regions in Germany, with countless walled cities ranging from the major fortifications of the Imperial city of Nuremberg (a Bavarian fortress until 1866) through smaller walled cities like Nördlingen, Rothenburg, Dinkelsbühl, and Weißenburg to small, weakly fortified towns like Spalt, Gunzenhausen, Erlangen, or Windsheim. The continued existence of the walls of such cities during the eighteenth century – long after most of them had lost their military value – demonstrates that city walls had always been much more than exclusively military defenses. Indeed, it was in Franconia and Swabia, more than in any other German region, that city walls remained unchanged during the eighteenth century: not a single Franconian or Swabian city was forced to demolish its walls before the Napoleonic Wars, and not a single one decided to do so of its own accord before the 1790s.

---

61 Bayer. HStA KA, C 2, 3, 10.

The situation began to change during the Revolutionary and Napoleonic Wars. Threatened by opposing armies and bankrupted by contributions and requisitions, Swabian and Franconian towns had no choice but to try new policies in order to survive. The Imperial city of Nördlingen (Bavarian Swabia) decided to demolish large parts of its military fortifications (excluding their innermost part, the medieval walls themselves) in 1803.[62] As in many other contemporaneous cases, this demolition was an attempt to prevent the city from becoming a lucrative target for the opposing armies in its vicinity as well as a way to fill the city's empty coffers. In the following years, large parts of the fortifications – wall sections, towers, entrenchments, and outer wards – were auctioned off to the highest bidder.[63] In the small Imperial city of Weißenburg (Middle Franconia), one finds similar developments. Weißenburg, overburdened with contributions, found itself in such dire financial straits that the city council had no choice but to raise some of the necessary money by selling parts of the walls – as well as other communal property – to the highest bidder. A local burgher described the situation in the city at the time. On August 4, 1801, the decision to sell communal buildings, the terrain of the moats, and even parts of the walls was made public, he reported, but immediately "many burghers assembled in front of the Upper Gate making such protests that one had to postpone the decision."[64] A week later, a special meeting of burghers was called in the city hall to discuss the same question, and the decision to fill in the moats and sell the terrain was reached by a majority vote despite the large number of burghers who protested against it.[65] The principal reason that large parts of Weißenburg's walls remained intact when Bavaria annexed Franconia a few years later was that selling them brought in much less money than had been hoped for. It was not the original decision to auction off the terrain of the former moats, large parts of the fortifications, and other buildings that saved parts of Weißenburg's walls; it was rather the fact that in the context of the financial depression caused by the wars there were simply not enough bidders to buy such properties.[66]

Weißenburg's case exemplifies the initial, intuitive opposition of many burghers to the decision to demolish all or even small parts of their cities'

---

62 Dietmar-H. Voges, *Nördlingen seit der Reformation: Aus dem Leben einer Stadt* (München: Beck, 1998), 208–09, n.61.

63 Ibid.

64 Georg Christoph Staudinger, "Chronica Weissenburg; Oder Geschichte der Kaiserlich-Freien-Reichsstadt Weissenburg am Nordgau mit einigen Umstaenden der herum liegenden Gegend," StdA Weissenburg. Quoted here is page 172 of the manuscript.

65 Ibid.	66 Ibid.

walls. Such a reaction was by no means restricted only to Swabia or Franconia. In Jena, hundreds of miles away, a similar incident occurred when Goethe – a minister in the city at that time – wanted to demolish part of the city walls that blocked the view from his library.[67] A similar incident took place in Ellwangen (Württemberg), when dozens of burghers protested the decision to demolish their town's walls. The walls, in the burghers' opinion, "could continue to stand for many years."[68] Some burghers, as was the case with the widows of Nikolaus David Scherrer and Johann Friedrich Kah, were polite in their request to put a stop to the demolition.[69] The majority of the burghers, however, were so extreme in their protest against the demolition decision and used such strong language in their letter to the local magistrate that in July 1806, sixty-two of them were charged with insubordination and insurrection against state authority.[70]

As a group, burghers either opposed the demolition of their town and city walls or reluctantly accepted it as a necessary evil. As individuals, however, they were often the main force behind it. Goethe's reasoning for the demolition of one part of Jena's walls was by no means exceptional. All over Franconia and Swabia (and, indeed, all over Germany), thousands and thousands of burghers' petitions were sent in the course of the nineteenth century to local magistrates, city councils, provincial authorities, and even the central government, asking for permission to demolish or alter parts of the walls.[71] The reasoning behind such requests were almost always particular, not communal: the opening of a small gate in the walls that would allow one to pass more quickly from one's house to the vegetable gardens outside the walls; the need to enlarge a house adjacent to the walls; the use of building materials from the walls for different purposes; the opening of windows in burghers' homes, of which the city walls constituted one side; or the transformation of a gate to allow larger vehicles easier access into and out of the city. In many cases, such changes were made without asking governmental permission, a cause for endless disputes between state, city, and individual burghers.

During the half century after Waterloo, most Franconian and Swabian towns did not reach an official decision about the overall demolition of their walls. In those towns that did reach such a decision (e.g., Weißenburg),

---

67 As noted in Chapter One, n. 1.

68 StA Ludwigsburg, Bestand F 154 I, Bü 441.

69 StA Ludwigsburg, Bestand D 2 Hofkammer Ellwangen, Bü 800.

70 StA Ludwigsburg, Bestand F 154 I, Bü 441.

71 Examples of such petitions can be found in formerly Prussian provincial archives: Br. LHA Potsdam, Rep. 2 A IHb Nr. 1163, Bd.I (Beskow) and Rep. 2A, Nr. 1164 (Angermünde); in the main state archive in Munich: Bayer. HStA München, Abt. IV, C 2,3, and 10; and in countless local archives such as StdA Gunzenhausen (Fach 70, Nr.1) and StdA Bad Windsheim (XVIII, Fach 158).

demolition projects were either opposed by the state or progressed very slowly due to a lack of buyers interested in wall components. But over the same decades, city councils, provincial bureaucrats, and even the central government, by allowing for small alterations to the walls, helped bring about a state of affairs in which the city walls were increasingly pierced by new gates, lost much of their height, and were even partially demolished. Piece by piece, the walls lost much of their robust physical character; piece by piece, cities became increasingly open, until a point had been reached when it was clear that though many parts of the walls were still standing the city itself was no longer a closed, protected place.

The history of almost every Franconian and Swabian town demonstrates the piecemeal development of these demolitions. In the small town of Gunzenhausen, for instance, large parts of the walls were demolished in 1816; the Weißenburger Gate Tower was demolished a few years later; then the Spitaltörlein (1853), Bürgerturm, (1866), and finally the rest of the walls.[72] In Bad Windsheim, large parts of the walls were sold to local burghers during the economic depression of 1816–1817; three new gates were opened in what remained of the walls about three decades later, in 1848; and another part of the walls was demolished as late as the 1870s.[73] Similar developments prevailed in other Franconian cities such as Altdorf, Erlangen, Roth, and Spalt.

When one visits Franconian and Swabian towns today, one can still see the results of the slow dismantling of their walls during the nineteenth century. In big cities like Munich or Hamburg, the defortification was also a long process, sometimes taking decades to complete. But the magnitude of the works and especially the circumstances of the Napoleonic Wars made for a very clear communal decision to demolish the walls. In such cases, it is possible to find a single document published on a single date that both announces the city's defortification decision and foresees the outlines of the defortification plan. In fortresses like Nuremberg, Ingolstadt, Ulm, or Cologne the situation was similar. The decision to demolish a fortress – much like earlier decisions to maintain, repair, or construct new fortresses – was reached by a relatively small group of people, at a specific date, and for a specific purpose. The result was an often single, regimented plan for the defortification of the fortress and clear urban planning principles for the following years. The situation in Franconian and Swabian home towns was different. Here defortification advanced very slowly, impelled mostly by individual petitions, with little in the way of a general defortification plan

---

72 StdA Gunzenhausen, Fach 70, Nr. 1.   73 StdA Bad Windsheim, XVIII, Fach 158.

or indeed a clear decision to defortify the city at all. The unregimented remnants of towers, gates, and long sections of walls that still characterize the rolling hills of urban Franconia and Swabia are the product of this sort of haphazard defortification, just as carefully laid-out public parks, promenades, and wide avenues characterize German cities whose defortification was planned and executed in an orderly fashion and according to a general plan.

As burghers in hundreds of German home towns slowly dismantled their ancient city walls, they were changing the boundaries of their towns, both physically and metaphorically. They not only dismantled the physical distinction between town and countryside; they also turned their communities into entities that were – as Charlotte in *Elective Affinities* so beautifully put it – not really cities at all. The blurring of the traditional distinctions and definitions the defortification of German home towns entailed was the reason there was initial opposition to the demolition of the walls in Weißenburg and Jena, places that had lost their strategic utility long ago. It is why few Franconian or Swabian towns ever officially ordered the complete demolition of their walls. Finally, it engendered endless bickering – between state, provincial, and city officials on the one hand, and local burghers on the other hand – about supposedly trivial matters such as the demolition of distant parts of the long-defunct fortifications, reduction of the height of the walls, or opening of a single window in a house adjacent to the walls.

As the state took over some of the wall's old functions – police, taxation, and defense, to name just three – the burghers did not remain idle. They opened little gates and windows in the walls, and took stones, lumber, and other building materials from the communal walls and used them for the enlargement or repartition of their homes. In short, they, too, helped undermine the symbolism and the physicality of the separation between city and countryside. It was now the walls of the burgher's home rather than the old walls of the community that gave nineteenth-century burghers a sense of belonging; it was the burgher's own walls that gave him a simultaneously actual and symbolic point of reference for what or who he was. Outside of the home, public security, law and order, and the maintenance of roads and other infrastructures had become the state's responsibility. State officers stood at the city gate, policed the city streets, and occupied themselves with matters of war, peace, and taxation. At home, however, the burgher ruled supreme. Here he was still sovereign.

The longer the demolition process continued, the more the city was defined less in terms of its physical boundaries than as a collection of property-owning individuals. It was less and less the city's honor, traditions, or privileges that defined a city as such; rather, the city was an amalgamation of properties – a collection of houses to be counted, individuals to be taxed, and people to be conscripted. Those sections of the walls that were still present had consequently become a representation of the city's past, not of its present or future. In the course of time, burghers learned to profit from the state's takeover of their walls, too. Rather than just passive objects of state policies, they were active agents in the transformation of their towns.

In the decades after Waterloo, German home towns were slowly becoming curious places in which both destruction and construction of boundaries were taking place. The fate of home towns' walls was both a metaphor for, and an example of, this dual process. While many parts of the walls were still visible, they no longer belonged to the present or future of the community. They were vestiges of a different time and a different city; they enjoyed a kind of surreal existence as physical signifiers of absence, representing what the city had been rather than what it now was. Perhaps no one sensed and better expressed this kind of surreal existence of city walls in Franconia and Swabia around the mid-nineteenth century than the Bavarian painter and poet Carl Spitzweg, who repeatedly visited Franconian cities during his life. In a series of paintings and drawings Spitzweg produced mid-century, he depicted over and over again the underlying tension between past and present in such places. In "On the Bastion" (*Auf der Bastei*, 1856),[74] Spitzweg depicted a lone grenadier standing yawning on decrepit city walls where laundry has been hung out to dry; a thick layer of vegetation covers the walls and a nearby cannon. In "Peace in the Land" (*Friede im Lande*, 1850/1855),[75] Spitzweg drew an old soldier sitting on half-demolished fortifications, knitting a sweater; and in the "Fortress's Commandant" (*Festungskommandant*, 1875/1880),[76] Spitzweg painted an old general sitting comfortably just outside a city's walls, covered by a red blanket, smoking his pipe, and reading a newspaper. These and other paintings by Spitzweg are saturated with a certain nostalgia for the lost world the walls represented. The age of Spitzweg's figures and their leisurely activities (yawning, knitting, reading, smoking) point to the widening gap between the city's past and present. The decrepit walls still exist physically in Spitzweg's paintings, but the world to which they belonged is either already dead or clearly dying. The visibility of nineteenth-century home town walls was directly related to the tension between past and present: they seemed out of place; they were a curious artifact from a bygone era when, as Goethe once put it, Germans fought against each other and "the burgher hid himself behind

---

74 Siegfried Wichmann, *Carl Spitzweg: Reisen und Wandern in Europa und der glückliche Winkel* (Stuttgart: Belser, 2002), 101.

75 Ibid., 109.   76 Ibid., 102.

Figure 20. Carl Spitzweg, *Es war einmal* (1845/1850). *Source:* Museum Georg Schäfer, Schweinfurt.

his city's walls."[77] In short, Spitzweg depicted less the spatial boundaries between city and countryside and more the temporal boundaries between ancient and modern.

The deteriorating state of city walls became increasingly visible not only because of the widening gap between past and present but also for a second reason Spitzweg illustrated. When, in "Once Upon a Time" (*Es war einmal*, 1845/1850, figure 20,)[78] Spitzweg depicted yet another officer on the decrepit ramparts of a Franconian town, he described him as usual as an old man, knitting a sweater. In this particular painting, however, Spitzweg's

77 Johann Wolfgang von Goethe, *Goethes Werke* (Weimar: Böhlau, 1895), 16:281.
78 Wichmann, *Carl Spitzweg*, 99.

officer also raises his head and looks beyond the horizon, at what (in another of his painting, titled *Kanonier*) is the smoke rising from a factory chimney. The first and obvious tension in *Once Upon a Time* is between present and past, between the current decrepit state of the walls and what they had once stood for; hence the painting's title. But Spitzweg also draws the viewer's attention to a second tension here, the tension between the provinciality of a local guard in a home town, who has nothing better to do than knit a sweater while on duty, and the distant sights and sounds of factories, traffic, people, and movement beyond the home town's horizon. This second tension reveals a new boundary that is not physical but nonetheless insistent and conspicuous, a boundary that would define the modern home town more than any other. It is the boundary separating home town from metropolis.

METROPOLIS

The concerns and actions that shaped the developments in fortresses, home towns, and metropolises in the period between 1815 and 1866 were common to all three types of cities. The first concern was the overall security of the state; this was the reason for the maintenance and construction of new fortresses after 1815 and the prohibition on the demolition of city walls in the home towns. A second concern was the question of the control of property, hence the opposition of burghers to turning their cities into fortresses and the slow defortification of many a home town after 1815. The third concern was that of internal security: the attempt to keep the city itself secure. This was above all the case of the metropolis.

The traditional narrative for the defortification of cities singles out expansion as its main catalyst. There are many versions of this narrative, but none equals the beauty of Victor Hugo's description of medieval Paris in *Notre Dame de Paris* (1834). It is worth quoting at some length:

Little by little the tide of houses, always thrust from the heart of the city outwards, overflows, devours, wears away, and effaces [the city walls]. Philip Augustus imprisons Paris in a circular chain of great towers, both lofty and solid. For the period of more than a century, the houses press upon each other, accumulate, and raise their level in this basin, like water in a reservoir. They begin to deepen; they pile story upon story; they mount upon each other; they gush forth at the top, like all laterally compressed growth, and there is a rivalry as to which shall thrust its head above its neighbors, for the sake of getting a little air. The houses finally leap over the walls and scatter joyfully over the plain, without order, and all askew, like runaways.... The city spreads to such an extent into the suburbs that a new wall becomes necessary. But a city like Paris is perpetually growing. It is only such cities that become capitals. They are funnels, into which all the geographical, political, moral, and intellectual water-sheds of a country, all the natural slopes of a people, pour; wells of civilization, so to speak, and also sewers, where commerce, industry, intelligence, population, – all that is sap, all that is life, all that is the soul of a nation, filters and amasses unceasingly, drop by drop, century by century.[79]

Any attempt to wall up a city like Paris, Hugo concludes, is doomed to failure. The city hates its wall: it "strides across it, passes beyond it, and runs farther."[80]

Hugo's description tells us little about the actual events in Philip Augustus's Paris. Medieval Paris was not a capital in the modern sense of the word, there was no such a thing as a "soul of the nation" in the Middle Ages, and medieval cities – as this book has repeatedly demonstrated – did not "hate their walls" – quite the contrary. But while the empirical value of Hugo's description of the history of the medieval city is very limited, it tells us a great deal about the image of metropolises in his own time. These metropolises were rapidly expanding and industrializing, drawing multitudes of people to their suburbs, in the process developing a set of social, economic, and political problems unseen in Europe since the fall of the Roman Empire. Moreover, in a Europe haunted by the specter of revolution illuminated by Karl Marx and Frederick Engels in the Communist Manifesto of 1848, the metropolis seemed the natural place for such a revolution to raise its head again. After all, it was in Hugo's Paris that the troubles had begun in 1789; Paris was where the revolution had broken out, where it progressed; Paris was the revolution. German generals, diplomats, and politicians of the Restoration period consequently looked with growing suspicion at their own expanding metropolises. The metropolis, more than any other sort of city in their states, needed to be secured and controlled. To have no physical barriers between the metropolis, its suburbs, and the surrounding countryside would have made no sense at all under such circumstances.

The least complicated case of the four great German metropolises that will be discussed here is that of Berlin. In 1800, Berlin was Germany's second largest city, with a population of over 170,000 inhabitants; half a century later, it already had more than 470,000.[81] Expansion and demographic growth, if they were indeed the main causes of the demolition of city walls, should have made Berlin into an open city very early. Yet in the first half of the nineteenth century, Berlin was still "imprisoned" by long walls. Indeed, it was exactly the exponential growth of its population that led to this state of affairs.

79 Victor Hugo, *Notre-Dame de Paris*, trans. Isabel F. Hapgood (New York: Crowell, 1888), 125–26.
80 Ibid.   81 DSB 2:584.

The walls enclosing Berlin in the early nineteenth century had little military value. Friedrich Wilhelm I, Frederick the Great's father and predecessor, had already transformed the fortifications around his residence back in the 1730s. Friedrich Wilhelm's reasons for the transformation of Berlin's fortifications derived from the city's unique history. Berlin, unlike most other German cities, did not have a historical center but was composed of several settlement or "villages": the historic towns of Berlin and Cöln on the one hand, and eighteenth-century additions like the Friedrichstadt (on the left bank of the Spree) on the other hand. To defend this large area through fortifications was consequently a very difficult challenge, much more so than defending any other contemporary German city, so Friedrich Wilhelm had already given up any attempt to do so in the 1730s. From that point on, Prussia and its capital would be protected by a strong standing army and a series of fortress towns along the borders, not by fortifying the king's residence city. The weakness of Berlin's fortifications in the eighteenth century explains why Friedrich Wilhelm III, even as he raged against the collapse of his fortresses during the campaign of 1806 and 1807, did not mention Berlin's commandant as one of the officers who had to be summarily executed. Berlin's capitulation was understandable: no one thought seriously about defending the city through its walls, not even the king.

In the 1780s, Berlin was encircled by new customs walls that stretched for almost eleven miles. These walls (of which the Brandenburger Gate was one part) helped control the movement of people in and out of the city and collect taxes from all travelers entering the city. Occupying Berlin in 1806, Napoleon's army had no reason to demolish the city's walls as it did, for instance, in Breslau. When the Napoleonic Wars ended, Berlin's walls remained intact.

After 1815, the military and police authorities in Berlin were concerned less with the military value of the walls than with their roles as the legal boundaries that separated the city from its expanding suburbs, observation posts for the local police, and checkpoints for state customs officers. Local magistrates in Berlin were disturbed by the reduction in the number of gate and night watchers in the city, characteristic to the immediate aftermath of the Napoleonic Wars. "From the perspective of the security of the state as a whole, and not just Berlin," wrote the mayor of Berlin in a typical letter in 1821, "the numbers [of such watchers] has to be increased rather than diminished."[82] Even more pressing was the question of the suburbs

---

82 LA Berlin, Pr. Br. 030 Nr. 7394.

and their role, to use John Merriman's term, as an "urban frontier."[83] After 1815, as the suburbs were filling quickly with immigrants whose occupations, whereabouts, and even exact identities were unknown to the state, they caused major headaches for local authorities concerned with social and political unrest. Police reports as well as burghers' complaints at this time reiterated the same points over and over: Berlin's suburbs were witnessing a precipitous rise in crime, and the entire area around the city was becoming a no-man's-land, a place where "prostitutes, ex-convicts, and other suspected persons" could be found, sometimes engaging in sexual activities behind trees and bushes and even in open fields.[84] Little wonder, then, that the police were ordered to raid the suburbs frequently and arrest any real or potential troublemakers (at one such raid no less than 250 people were apprehended and 40 of those taken "down town").[85] Under such circumstances, one can understand the continuing importance of the city's walls to the observation and control of the suburbs. They helped define where potential troublemakers might be located and keep such people out of the city itself.

Another major argument against any attempt to change Berlin's physical boundaries was economic in nature. Unlike American cities, many European suburbs – in the early nineteenth century, as today – were the poorest districts of the city. Here immigrants assembled in growing numbers in the late eighteenth and early nineteenth centuries because they were prohibited from settling in the city itself. To annex the suburbs to the legal sphere of the city would have meant a huge increase in the fiscal obligations of the urban community. Hence the latter's constant objections to any annexation of suburbs. When the question of the expansion of Berlin's city limits was discussed in the mid-1820s, for instance, the relevant administrators warned that if such an expansion were to take place, the city would have to assume and carry the financial and social burdens of the suburbs in question – the maintenance of roads, street lights, fire protection, and even relief for the poor (according to the Prussian Cities Ordinance of 1808, cities had to take care of their own poor population).[86] For the military, too, the walls could have been helpful. In the case of a revolution, even a weakly fortified city

---

83 John M. Merriman, *Margins of City Life: Explorations on the French Urban Frontier, 1815–1851* (New York: Oxford University Press, 1991).
84 "Sicherheit Zustand in Berlin," LA Berlin, Pr. Br. Rep. 030–05 Nr. 207; Pr. Br. Rep. 030 Nr. 7426.
85 LA Berlin, A Rep. 038–01 Nr. 48; and A Pr. Br. Rep. 030 Nr. 16926.
86 "Das Weichbild der Stadt bzw. Eingemeindung von Vororten," LA Berlin, A Rep. 000–02–01 Nr. 1612; and "Die Verhältnisse der außerhalb der Stadt belegenen Gebäude zur städtischen Feuer-sozietät," LA Berlin, A Rep. 000–02–01 Nr. 1745.

like Berlin could (and in 1848 would) be put under a state of siege decree. At least in theory, the city walls could help control the "revolutionary" population in the suburbs.[87]

Because of these considerations, Berlin retained its walls into the second half of the nineteenth century. In the social and political context of the first half of the century, the walls could still be used – at least in theory – to protect the monarch in case of a revolution; more important, they could be used to mark a distinct legal, administrative, and social distinction between the city and its rapidly expanding suburbs. The Prussian government, in brief, decided to maintain Berlin's walls for a few decades after 1815 not despite but because of the city's expansion.

The matrix of political, legal, social, and economic considerations that drove the Prussian government to keep Berlin's walls intact until the early 1860s was markedly different from the considerations that drove many a typical home town burgher to petition for defortification. In the home town, public order could be at least partly maintained by the population itself. The home town, as the historian Mack Walker reminds us, was a place where everybody knew everybody else, and where, consequently, it was very difficult to pretend you were not who you were.[88] In the suburbs of an expanding metropolis like Berlin, the situation was precisely the opposite. These were places with a growing population the state knew very little about. The state wanted to "see" these places better, hence the raids on the suburbs and hence also the continuing physical presence of city walls, which helped the state physically distinguish between the population of the city itself and the *sans-papiers* of the suburbs. There is little to suggest in all of this the sort of generalized, undivided soul of the nation Hugo describes. If anything, the maintenance of the physical boundaries around a metropolis like Berlin during the first half of the nineteenth century demonstrates the deep social divisions between Germans and their mutual suspicion of one another during the first decades after 1815.

The cases of Munich and Hamburg are slightly different from that of Prussia's capital city because these two cities, unlike Berlin, still had strong military fortifications when the Revolutionary and Napoleonic Wars began. Nonetheless, in both Munich and Hamburg one can discern concerns similar to those of Berliners about the internal security of the metropolis and trace how these concerns affected the metropolis's boundaries.

---

87 "Die Garnison in Berlin und die für besondere Fälle getroffenen militärischen Maßregeln," LA Berlin, A Rep. 000–02–01 Nr. 2151.
88 See Walker, *German Home Towns*, 108–42.

The previous chapter discussed how the first decision to defortify Munich had already been reached in the early 1790s, and that the Hamburgers, fearing a possible siege and occupation of their city, reached a similar decision in 1804 but were forced to see their city refortified between the springs of 1813 and 1814. When the wars were over, many Hamburgers feared that their city would be refortified because of its strategic location on the river Elbe. The representative of Hamburg's senate had to withstand pressures from the other powers in the Congress of Vienna to make Hamburg into a major fortress, which was also the reason for several articles published in 1814 and 1815 that opposed the refortification of the city.[89] These fears ultimately proved unfounded, and the decision about the fate of Hamburg's walls fell to its senate and city council alone.

Shortly after the last French soldier left the city, Hamburg's city council appointed a special committee to discuss renewed defortification, composed of city council representatives, military engineers, and even external experts.[90] The council reminded the committee that the consensus in Hamburg was for the rapid defortification of the city, but it was important, the council added, that the defortification plan be carefully thought through so as not to cause more damage to the internal security of the city than was absolutely necessary.[91] "At any rate," the council's secretary wrote, "we are talking here about a long process, so it is very important to reach a basic decision about the defortification itself as quickly as possible." "As to the nature of the works themselves," he added, "one needs to be aware that there are extremely important considerations to keep in mind here. The defortification of the city is directly related to the question of internal security in Hamburg as well as to direct taxation, other financial considerations, and even the beauty of the city."[92]

In the following years, the defortification committee both helped plan the defortification and supervised its execution. "Already in 1804," the senate later proclaimed, "we have decided to demolish the fortifications of this city. . . . The tragic events of the following years, which brought about the refortification of the city, made a recognition of this need [to defortify Hamburg] all the more pressing."[93] However, as in almost every defortification story, the question of property represented a stumbling block for the quick execution of the work. Whose property would have to be demolished

---

89 "Demolirung der Festungswerk nach der französischen Wiederherstellung derselben," in StA Hamburg, 111–1, Cl. VII, Lit. Cc Nr. 1 Vol. 4g 13.
90 Ibid.   91 Ibid.
92 Ibid.
93 Christian Daniel Anderson, ed., *Sammlung der Verordnungen der Freyen Hansestadt Hamburg seit deren Wiederbestehung im Jahre 1814* (Hamburg: G.F. Schniebes, 1819), 6:142.

by the defortification of Hamburg? Who would be compensated for the transfer and loss of property, by whom, and by what rate? Such questions were discussed in the committee over and over.[94] Even beyond such considerations, the committee also had to formulate a general defortification credo: an exposition of what the defortification was all about that would allow architects and engineers to follow a general vision for Hamburg's future.

Tackling this issue head on, the city council's defortification committee stated very early that "The importance of the questions at hand makes it absolutely necessary to clarify the term 'defortification of a city' [*Entfestigung eines Platzes*]."[95] "Under the term 'defortification,'" it continued, "one designates the process through which the fortification system of a city is transformed according to a clear plan and into such a state that makes it impossible to use it militarily." Defortifying a city could be done in two ways. One would be to demolish all the wall sections, towers, and gates of the city. In this case, the defortification would be clear and complete. But there was another way of defortifying a place. "The nature of urban fortifications is such," the committee wrote back to the city council, "that all its parts combine to create a complete system. It is not the walls or the moats in and of themselves that turn a city into a fortress. A city is a fortress only if walls, moats, and other buildings have close connections to one another, forming, as it were, a complete *system*."[96] Consequently, "if one only demolished the most important parts of the fortifications while keeping or only mildly transforming others, the aims of the defortification would also be reached." Taking all these arguments into account, the committee opted for the latter option. It would make Hamburg's fortifications useless from a military perspective, but help maintain the walls' role in keeping internal security and raising taxes.[97]

In the course of the next few decades, Hamburg followed this strategy. It kept large parts of its long wall sections and especially the gates intact, but demolished the bastions, outer wards, and other parts of the fortifications. It even lifted most of the restrictions on the construction of new buildings in the city's former glacis. But it still kept a physical separation between the city and its suburbs, still had police and customs officers at the gates, and still locked the gates every night, allowing in after dark only those travelers who

---

94 Ibid.
95 "Revidire Kriegs-Artikel für die Garnison der Stadt Hamburg," StA Hamburg, A 480, 307.
96 "Demolirung der Festungswerk nach der französischen Wiederherstellung derselben," in StA Hamburg, 111–1, Cl. VII, Lit. Cc Nr. 1 Vol. 4g 13.
97 Ibid.

were willing to pay a special tax.[98] Even "in the areas around the gates," a local described the situation in 1828, "mounted patrols keep an open eye on public security at night."[99] Hamburg was no longer a fortified place in the military sense of the term, but it was still a closed, protected city in terms of its police and taxation policies, and would remain so until the 1850s.

Munich's case was slightly different. Here, the physical destruction of the old fortifications started earlier and was much more thorough than in Hamburg. "If one were to visit Munich today after several years of not seeing it, one might think one is entering a completely new city," wrote one local professor a decade and a half after the defortification had begun.[100] But while Munich's fortified footprint had changed dramatically since the 1790s, police measures remained strict after 1815. Maximilian I, Karl Theodor's successor, bragged in 1824 about how the defortification of the city brought more peace to its inhabitants than their ancient walls.[101] But in fact, Munich was not a completely open city at the time. Only two years earlier, in August 1822, the Munich police decided to enclose Munich and its suburb Au with palisades because "of the many dangers caused by the fact that it is practically impossible to control and observe the many entrances to the city from a police perspective."[102] These palisades were meant, quite literally, to help "fortify the security of the city."[103] During the same year, as Maximilian I celebrated the defortification of the city in the early years of his reign and large parts of the building materials of the old fortifications were being sold to the highest bidder,[104] he also published a proclamation asserting that control of Munich's expanding population could not be maintained without enclosing the city and its suburbs with new fences. All around the city, units of the Bavarian army were stationed on the main roads, sometimes near newly constructed barriers and sometimes literally in the middle of the street.[105] In Munich as in Hamburg, therefore, the demolition of the old military fortifications did not mean the complete opening of the city. After about 1820, as part of the reactionary politics of the Restoration period, both Hamburg and Munich were still closed, protected cities, although most parts of their old walls were already gone. Attempts

98 Ibid.

99 Friedrich Georg Buek, *Handbuch der hamburgischen Verfassung und Verwaltung* (Hamburg: Hoffmann und Campe, 1828), 215.

100 Johann Georg Prändel, *Geographie der sämmtlichen kurpfalzbaierischen Erbstaaten* (Amberg: Uhlmann, 1806), 39.

101 Stadtmuseum München, Maillinger I, 3078.

102 "München. Umschließung mit Linien betr.," StdA München, Polizeidirektion, Nr. 197.

103 "Umschließung der Stadt mit Linien," StdA München, Polizeidirektion, Nr. 226.

104 "Versteigerung von Baumaterial," StdA München, Bauamt - Hochbau, Nr. 73.

105 "München. Umschließung mit Linien," StdA München, Polizeidirektion, Nr. 197.

were made to turn back the clock on the kind of openness envisaged by the first defortification of the two cities, attempts that were led primarily by concerns about the internal security of the expanding metropolis.

The bigger a German metropolis was in the first half of the nineteenth century the more massive were its walls: exactly the opposite of what the expansion thesis would imply.[106] Munich had about 40,000 inhabitants in 1800 and 100,000 half a century later. It was protected by weak lines of palisades. Hamburg had 130,000 inhabitants in 1800 (160,000 in 1850), and though it was defortified from a military perspective, it still retained large wall sections. Berlin had 170,000 inhabitants in 1815 (470,000 in 1850), and did not make any substantial alteration to its eighteenth-century customs walls. And Vienna, the largest city in central Europe, had 220,000 inhabitants in 1810 and well over half a million in 1850. It was also by far the best-fortified metropolis in Germany (figure 21 below).[107]

Countless visitors to Vienna in the early decades of the nineteenth century commented on the singularity of the city's footprint. William Howitt described the situation in the mid 1840s:

The city is great and compact, that is, so far as it is included within the walls, while far around there is an immense circle built upon, called the Vorstädte, or suburbs, forming in segments radiating from the centre of the city, six and thirty in number. The city itself is still surrounded by its lofty walls and broad moat. Without this moat lies a broad open space, called the Glacis, consisting of plots of grass divided by walks and roads, and by lines of trees; without this green open circle commence the Vorstädte. These are interspersed with gardens, public walks, churches, palaces, and theatres, so that as you walk round the ramparts, now converted into a public promenade surrounding the whole city, you behold within the city a dense mass of noble, though narrow streets, immense piles of princely buildings, and a crowding, bustling population.[108]

The permission to stroll on the city walls notwithstanding, Vienna still maintained a strict division between city and suburbs for security reasons.

The maintenance of the walls, moat, and city's glacis were directly related to the politics of restoration pursued in the Habsburg lands after 1815 by the Austrian emperors and Klemens von Metternich, the Austrian chancellor until the revolution of 1848.[109] To allow the population easy access to the inner city of Vienna – the place where many governmental buildings were

106 Compare, for instance, Jürgen Osterhammel, *Die Verwandlung der Welt: Eine Geschichte des 19. Jahrhunderts* (München: Beck, 2009), 201.
107 Statistics taken from Michael George Mulhall, *Dictionary of Statistics* (London: Routledge, 1892), 448.
108 Howitt, *The Rural and Domestic Life*, 363.
109 About Metternich, see Alan Warwick Palmer, *Metternich* (New York: Harper & Row, 1972); and Sheehan, *German History*, esp. 392–410.

Figure 21. Map of Vienna, 1857. *Source:* Courtesy of the University of Texas Libraries, The University of Texas at Austin, Map Collection.

located – was something to which the emperor, Metternich, and the military strongly opposed. This is all too understandable in a state where even the railway seemed like a political threat. "The railway brings revolution," the Austrian emperor is reported to have said at the time.[110]

A similar reactionary attitude dominated the question of Vienna's fortification in the half century after Waterloo. The rapid expansion of the city gave the authorities a tremendous headache. As late as 1850, a special commission urged the government to consider reducing the number of people living in the inner city so that the police could control them better.[111] "The most important protection of the inner city of Vienna are its walls," states

110 Palmer, *Metternich*, 278. 111 ÖStA KA, Gen. Genie-Dir. 1850 2/4.

another contemporary report. "When one controls the fortifications, one also controls the inner city and the great part of the suburbs; one is in a position to check the crowd from advancing on the city from the suburbs, and one is in a position to put out any spark of insurrection."[112] The result of such considerations was the maintenance not only of the inner city's walls but also of the more weakly fortified boundaries between the suburbs and the countryside (the Linienwall or "line wall").[113]

The same consideration that determined the fate of the city walls and the walls around the suburbs also affected the fate of Vienna's glacis. The breadth of this empty terrain, separating the inner city from its thirty-six suburbs, was calculated to allow the city's gunners enough room to shoot down any crowd approaching the city.[114] Even after 1822, when the Viennese were allowed to use the glacis and even the bastions themselves for promenading during the day, one tried to keep them clear of any obstacles that might obstruct the view of the inner city's garrison in case of a revolution.[115]

Perhaps nothing demonstrates better the close relationship between city planning and internal security concerns in Restoration Vienna than the debate about the landscape architecture model to be used in the glacis. In the 1830s, there were two options: to construct an English garden around the city (as in Munich's case) or use the French garden model. That the government decided to go with the by-then dated French model is explained by a very telling fact. The English garden, imitating nature by its multiplicity of trees and bushes laid out supposedly at random, would have allowed an insurrectionary mob to approach Vienna's walls easily, using the landscaping to hide itself from the garrison on the walls. The French model of landscape architecture was far better as far as the Austrian military was concerned. Based on straight lines and low vegetation, it could allow the garrison to shoot down anyone approaching the inner city's fortifications in the case of a revolution. Howitt's description of the glacis as "consisting of plots of grass divided by walks and roads, and by lines of trees" seems harmless enough at first sight, but when one realizes what motives lay behind this type of landscape architecture, it looks quite different. The important point is this: Vienna's overall plan – the maintenance of the inner city walls, wide

112 ÖStA KA, KM Präs. 264 ex 1850.

113 About the enclosure of the suburbs through the so-called *Linienwall*, see Wolfgang Mayer, *Der Linienwall: Von der Befestigungsanlage zum Gürtel* (Wien: Stadt- und Landesarchiv, 1986).

114 Walter Wagner, "Die Stellungnahme der Militärbehörden zur Wiener Stadterweiterung in den Jahren 1848–1857," *Jahrbuch des Vereins für Geschichte der Stadt Wien* 17/18 (1961/1962), 216–85.

115 For this and other anecdotes about the landscape architecture of Vienna's public gardens, see Géza Hajós, "Die Stadtparks der österreichischen Monarchie von 1765 bis 1867 im gesamteuropäischen Kontext," in *Stadtparks in der österreichischen Monarchie 1765–1918*, ed. Géza Hajós (Wien: Böhlau, 2008), 38–46.

glacis, palisades around the suburbs, even the landscape architecture of the gardens in the glacis – was directly related to the question of the internal security of the state and city. In a large, expanding city like Vienna, with its "crowding, bustling population," as Howitt put it, security considerations were of the highest importance. Hence the maintenance of Vienna's walls, moats, and glacis for over forty years after 1815.

In all the cases explored in this chapter – the maintenance of fortresses, prohibition on demolition of city walls in home towns, and fortifications of the metropolis – the politics of restoration pursued by German governments were, overall, hostile to the destruction of city walls. Such policies directly affected the number, shape, and location of city walls in Germany, although in both fortresses and home towns the burghers were far from passive onlookers on this process. They complained about the building restrictions in or near fortresses and they physically altered or even demolished the walls in home towns. The case of the metropolis is similar. The overall form of its fortifications in the first half of the nineteenth century was determined by central governments, but burghers did not remain idle. More and more of them objected to the police restrictions in and around their cities, contributing to a mounting political pressure to erase all physical boundaries in the metropolis.

In the decades after 1815, burghers in Munich, Hamburg, Berlin, and Vienna – whether they lived in the city itself or the suburbs – often complained about police measures in and around their cities. The most usual complaint was concerned with property: the wish, as in home towns and fortresses, to expand one's property at the expense of the fortifications.[116] There were, however, other concerns in metropolises that were less common elsewhere. One was the burghers' inability to move freely between different parts of the city. In Hamburg, for instance, we find a complaint by one burgher who wanted to enjoy the theaters in nearby Altona in the evening. He was prohibited from doing so because the gates were locked every night, meaning that he could enjoy the Altona theaters only if he spent the night there or paid a special fee upon reentering Hamburg after dark – to which, of course, he strongly objected.[117] In Munich, we find a similar complaint by an inhabitant in Au, Munich's suburb just north of the Isar. The lock out in the early evening meant that he could not stay late at

---

116 Examples for such disputes in Berlin and Munich can be found in LA Berlin, A Rep. 000–02–01 Nr. 1612, 1745; and A Rep. 002 Nr. 19; StdA München, Bauamt-Hochbau, Nr. 77.

117 "Acta betr. neue Einrichtungen an den Thoren u. Eingängen in die Stadt nach erfolgten Demolierung," StA Hamburg, 111–1, Cl. VII, Lit. Cc Nr. 1 Vol. 4g 9.

the Hofbräuhaus, Munich's famous local beer cellar, which distressed him greatly then as it would surely distress many Münchners today.[118]

Other common complaints included concerns about mayhem on the roads leading to the city just before the gates were locked, and an overall sense of being imprisoned within the city every evening. In the 1830s, one painter depicted the chaos at one of Hamburg's gates, a painting that was meant to draw attention to the dangers of large crowds pressing their way into the city just before lock out.[119] Indeed, an entire play was written in Hamburg at the time about the negative consequences of the lock out. It contains some unforgettable lines such as, "In this fantastic human-world/Where thousand barriers us withhold//One never finds the golden fleece/In taxes, customs, or meat-excise."[120] The city of Hamburg might close its gates every night, the playwright continues, but "When we climb to heaven's door/From the earthly valley's floor//There Peter stands, no slave is he/He'd let one in and charge no fee."[121]

The pressure to finally open the metropolis mounted in the years after the revolutions of 1848. It was not the houses themselves, "gasping for air," as Hugo put it, that caused this pressure. Rather, it was burghers' complaints about property, taxation, and the right to enjoy the entertainment of a nearby district, even after dark. And it was the revolution itself – its effects on local government and the geopolitical situation of many German cities. As in all the other, general developments discussed so far – the slow disintegration of the Holy Roman Empire in the eighteenth century, the rise of absolutist states, the Napoleonic experience, and the politics of restoration after 1815 – the changing geopolitical habitat of German cities after 1848 directly affected their form. Indeed, the period of 1848–1866 not only brought about a fundamental transformation in the geopolitics of Germany; it also set the stage for the final act in the history of the defortification of the German city.

---

118 This and similar complaints can be found in "Maxtor: Wiederherstellung, Brücke," StdA München, Bauamt – Hochbau, Nr. 69; and "Angertor – Wiederherstellung und Abbruch," StdA München, Bauamt – Hochbau, Nr. 78/2.

119 Museum für Hamburgische Geschichte. For Munich's case, see StdA München, Bauamt-Hochbau, Nr. 78/2.

120 Wilhlem Hocker, *Opfer der Thorsperre: Local Lustspiel mit Gesang* (Hamburg: Tramburg, 1840), 58.

121 Ibid., 59.

7

A Modern City, 1848–1866

The final chapter in the story of the defortification of the German city begins in 1848 and ends, for all practical purposes, in 1866. It is a chapter with many contradictions. It contains events characteristic of the earliest defortification waves of the seventeenth and eighteenth centuries, but also developments unique to the mid-nineteenth century. It signifies the final defeat of the walled, protected city, but also marks the ultimate triumph of urban ideas and culture in the modern world. Finally, although it includes some of the best-documented defortification cases in existing historiography, it continues to be understood only superficially by modern historians.

The importance of the events of 1848–1866 does not stem from the number of defortifications that took place in those years. By the late 1840s, most German cities had already been defortified, and some German fortresses, though few in number, would be defortified only after 1866. The importance of the period 1848–1866 lies instead in the radical reconceptualization of the relationship between the city and its habitat: a reconceptualization that for the first time made clear what the entire story of the defortification of the German city was all about. In the wake of the revolutions of 1848, the wars of German unification, and the accelerated industrialization of large parts of Germany the habitat of the German city completed a fundamental transformation. It was no longer a closed, hierarchical cosmos of bodies (corporations) but an open world in which people, commodities, and ideas were constantly moving. As this new world took on its recognizable form in the middle decades of the nineteenth century, the city finally managed to adapt to the post-corporative nature of its surroundings. The experience of the city's boundaries, their function and symbolism, and the definition of the city itself consequently took on a new and open form. By 1866, some German city walls were still standing, but the conception of the German city had already completed its evolution from walled, corporative body – the old city – to open, modern space.

The final stage in the defortification of the German city is connected to four important developments that affected mid-nineteenth-century Germany as a whole: the completion of the reconceptualization of the relationship between state and city; the 1848 revolutions, which resulted in the demolition of the metropolis's walls; the wars of unification in the 1860s, which caused a dramatic decrease in the number of fortress towns in central Europe; and the revolution in transportation which fundamentally altered the way in which boundaries of German cities were experienced and perceived.

STATE AND CITY RECONCEPTUALIZED

In the eighteenth century, it was usually sovereign, territorial states that physically demolished city walls, built open residence cities, or took over the maintenance of the walls from the burghers. By demolishing city walls, absolutist rulers undermined – both literally and figuratively – the ancient privileges that made the city into a walled, protected place, dealing a physical as well as symbolic blow to the definition of the German city as a corporative entity. Eighteenth-century defortifications expressed a political idea by physical means: there should be no internal divisions within the state, no estates or corporations, other than the boundary between prince and subjects, *Fürst* and *Untertanen*.

During the great defortification surge of the Revolutionary and Napoleonic Wars, the loss of the corporative nature of their communities became evident even to those German burghers who did not live in strong territorial states such as Prussia, Bavaria, or Austria. The massiveness of state armies, their new tactics, and the number of their artillery pieces allowed the French revolutionary armies and those of strong German states to overrun what remained of the Holy Roman Empire. French, Austrian, Prussian, and Bavarian occupation of cities and the dissolution of the Holy Roman Empire (1806) caused German burghers to recognize that city walls had become more dangerous than useful. The walls were not strong enough to defend the city but still attracted great armies, making it more likely that the city would be bombarded or occupied than if it were open and defenseless. Thus, even before Hamburg had been attacked, the city's senate ordered the demolition of the walls to avoid attracting French or Prussian armies to the city's strong fortifications. Defortification in such a case meant a recognition that the old world of the Holy Roman Empire was fast collapsing and that the city had to find new ways to survive in a post-Imperial, post-corporative world.

The collapse of the physical and symbolic boundaries of the German city in the eighteenth and early nineteenth centuries – their invasion and sub-jugation to external powers – was reflected in contemporary terminology. In the past, city burghers (*Stadtbürger*) and state subjects (*Untertanen*) were two separate groups.[1] The burghers formed a corporation that operated – and could only be fully understood – within the hierarchy of bodies of the Holy Roman Empire. Subjects, on the other hand, were defined in relation to sovereignty: the idea that the only clear boundary in a state should be the one between the prince and the rest of the population.[2] No wonder, therefore, that the more aggressive German states were in their dealings with city corporations the more ambiguous the distinction between burgher and subject became. Already in the 1790s, one finds German legal codes and scholars claiming that Stadtbürger and Untertanen are essentially synony-mous, an idea that would have shocked any early modern burgher.[3] The connection between these semantic developments and the defortification of cities is clear: whether conceptually or physically, state actions caused a reorganization of political boundaries, the replacement of old conceptual and physical distinctions (burgher versus subject; walled city versus open countryside) by new ones (sovereign versus subjects).

The Revolutionary and Napoleonic Wars and the huge surge in defor-tification they entailed caused German burghers to realize that the battle between state and city corporation had been lost. After 1815, no one seri-ously thought about resurrecting the Empire, and even burghers accepted the fact that their old, secluded lives were gone, never to return. But the defeat of the old city did not translate into the death of urban ideas and culture. Cities, just like people, "have all sorts of potential identities, which most of the time exist only as a set of possibilities."[4] In the half century after the end of the Napoleonic Wars, city dwellers worked to actualize exactly such a potential identity. While burghers could not hope to win the battle against the state, they could still wage and win battles within the state:

---

1 The following is based to a large extent on Manfred Riedel, "Bürger, Staatsbürger, Bürgertum," in *Geschichtliche Grundbegriffe: Historisches Lexikon zur politisch-sozialen Sprache in Deutschland*, eds. Otto Brunner, Werner Conze, and Reinhart Koselleck (Stuttgart: Klett, 1972), 1:672–725.
2 As, for instance, in Johann Heinrich Zedler, "Teutsches Staats-Raison oder Staats-Raison des Heiligen Römischen Reichs Teutscher Nation," in *Universal-Lexicon* (Halle, 1745), 4:1875. This would of course be repeated in the Restoration years. See, for instance, Carl Ludwig von Haller, *Restauration der Staatswissenschaft* (Winterthur, 1821), 97ff.
3 As, for instance, in the legal codexes in Austria and Prussia and in Gottlieb Hufeland, *Lehrsätze des Naturrechts* (Jena, 1790), 10.
4 David Graeber, *Toward an Anthropological Theory of Value* (New York: Palgrave, 2001), 39.

they could hope to achieve their political, economic, and even symbolic interests by transforming the state itself through peaceful means (political participation, economic development) or violent ones (revolution). It was in the context of this development that the term "Staatsbürger" (citizen; literally "state burgher" in German) ceased to sound like a contradiction in terms to German city dwellers and became a political battle cry.[5] "Staat" and "Bürger" were once two contradictory ways of imagining a political community, one related to sovereignty the other to privileges, corporations, and communal honor. By the mid-nineteenth century, with the demolition of the old political and physical boundaries within German states (not to be conflated with the boundaries between German states), a burgher could hope to remain a burgher only within the state, not outside of it. The demolition of the linguistic boundary between Staat and Bürger and the invention of the term "Staatsbürger" expressed in conceptual terms what defortification meant on the ground: the transformation of the relationship between city and state from one based on hierarchical organization to one based on horizontal coexistence. State and city now lived side by side, intermingling in a new struggle to define both politically and physically where the one began and the other ended.

The demolition of the old linguistic and physical boundaries between burghers and states and the need to find new ones were the source of some of the most important intellectual and political developments in eighteenth- and nineteenth-century Germany. Wilhelm von Humboldt devoted a whole book to the need for new boundaries within the state in 1810, and Johann Gottlieb Fichte claimed three years earlier that the most important task of contemporary political philosophers was to redefine the internal boundaries of Germany.[6] This was not a purely philosophical problem. In the late eighteenth and early nineteenth centuries, more and more Germans adopted a new terminology to describe the communal entities they felt must arise from the ashes of the old Empire. *Volk* (people), *Nation*, *Gesellschaft* (society), *Bürgertum* (roughly "bourgeoisie"), and *Proletariat* are only the most obvious examples of fundamental concepts through which Germans came to terms, literally, with the rearrangement of their country's internal political boundaries. It is to this rearrangement of boundaries and terms that one should perhaps ascribe the rise of that family group of ideas we

---

5 See Riedel, "Bürger, Staatsbürger, Bürgertum," 702–06.

6 Wilhelm von Humboldt, *Ideen zu einem Versuch die Grenzen der Wirksamkeit des Staates zu bestimmen* (1810), translated into English as Wilhelm von Humboldt, *The Limits of State Action*, ed. J. W. Burrow (Indianapolis: Liberty Fund, 1993); Johann Gottlieb Fichte, *Addresses to the German Nation*, ed. George Armstrong Kelly (New York: Harper, 1968), 190–91 (originally published in 1806–1807).

call liberalism and the new self-consciousness of burghers as a class rather than as an estate.[7] The rise of the bourgeoisie, liberal ideas, and even the industrialization of Germany are often described through economic, philosophical, or educational prisms, as if – to use Edward Soja's formulation – history takes place on a pinhead, without a spatial component.[8] But these very ideas and developments can also be understood in spatial terms. They signified a recognition that the old, walled nature of urban communities was a thing of the past, but also that once connected to one another in new ways, city dwellers could still demand or assert their liberties and pursue their political objectives within the state and even beyond its boundaries, in an international market. Goethe, as we saw, reminisced once that the traditional "burgher hid himself behind his city's walls."[9] By the mid-nineteenth century, the bourgeois artillery had changed from iron-cast cannons and city walls to political and economic measures. "The cheap prices of its commodities are the heavy artillery with which [the bourgoisie] batters down all Chinese Walls," wrote Marx and Engels in the Communist Manifesto (1848).[10] The times of *Bürgerschaft* – the quality of walled, protected burgher communities – was dying away; Bürgertum – the quality of burghers as a supraregional economic class within the state and even beyond its borders – became, literally, the order of the day.

THE 1848 REVOLUTION AND THE METROPOLIS'S WALLS

In 1848, the city rose up, making clear that although it had been defeated in its corporative form it had readapted to the new circumstances of its existence and was once again a political force to be reckoned with. Nowhere else was the rising power of the city more evident than in Germany's great metropolises. It was in the metropolis, therefore, that the confrontation between state and city took its most radical, violent form during the revolutionary year of 1848. It was in the metropolis, too, that a solution would be reached for this ongoing struggle between states and city dwellers in the years after the revolutions.

---

7 For the origins of liberal ideas in late eighteenth-century Germany, see James J. Sheehan, *German Liberalism in the Nineteenth Century* (Chicago: University of Chicago Press, 1978), 5–48; for the transformation from Bürgerschaft to Bürgertum, see Lothar Gall, *Von der ständischen zur bürgerlichen Gesellschaft* (München: Oldenbourg, 1993).

8 See Richard White and John M. Findlay, *Power and Place in the North American West* (Seattle: University of Washington Press, 1999), 233.

9 Johann Wolfgang von Goethe, *Goethes Werke* (Weimar: Böhlau, 1895), 16:281.

10 Karl Marx and Frederick Engels, *The Communist Manifesto: A Modern Edition*, ed. Eric Hobsbawm (New York: Verson, 1998), 39–40.

The walls that still surrounded German metropolises in 1848 were often viewed as symbols of the persistent repression of burghers by Restoration governments. The idea of the city in arms had died during the Napoleonic Wars, and Restoration governments had taken over the functions of the walls from local communities. By 1848, the very same monuments that had asserted and breathed life into the city's traditions, privileges, and honor in the early modern period became embarrassing reminders of the humiliation of the city by the state, representing the oppression of burghers rather than their old civic liberties. Attacking the city walls under such circumstances was no longer an attack on the old, symbolic form of the city; this symbolic form, after all, had already passed away. Rather, attacking the walls became tantamount to attacking the state: an attempt to question its sovereignty, deprive it of taxes raised at the gates, and wrest away from it the ability to police the city.

Verbal and physical attacks on city walls and gates became increasingly common in the years leading up to 1848. True, one can find examples of such attacks already in the late eighteenth century.[11] After about 1830, however, the attacks became more numerous and at times even violent. In the early 1830s, for instance, the city of Frankfurt still closed its gates at night, allowing latecomers in only upon payment of a special fee (known as *Sperrbatze* in Frankfurt and *Sperrgeld* in most other German cities). Burghers, who arrived after the gate's lock-out hour in the evening, found such restrictions enraging. At times, they confronted local gate watchers peacefully. During the July Revolution in France, local Frankfurt liberals spread revolutionary pamphlets in the city, calling for the abolition of all customs boundaries around the city.[12] A year later, the confrontation became violent. When a group of close to 1,000 Frankfurters missed the lock-out hour one autumn evening in 1831, the gate watchers demanded that they all pay the Sperrbatze. The result was the so-called *Sperrbatzen-Krawalle* (gate-fee riot), in which two local soldiers were killed and many more wounded. Two years later, in 1833, similar events occurred near the Hauptwache, one of the old entrances to the city, resulting once again in a riot that left casualties on both sides.[13]

Isolated incidents in cities like Frankfurt during the relatively peaceful 1830s became widespread during the revolutions of 1848. Garrison troops

---

11 Two examples are "Lästige Polizeianstalten vor Spaziergänger," *Kielisches Magazin* 2 (1784): 186–94; and Johann Rautenstrauch, *Das neue Wien, eine Fabel* (Wien: Mößle, 1785).
12 For a very lively description of these events in Frankfurt, see Johannes Moritz Proelss and Johannes Proelss, *Friedrich Stoltze und Frankfurt am Main* (Frankfurt am Main: Neuer Frankfurter Verlag, 1905), 97ff.
13 See Waldemar Kramer, *Frankfurt Chronik* (Frankfurt am Main: W. Kramer, 1987), 294–96.

stationed at the main entrances to big cities were an easy target for revolutionaries who, although they had disparate long-term expectations about the ultimate products of the revolution, still shared a common hatred for the arbitrariness of state power. Consider, for instance, the case of Hamburg. After 1815, Hamburg's city walls stopped possessing military functions, but the walls were still immensely important for the city in their legal, fiscal, and especially policing functions. Most important, the walls served to distinguish the city physically, legally, economically, and symbolically from its suburbs. During the 1848 revolution, it was these distinctions that became the targets of local revolutionaries who attacked the old form of the city (its walls) in the name of liberal principles of openness, commerce, and freedom of movement.

Sir George Floyd Hodges, the British envoy in Hamburg between 1841 and 1860, described the political conflicts arising from the physical separation between city and suburbs in the revolutionary year of 1848. "During the last twenty years," he wrote to London in one of his dispatches, "the increase of House property without the Walls, but still on Hamburgh territory, has been enormous. There is an instance of one family possessing house property to the extent of thirty five Houses within five minutes walk of the City Gates ... who have nevertheless no vote by right of that property at the Burgerschaft, and yet they are compelled to submit to every species of taxation consented to, or imposed upon them, by persons owning perhaps a single House each, within the Walls." This situation was not the lot of only one family, Hodges emphasized in his letter. "The old City of Hamburgh is surrounded by valuable property, manufactories, public works, and dwellings, all of which are in the same predicament, and one of the charges alleged by their owners against the present system, is the retention of exorbitant Tolls levied after night fall at the Gates of the City."[14]

For Hodges, all of this was a sign of class conflicts between the old burghers within the city and working class Hamburgers in the suburbs. "This class legislation [the raising of taxes at the city gates] is one of the great inducements for parties, having now no voice in the enactment of Laws, desiring to alter the principle upon which the suffrage is based. They are very cordially seconded by the numerous Inhabitants of the City itself, who are now disqualified from participating in the proceedings of the Burgherschaft." "The latter," Hodges continued, "feel the effect of their disqualification in other ways, in the retention of the Guilds and patent

---

14 Sabine Freitag, Peter Wende, and Markus Mösslang, eds., *British Envoys to Germany, 1816–1866* (New York: Cambridge University Press, 2000), 187.

privileges with which Hamburgh abounds, and by which heavy taxes are imposed upon them for the benefit of particular classes."[15]

The physical separation between city and suburbs had economic consequences, Hodges explained. Dwellings outside the walls were more affordable and property prices within the walls spiked. For Hodges, however, these economic factors represented much more than the ebbs and flows of property prices; they represented an essentially political conflict about suffrage, taxation, and divisions between different classes in Hamburg. The continued existence of the walls, in other words, represented a larger political conflict.

During the revolution, Hamburg's walls and gates were attacked by local revolutionaries. "For several days past," Hodges wrote in another dispatch to London, "there have been rumours of the intention of the working classes to destroy the Stein Gate of this city and the Altona Gate. It appears that these rumours were not attended to by the Hamburgh authorities. However, last evening some slight disturbance took place at the Thalia, a minor Theatre.... The performance was interrupted, and the rioters proceeded to the Stein Gate, where they were joined by a large concourse of people, which evidently proves that their movements were concerted." The rioters then "drove the National Guard on duty, as well as the collectors of the excise, from their posts, took possession of the buildings at the Gate, and set fire to them. It was nearly two hours before a sufficient force of National Guards could be collected together, and when they did arrive, the buildings were reduced to ashes, and the guards were received with derisive cheers by the populace." "The avowed object of these proceedings," Hodges concluded, "was to obtain the abolition of the Thorsperre, which certainly is very oppressive on the working classes. It is feared that renewed attacks will be made on the other Gates tonight."[16] British envoys in Germany reported similar disturbances in Vienna (April 1848) and Berlin (June), resulting in more casualties.[17] In Konstanz (Baden), local liberals even managed to destroy most of the city's old walls during the revolution.[18]

The walls of German metropolises in the early nineteenth century were meant to defend the state and the inner city from the threat of revolution. But as the revolution progressed, it became increasingly clear not only that they were useless in this respect but that they presented an easy target for

---

15 Ibid.   16 Ibid., 190.
17 Ibid., 124, 403–04.
18 Alfred Georg Frei and Kurt Hochstuhl, *Wegbereiter der Demokratie: Die badische Revolution 1848/49* (Karlsruhe: Braun, 1997), 58.

revolutionaries who wanted to attack state troops (burning down of gates) or mock the state's symbols of power (revolutionaries in Hamburg ridiculing the local garrison). At times, the metropolis's fortifications could even be used against the powers that be, if control of them fell into the hands of the revolutionaries. This was the case in Vienna, Berlin, and the fortress of Rastatt, where the German revolution began in February 1848 with the insurrection of the local garrison.[19] In such cases, the revolution made clear to German monarchs that the maintenance and restoration of urban fortifications, which after 1815 were meant to assert state sovereignty, could actually undermine it.

In cities overtaken by revolutionaries, the local population was armed, a development that reminded some contemporaries of the ancient idea of the city in arms.[20] German governments had to declare a state of siege in many cities, and in cases where a city was seized by revolutionaries, they had to force their way back in.[21] Some of these confrontations took place near city gates. In Vienna, state troops and local revolutionaries clashed next to the Hofburg Gate, which had been demolished by Napoleon in 1806 but rebuilt by the Habsburgs shortly thereafter. In Berlin, similar events took place next to the Brandenburger Gate in the west.[22]

Despite attempts by revolutionaries to defend cities they occupied through or at the city walls, the revolutions of 1848 were not a simple return to pre-nineteenth century conditions; too much had happened and changed in the previous century for that to take place. The city in arms was not reborn; the corporative structure of the old Empire was not resurrected. German liberals knew better; the old city had already been defeated and it was senseless to try to resurrect it. What the revolutionaries now wanted was to find a general, all-German solution to their political demands by the creation of a liberal constitution in specific German states (e.g., Prussia, Austria, Baden, etc.) and in Germany as a whole.[23] Such demands were closely linked to the transformation the city had undergone in the previous century. Isolated cities could no longer face territorial, sovereign states, but as a class and nation, as an all-German movement, city dwellers could reasonably hope to turn things in their favor. The nineteenth-century German

---

19 For the events of the revolution in Rastatt, see Peter Hank, Heinz Holeczek, and Martina Schilling, *Rastatt und die Revolution von 1848/49* (Rastatt: Rastatt Stadtarchiv, 2001).
20 As, for instance, Friedrich Freiligrath's famous poem, "Schwarz-Rot-Gold" (below, n. 24); and Christopher B. With, "Adolph von Menzel and the German Revolution of 1848," *Zeitschrift für Kunstgeschichte* 42, H. 2/3 (1979): 195.
21 This was the case in Berlin, Vienna, Cologne, and Erfurt, among many other cities.
22 Freitag et al., *British Envoys to Germany*, 124, 403–04.
23 See, most importantly, Sheehan, *German Liberalism*, 51–76.

nationalist Ferdinand Freiligrath expressed this idea in "Black-Red-Gold,"
a poem he published in mid-March, 1848 (later to be set to music by Robert
Schumann):

> It's not the freedom that we seek
> And ought all Germans to befall
> When only one armed city [Gr. *Stadt in Waffen*] speaks
> Behind its gates and wall.[24]

For Freiligrath and many of his fellow revolutionaries, the issue of German
freedom was no longer – and could no longer be – related to this or that
specific city. Rather, it was the issue of German city burghers as a class and
Germany as a whole. Freedom in his times, Freiligrath explained, was not
identical with the privileges of the old world of yesteryear, privileges that
had always been local and based on seclusion of one group from another.
Freedom was a universal demand, a republican demand, he wrote:

> True freedom breaks the yokes of gall
> Lets none for justice wait
> And offers up to auction
> All the fripperies of state
> For freedom's universal right
> Republicans alone can fight![25]

During the revolution, German burghers attacked specific gates and wall
sections and at times even used urban fortifications to defend themselves
from state armies. They took for granted that the old form of the city was
gone, and so sought a solution to their political demands within the state,
not through resurrecting the city in arms in this or that specific place. By
1848, the old, walled form of the German city had already passed away. But
if German burghers could find a way to adapt to the new political realities
of the times, city inhabitants and the city as an idea could still win the battle
against absolutism. Assumptions about the defeat of the old city and hopes
about the eventual triumph of a new city were complementary facets of
the revolutions of 1848. The same was true for German states, but in an
inverted form: while they eventually managed to squelch the revolutionary
movement of 1848, they realized that although they might have won the
battle against the old city and Bürgerschaft, they could still lose the war
against the newly reincarnated, *bürgerliche*, post-corporative, liberal city. To

---

24 Werner Ilberg, ed., *Freiligraths Werke in einem Band*, 3rd. ed. (Berlin: Aufbau-Verlag, 1976), 118ff.
   My translation.
25 Ibid.

put it in dialectical terms: state sovereignty was the thesis, and the rise of the bourgeoisie and the spread of liberal ideas were the antithesis. A synthesis was needed.

TWO UNIFICATIONS

How specific states dealt with the question of the metropolis's walls varied from state to state and city to city. Local authorities in Bremen abolished the Torsperre in 1848, while in nearby Hamburg it took the local senate five more years to stop locking the gates every night.[26] In Vienna, military authorities continued to oppose the demolition of the inner city's fortification for almost ten years after the revolution, and in Berlin it was not until 1862 that a final decision to demolish the old customs barriers around the city was reached.[27] Although the process took different shapes in different places, the final demolition of the boundaries around German metropolises was based on the same realization: the relationship between state and city could no longer be based solely on the interests of German states. State and city, sovereignty and Bürgertum had to be united.

Nowhere was this kind of unification between state and city more evident than in Vienna, the biggest German city of the mid-nineteenth century.[28] Even into the 1850s, Viennese officials continued to debate the question of the maintenance of the inner city's fortifications and glacis. The military continued to oppose the inner city's defortification, and burghers continued to support it. With arguments for and against defortification before him, Emperor Franz Joseph faced the same dilemma Goethe's Charlotte and her interlocutor had pondered half a century earlier in *Elective Affinities*: should Vienna's inner city continue to be fortified or should its fortifications be demolished? In late 1857, Franz Joseph finally reached the decision to demolish Vienna's fortification, a decision he opened with four famous words that encapsulate one of the most important arguments of this book: it was not expansion, industrialization, or even progress in military technology that caused defortification. Rather, it was human agency and human actions.

---

26 Franz Buchenau, "Die Entwicklung der Stadt Bremen," *Bremisches Jahrbuch*, no. 17 (1896): 30; the case of Hamburg is well documented. See Burghart Schmidt, "Die Torsperre in Hamburg: Staatliches Kontrollinstrument, finanzielle Einnahmequelle oder 'Überbleibsel aus der Knechtschaftszeit,'" *Mitteilungen des Hamburger Arbeitskreises für Regionalgeschichte*, no. 37 (2000), 26–37.

27 For the opposition of the military to Vienna's defortification, see Walter Wagner, "Die Stellungnahme der Militärbehörden zur Wiener Stadterweiterung in den Jahren 1848–1857," *Jahrbuch des Vereins für Geschichte der Stadt Wien* 17/18 (1961/62): 216–85; about Berlin, see Claus Bernet, "The 'Hobrecht Plan' (1862) and Berlin's Urban Structure," *Urban History* 31, no. 3 (2004): 400–19.

28 Vienna's defortification is extremely well documented. See above, Introduction, n. 2.

"*Es ist mein Wille,*" Franz Joseph wrote in the demolition order – "It is my will."[29]

In its wording, Franz Joseph's declaration resembled the earliest defortification decisions in France and Germany, which had also been based on the assertion of a monarch's supreme political will or sovereignty.[30] Unlike the early defortification waves, however, the defortification of Austria's capital after 1857 did not constitute an attack on the corporative character of the city – this character, after all, had long been gone. Instead, the defortification signified an opening of an already bourgeois city: the opening of a city that wanted to be opened. Throughout most of the defortification waves of the eighteenth and nineteenth centuries, defortification meant contestation; in Vienna, it meant a reconciliation, even a celebration. The government's newspaper *Wiener Zeitung*, the conservative paper *Die Presse*, the unaffiliated journal *Der Wanderer*, and the liberal newspaper *Neue Freie Presse* celebrated the demolition of the inner city's fortifications with similar pronouncements. The *Wiener Zeitung* thanked the emperor for "his great gift" to the city; *Der Wanderer* celebrated the demolition as the city's own triumph, its ability at long last to continue its natural growth; *Die Presse* spoke of the demolition of "a stone belt" around the city, a sign of the growth of "the state organism" and a young, flourishing culture; and the *Neue Freie Presse* heralded the defortification as the breaking down "of the old cincture of stone which for many centuries kept Vienna's noble limbs imprisoned in an evil spell."[31] Indeed, some newspapers published caricatures about the demolition of the walls (see figure 22), and Johann Strauss II even composed a short Polka in celebration.[32]

The importance of such reactions is twofold. First, they demonstrate how city and state were no longer on opposite sides of the defortification question. In this respect, Vienna's case is the culmination of the defortification waves, despite – and perhaps precisely because of – its uniqueness. By the mid-nineteenth century, state and city found themselves on the same side, both physically (thanks to the demolition of the physical barriers between them) and politically (given the broad consensus in favor of demolition). The enthusiastic reactions to Franz Joseph's defortification decision are also important because they show that the old idea of the city as an organism was still alive, even after the demolition of the walls that had for so long

29 As quoted in the Wiener Zeitung, "Amtlicher Theil," *Wiener Zeitung*, December 25, 1857.
30 For the argument that the defortification of Vienna was based on absolutist principles, see Carl Schorske, *Fin-de-siècle Vienna: Politics and Culture* (New York: Vintage Books, 1981), 29–30.
31 "Die Stadterweiterung," *Wanderer*, December 19, 1857; "Erweiterung der Stadt Wien," *Die Presse*, December 29, 1857.
32 Demolierer, Polka Francaise, op. 269.

Figure 22. The demolition of Vienna's walls as a caricature. *Source: Figaro: Humoristisches Wochenblatt*, April 16, 1859.

defined it. "Natural growth," "iron belts," "the city's noble limbs" – such expressions indicate how Viennese burghers came to terms with defortification by casting it as the urban organism's own triumph.

This last point is especially important to our story because it explains why expansion and defortification are often conflated. Expansion was not the cause of most defortification cases in the eighteenth and early nineteenth centuries. Even in 1857 Vienna, it was not expansion itself that caused the demolition but Franz Joseph's political decision. The importance of expansion to the story of the defortification of German cities does not lie therefore in its causal links to the demolition of city walls, but elsewhere. In the context of the mid-nineteenth century, the idea of the natural growth or expansion of cities allowed Germans to speak about defortification not as an imposition from the outside but as the victory of the (new) city over the (old) city: as a natural, evolutionary development related to the old idea of the city as an organism. Expansion was important more as a concept than as a physical factor in the demolition of city walls. It allowed the Viennese, and German burghers more generally, to construct a story about the transformation of their communities that ascribed agency to the city itself, a story in which the city was the protagonist and the winner – and not the object or the victim – of its own modernization.

Were we to walk along the Ringstrasse in the late nineteenth century, we could discern the reconfiguration of the relationship between city and state characteristic to this period. The Ringstrasse, laid out in Vienna's old glacis, contains state and bourgeois institutions side by side. On the one hand, the boulevard contains a large complex of military buildings and the Votive Church; these are signs of the monarchy's military power and the unity of throne and altar in Austria. On the other hand, the Ringstrasse also includes what historian Carl Schorske once called "the great representational buildings of the bourgeoisie": the parliament, city hall, Hofburg Theater, opera house, university, and new apartment complexes.

Many nineteenth-century travelers commented on the parallel existence of state buildings and bourgeois institutions along the Ringstrasse. The Ringstrasse "is a broad avenue," wrote one American traveler in the late nineteenth century, "part promenade and part street, extending around the entire city with double lines of lindentrees down the centre ... [it] encircles the whole interior of the city, or rather it is the boundary line between Old Vienna and New Vienna. On this broad avenue are being located the most elegant and imposing structures: those of private individuals and companies vie in elegance with government structures."[33] Another traveler agreed: "The Ringstrasse, broad, and almost encircling as it docs the old town in a stretch of one and three-quarter mile, is a highly suitable field for connecting together the details of this plan of embellishment." This was especially apparent in the kind of buildings planned for the street: "a

---

33 Charles Carroll Fulton, *Europe Viewed through American Spectacles* (Philadelphia: Lippincott, 1874), 30.

new university, quadrate in form, with court, and of magnificent style and proportions; a theatre, corresponding to the opera-house; a city hall; new Parliament buildings; two imperial museums; and, as a climax to all, a new, extensive palace, with imposing wing-arches extending across the avenue itself. These embryonic architectural wonders are to succeed one another along the street, separated, and so surrounded with, parks as to display each to the best advantage."[34]

These descriptions make clear that the Ringstrasse was a place that signified the reconfiguration of the relationship between state and city in precisely the same location where the old, physical manifestations of the corporative period – that is, the city walls – had once stood. The Ringstrasse marks the boundary between old and new, but also relates them to one another, "connecting together" state and bourgeois institutions. State and city, monarchy and bourgeoisie live side by side on the Ringstrasse, two aspects of a political synthesis, of a reconciliation that expressed itself in the form of two parallel sets of institutions along the boulevard. The Ringstrasse demonstrates that neither side was the absolute victor in the confrontation between state and city that characterized their relationship in the previous century. The city walls as an expression of communal honor are gone, as are the metropolis's walls of the early nineteenth century, which signified the "divide and rule" politics of the Restoration era. But neither city nor state loses drastically in this struggle: the monarchy is still intact (state museums, Votive Church, palace), and bourgeois culture is ubiquitous (university, theater, apartment complexes). What the replacement of Vienna's old fortifications with the Ringstrasse signified was a particular sort of unification: not the unification of German states, but the unification of city and monarchy within a German state.

Vienna's Ringstrasse is one place where the story of the defortification of the German city ends. It is the climax, reconciliation, and synthesis of sovereign and bürgerliche ideas that, as long as they were viewed as opposites, caused much of the debates and friction during the long process of the defortification of German cities in the eighteenth and nineteenth centuries. But there are at least two additional endings to our story, which – while they do not contradict the resolution reached in Vienna – shed important light on it from a far less favorable angle. The first of these endings takes us away from the open metropolis and to the question of fortress towns, the last fully functional urban fortifications in the German lands, still present even after the defortification of home towns and metropolises.

---

34 "Art Notes," *Appleton's Journal of Literature, Science, and Art* 10, no. 242 (1873): 603.

The rise of territorial states in the seventeenth and eighteenth centuries affected the number and location of fortified cities. In seventeenth-century France, absolutist principles led the state to embrace a dialectical approach toward the question of city walls. On the one hand, the state needed to assert its monopoly over the use of power (sovereignty) and strove to deprive local magnates in their chateaux and burghers in their fortified urban communes of their ability to oppose the king. One such assertion of state power led to the demolition of hundreds of chateaux and urban fortifications in France's interior during the seventeenth century; another led to the first defortification waves in eighteenth-century Germany. On the other hand, in order to defend itself from its external enemies, the state also needed strong fortress towns along its external borders. That was the logic behind the construction of Vauban's ceinture de fer in northeastern France and the many fortresses built or maintained by German states and later, in the nineteenth century, maintained by the German Confederation.

The dialectics of urban form was most prevalent in seventeenth-century France where, by the 1690s, the country itself had become a fortress of sorts: it was demilitarized internally, defended by fortification lines along its land borders, and even possessed a moat (the Rhine) and a glacis (the river's right bank). The same phenomenon can be observed in Germany during the second half of the nineteenth century. With the unification wars of the 1860s, the changing geopolitics of central Europe meant that many German fortresses lost their strategic value. The fortresses of Nuremberg and Augsburg were strategically important only as long as Bavaria needed to defend its northern borders. Following the wars of unification there was no such need, and Nuremberg and Augsburg's walls lost their strategic importance and were razed to the ground (1866; see figure 23). Similar defortification of fortress towns in the German hinterland became pervasive in the decades following the wars of unification. Braubach (Palatinate) and Stade (Lower Saxony) were defortified in the late 1860s; the walls of Landau and Wittenberg were demolished in the 1870s; those of Cologne, Saarlouis, and Torgau in the 1880s; and those of Rastatt, Koblenz, and Magdeburg in 1890. With the stabilization of the Second Empire's external borders, the physical boundaries of fortress towns in the country's interior also changed. The stronger the former were the weaker the latter could become; the two processes relied on one another, just as in seventeenth-century France.

Unlike defortification in seventeenth-century France, however, the defortification of late-nineteenth-century German cities was supported and accelerated by the local population. In the early 1860s, a visitor in Freiberg

Figure 23. The demolition of Nuremberg's fortifications, ca. 1870. *Source*: Stadtarchiv Nürnberg, A47_KS_058_06.

(Saxony) described in great detail the "honorable city walls and towers of this place," but also his melancholic feeling as a patriot, "who keeps before his eyes the bravery, loyalty, and piety" of past generations, at the tendency of local burghers to demolish the walls of this "last place [in Saxony], where medieval fortifications can still be seen." Unlike past generations, for whom the walls were symbols of honor, heritage, and local patriotism, by now the average burgher "is no longer a friend of old fortifications."[35] A similar observation was made by a military painter (there was such a thing back in the mid-nineteenth century) sent by the Bavarian army to Augsburg, just before the defortification of that city began, to document the walls before their demolition. The painter, knowing full well that once the Bavarian government permitted Augsburgers to demolish their city walls they would go about it quickly and thoroughly, was melancholic. "I draw these pictures," he wrote on the back of one of his drawings, "so that these beautiful

---

35 Eduard Heuchler, "Altes und Neues aus Freiberg," *Sachsengrün: Culturgeschichtliche Zeitschrift*, no. 7 (January, 1861), 72–74.

walls would continue to exist in memory, if not in actual reality, once the Augsburgers demolish them."[36]

Such descriptions highlight, once again, the radical change in the way defortification was perceived in the transition between the eighteenth and nineteenth centuries. In the past world of bodies and communal honor characteristic of the Holy Roman Empire, the demolition of a city's walls was often a traumatic event. In the late-nineteenth-century bourgeois world, defortification was an affirmative act, supported by the local population to such an extent that they seem to have completely forgotten how physically and symbolically important their cities' walls had been for so many centuries. This is why Freibergers and Augsburgers would go about demolishing their walls with haste as soon as they were allowed, and why Eduard Heuchler (the visitor in Freiberg) and the Bavarian military painter were so mournful about it.

Even in those late-nineteenth-century fortresses where the walls were not physically demolished one could still witness the effects of unification. One such place was the Saxon fortress of Königstein, which was incorporated into the Second Empire's lines of fortification after 1871, but was not as tightly guarded as it had been in the past. In 1893, it could be visited by any tourist who wanted to enjoy the "charming views" from the ramparts. Tickets could be bought at the fortress's entrance for four marks per person; refreshments could be found in the fortress and outside the main gate; and a guided tour took about two and a half hours.[37] Only the stabilization of Germany's internal borders through unification can explain this laxity. Other fortresses (and even certain sections within Königstein) would turn into something quite different from tourist attractions. The fortress's ability to keep people out also meant that it could be used to keep people in; hence the widespread adaptation of late-nineteenth-century fortresses into prisons. Some of Germany's most famous prisons were originally built as, or within, fortresses: Weichselmündung (Danzig), Spandau (where Nazi war criminals such as Rudolph Hess and Albert Speer would be incarcerated after WWII), Landsberg am Lech in Bavaria (where Adolf Hitler wrote *Mein Kampf* while serving a sentence for his Beer Hall Putsch of 1923), Kufstein (Tyrol), and perhaps most important, Theresienstadt.

Such fortress prisons epitomize the radical transformation city walls had undergone in the eighteenth and nineteenth centuries, and they are as good an ending point for our story as the Ringstrasse. In the world of

---

36 "Augsburg: Entfestigung, Mauer, Tore," Bayer. HStA KA, Plansammlung, Augsburg 199–211.
37 Karl Baedeker (Firm), *Northern Germany: As far as the Bavarian and Austrian Frontiers* (London: Karl Baedeker, 1890), 324.

corporations that constituted the Holy Roman Empire, not belonging to a place was tantamount to being deprived of one's liberties. City walls consequently stood for one's identity and privileges, marking an area that literally "made one free" (*Stadtluft macht frei*). Modern central Europe, on the other hand, became a world not of Bürger but of Staatsbürger, a world where liberty, honor, and rights find their origins outside of the city, in the state, and not in seclusion from it. In such a world, living behind a fortress's walls signifies incarceration, punishment, dishonor – exactly the opposite of what the walled, early modern city was all about. If one understands the city as the sum total of its liberties, traditions, and honor, the modern city is the state itself, the "outside" in which civic rights, honor, and privileges are to be found, while it is now in the seclusion of the fortress prison that one ceases to be a Bürger. There is perhaps no better place than Theresienstadt to witness the radical transformation of the relationship between city and habitat in the eighteenth and nineteenth centuries. In the late nineteenth century (and of course in the twentieth century as well), it remained one of the last places that physically resembled the old, walled form of the German city while simultaneously symbolizing social practices that appeared as a dystopic mirror image of what the early modern city was all about.

The fortress prison thus exemplifies in negative terms what the 1848 revolution, the Ringstrasse, and even the term Staatsbürger exemplify in positive terms. In the world of the Holy Roman Empire, the worst thing that could happen to a person was to be outside: outside of the corporative order (and therefore deprived of political rights) and outside of a castle or a city's walls – those quintessential signs of political membership. In the modern world, political rights are not located in specific, fortified places but in abstract terms, state sovereignty, the very same outside that in the early modern period signified the lack of rights. To be a part of the open space of the state became a sign of membership in modern Germany (the Ringstrasse, the open city), while seclusion from it became a sign of dishonor and lack of political rights (the fortress prison). When we look at this transformed world in the decades after the German unification, when we visit the city's broad avenues and even state prisons, we appreciate the radical transformation that both city and habitat underwent through the demolition of city walls and other typical early modern boundaries in the eighteenth and nineteenth centuries. It is a world in which the perception and experience of boundaries is both more uniform and more diverse than in earlier times. More uniform in the sense that older divisions such as the clear physical line between city and countryside have lost their salience; more diverse in the sense that other boundaries have become more sharply drawn and new political, social, and cultural divisions have become more clearly defined. Indeed, it was exactly this simultaneous process of demolition and construction of boundaries that drew the attention of late-nineteenth-century travelers in Germany.

TRANSPORTATION

The first ending point of our story is the Ringstrasse; the second is the fortress prison. Though very different from each other, both the wide boulevard of the open city and the closed character of the fortress prison point in the same direction: each expresses the radical and dialectical recon-ceptualization of political and social boundaries characteristic of the eigh-teenth and nineteenth centuries. The same is true for our third – and final – ending point: the train station. The railway is sometimes associated with the demolition of city walls,[38] but as we shall shortly see, not exactly for the right reason.

By the mid-nineteenth century, gone were the days when a traveler to a German city approached it slowly, crossing its emerging boundaries one by one – the city's legal limits, suburbs, city walls – paying respect each time to the physical signs that indicated the presence of the city as a noble cor-porative body. Instead, the train came to town, flying over boundaries at an unnatural pace, leaving a dark trail of smoke in its path, and delivering its pas-sengers, finally and almost unexpectedly, inside the city, at the train station.[39]

In his poem *On the Night Train* (*Im Nachtzug*, 1887), Gerhart Hauptmann reflected on how the train affected physical as well as subjective boundaries. Still awake among a group of snoring passengers, the poet looks out at the nocturnal landscape through the window that separated the lighted compartment from the dark countryside, when he suddenly recognized his own face reflected in the glass:

> I watch as it races as one with the train
> Leaving clearings and forests behind,
> Over walls, palisades, and tollbooths in the plain,
> Its forehead increasingly lined.[40]

---

38 As, for instance, in Michael Wolfe, *Walled Towns and the Shaping of France: From the Medieval to the Early Modern Period* (New York: Palgrave MacMillan, 2009), 170.

39 On the effects of the railroad on nineteenth-century travel and perception of time and space, see Wolfgang Schivelbusch, *The Railway Journey: The Industrialization of Time and Space in the 19th Century* (Berkeley: University of California Press, 1986). There is extensive literature on the effects of the railroad on specific cities in Germany and abroad. A cultural history of the case of Mainz is Wolfgang Bickel, *Der Siegeszug der Eisenbahn* (Worms: Wernersche Verlagsgesellschaft, 1996). An example for the symbolism of train station architecture can be found in Manfred Berger, *Hauptbahnhof Leipzig: Geschichte, Architektur, Technik* (Berlin: Transpress, 1990).

40 Gerhart Hauptmann, *Sämtliche Werke* (Berlin: Propyläen Verlag, 1962), 4:54–56.

Watching the nocturnal landscape and his own face change as one, Haupt-mann felt the train demolished boundaries and created new ones simulta-neously. It flew over fences and walls and palisades, but also extended and highlighted the distance between the compartment and the world through which it raced. Inside the compartment there was light and peace; the only noise breaking the monotonous rattle of the train was the snores of the dozing passengers around the poet. But outside, just beyond the win-dow – close and far at the same time – Hauptmann felt the presence of a very different world: a world of spirits, magic, and demolished boundaries; the world of yesterday, when travelers had not only observed the landscape through a glass window but had also acted within it. The thought brought tears to the poet's eyes, and a longing to be there, among the moving silhou-ettes of the night.[41] The train, in Hauptmann's poem, both demolishes and constructs boundaries, allowing passengers to travel over physical barriers as never before while also highlighting the growing distances between man and nature and present and past.

The relationship between the spread of the railroad network and the demolition of boundaries, so beautifully described by Hauptmann, was on many people's minds in mid-nineteenth-century Germany. The pace of life, the movement of people, commodities, and ideas – the pace, indeed, of time itself – was accelerating.[42] The train stood as the quintessential symbol of this acceleration. The first railway line in Great Britain was opened in 1828, followed in 1832 by the first French one. In 1835, the first railway line reached a German city, a short span of less than five miles between Nuremberg and Fürth. Only fifteen years later, Germany already boasted over 3,000 miles of railroad tracks; by 1860, over 7,000 miles had been laid.[43] German cities – the focal points that held national railroad networks together – became ever more tightly bound up with one another, making distinctions among cities less clear than in earlier times. "The railway operation," wrote Constantin Pecqueur in 1841 about the effects of the railway in France, "causes distances to diminish. . . . Lille suddenly finds itself transported to Louvres; Calais to Pontoise; le Havre to Poissy; [and] Rouen to Sèvres or to Asnières."[44] The same was true in the case of mid-nineteenth-century German cities: they were closer than ever before, exchanging ideas, books, newspapers, people, commodities, and raw

---

41 Ibid.
42 The term "acceleration" (or *Beschleunigung* in German) is of considerable importance in recent research about modernity in German studies. For a full theory of acceleration and its importance, see Hartmut Rosa, *Beschleunigung: Die Veränderung der Zeitstrukturen in der Moderne* (Frankfurt am Main: Suhrkamp, 2005).
43 Sheehan, *German History*, 466.   44 Schivelbusch, *The Railway Journey*, 33.

materials that highlighted their interdependence. This is why, even though the railway journey took place, physically, in the countryside, between cities, it is associated with the city and not with the village. The railway was primarily an urban phenomenon.

Nineteenth-century Germans constantly commented on the railroad and how it affected their world, referring over and over again to its ability to transcend boundaries. "The effects of the railway are wonderful," wrote one contemporary. "It opens an opportunity for everyone, including the lower classes, to travel to new countries and cities, it spreads new ideas and insights, demolishes prejudices, helps distant peoples and nations know and befriend one another."[45] "The train," a representative in the Landtag in Hessen claimed, "brings friends and acquaintances together. Through the railway, distances are shortened, political and religious barriers are destroyed, prejudice disappears, and the evils of the provincial cities are annihilated."[46] "The railroad," concludes a third German in 1841, simply "annihilates space."[47] "Annihilation of space," "destruction of prejudices," and "demolition of social and political barriers" – such terms and expressions show the inherent relationship between the experience and symbolism of the train and the question of boundaries. More importantly, they demonstrate that the demolition of boundaries in the mid-nineteenth century was perceived by many as a positive development, a triumph of modern ideas over antiquated ones.

It is easy to take such typical descriptions of the railway's agency in the dissolution of boundaries at face value – easy to see the train as a major factor in the destruction of physical boundaries such as city walls. Are not walls, together with palisades and tollbooths, what the train was cutting through in Hauptmann's poem? Was not the construction of the railroad and the industrialization of German cities and towns more generally, a major, physical factor in the demolition of physical barriers such as city walls in mid-nineteenth-century Germany? Many nineteenth-century Germans, and even some modern historians, have claimed that such a connection existed: the railway physically altered the boundaries of cities and communities, demolishing walls in its path, perhaps even contributing to Germany's unification.[48]

45 Friedrich Haupt, *Die Weltgeschichte* (Zürich: Drell, 1843), 64.
46 *Verhandlungen der zweiten Kammer der Landstände des Grosherzogthums Hessen* (Darmstadt: Carl Wilhelm Leske, 1842), 27.
47 *Magazin der Literatur des Auslandes*, March 10, 1841, 119.
48 Some examples can be found in Alexa Geisthövel and Habbo Knoch, *Orte der Moderne: Erfahrungswelten des 19. und 20. Jahrhunderts* (Frankfurt am Main: Campus, 2005), 20–21; and Sheehan, *German History*, 468–69.

Strictly speaking, such accounts are incorrect. This is first of all a matter of historical record, which reveals a mixed picture about the spread of the railway and the destruction of physical boundaries such as city walls. Most city walls in Germany had already been demolished – completely or very substantially – by the time the first railway line between Nuremberg and Fürth was constructed. Defortification, as we saw throughout this book, was the result of the rise of absolutist states in the eighteenth century and the ubiquitous collapse of political and physical boundaries caused by the Napoleonic experience – not the result of changes in transportation technology. Even after the introduction of the railway, the correlation between the opening of a railway line in a specific city and the demolition of its walls is often weak. The railroad line between Nuremberg and Fürth was constructed in 1835, but Nuremberg remained a fortress until 1866 (Fürth was never a fortified city); the line between Berlin and Potsdam was already operative in 1838, but Berlin retained its walls until 1862 and Potsdam until the 1890s; and although the line between Cologne and Herbesthal was opened in 1839, Cologne remained fortified for the next half century. What was true in large cities like Nuremberg, Berlin, or Cologne was often the case in German home towns as well. In the small city of Angermünde (Brandenburg), a place where for centuries travelers had to cross the city on their way from Berlin to Mecklenburg, the opening of a train station outside the city walls diverted traffic from the city itself, helping to preserve Angermünde's walls, not causing their destruction.[49]

The assumption that it was the railroad that destroyed city walls is problematic for a second reason. Such accounts might lead one to believe that the train has its own agency: it crosses, connects, demolishes, and destroys. The train is a sovereign, animate being in such descriptions – a subject that acts of its own volition – turning the countryside, city, and individual into objects it can command, change, and at times even annihilate. But the train is not a person: it does not destroy objects of its own accord; it does not break walls or annihilate space of its own volition, and despite what some mid-nineteenth-century Germans were led to believe, it does not, unfortunately, erase social, political, and religious barriers so easily.[50] Walls, palisades, and tollbooths had to be demolished by human beings before the train could pass over them. The "space" through which the train was passing,

---

49 Carl Ferdinand Friedrich Lösner, *Chronik der Kreisstadt Neu-Angermünde* (Schwedt, 1845), 282ff., StdA Angermünde, Baukommission, 1831–1887.

50 As some contemporaries such as Hauptmann were quickly to realize. See also Arthur von Mayer, *Geschichte und Geographie der deutschen Eisenbahn von ihrer Entstehung bis auf die Gegenwart* (Berlin: Baensch, 1891), 2:535.

breaks in the walls, diminishing importance of political and economic boundaries: all these had to be destroyed or at least substantially weakened for the railway to connect disparate peoples, cities, and states as it in fact did.

When read closely, contemporary descriptions of the railroad point to this preindustrial destruction of boundaries. Mid-nineteenth-century Germans claimed, as we just read, that the train "annihilates space" and demolishes "social boundaries." But these very terms should give one pause. The world of the Holy Roman Empire was corporative in nature; it was not a world of "spaces" but a world of bodies. (Can a space have a voice? Can a space be represented in the Imperial Diet? Can a space wake up in the morning and fall asleep at night?). The same is true for the term "social." Early modern Germans (and early modern Europeans in general) did not view themselves as members of a common society.[51] They belonged to estates (one was an elector, prince, free knight, burgher of a free city, etc.) or to corporations (guilds, towns, etc.); they were not members of a general society in the modern sense of the term. To speak about the annihilation of space and destruction of social barriers is consequently already to use terms belonging to the modern, post-corporative world, a world which, at least in theory, consists of open spaces rather than walled, protected places; a world with relatively free movement (space, society) rather than of the strictly vertical world of the early modern period (place, estates).

This point is not merely semantic. Consider how difficult it would have been to introduce the railway into the corporative world of the Holy Roman Empire in the early eighteenth century. Permission would have had to be granted by every state, prince, local magnate, city, monastery, or market village along the way. Guilds would bicker about who would lay the tracks, at what rate, and by what method, and trains would have had to stop every few miles when crossing any of the innumerable internal boundaries in Germany to allow locals to tax the passengers. The landscape mid-nineteenth-century passengers viewed from their seats inside the train compartments as well as the words they used to describe it were already those of a post-corporative

---

51 For the history of the concept of society see, most importantly, Keith Michael Baker, "Enlightenment and the Institution of Society," in *Main Trends in Cultural History: Ten Essays*, ed. W. Melching and Wyger Velema (Amsterdam: Rodopi, 1994), 95–120. For the emergence of the term "social" in the mid-eighteenth century, see Yair Mintzker, "'A Word Newly Introduced into Language:' The Appearance and Spread of 'Social' in French Enlightened Thought, 1745–1765," *History of European Ideas* 34, no. 4 (2008), 500–13. A classic essay on the conceptual transformation from community to society in the German case is Ferdinand Tönnies, *Gemeinschaft und Gesellschaft* (Leipzig: Fues, 1887).

world. In short, the train did not cause the demolition of corporative boundaries; it only made its scope and consequences apparent.

All of this is not to deny that the railroad accelerated the rate of change in and around mid-nineteenth-century German cities. The railway line between Nuremberg and Fürth allowed many Jews living in Fürth to commute to Nuremberg (which still did not allow Jews to settle in the city) every day for work,[52] and once new railroad tracks were laid inside the city or between the city and its suburbs, movement within the urban sphere changed dramatically as well.[53] Changes to the city's appearance and the physical state of those wall sections still standing by mid-century were also conspicuous. It was a common practice, for instance, to take stones from decrepit walls for the construction of railway bridges or train stations.[54] In some cases, the very architecture of the train station highlighted this connection: railway stations in nineteenth-century Germany often resembled a monumental city gate and indeed took over some of the functions of the old gates. It was now at the train station that one welcomed or bid farewell to guests, much in the same way that in the old world the city gates had represented rites of passage for burghers and foreigners.[55] While it is undeniable that the construction of the railroad spurred change, one must emphasize chiefly that these changes were caused by human beings rather than by the train, and that the roots of the changes were much older than the railroad itself.

There is a second crucial point one must understand about the relationship between the railroad, city, and city walls. In the eighteenth and early nineteenth centuries, the demolition of walls was often a traumatic event. In the eighteenth century, it usually signified an attack by absolutist states on the corporative structure of urban communities, and the demolition of walls during the Napoleonic Wars was a reflection of the general collapse of the cosmos of bodies that made up the Holy Roman Empire. This, we saw, was the reason why the Brückenturm in Frankfurt was literally laid to rest in 1801, why Münchners urged Karl Theodor to spare their walls in the 1790s, and why the burghers of Jena opposed any attempt to demolish their city walls in the early nineteenth century.

In mid-nineteenth-century Germany, one finds a very different reaction to the demolition of walls. Contemporary descriptions of such destructions

52 Sheehan, *German History*, 466.
53 Schivelbusch, *The Railway Journey*, 178–87.
54 This, for instance, was the case in Berlin. "Der Abbruch der Stadtmauer sowie die Regulierung, Pflasterung und Unterhaltung der hierdurch frei werdenden Straßen, 1859–1882," LA Berlin, A Rep. 000–02–01 Nr. 1579.
55 Cf. Geisthövel and Knoch, *Orte der Moderne*, 20; Schivelbusch, *The Railway Journey*, 171–76.

are suddenly saturated with euphoria. A mural in Munich's train station (1862) depicts the train as a winged angel, demolishing barriers, conquering space, and breaking the chains of the past, its symbols, and even its ideas.[56] For Heinrich Brüggemann, the opening of a new line signified a "liberal joy, a pleasure over new triumphs which will increase the power of liberal and humane principles."[57] And in many cases, the design of entrances to train stations resembled less the layout of a medieval city gate than that of a triumphal arch: a sign of victory over space, rather than the seclusion of the urban community.[58]

Middle-class Germans, whose grandparents still opposed the demolition of their cities' walls and took pride in the seclusion of their communities from the surrounding countryside, called now for more demolitions. Indeed, they were celebrating the demolition of the city's seclusion, which they viewed as "the evils of provincial cities." The very process of the demolition of the old borders of the German city was viewed as a triumph of the city and not, as in the past, an imposition from the outside. Here is perhaps the most important aspect of the railroad's introduction to our story. Its significance goes well beyond the supposed (and factually problematic) causal link between the genesis of the railroad and the boundaries of the German city. The railroad signified an urban phenomenon. It was associated with liberal ideas about openness, industry, commerce, and indeed society itself – all ideas that were associated with the city and stemmed from city inhabitants. The railroad consequently symbolized the final defeat of the old city (seclusion), but also the triumph of a new, liberal conception of the city (industry, commerce, urban culture and ideas). The annihilation of the physical boundaries of the old city was perceived now as the triumph of the city over itself. The old city died with the rest of the bodies that made up the old, corporative world, but the idea of the city somehow came back to life in a new, liberal, modern iteration: conquering, demolishing, triumphing.

The railroad did not cause the demolition of boundaries such as city walls. Instead, it showed contemporaries the scope of the demolition (e.g., Hauptmann looking through the window at the old world of boundaries) and gave them a language with which to describe this demolition as the city's own triumph: a triumph of urban ideas, commerce and industry, and ingenuity – a triumph of the city over the city. Here again is the same

56 Reproduced in Bickel, *Der Siegeszug der Eisenbahn*, 7.
57 Quoted in Sheehan, *German History*, 468.
58 See, for instance, André Corboz, *Die Kunst, Stadt und Land zum Sprechen zu Bringen* (Berlin: Birkhäuser, 2001), 104.

phenomenon we witnessed in the case of the metropolis and fortress town: the consolidation of a new habitat for German cities in the mid-nineteenth century that was as much conceptual as physical. By the mid-nineteenth century, German burghers already realized that the habitat in which the old city had lived was gone. This was the source of the language they used (space, society) and the reasons for Hauptmann's nostalgic tears when he looked out through his compartment window. This destruction, however, was also a sign of the city's triumph, the conquest of a new, post-corporative habitat by the city. Like a phoenix, the city died and was resurrected, or perhaps even better: like a king, the physical body of the city – its walls – passed away, but the idea of the city marched on.

THE DEFINITION OF THE CITY

The final reconceptualization of the relationship between city and habitat typical to the middle decades of the nineteenth century explains a curious fact. The modern world is an urban world. It is epitomized by great urban centers, ideas, ingenuity, even strife. But while the importance of the city to German and European history in the nineteenth and twentieth centuries is unquestionable, a definition of what a city is or ought to be has become notoriously hard to find. Countless bureaucrats and scholars have attempted to find it, only to realize time and time again how elusive such a definition is.[59] Why that is the case relates to the story of the defortification of the German city in three interconnected ways: physical, historical, and discursive. With their walls demolished, the physical boundaries that characterized and constituted German cities became amorphous. If, as Fernand Braudel once claimed, to define is to encircle or draw boundaries around an object or a phenomenon, then the demolition of the city's ancient boundaries made the city much harder to define for the simple reason that the defortified city lacked clear boundaries, thus escaping a simple attempt to encircle or encompass it in the mind's eye.[60] With its borders wide open and ever changing, the city lost that fundamental aspect of its footprint that had made it readily and definitively definable before the modern period.

The difficulties in defining the modern city also relate to the city's history. *Omnis determinatio est negatio*, Spinoza famously said: to define is to negate; it is to characterize an object, event, or phenomenon in terms of what it

---

59 On the attempts to define the modern city see, most importantly, Peter Johanek and Franz-Joseph Post, eds., *Vielerlei Städte: Der Stadtbegriff* (Köln: Böhlau, 2004).

60 As quoted in James J. Sheehan, "What is German History? Reflections on the Role of the Nation in German History and Historiography," *The Journal of Modern History* 53, no. 1 (1981): 1.

is not, in terms of what lies beyond it. We come to terms with concepts such as "a woman," "German," or even "a city" by determining what these concepts are not (a woman is not a man; to be German is not to be French or British; a city is not a village, etc.). In the seventeenth, eighteenth, and early nineteenth centuries, however, the world around the city – its habitat – had collapsed. By the middle decades of the nineteenth century, the hierarchical world of boundaries and bodies characteristic of the Middle Ages and the early modern period had ceased to exist. Attempts to find a general definition of both the early modern and the modern city – like Max Weber's, for instance[61] – consequently encounter a fundamental challenge: the habitat against which the city was defined in the early modern period is not the same as the environment against which it can be understood in the modern world. To define the city as a walled place makes sense in the early modern period but not in the modern world, much in the same way that to call the city a social phenomenon or a space makes sense in the nineteenth and twentieth centuries but not in premodern Germany, where the city was a member in a body (not in society) and was perceived as a specific place rather than as a space. In this respect, it is not the lack of physical boundaries that makes a general definition of the city so hard to find today, but the discontinuity of its history between the early modern and modern periods.

Finally, and perhaps most importantly, definitions of the modern city also have to take into account the very success of the city in the modern world. Throughout this chapter, we saw that as the old, corporative, walled city of the past was passing away, the new, modern, and open city was becoming a blueprint for society as a whole. The secluded urban communities of the Middle Ages and early modern period were dying away, but urban ideas (industry, liberalism), culture (Biedermeier, Bürgertum), and use of metaphors (citizenship, market) reached unprecedented dimensions. Consequently, it has become immensely difficult in the modern world to locate and isolate – to define – what a city is. Modern cities are connected through transportation networks, common phenomena, and a common political vocabulary. Simply because cities are so closely related to one another, because they are so fundamental to any attempt to imagine modern societies, it becomes immensely difficult to delineate them not only in terms of their physical borders but as human phenomena with stable locations. Urban culture, defeated in its premodern form, permeates contemporary society in its novel, modern manifestation: in political ideas and

---

61 Max Weber, *The City*, trans. Don Martindale and Gertrud Neuwirth (Glencoe, IL: Free Press, 1958), 65–89.

terminology (indeed, in the term "politics" itself – from "polis" or city in Greek); in state law (Staatsbürgerschaft); in specific, local markets and in the market as an abstract idea; in train stations in cities, and on the train moving through the countryside; along the great boulevards of metropolises such as the Ringstrasse, and in fortress prisons. To try to restrict the urban only to the city is therefore to miss one of the major developments the idea of the city underwent in the eighteenth and nineteenth centuries. Indeed, it is to miss what is so unique about the place of the city in modern imagination: it permeates our world and our *Weltanschauung* to such a degree that any attempt to reduce the urban to any actual, physical city is doomed to failure.

The impossibility of finding an agreed-upon definition of the modern city draws our attention once more to the inherent dialectics of city form we saw throughout this book, a process through which the old, walled character of the early modern city was destroyed at the same time that urban ideas and culture continued to prosper. The difficulty of defining what a modern city thus relates directly to the topic of this book. With its walls demolished, history fractured, and the world around it transformed almost beyond recognition, the defortified, wall-less, modern city eludes attempts to define it; yet at the same time, its importance to our culture is accepted by all. Modeling Justice Potter Stewart's approach to pornography, we can't define the modern city, but "we know it when we see it." Or perhaps better, modeling St. Augustine's concept of time, we know intuitively what a modern city is – until we are asked to put it into words.

Two centuries and over 250 pages ago, this book set out to explore the demolition of city walls in German-speaking central Europe. In light of all it has described – from events in seventeenth-century France through the early defortification waves in eighteenth-century Germany, the Napoleonic experience, and Restoration politics to the post-1848 era – what was the significance of the transformation of the physical and symbolic form of the German city from a walled to open place? What was the tragic end of the walls Hans Wachenhusen referred to in 1867? What, in other words, was defortification, and what was its historical significance?

The first chapter of this book claimed that monuments are hardly ever silent. The old city walls spoke to travelers and locals, constituting rites of passage that breathed life into the idea of the city as a living, pulsating body. The demolition of walls was consequently as much symbolic as it was physical. The old city walls and the open city, urban fortifications and the Ringstrasse not only function in a certain practical way. They also stand for ideas about identity, honor, and political participation: they are structures that make arguments. Of course, the opposite is also true. Arguments have structures: they progress, build up, reach – both literally and figuratively – an endpoint, a conclusion. This book has treated different aspects or leitmotifs in various defortification stories: key terms such as openness, disenchantment, and state-building; ideas such as the defortification as a physical break in the cityscape but also as a temporal break between an old and new city; political processes such as the collapse of Bürgerschaft and the rise of Bürgertum; and fundamental narratives about industrialization and urban expansion. When all the various components of this story are added up, one reaches perhaps the most fundamental conclusion about defortification, the structure of the argument of the entire story of the defortification of the German city. Defortification was part of the process by which the German city entered the modern world, the process by which the German city became a modern city. Not because the defortified city was industrialized or because it was necessarily bigger than the premodern city, but because through defortification the city came to be understood and experienced through the same symbols, metaphors, and terms that define the modern world as such: an open, post-corporative, disenchanted world that had severed itself from its past. As in earlier crucial periods in European history – the growth of the Greek polis, the changing urban environment in late antiquity, and the flourishing urban culture of the high Middle Ages – the city's changing appearance in the transition to the modern era was a canary in the mine. It was an indication of a much larger, general change.

Understanding the defortification of the German city as part of the process by which the city became modern explains the predominance of especially the expansion thesis in defortification stories up until now. Strictly speaking, such a thesis is a rather weak tool in explaining the emergence of "invention" of the open city: there is little or no correlation between expansion and defortification in the eighteenth and early nineteenth centuries, and, even more importantly, expansion as such could never have been the cause of the demolition of city walls. Human beings had to decide and have the political will and financial means to defortify cities; abstract demographic forces have neither wills nor coffers. The importance of the expansion thesis lies instead in the fact that it would be retrospectively applied to defortification at all. It signifies an attempt to come to terms with an often traumatic event in the history of German cities – a tragedy, as Hans Wachenhusen put it – by constructing a narrative in which the city is the protagonist, the agent of its own affirmative change. To conflate expansion and defortification is therefore not just a mistake, but an interesting and telling mistake. It is to construct a narrative that is historically largely incorrect but psychologically enlightening; it is an attempt to narrate away the trauma and melancholy of modernization by claiming that it was precisely the victim of modernization – the walled city – that had won the battle against itself and its surroundings; it is to celebrate the destruction of the old city in the name of a new one.[62]

Perhaps such a positive narrative is essential for any successful modernization story: a story that tells the history of the invasion of early modern places and the replacement of early modern practices by a new world of ideas, imagination, and forms of power by ascribing agency to the very same people, communities, and ways of life the modern world has done so much to destroy. Through defortification, the old city died, but a new city emerged; through defortification, the city was invaded, but through expansion it became triumphant again. Through the defortification-as-expansion thesis, we are urged to reflect how even the worst of times can be the beginning of the best of times. Perhaps no monument to the world of the Holy Roman Empire had been as physically and violently assaulted as the walls of early modern German cities in the eighteenth and nineteenth centuries. But this same assault, this very demolition, was transformed by modern historians and laypersons alike into a mere stage in the long history of that living, breathing, pulsating organism we call a city. When all is said and done, this dialectics of old and new, demolition and construction, defeat and triumph, defortification and expansion, is perhaps the most important aspect of the story that was told in the pages of this book. Defortification contains all these contradictions and in an important way is the story of these contradictions. It constitutes the extended moment when the old German city died and was resurrected, the process through which Germany as a whole and so many of its cities entered a new stage in their centuries-old relationship, leaving behind the vertical, corporative world of places and physical boundaries typical to the early modern period and entering – not without conflict, trepidation, and even trauma – that horizontal, open, social world in which they continue to exist to the present day.

---

62 The theme of melancholy and modern urban life has been one of Walter Benjamin's most important contributions to the discussion about the modern city. See Walter Benjamin, *The Arcades Project*, trans. Howard Eiland and Kevin McLaughlin (Cambridge, MA: Harvard University Press, 1999), 10–11.

Bibliography

The literature about urban fortifications – let alone about early modern and nineteenth-century Germany – is vast. The archival collections and printed sources listed in this bibliography are only the ones cited in the notes.

Manuscript Collections

Angermünde, Stadtarchiv (abbreviated as StdA Angermünde)

Baukommission, 1831–1887.

Bad Windsheim, Stadtarchiv (StdA Bad Windsheim)

XVIII, Fach 158.

Berlin, Geheimes Staatsarchiv Preußischer Kulturbesitz (GStA PK)

HA I, Rep. 77 (Ministerium des Innern, Militärabteilung Sekt. 1, 2), 263.
HA I, Rep. 77 (Ministerium des Innern, Militärabteilung Sekt. 1, 2), 330a.
HA III, MdA Abt. I, 10324.
HA VI, NL Friedrich Wilhelm III, 45/I.

Berlin, Landesarchiv (LA Berlin)

A IHb 1163–1165.
A Rep. 000–02–01.
A Rep. 038–01.
Berlin, 2840.
Pr. Br. Rep 030–05.
Pr. Br. Rep. 030.
Rep 002 Nr. 19.
Rep. 2 A IHb 1163 (Beskow).
Rep. 2 A, 1164 (Angermünde).
Rep. 2 B 71.
S Nr. 11.

Bremen, Staatsarchiv (StA Bremen)

P-9.d.3.a.13.
2-P.2.f.6.b.1.d.
2-P.1.265; 268.

Breslau, Staatsarchiv (StA Breslau)

StA Breslau, Akten der Stadt Breslau, (985) 11; (991) 11; (1136) 11; (1680) 12; (1682) 12; (1702) 12; (1703) 12; (1747) 12.

Frankfurt am Main, Historisches Museum (Hist M. Frankfurt am Main)

Grafische Sammlung.

Frankfurt am Main, Institut für Stadtgeschichte (ISG Frankfurt am Main)

Kriegszeugamt, Nr. 5.
Revolutions- und Befreiungskriege, Nr. 65; 81; 122; 130; 139.

Freiburg im Breisgau, Stadtarchiv (StdA Freiburg)

B 5 VI a.

Gunzenhausen, Stadtarchiv (StdA Gunzenhausen)

Fach 70, Nr. 1.

Hamburg, Staatsarchiv (StA Hamburg)

Instruction für die Wächter an Thoren und Bäumen (ohne Signatur).
111–1 (Senat).
A 480.
Cl. I, Lit. Pb 8.
Cl. VII, Lit. Cc 1.

Karlsruhe, Generallandesarchiv (GLA Karlsruhe)

Abt. 65, Nr. 1443.

Koblenz, Landeshauptarchiv (LHA Koblenz)

655,047.
1C 9391; 9433.

Koblenz, Stadtarchiv (StdA Koblenz)

623, Nr. 1451.

Ludwigsburg, Staatsarchiv (StA Ludwigsburg)

F 154 I.
D 2 Hofkammer Ellwangen.

Munich, Bayerisches Hauptstaatsarchiv (Bayer. HStA)

Gl 2747/870.
Gl 2751/911.
Gl 2756/973.

Munich, Bayerisches Hauptstaatsarchiv, Abteilung Kriegsarchiv (Bayer. HStA KA)

A XIII
B 267
C 1; 2; 3; 9g; 10; 132; 136–38.
MKr 7791; 9165; 8046; 9605–9674;
Plansammlung, Augsburg.

Munich, Bayerische Staatsbibliothek (BSB)

2 Mus.pr. 1722–29.

Munich, Stadtarchiv (StdA München)

Bauamt – Hochbau, Nr. 73; 77; 78.
Bürgermeister und Rat, Nr. 61.
Polizeidirektion, Nr. 20; 21; 197; 226.
Stadtverteidigung, Nr. 288.

Munich, Stadtmuseum

Maillinger I.

Paris-Vincennes, Service historique de l'armée de terre (S.H.A.T.)

Mémoires Historiques, 171; 1045; 1746; 1752.
Article 14: "Hambourg," "Breslau."

Potsdam, Brandenburgisches Landeshauptarchiv (Br. LHA Potsdam)

Rep. 2 A.
Rep. 2 B 71.
Rep. 2 S 11.

Vienna, Österreichisches Staatsarchiv, Abteilung Kriegsarchiv (ÖStA KA)

KM Präs. 264
Gen. Genie-Dir. 1850 2/4.

Weissenburg, Stadtarchiv (StdA Weissenburg)

Georg Christoph Staudinger, "Chronica Weissenburg; Oder Geschichte der Kaiserlich-Freien-Reichsstadt Weissenburg am Nordgau mit einigen Umstaenden der herum liegenden Gegend," manuscript.

Printed Sources

"A Picturesque Description of the Rhine." *The Edinburgh Magazine* 6 (1795): 89.

Adams, John Quincy. *Letters on Silesia: Written During a Tour Through That Country in the Years 1800, 1801.* London: Printed for J. Budd, 1804.

Agamben, Giorgio. *State of Exception.* Translated by Kevin Attell. Chicago: Chicago University Press, 2005.

———. "Amtlicher Theil." *Wiener Zeitung*, December 25, 1857.

Anderson, Christian Daniel, ed. *Sammlung der Verordnungen der Freyen Hansestadt Hamburg seit deren Wiederbestehung im Jahre 1814.* Vol. 6. Hamburg: G.F. Schniebes, 1819.

Angelow, Jürgen. *Von Wien nach Königgrätz: Die Sicherheitspolitk des Deutschen Bundes im europäischen Gleichgewicht, 1815–1866.* München: Oldenbourg, 1996.

Archambault, Paul. "The Analogy of the Body in Renaissance Political Thought." *Bibliothèque d'humanisme et renaissance* 29, no. 1 (1967): 21–53.

Aretin, Karl Otmar von. *Heiliges Römisches Reich 1776–1806.* 2 vols. Wiesbaden: F. Steiner, 1967.

———. *Das Alte Reich, 1648–1806.* 3 vols. München: Bayerischer Schulbuchverlag, 1981.

Arnim, Achim von. *Isabella von Ägypten und andere Erzählungen.* Zürich: Manesse Verlag, 1959.

Arnim, Bettina von. *Dies Buch gehört dem Könige.* Frankfurt am Main: Inselverlag, 1982.

———. "Art Notes." *Appleton's Journal of Literature, Science, and Art* 10, no. 242 (1873): 603.

d'Aucour, Barbier. *Ode sur la prise de Philipsbourg.* Paris, 1689.

Avenel, Denis-Louis-Martial, ed. *Lettres, Instructions diplomatiques et papiers d'État du Cardinal de Richelieu.* 8 vols. Paris: Imprimerie Impériale, 1853–1877.

Baedecker, Karl. *Northern Germany: As far as the Bavarian and Austrian Frontiers, with Excursions to Copenhagen and the Danish Islands. Handbook for Travellers.* London: Baedecker, 1890.

Baker, Keith Michael. *Inventing the French Revolution: Essays on French Political Culture in the Eighteenth Century.* Cambridge: Cambridge University Press, 1990.

———. "Enlightenment and the Institution of Society." In *Main Trends in Cultural History: Ten Essays*, edited by W. Melching and Wyger Velema. Amsterdam: Rodopi, 1994, 95–120.

Barkan, Leonard. *Nature's Work of Art: The Human Body as Image of the World.* New Haven: Yale University Press, 1975.

Bathurst, C. *The Modern Part of an Universal History, From the Earliest Accounts to the Present Time.* 60 vols. London 1779–1784.

Battonn, Johann Georg. *Oertliche Beschreibung der Stadt Frankfurt am Main.* Frankfurt am Main: Verein für Alterthumskunde, 1861.

Bauer, Richard. *Geschichte der Stadt München.* München: Beck, 1992.

Beales, Derek. *Joseph II: Against the World.* Cambridge: Cambridge University Press, 2009.

Béguillet, Edmé. *Description historique de Paris.* Paris: Frantin, 1779.

Bell, David. *The First Total War: Napoleon's Europe and the Birth of Warfare as We Know It.* Boston: Houghton Mifflin, 2007.

"Bemerkungen über die neuen Anlagen und Kunst-Sammlungen in Gotha." *Journal des Luxus und der Moden* 25 (1810): 756–68.

Benevolo, Leonardo. *Die Stadt in der europäischen Geschichte.* Translated by Peter Schiller. München: Beck, 1993.

Benjamin, Walter. *The Arcades Project.* Translated by Howard Eiland and Kevin McLaughlin. Cambridge, MA: Harvard University Press, 1999.

Berenhorst, Georg Heinrich von. *Annalen des Krieges und der Staatskunde.* 2 vols. Berlin: Himburg, 1806.

Berger, Manfred. *Hauptbahnhof Leipzig: Geschichte, Architektur, Technik.* Berlin: Transpress, 1990.

"Berichtigung eines Aufsatzes im Kiel. Mag. II B. 2St. S. 186 die Thorpolicey in Coburg betreffend." *Journal von und für Deutschland* 10 (1785): 380–82.

Bernard, Richard Boyle. *A Tour Through Some Parts of France, Switzerland, Savoy, Germany and Belgium.* Philadelphia: Edward Earle, 1815.

Bernet, Claus. "The 'Hobrecht Plan' (1862) and Berlin's Urban Structure." *Urban History* 31, no. 3 (2004): 400–19.

Béthouart, Antoine. *Le prince Eugène de Savoie: soldat, diplomate et mécène.* Paris: Perrin, 1975.

Bickel, Wolfgang. *Der Siegeszug der Eisenbahn.* Worms: Wernersche Verlagsgesellschaft, 1996.

Blanning, T.C.W. *The French Revolution in Germany: Occupation and Resistance in the Rhineland, 1792–1802.* Oxford: Clarendon Press, 1983.

Bodin, Jean. *The Six Bookes of a Commonweale.* Edited by Kenneth D. McRae. Cambridge, MA: Harvard University Press, 1962.

Boldt, Hans. *Rechtsstaat und Ausnahmezustand. Eine Studie über den Belagerungzustand als Ausnamezustand des bürgerlichen Rechtsstaates im 19. Jahrhundert.* Berlin: Duncker & Humboldt, 1967.

Bonaparte, Napoléon. *De l'importance des places fortes. Notes de Napoléon sur un écrit du Lieutenant-Général Sainte-Suzanne.* Paris: Moreau, 1826.

———. *Correspondance de Napoléon.* Edited by J.B.P. Vaillant. 32 vols. Paris: Impr. Impériale, 1858–1869.

———. *Correspondance de Napoléon I, publiée par ordre de l'Empereur Napoléon III.* 32 vols. Paris: Henri Plon and J. Dumaine, 1858–1870.

Böning, Holger. "Gotha als Hauptort volksaufklärischer Literatur und Publizistik." In *Ernst II. von Sachsen-Gotha-Altenburg*, edited by Werner Greiling, Andreas Klinger, and Christoph Köhler, 325–44. Köln: Böhlau, 2005.

Bönnen, Gerold, ed. *Geschichte der Stadt Worms*. 2 vols. Stuttgart: Theiss, 2005.

Brady, Jr., Thomas A. *German Histories in the Age of Reformations, 1400–1650*. New York: Cambridge University Press, 2009.

———. *Ruling Class, Regime, and Reformation at Strasbourg, 1520–1555*. Leiden: Brill, 1978.

Braun, Rainer. "Garnisonsbewerbungen." In *Bayern und seine Armee: Eine Austellung des bayerischen Hauptstaatsarchivs aus den Beständen des Kriegsarchivs*, edited by Rainer Braun, 217–24. München: Bayerisches Hauptstaatsarchiv, 1987.

———. "Anfänge der Denkmalpflege." In *Bayern und seine Armee: Eine Austellung des bayerischen Hauptstaatsarchivs aus den Beständen des Kriegsarchivs*, edited by Rainer Braun, 240–49. München: Bayerisches Hauptstaatsarchiv, 1987.

Bredekamp, Horst. *Thomas Hobbes visuelle Strategien*. Berlin: Akademie Verlag, 1999.

Breslauische Erzähler 8, no. 2: 18–21; n. 3: 34–41.

"Breslau's abgetragene Wälle und deren Verschönerung." *Schlesische Provinzialblätter* 60 (1814): 324–28.

Brindley, J. *An Introduction to the Art of Fortification*. London 1745.

Brossault, Colette. *Les intendants de Franche-Comté, 1674–1790* Paris: Boutique de l'Histoire, 1999.

Brown, Sanborn C. *Benjamin Thompson, Count Rumford*. Cambridge, MA: MIT Press, 1979.

Brown, Wendy. *Walled States, Waning Sovereignty*. Cambridge, MA: MIT Press, 2010.

Buchenau, Franz. "Die Entwicklung der Stadt Bremen." *Bremisches Jahrbuch*, no. 17 (1896): 1–32.

Bücher, Karl. *Beiträge zur Wirtschaftsgeschichte*. Tübingen: H. Laupp'sche Buchhandlung, 1922.

Buek, Friedrich Georg. *Handbuch der hamburgischen Verfassung und Verwaltung*. Hamburg: Hoffmann und Campe, 1828.

Burk, Kurt. *Handbuch zur Geschichte der Festungen des historischen deutschen Ostens*. Osnabrück: Biblio, 1995.

Büsch, Otto. *Militärsystem und Sozialleben im alten Preußen, 1713–1807: Die Anfänge der sozialen Militarisierung der preußisch-deutschen Gesellschaft*. Berlin: de Gruyter, 1962.

Byron, George Gordon. *Byron: Selected Poetry and Prose*. Edited by Donald A. Low. New York: Routledge, 1995.

Calvino, Italo. *Le città invisibili*. Torino: Einaudi, 1972.

Casse, A. du. *Histoire des négociations diplomatiques relatives aux Traités de Mortfontaine, de Lunéville et d'Amiens*. 10 vols. Paris: Dentu, 1853–1855.

The Changing Face of Boston Over 350 Years. Boston: Massachusetts Historical Society, 1980.

Churbayerisches Regierungsblatt. München, 1803.

Church, William F. *Richelieu and Reason of State*. Princeton: Princeton University Press, 1972.

Clark, Christopher M. *Iron Kingdom: The Rise and Downfall of Prussia, 1600–1947.* Cambridge, MA: Harvard University Press, 2006.

Clausewitz, Carl von. *On War.* Translated by Michael Howard and Peter Paret. Princeton: Princeton University Press, 1976.

Cogan, Thomas. *The Rhine: Or, a Journey from Utrecht to Francfort.* 2 vols. London: G. Woodfall, 1794.

Corboz, André. *Die Kunst, Stadt und Land zum Sprechen zu Bringen.* Berlin: Birkhäuser, 2001.

Craig, Gordon. *The Politics of the Prussian Army 1640–1945.* Oxford: Clarendon Press, 1955.

Creveld, Martin Van. *Supplying War: Logistics from Wallenstein to Patton.* New York: Cambridge University Press, 1977.

Decker, Karl von. *Die Artillerie für alle Waffen oder Lehrbuch der Gesammten reinen und ausübenden Feld- und Belagerungs-artilleriewissenschaft.* Berlin: Mittler, 1816.

DeJean, Joan E. *Literary Fortifications: Rousseau, Laclos, Sade.* Princeton: Princeton University Press, 1984.

"Description of the city of Frankfort am Main." *The Lady's Magazine* 27: 247.

"Die Befestigung und Entfestigung Hamburgs." *Sonderbeiträge zum Hamburger Adressbuch* (1929): 58–64.

"Die Berge gebären! – die Wälle fallen!" *Schlesische Provinzialblätter* 61 (1815): 433–39.

"Die Stadterweiterung." *Wanderer*, December 19, 1857.

Dietrich. *Gedanken über die Frage: Wann und wie sind die Reichsstände verpflichtet, in die in ihren Landen befindlichen Festungen . . . Reichstruppen zur Besatzung einzunehmen?* Frankfurt am Main, 1794.

Dotzauer, Winfried. "Die Ankunft des Herrschers: Der fürstliche 'Einzug' in die Stadt (bis zum Ende des Alten Reiches)." *Archiv für Kulturgeschichte* 55, no. 2 (1973): 245–88.

Duchhardt, Heinz. "Dalbergs politische Publizistik." *Jahrbuch der Vereinigung 'Freunde der Universität Mainz'* 23/24 (1974/1975): 47–72.

Dülmen, Richard van. *Kultur und Alltag in der frühen Neuzeit.* 3 vols. München: Beck, 1990.

Dürer, Albrecht. *Etliche underricht/zu befestigung der Stett/Schloßz/und flecken.* Nürnberg, 1527.

Durkheim, Emile. *The Elementary Forms of Religious Life.* Translated by Karen E. Fields. New York: Free Press, 1995.

Eichendorff, Joseph von. *Werke in einem Band.* München: Carl Hanser, 2007.

Eigentliche Beschreibung der Stadt Speyer/Wie tyrannisch und unchristlich die Barbarischen Franzosen mit derselben Stadt und Innwohnern verfahren wird. Nürnberg, 1689.

Ekirch, A. Roger. *At Day's Close: Night in Times Past.* New York: Norton, 2005.

Ennen, Edith, ed. *Geschichte der Stadt Bonn in vier Bänden.* 4 vols. Bonn: Dümmler, 1989.

"Erweiterung der Stadt Wien." *Die Presse*, December 29, 1857.

Fallois, Joseph de. *L'École de la Fortification ou les éléments de la fortification permanente, régulière et irrégulière.* Dresden, 1768.

Färber, Konrad Maria. *Kaiser und Erzkanzler: Carl von Dalberg und Napoleon am Ende des Alten Reiches.* Regensburg: Mittelbayerische Druckerei- und Verlags-Gesellschaft, 1988.

Favier, René. *Les villes du Dauphiné aux XVIIe et XVIIIe siècles: la pierre et l'écrit.* Grenoble: Presses universitaires de Grenoble, 1993.

Feyerlein, Friedrich Siegmund. *Ansichten, Nachträge und Berichtigungen zu A. Kirchners Geschichte.* 2 vols. Frankfurt am Main, 1809.

Fichte, Johann Gottlieb. *Addresses to the German Nation.* Edited by George Armstrong Kelly. New York: Harper, 1968.

Fontaine, Jean de La. *Œuvres de J. de La Fontaine.* Edited by Henri Régnier. 11 vols. Paris: Hachette, 1883–1897.

Forbes, John. *Sight-Seeing in Germany and the Tyrol in the Autumn of 1855.* London: Smith, 1856.

Forrest, Alan, Karen Hagemann, and Jane Rendall, eds. *Soldiers, Citizens, and Civilians: Experiences and Perceptions of the Revolutionary and Napoleonic Wars, 1790–1820.* New York: Palgrave Macmillan, 2009.

Frankfurter Frag- und Anzeigungsnachrichten, September 13, 1804.

Frederick the Great. "Forms of Government and the Duties of Rulers (1777)." In *The Foundations of Germany: A Documentary Account Revealing the Causes of Her Strength, Wealth, and Efficiency,* edited by J. Ellis Baker, 21–22. London: John Murray, 1918.

———. "Political Testament (1752)." In *The Habsburg and Hohenzollern Dynasties in the Seventeenth and Eighteenth Centuries,* edited by Carlile Aylmer Macartney, 331-45. New York: Walker, 1970.

Frei, Alfred Georg and Kurt Hochstuhl. *Wegbereiter der Demokratie: Die badische Revolution 1848/49.* Karlsruhe: Braun, 1997.

Freitag, Sabine, Peter Wende, and Markus Mösslang, eds. *British Envoys to Germany, 1816–1866.* New York: Cambridge University Press, 2000.

Fresenius, Johann Christian Ludwig. *Reichsfriede, Deutschland, Frankfurt: Neujahrgeschenk für deutsche Mitbürger.* Frankfurt am Main, 1799.

Freyberg, Pankraz von. *200 Jahre Englischer Garten München.* München: Knürr, 1989.

Friedrichs, Christopher. *The Early Modern City.* New York: Longman, 1995.

———. "But Are We Any Closer to Home? Early Modern German Urban History Since 'German Home Towns.'" *Central European History* 30, no. 2 (1997): 163–85.

Fuchs, Michael G. *Beschreibung der Stadt Elbing und ihre Gebiete.* 3 vols. Elbing: Hartmann, 1818.

Fulton, Charles Carroll. *Europe Viewed through American Spectacles.* Philadelphia: Lippincott, 1874.

Gagliardo, John G. *Reich and Nation: The Holy Roman Empire as Idea and Reality, 1763–1806.* Bloomington: Indiana University Press, 1980.

Gall, Lothar. *Von der ständischen zur bürgerlichen Gesellschaft.* München: Oldenbourg, 1993.

"Gedanken über die Verschönerung Breslau's, in Hinsicht der abgetragenen Wälle." *Schlesische Provinzialblätter* 60 (1814): 423–31.

Geisthövel, Alexa, and Habbo Knoch. *Orte der Moderne: Erfahrungswelten des 19. und 20. Jahrhunderts.* Frankfurt am Main: Campus, 2005.

Gerning, Johann Isaak von. *Skizze von Frankfurt am Main.* Frankfurt am Main, 1800.

Gesetzsammlung für die Königlichen Preußischen Staaten. Berlin, 1828.

Gesetzsammlung für die Königlichen Preußischen Staaten. Berlin, 1830.

Gieraths, Günther. *Breslau als Garnison und Festung 1241–1941.* Hamburg: Helmut Gerhard Schulz, 1961.

Gigl, Caroline. *Die Zentralbehörden Kurfürst Karl Theodors in München 1778–1799.* München: Beck, 1999.

Goethe, Katharina Elisabeth. *Briefe an ihren Sohn Johann Wolfgang, an Christiane und August von Goethe.* Stuttgart: Reclam, 1999.

Goethe, Johann Wolfgang von. *The Autobiography of Goethe; Truth and Poetry: From My Life.* Translated by Parke Godwin. New York: Wiley and Putnam, 1846.

———. *Faust: A Tragedy.* Translated by Bayard Taylor. Leipzig: Brockhaus, 1872.

———. *Goethes Werke.* 55 vols. Weimar: Böhlau, 1887–1912.

———. *Gespräche.* Edited by Woldemar Freiherr von Biedermann. Leipzig: Biedermann, 1890.

———. *Hermann and Dorothea.* Translated by Daniel Coogan. New York: Frederick Ungar, 1966.

———. *Elective Affinities.* Translated by R.J. Hollingdale. Harmondsworth: Penguin, 1971.

———. *Sämtliche Werke nach Epochen seines Schaffens, Münchner Ausgabe.* Edited by Karl Richter. Vol. 9. München: C. Hanser, 1985.

———. *From My Life.* Translated and edited by Thomas P. Peine and Jeffrey L. Sammons. New York: Suhrkamp, 1987.

———. *Die Leiden des jungen Werthers.* Stuttgart: Reclam, 1999.

Goldschmidt, Robert. *Die Stadt Karlsruhe: Ihre Entstehung und ihre Verwaltung.* Karlsruhe: Müllersche Hofbuchhandlung, 1915.

Graeber, David. *Toward an Anthropological Theory of Value.* New York: Palgrave, 2001.

Gray, Robert. *Letters During the Course of a Tour Through Germany, Switzerland, and Italy.* London, 1794.

Gregory, Brad S. *Salvation at Stake: Christian Martyrdom in Early Modern Europe.* Cambridge, MA: Harvard University Press, 1999.

Griep, Wolfgang and Hans-Wolf Jäger. *Reisen im 18. Jahrhundert.* Heidelberg: Winter, 1986.

Grillon, Pierre, ed. *Les papiers de Richelieu: section politique intérieure, correspondance et papiers d'état.* 6 vols. Paris: Pedone, 1982.

Grobe, Peter. *Die Entfestigung Münchens* München: München Stadtarchiv, 1987.

Grotius, Hugo. *The Most Excellent Hugo Grotius, His Three Books treating of the Rights of War and Peace.* 3 vols. London, 1682.

Hahn, Anne. *Die Entfestigung der Stadt Saarlouis.* St. Ingbert: Röhrig, 2000.

Hajós, Géza. "Die Stadtparks der österreichischen Monarchie von 1765 bis 1867 im gesamteuropäischen Kontext." In *Stadtparks in der österreichischen Monarchie 1765–1918,* edited by Géza Hajós, 38–46. Wien: Böhlau, 2008.

Haller, Carl Ludwig von. *Restauration der Staatswissenschaft.* Winterthur, 1821.

Hamburg und Altona: Eine Zeitschrift 4 (1802): 354–59.

Hank, Peter, Heinz Holeczek, and Martina Schilling. *Rastatt und die Revolution von 1848/49: Vom Rastatter Kongress zur Freiheitsfestung.* Rastatt: Rastatt Stadtarchiv, 1999.

Hanway, Jonas. *An Historical Account of the British Trade over the Caspian Sea, With a Journal of Travels from London through Russia into Persia and Back Again through Russia, Germany, and Holland.* Dublin, 1754.

Harster, Wilhelm. "Materialien zur Geschichte der Zerstörung der Stadt Speyer 1689." *Mitteilungen des Historischen Vereins der Pfalz* 14 (1889).

Hartwich, Wolfgang. "Speyer vom 30jährigen Krieg bis zum Ende der napoleonischen Zeit." In *Geschichte der Stadt Speyer*, edited by Wolfgang Eger, 5–133. Stuttgart: Kohlhamer, 1983.

Haupt, Friedrich. *Die Weltgeschichte.* Zürich: Drell, 1843.

Hauptmann, Gerhart. *Sämtliche Werke.* Vol. 4. Berlin: Propyläen Verlag, 1962.

Hautmont, B. de. *Ode à Monseigneur sur la prise de Philipsbourg.* Paris, 1688.

Helmig, Guido. "Die Befestigung der Basler Vorstädte und ihre Integration in den äusseren Mauerring." In *Die Befestigung der mittelalterlichen Stadt*, edited by Gabriele Isenberg and Barbara Scholkmann, 167–78. Köln: Böhlau, 1997.

Hess, Jonas Ludwig von. *Topographisch-politisch-historische Beschreibung der Stadt Hamburg.* 2 vols. Hamburg, 1796.

Heuchler, Eduard. "Altes und Neues aus Freiberg." *Sachsengrün: Culturgeschichtliche Zeitschrift*, no. 7 (1861): 72–74.

Hocker, Wilhlem. *Opfer der Thorsperre: Local Lustspiel mit Gesang.* Hamburg: Tramburg, 1840.

Hoffmann, Alfred, ed. *Österreichisches Städtebuch.* Multiple vols. Wien: Verlag der Osterreichischen Akademie der Wissenschaften, 1968–.

Hoffmann, E.T.A. *Poetische Werke in sechs Bänden.* 6 vols. Berlin: Aufbau Verlag, 1958.

Hofmann, Klaus Martin "Festungsstädte im Rahmen Regional- und Stadtgeschichtlicher Konzeptionen." In *Festung, Garnison, Bevölkerung: historische Aspekte der Festungsforschung*, edited by Volker Schmidtchen, 31–44. Wesel: Deutsche Gesellschaft für Festungsforschung, 1982.

Hohenberg, Paul M. and Lynn Hollen Lees. *The Making of Urban Europe, 1000–1950.* Cambridge, MA: Harvard University Press, 1985.

Holt, Mack P. *The French Wars of Religion, 1562–1629.* New York: Cambridge University Press, 1995.

Howitt, William. *The Rural and Domestic Life of Germany.* London: Longman, Brown, Green, and Longmans, 1842.

Huber, Ernst Rudolf, ed. *Dokumente zur deutschen Verfassungsgeschichte.* 3rd ed. 5 vols. Stuttgart: Kohlhammer, 1978–1997.

Hübner, Lorenz. *Beschreibung der kurbaierischen Haupt- und Residenzstadt München.* 2 vols. München, 1803–1805.

Hufeland, Gottlieb. *Lehrsätze des Naturrechts.* Jena, 1790.

Hugo, Victor. *Notre-Dame de Paris.* Translated by Isabel F. Hapgood. New York: Crowell, 1888.

Humboldt, Wilhelm von. *The Limits of State Action.* Edited by J.W. Burrow. Indianapolis: Liberty Fund, 1993.

Hüsgen, Heinrich Sebastian. *Getreuer Wegweiser von Frankfurt am Main und dessen Gebiete für Einheimische und Fremde.* Frankfurt am Main: Behrensche Buchhandlung, 1802.

Huxley, Aldous. *The Devils of Loudun.* New York: Harper, 1952.

Ilberg, Werner, ed. *Freiligraths Werke in einem Band.* 3rd ed. Berlin: Aufbau-Verlag, 1976.

Isenberg, Gabriele and Barbara Scholkmann, eds. *Die Befestigung der mittelalterlichen Stadt.* Köln: Böhlau, 1997.

Ist es gut und nothwendig, Große und Handelsstädte zu Festungen zu machen? Berlin: Societätsverlag, 1815.

Ist es nützlich und ausführbar, Hamburg zur Festung zu machen? Hamburg: Perthes und Besser, 1814.

Jacobs, Allan B., Elizabeth Macdonald, and Yodan Rofé. *The Boulevard Book: History, Evolution, Design of Multiway Boulevards.* Cambridge, MA: MIT Press, 2002.

Janitsch, Aemilian. *Merkwürdige Geschichte der Kriegsvorfälle zwischen Oesterreich und Frankreich im Jahr 1809.* Wien: C. Gräffer, 1809.

Jany, Curt. *Geschichte der preußischen Armee vom 15. Jahrhundert bis 1914.* 2nd ed. 4 vols. Osnabrück: Biblio, 1967.

Johanek, Peter and Franz-Joseph Post, eds. *Vielerlei Städte: Der Stadtbegriff.* Köln: Böhlau, 2004.

Jones, Archer. *The Art of War in the Western World.* Urbana: University of Illinois Press, 1987.

Jones, Colin. *Paris: Biography of a City.* London: Allen Lane, 2004.

Jung, Rudolf. "Die Niederlegung der Festungswerke in Frankfurt am Main 1802–1807." *Archiv für Frankfurts Geschichte und Kunst* 30 (1913): 117–90.

Justi, Johann Heinrich Gottlob von. *Staatswirtschaft.* Vol. 1. Leipzig: B.C. Breitkopf, 1758.

Kaeber, Ernst. "Das Weichbild der Stadt Berlin seit der Steinschen Städteordnung." In *Ernst Kaeber: Beiträge zur Berliner Geschichte,* edited by Ernst Vogel, 234–376. Berlin: Alter de Gruyter & Co., 1964.

Kaiserlich und Kurbayerisch priviligierte Allgemeine Zeitung, December 28, 1804.

Kall, Peter, Harald Moritzen, and Lambert Frank. *Zolldienstkleidung einst und heute.* Bonn: Bundesministerium für Wirtschaft u. Finanzen, 1972.

Kammerl, Reiner. "Die Reichsstadt Weissenburg an der Wende zum 19. Jahrhundert." In *Das Ende der kleinen Reichsstädte im süddeutschen Raum,* edited by Rainer A. Müller, Helmut Flachenecker, and Reiner Kammerl, 288–319. München: Beck, 2007.

Kant, Immanuel. *Prolegomena to Any Future Metaphysics.* Translated by James W. Ellington. Indianapolis: Hackett, 2001.

Keegan, John. *A History of Warfare.* New York: Knopf, 1993.

Keyser, Erich and Heinz Stoob, eds. *Deutsches Städtebuch, Handbuch städtischer Geschichte.* Multiple vols. Stuttgart: Kohlhammer, 1939–.

Keyssler, Johann Georg. *Neueste Reise durch Teutschland.* Hannover, 1740.

Kirchberg, Burggraf von. *Pro-Memoria von Seite des Burggrafen von Kirchberg des Landesherren der Grafschaft Sayn-Hachenburg an die Reichsversammlung.* 1797.

Klebe, A. "Beobacthungen eines Reisenden in den untern Rheingegenden." *National-Chronik der Teutschen*, February 3, 1802.

Knobloch, Heinz. *Herr Moses in Berlin: Auf den Spuren eines Menschenfreundes*. Berlin: Der Morgen, 1979.

Kohl, J.G. *Denkmale der Geschichte und Kunst der Freien Hansestadt Bremen*. Bremen: C. Ed. Müller, 1870.

König, Johann Carl. *Grüundliche Abhandlung von denen Teutschen Reichs-Tägen überhaupt und dem noch fürwährenden zu Regensburg insbesondere*. Vol. 1. Nürnberg, 1738.

Koschorke, Albrecht, Susanne Lüdemann, Thomas Frank, and Matal de Mazza Ethel, eds. *Der fiktive Staat: Konstruktion des politischen Körpers in der Geschichte Europa*. Frankfurt am Main: Fischer, 2007.

Krabbe, Wolfgang R. *Die deutsche Stadt im 19. und 20. Jahrhundert*. Göttingen: Vandenhoeck & Ruprecht, 1989.

Kramer, Waldemar. *Frankfurt Chronik*. Frankfurt am Main: W. Kramer, 1987.

Kraus, Andreas. *Geschichte Bayerns: Von den Anfängen bis zur Gegenwart*. München: Beck, 2004.

Kreis, Georg. "Der Abbruch der Basler Stadtmauern." In *Stadt- und Landmauern*, edited by Brigitte Sigel, 135–43. Zürich: Institut für Denkmalpflege an der ETH Zürich, 1993.

Kurtze Relation und Entwurff der Röm. Kayserl. Mayest. Leopoldi, zu Nürnberg gehaltenen Einzugs den 6. (16.) Augusti 1658. Nürnberg, 1658.

Küttner, Carl Gottlob. *Reise durch Deutschland, Dänemark, Schweden, Norwegen und einen Theil von Italien*. 4 vols. Leipzig: Göschen, 1797–1801.

La Mare, Nicholas de. *Traité de la police*. 2nd ed. 4 vols. Amsterdam, 1729.

Lahne, Werner. *Magdeburgs Zerstörung in der zeitgenössischen Publizistik*. Magdeburg: Magdeburger Geschichtsverein, 1931.

"Lästige Polizeianstalten vor Spaziergänger." *Kielisches Magazin* 2 (1784): 186–94.

Lehmbruch, Hans. *Ein neues München: Stadtplanung und Stadtentwicklung um 1800*. Buchendorf: Buchendorf Verlag, 1987.

Letres d'vn solitaire av Roy, princes, et seigneurs faisans la guerre aux Rebelles. Poitiers, 1628.

Lindemann, Mary. *Patriots and Paupers: Hamburg, 1712–1830*. New York: Oxford University Press, 1990.

Lipowsky, Felix Joseph. *Karl Theodor, Churfürst von Pfalz-Bayern*. Sulzbach: Seidel, 1828.

Lohmann, Peter David, ed. *Rath- und Bürgerschlüsse vom Jahre 1801 bis zu Ende des Jahres 1825*. Vol. 1. Hamburg, 1828.

Lösner, Carl Ferdinand Friedrich. *Chronik der Kreisstadt Neu-Angermünde*. Schwedt 1845.

Lucian. *Lucian von Samosata sämtliche Werke*. Vol. 4. Wien: Franz Haas, 1798.

Machiavelli, Niccolò. *The Prince*. Translated by Peter Bondanella and Mark Musa. New York: Oxford University Press, 1984.

Magazin der Literatur des Auslandes, March 10, 1841: 119.

Mai, Bernhard. "Das befestigte Magdeburg." In *Magdeburg: Die Geschichte der Stadt 805–2005*, edited by Matthias Puhle, Peter Petsch, and Maik Hattenhorst, 493–510. Dössel: Stekovics, 2005.

Maigret, M. *Traité de la sûreté et conservation des états, par le moyen de forteresses.* Paris, 1725.

Marani, Pietro C. *L'architettura fortificata negli studi di Leonardo da Vinci.* Firenze: Leo S. Olschki, 1984.

Marx, Karl and Frederick Engels. *The Communist Manifesto: A Modern Edition.* Edited by Eric Hobsbawm. New York: Verson, 1998.

Mayer, Arthur von. *Geschichte und Geographie der deutschen Eisenbahn von ihrer Entstehung bis auf die Gegenwart.* Vol. 2. Berlin: Baensch, 1891.

Mayer, Walfgang. *Der Linienwall: Von der Befestigungsanlage zum Gürtel.* Wien: Wiener Stadt- und Landesarchiv, 1986.

McIntosh, Terence. *Urban Decline in Early Modern Germany: Schwäbisch Hall and Its Region, 1650–1750.* Chapel Hill: University of North Carolina Press, 1997.

Meeder, W.L. *Geschichte von Hamburg: Vom Entstehen der Stadt bis auf die neueste Zeit.* 2 vols. Hamburg: Wörmer, 1838–1839.

Mercier, Louis-Sébastien. *Panorama of Paris: Selections from the Tableau de Paris.* Translated and edited by Jeremy D. Popkin. University Park: University of Pennsylvania Press, 1999.

Merriman, John M. *Margins of City Life: Explorations on the French Urban Frontier, 1815–1851.* New York: Oxford University Press, 1991.

Mieck, Ilja. "Von der Reformzeit zur Revolution (1806–1847)." In *Geschichte Berlins von der Frühgeschichte bis zur Industrialisierung,* edited by Wolfgang Ribbe, 405–602. München: Beck, 1987.

Mintzker, Yair. "'A Word Newly Introduced into Language:' The Appearance and Spread of 'Social' in French Enlightened Thought, 1745–1765." *History of European Ideas* 34, no. 4 (2008): 500–13.

Mirabeau, Honoré Gabriel Riqueti Comte de. *De la monarchie prussienne sous Frédéric le Grand.* 4 vols. London, 1788.

Montecucolli, Raimondo. *Mémoires.* Strasbourg, 1735.

Moreri, Louis. *Le grand dictionnaire historique.* 10 vols. Basel, 1731.

Moser, Johann Jacob. *Von Teutschland und dessen Staats-Verfassung überhaupt.* Stuttgart, 1766.

Muenster-Meinhövel, Amalie. *Amaliens poetische Versuche.* Leipzig: Voss, 1796.

Mumford, Louis. *The City in History.* New York: Harcourt, 1961.

Neuhaus, Helmut. "Das Problem der militärischen Exekutive in der Spätphase des Alten Reiches." In *Staatsverfassung und Heeresverfassung in der europäischen Geschichte der frühen Neuzeit,* edited by Johann Kunisch, 297–346. Berlin: Duncker & Humboldt, 1986.

Nicolai, Christoph Friedrich. *Beschreibung einer Reise durch Deutschland und die Schweiz im Jahre 1781.* 12 vols. Stetting und Berlin, 1783–1796.

Nora, Pierre, ed. *Les Lieux de Mémoire.* Paris: Gallimard, 1984.

d'Orléans, Charlotte-Elizabeth. *Life and Letters of Charlotte Elizabeth, Mother of Philippe d'Orléans.* London: Chapman and Hall, 1889.

Osterhammel, Jürgen. *Die Verwandlung der Welt: Eine Geschichte des 19. Jahrhunderts.* München: Beck, 2009.

Pahl, Johann Gottfried. *Geschichte von Schwaben.* Nördlingen: Beck, 1802.

Palmer, Alan Warwick. *Metternich.* New York: Harper & Row, 1972.

Paret, Peter. *Clausewitz and the State: The Man, His Theories, and His Times*. Princeton: Princeton University Press, 1976.

Parker, Geoffrey. *The Military Revolution: Military Innovation and the Rise of the West, 1500–1800*. New York: Cambridge University Press, 1996.

———. ed. *The Thirty Years' War*. London: Routledge, 1998.

———. *The Cambridge History of Warfare*. New York: Cambridge University Press, 2005.

Paula, Mörz de. *Der Österreisch-Ungarische Befestigungsbau, 1820–1914*. Wien: Stöhr, 1997.

Paurmeister, Tobias. *De iurisdictione imperii Romani*. Vol. 2. Hannover, 1608.

Pelc, Ortwin. *Im Schutz von Mauern und Toren*. Heide: Boyens, 2003.

Picot, George-Marie-René. *Histoire des États généraux considérés au point de vue de leur influence sur le gouvernement de la France de 1355 à 1614*. 4 vols. Paris: Hachette, 1872.

Piépape, Léonce de. *Histoire de la réunion de la Franche-Comté à la France*. 2 vols. Genève: Mégariotis, 1881.

Platt, Colin. *The English Medieval Town*. London: Secker & Warburg, 1976.

Prändel, Johann Georg. *Geographie der sämmtlichen kurpfalzbaierischen Erbstaaten*. Amberg: Uhlmann, 1806.

Preitz, Max, ed. *Friedrich Schlegel und Novalis: Biographie einer Romantikerfreundschaft in ihren Briefen*. Darmstadt: Gentner, 1957.

Privilegirte wochentliche gemeinnützige Nachrichten von und für Hamburg, August 7, 1805.

Proelss, Johannes Moritz and Johannes Proelss. *Friedrich Stoltze und Frankfurt am Main*. Frankfurt am Main: Neuer Frankfurter Verlag, 1905.

Pütter, Johann Stephan. *An Historical Development of the Present Political Constitution of the German Empire*. Translated by Josiah Dornford. Vol. 3. London: T. Payne, 1790.

Radcliffe, Ann Ward. *A Journey Made in the Summer of 1794: Through Holland and the Western Frontier of Germany*. London, 1796.

Raumer, Kurt. *Die Zerstörung der Pfalz*. München: Oldenbourg, 1930.

Rautenstrauch, Johann. *Das neue Wien, eine Fabel*. Wien, 1785.

"Regensburg, vom 11. Nov." *Frankfurter Kaiserl. Reichs-Ober-Post-Amts Zeitung*, November 15, 1805.

Regierungsblatt für das Königreich Bayern. München, 1826.

Richter, Joseph. *Original Eipeldauer Briefe*. Wien, 1805.

Riedel, Manfred. "Bürger, Staatsbürger, Bürgertum." In *Geschichtliche Grundbegriffe: Historisches Lexikon zur politisch-sozialen Sprache in Deutschland*, edited by Otto Brunner, Werner Conze, and Reinhart Koselleck, 672–725. Stuttgart: Klett, 1972.

Riehl, Wilhelm Heinrich. *Land und Leute*. 2nd ed. Stuttgart, 1855.

Riesbeck, Johann Kaspar. *Briefe eines Reisenden Franzosen über Deutschland*. 2 vols. Paris, 1783–1784.

———. *Travels Through Germany, in a Series of Letters*. Vol. 3. London, 1787.

Ritter, Gerhard. *Frederick the Great*. Translated by Peter Paret. Berkeley: University of California Press, 1974.

Roberts, Michael. "The Military Revolution, 1560–1660." In *The Military Revolution Debate: Readings on the Military Transformation of Early Modern Europe*, edited by Clifford J. Rogers, 13–36. Boulder: Westview Press, 1995.

Robinson, James Harvey, ed. *The Napoleonic Period.* 2 vols. Philadelphia: University of Pennsylvania Press, 1895.

Rochas d'Aiglun, Albert de. *Vauban, sa famille et ses écrits, ses oisivetés et sa correspondance: analyse et extraits.* 2 vols. Genève: Slatkine Reprints, 1972.

Rosa, Hartmut. *Beschleunigung: Die Veränderung der Zeitstrukturen in der Moderne.* Frankfurt am Main: Suhrkamp, 2005.

Rosenberg, Hans. *Bureaucracy, Aristocracy, and Autocracy: The Prussian Experience, 1660–1815.* Cambridge, MA: Harvard University Press, 1958.

Rosenbohm, Rolf. "Die Straßensperren in den niederdeutschen Städten." *Lüneburger Blätter* 9 (1958): 21–38.

Rosmann, P. and Faustin Ens. *Geschichte der Stadt Breisach.* Freiburg: Friedrich Wagner, 1851.

Rousseau, Jean-Jacques. *The Political Writings of Jean Jacques Rousseau.* Translated by C. E. Vaughan. 2 vols. Oxford: Blackwell, 1962.

———. *Confessions.* Translated by Angela Scholar. Edited by Patrick Coleman. New York: Oxford University Press, 2000.

Rousset, Camille. *Histoire de Louvois et de son administration politique et militaire.* 3 ed. 4 vols. Paris: Didier, 1863.

Runde, Christian Gottlieb August. *Rundes Chronik der Stadt Halle, 1750–1835.* Halle (Saale): Gebauer Schwetschke Druckerei, 1933.

Russell, John. *A Tour in Germany and Some of the Southern Provinces of the Austrian Empire.* 3d ed. Vol. 2. Edinburgh: Longman, Rees, Orme, Brown, and Green, 1827.

Sahlins, Peter. *Boundaries: The Making of France and Spain in the Pyrenees.* Berkeley: University of California Press, 1989.

Saint-Foix, Germain-François Poullain de. *Œuvres Complettes.* 6 vols. Paris, 1778.

Salisbury, John of. *The Statesman's Book.* Translated by John Dickinson. New York: Knopf, 1927.

Saxe, Maurice de. "Reveries on the Art of War." In *The Art of War in World History*, edited by Gérard Chaliand. Berkeley: University of California Press, 1994.

Schama, Simon. *Citizens: A Chronicle of the French Revolution.* New York: Vintage, 1990.

Scharnhorst, Gerhard von. "Entwicklung der allgemeinen Ursachen des Glücks der Franzosen in dem Revolutionskriege." In *Scharnhorst: Ausgewählte militärische Schriften*, edited by Freiherrn v.d. Goltz. Berlin: Schneider, 1881.

Schäuffelen, Otmar. *Die Bundesfestung Ulm und ihre Geschichte: Europas grösste Festungsanlage.* Ulm: Vaas, 1980.

Scherer, Karl, ed. *Pfälzer – Palatines: Beiträge zur Volkskunde und Mundartforschung der Pfalz und der Zielländer pfälzischer Auswanderer im 18. und 19. Jahrhundert.* Kaiserslautern: Heimatstelle Pfalz, 1991.

Scheuermann, Gerhard, ed. *Das Breslau-Lexikon.* 2 vols. Dülmen: Laumann, 1994.

Schivelbusch, Wolfgang. *The Railway Journey: The Industrialization of Time and Space in the 19th Century.* Berkeley: University of California Press, 1986.

Schmidt, Burghart. *Hamburg im Zeitalter der Französischen Revolution und Napoleons (1789–1813)*. 2 vols. Hamburg: Verein für Hamburgische Geschichte, 1998.

———. "Die Torsperre in Hamburg: Staatliches Kontrollinstrument, finanzielle Einnahmequelle oder 'Überbleibsel aus der Knechtschatszeit.'" *Mitteilungen des Hamburger Arbeitskreises für Regionalgeschichte*, no. 37 (2000): 27–36.

Schmitt, Carl. *Die Diktatur: Von den Anfängen des modernen Souveränitätsgedankens bis zum proletarischen Klassenkampf*. München und Leipzig: Duncker & Humboldt, 1921.

Schorske, Carl. *Fin-de-siècle Vienna: Politics and Culture* New York: Vintage Books, 1981.

Schulte, Aloys. *Markgraf Ludwig Wilhelm von Baden und der Reichskrieg gegen Frankreich, 1693–1697*. 2 vols. Karlsruhe: J. Bielfeld, 1892.

Schütz, Friedrich. "Provinzialhauptstadt und Festung des Deutschen Bundes (1814/1816–1866)." In *Mainz: Die Geschichte der Stadt*, edited by Franz Dumont, Ferdinand Scherf, and Friedrich Schütz, 375–426. Mainz: Zabern, 1998.

Schwarzälder, Herbert. *Geschichte der freien Hansestadt Bremen*. 4 vols. Bremen: Röver, 1975–1985.

———, ed. *Bremen in alten Reisebeschreibungen, Briefe und Berichte von Reisenden zu Bremen und Umgebung, 1581–1847*. Bremen: Temmel, 2007.

Scott, James C. *Seeing Like a State: How Certain Schemes to Improve the Human Condition Have Failed*. New Haven: Yale University Press, 1998.

Sennett, Richard. *Flesh and Stone: The Body and the City in Western Civilization*. New York: Norton, 1994.

Sheehan, James J. *German Liberalism in the Nineteenth Century*. Chicago: University of Chicago Press, 1978.

———. "What is German History? Reflections on the Role of the Nation in German History and Historiography." *The Journal of Modern History* 53, no. 1 (1981): 1–23.

———. *German History, 1770–1866*. New York: Oxford University Press, 1989.

Soldan, Friedrich. *Die Zerstörung der Stadt Worms im Jahre 1689*. Worms: J. Stern, 1889.

Solières, F. Bertout de. *Les fortifications de Paris à travers les âges*. Paris: Girieud, 1906.

Soll, Jacob. *The Information Master: Jean-Baptiste Colbert's Secret State Intelligence System*. Ann Arbor: University of Michigan Press, 2009.

Sparrow, W.J. *Count Rumford of Woburn, Mass*. New York: Thomas Y. Crowell, 1965.

Staats, Reinhart. *Theologie der Reichskrone: Ottonische "Renovatio Imperii" im Spiegel einer Insignie*. Stuttgart: Anton Hiersemann, 1976.

Stahleder, Helmuth. *Erzwungener Glanz: Die Jahre 1706–1818*. München: Dolling und Galitz, 2005.

Stamm-Kuhlmann, Thomas. *König in Preussens grosser Zeit: Friedrich Wilhelm III, der Melancholiker auf dem Thron*. Berlin: Siedler, 1992.

Steffens, Henrich. *Was ich erlebte*. 10 vols. Breslau: Joseph Max, 1840–1844.

Stollberg-Rilinger, Barbara. *Der Staat als Maschine: Zur politischen Metaphorik des absoluten Fürstenstaats*. Berlin: Duncker & Humblot, 1986.

———. "Zeremoniell als politisches Verfahren. Rangordnung und Rangstreit als Strukturmerkmale des frühneuzeitlichen Reichstags." In *Neue Studien zur frühneuzeitlichen Reichsgeschichte*, edited by Johannes Kunisch, 91–132. Berlin: Duncker & Humblot, 1997.

———. *Das Heilige Römische Reich Deutscher Nation: Vom Ende des Mittelalters bis 1806.* München: Beck, 2006.

———. *Des Kaisers alte Kleider: Verfassungsgeschichte und Symbolsprache des Alten Reiches.* München: Beck, 2008.

Tackett, Timothy. *When the King Took Flight.* Cambridge, MA: Harvard University Press, 2003.

Takeda, Junko. *"Between Conquest and Plague": Marseillais Civic Humanism in the Age of Absolutism 1660–1725.* PhD Dissertation, Stanford University, 2006.

Tantner, Anton. *Ordnung der Häuser, Beschreibung der Seelen. Hausnummerierung und Seelenkonskription in der Habsburgermonarchie.* Wien: Studienverlag, 2007.

Textor, Fritz. *Entfestigung und Zerstörungen im Rheingebiet während des 17. Jahrhunderts als Mittel der französoschen Rheinpolitik.* 2 vols. Bonn: Ludwig Röhrscheid, 1937.

The Theatre of the Present War upon the Course of the Rhine. London, 1745.

Thompson, Benjamin. *Collected Works of Count Rumford.* Edited by Sanborn C. Brown. 5 vols. Cambridge, MA: Belknap, 1970.

Tieck, Ludwig. *Schriften in zwölf Bänden.* Edited by Manfred Frank. 12 vols. Frankfurt am Main: Deutscher Klassiker Verlag, 1985–1991.

Tippach, Thomas. "Die Rayongesetzgebung in der öffentlichen Kritik." In *Die Stadt und ihr Rand*, edited by Peter Johanek, 213–34. Köln: Böhlau, 2008.

Tönnies, Ferdinand. *Gemeinschaft und Gesellschaft.* Leipzig: Fues, 1887.

Tracey, James D., ed. *City Walls: The Urban Enceinte in Global Perspective.* New York: Cambridge University Press, 2000.

Traux, Maximilian von. *Die beständige Befestigungskunst.* Wien: Fritsch, 1817.

U., J. *Ueber die Entfestigung Lübecks.* Lübeck: Rohdensche Buchhandlung, 1838.

Über Befestigung und Bewaffnung grosser Handelsstädte. n.p., 1814.

"Ueber die Bepflanzung öffentlicher Lustörter mit Bäumen, mit Rücksicht auf Breslau's Verschönerungen." *Schlesische Provinzialblätter* 60 (1814): 503–10.

Valazé, Éléonore-Bernard-Anne-Christophe-Zoa Dufriche de. *Des places fortes et du système de guerre actuel.* Paris: Leneveu et Riant, 1845.

Verhandlungen der zweiten Kammer der Landstände des Grosherzogthums Hessen. Darmstadt: Carl Wilhelm Leske, 1842.

Vernon, Jean Louis Camille Gay de. *Mémoire sur les opérations militaires des Généraux en Chef Custine et Houchard, pendant les années 1792 et 1793.* Paris: Firmin Didot Frères, 1844.

Vetter, Roland. *"Kein Stein soll auf dem andern bleiben." Mannheims Untergang während des Pfälzischen Erbfolgekrieges im Spiegel französischer Kriegsberichte.* Heidelberg: Regionalkultur, 2002.

Virilio, Paul. *Speed and Politics: An Essay on Dromology.* Translated by Mark Polizzotti. New York: Columbia University Press, 1986.

Voges, Dietmar-H. *Nördlingen seit der Reformation: Aus dem Leben einer Stadt.* München: Beck, 1998.

Wachenhusen, Hans. *Berliner Photographien.* Vol. 2. Berlin: Hausfreund Expedition, 1867.

Wagner, Walter. "Die Stellungnahme der Militärbehörden zur Wiener Stadter-weiterung in den Jahren 1848–1857." *Jahrbuch des Vereins für Geschichte der Stadt Wien* 17/18 (1961/1962): 216–85.

Wagner-Rieger, Renate. *Die Wiener Ringstrasse, Bild einer Epoche: Die Erweiterung der inneren Stadt Wien unter Kaiser Franz Joseph.* 8 vols. Wien: H. Böhlaus, 1969.

Walker, Mack. *German Home Towns: Community, State, and General Estate, 1648–1871.* 2nd ed. Ithaca: Cornell University Press, 1998.

Walter, Jacob. *The Diary of a Napoleonic Foot Soldier.* Edited by Marc Raeff. New York: Doubleday, 1991.

Weber, Carl Julius. *Deutschland oder Briefe eines in Deutschland reisenden Deutschen.* Stuttgart: Hallberger, 1834.

Weber, Karl-Klaus. "Stadt und Befestigung: Zur Frage der räumlichen Wachstums-beschränkung durch bastionäre Befestigungen im 17. und 18. Jahrhundert." *Die alte Stadt* 22, no. 4 (1995): 301–21.

Weber, Klaus T., ed. *Was ist Neuere Befestigung?* 2 vols. Berlin: dissertation.de, 2002.

Weber, Max. *The City.* Translated by Don Martindale and Gertrud Neuwirth. Glencoe, IL: Free Press, 1958.

Wedgwood, C.V. *The Thirty Years War.* 2nd ed. New York: New York Review of Books, 2005.

Weigel, Johann Adam Valentin. *Geographische, naturhistorische und technologische Beschreibung des souverainen Herzogthums Schlesien.* 10 vols. Berlin: Hamburgis-che Buchhandlung, 1800–1806.

Weinhagen, Napoleon. *Studien zur Entfestigung Kölns.* Köln: Selbstverlag des Ver-fassers, 1869.

Westenrieder, Lorenz. *In München Anno 1782.* München: Süddeutscher Verlag, 1970.

Westerburg, Albert. *Ueber die rechtliche Natur der Frankfurter sogenannten Wallservitut, zugleich ein Beitrag zur Geschichte des deutschen Baurechts.* Frankfurt am Main: Ludwig Ravenstein, 1887.

White, Richard and John M. Findlay. *Power and Place in the North American West.* Seattle: University of Washington Press, 1999.

Wichmann, Siegfried. *Carl Spitzweg: Reisen und Wandern in Europa und der glückliche Winkel.* Stuttgart: Belser, 2002.

Wienhöfer, Elmar. *Das Militärwesen des Deutschen Bundes und das Ringen zwischen Österreich und Preussen um die Vorherrschaft in Deutschland, 1815–1866.* Osnabrück: Biblio, 1973.

Wissenbach, Björn. *Mauern zu Gärten: 200 Jahre Frankfurter Wallanlagen.* Frankfurt am Main: Societätverlag, 2010.

With, Christopher B. "Adolph von Menzel and the German Revolution of 1848." *Zeitschrift für Kunstgeschichte* 42, no. 2/3 (1979): 195–214.

Wolfe, Michael. "Walled Towns During the French Religious Wars." In *City Walls: The Urban Enceinte in Global Perspective*, edited by James D. Tracey, 317–48. New York: Cambridge University Press, 2000.

———. *Walled Towns and the Shaping of France: From the Medieval to the Early Modern Period.* New York: Palgrave MacMillan, 2009.

Wood, Allen W. *Kant.* Walden, MA: Blackwell, 2005.

Zedler, Johann Heinrich. "Teutsches Staats-Raison oder Staats-Raison des Heiligen Römischen Reichs Teutscher Nation." In *Universal-Lexicon*, edited by Johann Heinrich Zedler, 1875. Halle, 1745.

Zeller, Gaston. *L'organisation défensive des frontières du nord et de l'est au dix-septième siècle*. Paris: Berger-Levrault, 1928.

Zeumer, Karl, ed. *Quellensammlung zur Geschichte der Deutschen Reichsverfassung in Mittelalter und Neuzeit*. Vol. 2. Tübingen: J.C.B. Mohr, 1913.

Zschocke, Helmut. *Die Berliner Akzismauer: Die vorletzte Mauer der Stadt*. Berlin: Story Verlag, 2007.

Zysberg, André. *Marseille au temps du Roi-Soleil: La ville, les galères, l'arsenal, 1660 à 1715*. Marseille: Laffitte, 2007.

Index

CPSIA information can be obtained at www.ICGtesting.com
Printed in the USA
BVOW02s1323290115

385571BV00001B/10/P